I0794847

Lives and Writings of the Great Fathers of the Lutheran Church

Lives and Writings of the Great Fathers of the Lutheran Church

Edited by Timothy Schmeling
with an Introduction by Robert Kolb

Concordia Publishing House • Saint Louis

3558 S. Jefferson Avenue, St. Louis, MO 63118-3968

1-800-325-3040 • www.cph.org

Manufactured in the United States of America

Library of Congress Cataloging-in-Publication Data

Names: Schmeling, Timothy, editor.
Title: Lives and writings of the great fathers of the Lutheran Church / edited by Timothy Schmeling.
Description: St. Louis : Concordia Publishing House, 2016. | Includes bibliographical references and index.
Identifiers: LCCN 2016030599 (print) | LCCN 2016032793 (ebook) | ISBN 9780758649430 (alk. paper) | ISBN 9780758649447
Subjects: LCSH: Lutheran Church—History. | Lutheran Church—History—Sources. | Lutherans—Biography. | Lutheran Church—Doctrines—History.
Classification: LCC BX8018 .L67 2016 (print) | LCC BX8018 (ebook) | DDC 284.1092/2--dc23
LC record available at https://lccn.loc.gov/2016030599

5 6 7 8 9 10 29 28 27 26 25

Contents

Abbreviations

AE	Luther, Martin. *Luther's Works*. American Edition. Vols. 1–30: Edited by Jaroslav Pelikan. St. Louis: Concordia, 1955–76. Vols. 31–55: Edited by Helmut Lehmann. Philadelphia: Muhlenberg/Fortress, 1957–86.
ESV	English Standard Version
FC	Formula of Concord
LSB	*Lutheran Service Book* (St. Louis: Concordia, 2006)
LW	*Lutheran Worship* (St. Louis: Concordia, 1982)
SD	Solid Declaration of the Formula of Concord
TLH	*The Lutheran Hymnal* (St. Louis: Concordia, 1941)
WA	*D. Martin Luthers Werke: Kritische Gesamtausgabe*. 73 vols. in 85. Weimar: Hermann Böhlau, 1883–.

Introduction

Continuities and contrasts mark all eras of human history. Luther's (1483–1546) call for reform in the first quarter of the sixteenth century initiated a movement that became institutionalized in churches claiming the name "Lutheran" during a half century of discovery and definition of the biblical message as Luther and his colleagues in Wittenberg, especially Philipp Melanchthon (1497–1560), had proclaimed and formulated it. History is, like the unchanging Creator as Scripture portrays him, always on the move. Thus, debates about the exact meaning of the Wittenberg way of speaking the Gospel of Jesus Christ slowly arrived at a definition of issues controverted among Luther's and Melanchthon's students. This delineation took written form in 1580 with the acceptance of the Book of Concord by roughly two-thirds of those who claimed to be following the Wittenberg way.

With its adoption, a new era began, bearing many marks of the Reformation period out of which it came, but also moving on in new contexts to new expressions of the biblical message and new formulations to address old and new issues raised by the time. The ecclesiastical culture that arose out of the Reformation, with roots from the 1520s and 1530s and a trunk forged in the next half century, lasted, despite ongoing shifts and adjustments of its common core, into the eighteenth century. This "long" seventeenth century has sometimes been labeled "Lutheran Orthodoxy." This period is often misrepresented as a theologically sterile monolith and a dogmatic system alienated from the needs of the faithful.

The adjective "orthodoxy" has expressed the conviction of the Christian Church throughout history that public teaching matters, and that the biblical message demands accurate and sensitive application of its call for repentance, restoration of the fullness of humanity through the forgiveness of sins, and instruction for living as the forgiven children of God. Reflecting the ancient division of the Roman Empire into western and eastern regions, many segments of the "Eastern" Church claim the title "Orthodox" as part of their official designation. But "orthodoxy" also became a term for seventeenth-century Protestant theologies and ecclesiastical cultures, Lutheran and Reformed, in the modern period. Scholars dispute the usefulness of this term today because it has come to suggest a sterile uniformity and a concentration on an elite form of exercising theological thinking. These depictions distort our understanding of the dynamic of the church's life in the period. Ernst Koch has labeled the period simply "the confessional era."[1]

QUID EST?

Certainly, the intellectual analysis and application of Scripture constituted a vital element of this culture. The seventeenth-century Lutheran professors of dogma followed the pattern set down by Philipp Melanchthon in his doctrinal handbook, *Commonplaces* (*Loci Communes*), and even by Luther in his Small Catechism, which asks first for a definition of the topic at hand: "What is this?" (in Latin, *quid est?*). Students of the period encounter two definitions: one concentrates on its academic theology, particularly the systems of organizing biblical teaching within a framework shaped significantly by Aristotelian rhetorical and logical categories; the other views "orthodoxy" as a wider phenomenon, embracing the practice of the Christian faith in the many aspects of its teaching, proclamation, biblical interpretation, family devotions, liturgical expressions, church governance, as well as the impact of the worldview that was formed from biblical teaching on the political, social, economic, and cultural life of the larger society. The two definitions are obviously interrelated, and it seems best to take the second as a working framework for ascertaining how the inhabitants of the period experienced it.[2]

The pioneer in the fresh exploration of aspects of the phenomenon often labeled "Lutheran Orthodoxy," called for in 1933 by Breslau professor Hans Leube,[3] was the Swedish church historian Bengt Hägglund.[4] His

---

[1] Ernst Koch, *Das konfessionelle Zeitalter - Katholizismus, Luthertum, Calvinismus (1563–1675)* (Leipzig: Evangelische Verlagsanstalt, 2000).

[2] See Johannes Wallmann, "Lutheran Orthodoxy," in *Religion Past and Present*, ed. Hans-Dieter Betz et al., 4th ed. (Leiden: Brill, 2007–13), 9:406–10; Markus Matthias, "Lutherische Orthodoxie," in *Theologische Realencyklopädie*, ed. Gerhard Müller (Berlin: de Gruyter, 1977–2004), 25:464–85; Robert Kolb, ed., *Lutheran Ecclesiastical Culture, 1550–1675* (Leiden: Brill, 2008); Hans-Christoph Rublack, "Zur Problemlage der Forschung zur lutherischen Orthodoxie in Deutschland," in *Die lutherische Konfessionalisierung in Deutschland*, Wissenschaftliches Symposion des Vereins für Reformationsgeschichte, ed. Hans-Christoph Rublack (Gütersloh: Mohn, 1992), 13–32; Johannes Wallmann, "Lutherische Konfessionalisierung—Ein Überblick," in *Die lutherische Konfessionalisierung in Deutschland*, 33–53; and Robert Kolb, "Lutheran Theology in Seventeenth-Century Germany," *Lutheran Quarterly* 20 (2006): 446–73.

[3] Hans Leube, "Die altlutherische Orthodoxie: Ein Forschungsbericht," in Hans Leube, ed., *Orthodoxie und Pietismus: Gesammelte Studien* 13 (Bielefeld: Luther-Verlag, 1975), 19–35.

[4] Bengt Hägglund, *Die Heilige Schrift und ihre Deutung in der Theologie Johann Gerhards. Eine Untersuchung über das altlutherische Schriftverständnis* (Lund: CWK Gleerup, 1951).

study of Johann Gerhard was followed within a decade by focused investigations from Robert Preus, Johannes Wallmann, Jörg Baur, and Hermann Schüssler.[5] More comprehensive overviews of the theology of the post-Reformation period appeared in the following decade, authored by Carl Heinz Ratschow and Robert Preus.[6]

The picture painted of Lutheran thinking in this period as sterile, caught in the grip of Aristotle, and unrelated to the daily life of parishioners, is simply false. The extensive use of Aristotle's teachings and their advancement in late sixteenth-century Lutheran teaching and thinking indicates first of all the deep ecumenical commitment of the theologians of this era, for Lutheran theologians continued to strive to call the whole household of faith—including Roman Catholic, Anglican, and Reformed conversation partners—to their confession of the biblical message. Aristotle provided the common language and theoretical framework that both Jesuits and Calvinists used. It is true that efforts to fit biblical material into Aristotelian categories did sometimes distort the former with attempts to answer questions that Scripture neither asks nor answers. It is also true that these Aristotelian concepts or expressions did not transfer easily into preaching. Furthermore, the focus on the dogmatic works of the most prominent professors and pastors has overshadowed other aspects of this ecclesiastical culture, sometimes giving an impression of deadening detail and ideas frozen in place. But the university life behind these works demonstrated a lively sense of experimentation with the formulation of public teaching, as professors and students conducted formal disputations to test such new expressions and applications of the theological core at the heart of their deliberations.[7] Furthermore, at least one probe of the preaching of the period demonstrates that the ideas of

---

[5] Robert D. Preus, *The Inspiration of Scripture* (Edinburgh: Oliver and Boyd, 1957); Hermann Schüssler, *Georg Calixt, Theologie und Kirchenpolitik. Eine Studie zur Ökumenizität des Luthertums* (Wiesbaden: Steiner, 1961); Johannes Wallmann, *Der Theologiebegriff bei Johann Gerhard und Georg Calixt* (Tübingen: Mohr/Siebeck, 1961); Jörg Baur, *Die Vernunft zwischen Ontologie und Evangelium. Eine Untersuchung zur Theologie Johann Andreas Quenstedts* (Gütersloh: Mohn, 1962).

[6] Carl Heinz Ratschow, *Lutherische Dogmatik zwischen Reformation und Aufklärung*, 2 vols. (Gütersloh: Mohn, 1964, 1966); Robert D. Preus, *The Theology of Post-Reformation Lutheranism*, 2 vols. (St. Louis: Concordia, 1970–72).

[7] Kenneth G. Appold, *Orthodoxie als Konsensbildung. Das theologische Disputationswesen an der Universität Wittenberg zwischen 1570 und 1710* (Tübingen: Mohr Siebeck, 2004).

the grand dogmatic works could be and were translated into effective homiletical application to the lives of the common people.[8]

Furthermore, the concord established in 1580 was disturbed by at least four major controversies during the following century and a half. The Formula of Concord's solution to discussions of God's election of his own to salvation did not end questions regarding the predestination of the saved. Aegidius Hunnius (1550–1603) and Samuel Huber (1547–1624) of the University of Wittenberg debated the nature of God's predestining counsel in the 1590s,[9] and without much public disagreement the view of predestination "in view of faith" (*intuitu fidei*) crept into later seventeenth-century Lutheran dogmatic works. The Formula of Concord's article on Christology had also left the door open to questions raised between theologians at Giessen and Tübingen regarding the best way to describe the role of Christ's divinity in his life on earth, as a "hiding" or an "emptying" of the divine nature.[10] Hermann Rahtmann (1585–1628), pastor in Danzig, fell into the crossfire of most other theologians with his views of the relationship of the Holy Spirit and Scripture, which posited an independent working of the Spirit apart from the written Word of God.[11] The most divisive and bitter controversy that erupted among Lutheran theologians in this period took place when Georg Calixt (1586–1656) advanced irenic suggestions for a coming together of the Roman Catholic and Reformed churches with the Lutheran churches.[12]

---

[8] Bernhard Liess, *Johann Heermann (1585–1647): Prediger in Schlesien zur Zeit des Dreißigjährigen Krieges* (Münster: LIT Verlag, 2003), 185–86.

[9] Gottfried Adam, *Der Streit um die Prädestination im ausgehenden 16. Jahrhundert, eine Untersuchung zu den Entwürfen vom Samuel Huber und Aegidius Hunnius* (Neukirchen: Neukirchener Verlag, 1970); Rune Söderlund, *Ex praevisa fide. Zum Verständnis der Prädestinationslehre in der lutherischen Orthodoxie* (Hannover: Lutherisches Verlagshaus, 1983).

[10] Joar Haga, *Was There a Lutheran Metaphysics? The Interpretation of communicatio idiomatum in Early Modern Lutheranism* (Göttingen: Vandenhoeck & Ruprecht, 2012); Jörg Baur, "Auf dem Wege zur klassischen Tübinger Christologie. Einführende Überlegungen zum sogenannten Kenosis-Crypsis-Streit," in *Luther und seine klassischen Erben, Jörg Baur* (Tübingen: Mohr Siebeck, 1993), 204–89.

[11] Heinrich Halverscheid, "Lumen Spiritus prius quam Scriptura intellecta: Hermann Rathmanns Kritik am lutherischen Schriftprinzip" (Th.D. diss., University of Marburg, 1971).

[12] In addition to the works of Wallmann and Schüssler listed above (nn. 2 and 5), see Timothy R. Schmeling, "Slaying the Syncretistic Chimera. A Study of the Consensus Repetitus in Light of the Confessionalization Theory" (Ph.D. diss., Concordia Seminary, 2014); Heinz Staemmler, *Die Auseinandersetzung der kursächsischen Theologen mit dem Helmstedter Synkretismus. Eine Studie zum "Consensus repetitus fidei vere Lutheranae" (1655) und den Diskussionen um ihn* (Waltrop: Spenner, 2005); and Peter Engel, *Die eine*

These discussions were drawn into the area of political maneuvering between electoral Saxony and other Lutheran governments, and this affected the course of the debate.[13]

In addition, the infusion of forms of medieval mysticism, especially in the concept of union with Christ,[14] but also more widely in devotional literature, lent a varied texture to much of the popular piety and also to the theological deliberations of seventeenth-century Lutherans at every level. Johann Arndt (1555–1621), finally superintendent of the churches of the duchy of Braunschweig-Lüneburg, gives evidence of a surrender to such "mystical" theological currents in some of his writings,[15] but interestingly, the sermons in his postil emphasize the necessity of the outward proclamation and reception of God's Word as conveyed in Scripture in ways that do not distinguish him from his catechumen and friend, Johann Gerhard (1582–1637).[16] The reliance on allegorical interpretations of Scripture in preaching was part of this larger return to certain medieval expressions of the Christian faith,[17] as was a turn to calls for an ascetic way of practicing it (e.g., in the devotional writings of Martin Moller [1547–1606]).[18]

The concentration on the dogmatic works of post-Reformation ecclesiastical culture has also obscured the fact that the theological curriculum of the seventeenth-century university in Lutheran lands continued to

---

Wahrheit in der gespaltenen Christenheit. Untersuchungen zur Theologie Georg Calixts (Göttingen: Vandenhoeck & Ruprecht, 1976).

[13] Schmeling, "Slaying the Syncretistic Chimera."

[14] Theodor Mahlmann, "Die Stellung der unio cum Christo in der lutherischen Theologie des 17. Jahrhunderts," in *Unio. Gott und Mensch in der nachreformatorischen Theologie*, ed. Matti Repo and Rainer Vinke (Helsinki: Luther-Agricola Gesellschaft, 1996), 72–199.

[15] Most radically argued by Hermann Geyer, *Verborgene Weisheit. Johann Arndts "Vier Bücher vom Wahren Christentum" als Programm einer spiritualistisch-hermetischen Theologie*, 3 vols. in 2 (Berlin: de Gruyter, 2001).

[16] Eric Lund, "Modus docendi mysticus: The Interpretation of the Bible in Johann Arndt's Postils," *Hermeneutica Sacra. Studien zur Auslegung der Heiligen Schrift im 16.- und 17. Jahrhundert / Studies of the Interpretation of Holy Scripture in the Sixteenth and Seventeenth Centuries*, ed. Torbjörn Johansson, Robert Kolb, and Johann Anselm Steiger (Berlin: de Gruyter, 2010), 223–45.

[17] Robert Kolb, "'A Time of Shadows and Signs': Johann Gerhard's Use of the Old Testament in Early Homiletical and Devotional Writings," in *Konfession, Politik und Gelehrsamkeit: Der Jenaer Theologe Johann Gerhard (1582–1637) im Kontext seiner Zeit*, ed. Markus Friedrich, Sascha Salatowsky, and Luise Schorn-Schütte (Stuttgart: Steiner Verlag, forthcoming).

[18] Elke Axmacher, *Praxis Evangeliorum: Theologie und Frömmigkeit bei Martin Moller (1547–1606)* (Göttingen: Vandenhoeck & Ruprecht, 1989).

consist largely of exegetical lectures. The grounding of biblical studies in hermeneutics, initiated by Matthias Flacius Illyricus (1520–75) in his *The Key to Sacred Scripture* (*Clavis scripturae sacrae*), had set in motion a tradition of sophisticated discussion of the principles of biblical interpretation that took form in essays or books by Johann Gerhard, Wolfgang Franz (1564–1628) of Wittenberg, and Salomon Glass (1593–1656) of Jena.[19] The investigation of parish and pastors' libraries could provide information regarding the place of commentaries alongside (or perhaps instead of) the great dogmatic works. The commentaries of Johann Tarnow (1586–1629) of Rostock and Sebastian Schmidt (1617–1696) of Strassburg, as well as of the dogmatics masters such as Johann Gerhard, await analysis. Abraham Calov's (1612–86) annotated Bible has received careful attention[20] but invites more study.

When Did Lutheran "Orthodoxy" Begin and End?

In order to simplify matters for easy digesting by those who learn, scholars cast history into periods, but every attempt at periodization represents only a certain set of concerns and perspectives. The flow of human experience is not in fact so easily chopped up. This volume begins with figures who taught the Gospel message and led the church in the era that begins with the adoption of the Book of Concord as the accepted, official definition of the teaching of the Wittenberg Reformation in 1580. Up to that time, the theologians within the circle formed around Luther, Melanchthon, and their Wittenberg colleagues were sorting out the legacy they had received, in what may be called "the Late Reformation," the period after the Smalcald War (1546–47) and the imperial promulgation of the "Augsburg Interim" (1548). These events initiated a new period of intensive debate over certain key issues in teaching and practice, made rancorous by feelings of betrayal and duplicity on both sides of most questions.[21] In the years between 1580 and the arrival of Johann Gerhard

---

[19] Bengt Hägglund, "Pre-Kantian Hermeneutics in Lutheran Orthodoxy," *Lutheran Quarterly* 20 (2006): 318–36; Christoph Bultmann and Lutz Danneberg, eds., *Hebraistik – Hermeneutik – Homilitek: Die "Philologia Sacra" im frühneuzeitlichen Bibelstudium* (Berlin: de Gruyter, 2011), with a concentration on Glass.

[20] Volker Jung, *Das Ganze der Heiligen Schrift: Hermeneutik und Schriftauslegung bei Abraham Calov* (Stuttgart: Calwer Verlag, 1999).

[21] On defining the period as "Late Reformation," see Peter F. Barton, *Um Luthers Erbe: Studien und Texte zur Spätreformation: Tilemann Heshusius (1527–1559)* (Witten: Luther-Verlag, 1972), 7–15; on the course of these controversies, see the summary of Irene Dingel,

at the University of Jena to teach theology in 1616, Lutheran thinkers endeavored to integrate the insights of the Reformation and their interpretation of the Book of Concord into the lives of the common people. Gerhard initiated a new era in teaching theology and promoted the devotional life of the faithful with popular writings. This era ends with the teaching careers of Johannes Musaeus (1613–81), Abraham Calov (1612–86), and Johann Andreas Quenstedt (1617–88). Imaginative application of the Wittenberg legacy within a variety of structures and genre, from hymns and devotional literature to dogmatic treatises and polemical treatises, marked this period, as did the closest cooperation of church and secular governmental authorities. Already in this period, challenges from new forms of thinking began to challenge presuppositions of the theology fostered by the Lutheran Confessions. Socinianism, the stream of thought that took its name from the anti-Trinitarian theologians Laelio (1525–62) and Fausto Sozzini (1539–1604) and that developed into a church in Poland, produced a number of intellectuals whose works challenged Lutheran theologians throughout the seventeenth century. The Socinian emphasis on reason as the master of Scripture led to their rejection of the doctrine of the Trinity and the atoning work of Christ. These confrontations fit into the broader discussions raised by some new scientific discoveries, even though much of the advancement of scientific experimentation and theorizing proceeded from churchly circles, particularly in England and the Netherlands. Furthermore, the rise of biblical criticism from figures such as the Roman Catholic Richard Simon (1638–1712), who claimed to be trying to undermine the Protestant appeal to the sole authority of Scripture with his critical studies, attracted support from some individuals in Lutheran circles. These included the Hamburg educator Hermann Samuel Reimarius (1694–1768), who in fact had little to do with the church, and theology professor Johann Salomo Semler (1725–91). Both developed their own critical stances toward the biblical text. Such intended and unintended undermining of the credibility and authority of Scripture merged with the increasing use of arguments from natural theology to further weaken the stand of orthodoxy in Lutheran theological faculties.

Indeed, the Aristotelian argumentation that had come to dominate dogmatic discussions may have helped pave the way for the Enlightenment (and "Enlightened" Germans were in general much more friendly toward and active in the church than French or English Enlightenment

---

"The Culture of Conflict in the Controversies Leading to the Formula of Concord (1548–1580)," in Kolb, *Lutheran Ecclesiastical Culture*, 15–64.

figures),[22] but theologians, including Johannes Musaeus, reacted to their undermining of fundamental principles implicit in much of the new philosophies,[23] and Ernst Valentin Loescher (1674–1749) a century later typifies the reaction to ever more serious challenges to the faith from them.[24] Study of the mediating and accommodating theological proposals, including the appeals of irenic voices for reunion of Western Christendom and the arguments mounted to preserve something of the tradition while speaking the language of reason, has hardly begun.[25]

From the 1680s on, theology increasingly lost its place in the intellectual discussions of the period as "Enlightened" thinking advanced at the universities, and the rise of Pietism shifted accents in pastoral care and preaching. The works of "Orthodox" theologians continued to influence the eighteenth century, both through their continued use at the university as reference works and also through their place on the shelves of pastors and teachers. But with the deaths of Ernst Salomon Cyprian (born 1673)[26] in 1745 and of Valentin Ernst Loescher in 1749, the public voice of this way of conveying the legacy of Luther, Melanchthon, and their colleagues was softened dramatically, if not stilled.

The relationship of "Orthodox" methods and processes to the Enlightenment invites further study as do the continuities and discontinuities with Pietism. The "Orthodox" leaders of the church had continually sought to foster the faith and pious practices in the daily lives of the laity through preaching and publications. In Rostock, for example, both pro-

---

[22] Irene Dingel, "Recht und Konfession bei Samuel von Pufendorf," in: *Recht - Macht - Gerechtigkeit*, ed. Joachim Mehlhausen, *Veröffentlichungen der Wissenschaftlichen Gesellschaft für Theologie*, no. 14 (Gütersloh: Gütersloher Verlagshaus, 1998), 516–40; Irene Dingel, "Toleranz und Ökumene: Zum Erscheinen von Band 7 der Politischen Schriften von Leibniz," in *Drehscheibe des Wissens – und Zierde für jede Bibliothek*, ed. Wenchao Li (Hannover: Wehrhahn, 2012), 27–43; Friedrich Beiderbeck and Stephan Waldhoff, eds., *Pluralität der Perspektiven und Einheit der Wahrheit im Werk von G. W. Leibniz* (Berlin: Akademie-Verlag, 2010).

[23] Harry Mathias Albrecht, *Wesen und Einheit der Kirche nach der Lehre des Johannes Musäus (1613–1681): Lutherische Orthodoxie und Kirchliche Wiedervereinigung* (Mainz: von Zabern, 2003).

[24] Solveig Strauch, *Veit Ludwig von Seckendorff (1626–1692): Reformationsgeschichtsschreibung – Reformation des Lebens – Selbstbestimmung zwischen lutherischer Orthodoxie, Pietismus und Frühaufklärung* (Münster: LIT Verlag, 2005).

[25] But see Wolf-Friedrich Schäufele, *Christoph Matthäus Pfaff und die Kirchenunionsbestrebungen des Corpus Evangelicorum 1717–1726* (Mainz: Zabern, 1998).

[26] *Ernst Salomon Cyprian (1673–1745) zwischen Orthodoxie, Pietismus und Frühaufklärung*, ed. Ernst Koch und Johannes Wallmann (Gotha: Forschungs- und Landesbibliothek, 1996).

fessors and pastors campaigned for improvement of faithful Christian liberty in the seventeenth century.[27] The repetition of "Orthodox" teaching and concerns by leading "Pietists" and the strenuous efforts to cultivate piety similar to that advanced by Pietists (such as Philipp Jakob Spener [1635–1705]) by "Orthodox" pastors and professors suggests that it is necessary to rechart the analysis of the developments that lie behind these designations.

Where Can Lutheran "Orthodoxy" Be Found?

One focal point for investigating seventeenth-century ecclesiastical culture is certainly in the theological faculties of the universities, where pastors learned the tradition and how to proclaim it aptly in their own parishes.[28] The majority of village priests in the Middle Ages had no university training whatsoever. The evangelical emphasis on preaching and God's Word brought more and more prospective pastors to the universities, but into the seventeenth century the number of semesters they spent there and the time they devoted specifically to theological studies, offered largely in the form of exegetical lectures and exercises in logical thinking (the disputations) and homiletics, was often quite limited. For admission to the theological faculty, requirements included presumed command of Greek, Hebrew, and Latin, as well as ancient literature, the tools of dialectic and rhetoric, and some knowledge of other disciplines, especially mathematics and natural science.[29] Only slowly did the number of pastors who had more than a semester or two at the theological faculty grow.

Wittenberg's faculty remained prominent throughout the seventeenth and eighteenth centuries after its restoration in the late 1570s,[30] but other faculties also became centers of the formulation of the church's public teaching. Jena, Leipzig, and Tübingen exercised wide influence throughout much of the period. The teachers of future pastors and teach-

---

[27] Jonathan Strom, *Orthodoxy and Reform: The Clergy in Seventeenth Century Rostock* (Tübingen: Mohr Siebeck, 1999).

[28] Kenneth G. Appold, "Academic Life and Teaching in Post-Reformation Lutheranism," in Kolb, *Lutheran Ecclesiastical Culture*, 65–115.

[29] Luise Schorn-Schütte, *Evangelische Geistlichkeit in der Frühneuzeit, Deren Anteil an der Entfaltung frühmoderner Staatlichkeit und Gesellschaft Dargestellt am Beispiel des Fürstentums Braunschweig-Wolfenbüttel, der Landgrafschaft Hessen-Kassel und der Stadt Braunschweig* (Gütersloh: Gütersloher Verlagshaus, 1996), 159–226.

[30] Ulrike Ludwig, *Philippismus und orthodoxes Luthertum an der Universität Wittenberg: Die Rolle Jakob Andreäs im lutherischen Konfessionalisierungsprozeß Kursachsens (1576–1580)* (Münster: Aschendorff, 2009); Appold, *Orthodoxie als Konsensbildung*, 15–35.

ers in Rostock, Greifswald, and Königsberg on the Baltic coast, as well as in Copenhagen and Uppsala, published significant works. Helmstedt's turn to metaphysics[31] and the subsequent irenicism of its professor, Georg Calixt, made it a focal point of theological discussion. Marburg shifted between Lutheran and Calvinist positions as its rulers dictated, and Giessen came into existence in 1607 as a Lutheran counter-weight while brothers and cousins among the descendants of Philipp I of Hesse (1504–67) struggled to defend their own convictions. Strassburg transformed its academy into a university in 1621, and its instructors also shaped elements of the ongoing discussions within Lutheran theological exchange.

But the heartbeat of the period comes rather from the parsonage and pulpit of local congregations and from the tables in the homes in which parents led their children and servants in Bible reading, hymn singing, and prayer. While many lay people were undoubtedly lackadaisical about practicing their faith, some understood rather complex doctrinal disputes and held firm opinions that enabled them to remain faithful to their convictions and resist secular government's pressures.[32] Indeed, what has been discussed in scholarship on Lutheran ecclesiastical culture to date has focused above all on the universities and their theological faculties, hymnwriters, the authors of devotional literature, and preachers who commanded some attention. Preachers at princely courts, such as Matthias Höe von Höenegg (1580–1645) and Jakob Weller (1602–64) (both in Dresden), Salomon Lentz (1584–1647) (in Magdeburg), and Basilius Sattler (1549–1624) and Joachim Lütkemann (1608–55) (both in Wolfenbüttel), not only made significant contributions to public theology but also wielded a great deal of political influence.[33] Pastors, often those with responsibilities as superintendents over territorial churches or regions within them, turned their preaching and teaching into handbooks for individual meditation, collections of sermons used in family devotions as well as sermon preparation by other pastors, and prayerbooks or meditative exercises. Johann Arndt, Philipp Nicolai (1556–

---

[31] Walter Sparn, *Wiederkehr der Metaphysik: Die ontologische Frage in der Lutherischen Theologie des frühen 17. Jahrunderts* (Stuttgart: Calwer Verlag, 1976).

[32] See Robert Christman, *Doctrinal Controversy and Lay Religiosity in Late Reformation Germany: The Case of Mansfeld* (Leiden: Brill, 2012); more general on the popular piety of the time, see Robert Christman, "The Pulpit and the Pew: Shaping Popular Piety in the Late Reformation," in Kolb, *Lutheran Ecclesiastical Culture*, 259–303.

[33] E.g., see the studies in Wolfang Sommer, *Die lutherischen Hofprediger in Dresden: Grundzüge ihrer Geschichte und Verkündigung im Kurfürstentum Sachsen* (Stuttgart: Steiner, 2006).

1608),[34] Paul Gerhardt (1607–76), and Johannes Heermann (1585–1647) are but four examples of such pastors.

The tenor and texture of the life of the Lutheran church in the seventeenth century emerges for today's student largely from printed literature, although a wealth of manuscript sources for more average sermons than those printed lies untouched in archives, along with personal records of pious and not-so-pious lay people. The several genres of seventeenth-century published works that continue to await study include the postils (sermons for the appointed lessons of the Church Year), other collections of sermons,[35] commentaries,[36] pastoral manuals and summaries of decisions on cases of casuistry,[37] poetry and drama, works for personal meditation, hymns,[38] polemical attacks and responses, and catechetical tools and treatises.[39]

Seventeenth-century Lutheran ecclesiastical culture was an international phenomenon. Indeed, it spread throughout many—though not all—parts of the "German lands." There was no "German state" at this time. The "Holy Roman Empire of the German Nation" embraced much of the territory in which German was spoken. Some territories beyond modern German national borders were thoroughly German: Alsace and (at least theoretically) parts of Lorraine in the west; Prussia, Silesia, and

---

[34] Anne M. Steinmeier-Kleinhempel, *"Von Gott kompt mir ein Frewdenschein": Die Einheit Gottes und des Menschen in Philipp Nicolais "FrewdenSpiegel deß ewigen Lebens"* (Frankfurt/M: Lang, 1991).

[35] Mary Jane Haemig and Robert Kolb, "Preaching in Lutheran Pulpits in the Age of Confessionalization," in Kolb, *Lutheran Ecclesiastical Culture*, 117–57.

[36] Johann Anselm Steiger, *Philologia Sacra: Zur Exegese der Heiligen Schrift im Protestantismus des 16. bis 18. Jahrhunderts* (Neukirchen-Vluyn: Neukirchener Verlag, 2011) grows out of the author's extensive work on the exegesis of the period and points in further directions.

[37] Benjamin T. G. Mayes, *Counsel and Conscience: Lutheran Casuistry and Moral Reasoning after the Reformation* (Göttingen: Vandenhoeck & Ruprecht, 2011).

[38] Christopher Boyd Brown, "Devotional Life in Hymns, Liturgy, Music, and Prayer," in Kolb, *Lutheran Ecclesiastical Culture*, 205–58; Ferdinand van Ingen and Cornelia Niekus Moore, eds., *Gebetsliteratur der frühen Neuzeit als Hausfrömmigkeit: Funktionen und Formen in Deutschland und den Niederlanden* (Wiesbaden: Harrassowitz, 2001). Among recent studies of seventeenth-century hymnody, see Lukas Lorbeer, *Die Sterbe- und Ewigkeitslieder in deutschen lutherischen Gesangbüchern des 17. Jahrhunderts* (Göttingen: Vandenhoeck & Ruprecht, 2012).

[39] Gerhard Bode, "Instruction of the Christian Faith by Lutherans after Luther," in Kolb, *Lutheran Ecclesiastical Culture*, 159–204; Gerhard Bode, "Conrad Dieterich (1575–1639), and the Instruction of Luther's Small Catechism," (Ph.D. diss., Concordia Seminary, 2005); Andreas Ohlemacher, *Lateinische Katechetik der frühen lutherischen Orthodoxie* (Göttingen: Vandenhoeck & Ruprecht, 2010).

Pomerania, as well as the Habsburg domains centered in Austria in the east. In addition, German language and culture had spread with populations moving east, into the kingdom of Poland, the Baltic region, Transylvania, and other points. In many of these areas, as well as in key parts of the Empire, Lutheran preaching won over the population and often the ruling authorities.

Luther's theology and program of reform appealed to many beyond those who spoke German. Students from various parts of Western Europe came to Wittenberg to study with Luther and Melanchthon. Some hailed from lands in which Luther's thought and/or the theology of the Formula of Concord did not attain a dominant position. William Tyndale (ca. 1490–1536) and Robert Barnes (1495–1540) had few successors in England, for example. But students from the kingdom of Denmark, which included Norway and Iceland, and from the kingdom of Sweden, including Finland, quickly brought the Wittenberg message to their homelands and introduced the Lutheran Reformation with the aid of their rulers.[40] German nobility governed much of the Baltic lands that now constitute Estonia and Latvia. Although the Reformation only slowly penetrated the "not-German" population, as seventeenth-century Latvians were taught to label themselves, the literature of both the Estonian and Latvian peoples emerged in print in Luther's Small Catechism, hymns and other devotional literature, the Bible, and a Latvian postil by the mid-seventeenth century.[41] Governing officials were more hostile in areas to the East, in what is today Poland, Slovakia, and Hungary, but the way of thinking and practicing the faith learned in Wittenberg spread in all three and became dominant among Slovak-speakers until the Counter-Reformation sent pastors into exile and forbade Lutheran worship and instruction.[42] By the end of the seventeenth century, Lutheran attempts at mission and confession of the faith outside traditional lands in Europe had begun, although the first actual planting of a church "overseas" took place in 1706 as Bartholomäus Ziegenbalg (1683–1719) and Heinrich Plütschau (1676–1752) took the Gospel to southeast India, soon

---

[40] A good overview is provided by Eric Lund, "Nordic and Baltic Lutheranism," in Kolb, *Lutheran Ecclesiastical Culture, 1550–1675*, 411–54.

[41] Jānis Krēsliņš, *Dominus narrabit in scriptura populorum: A Study of Early Seventeenth-Century Lutheran Teaching and Preaching in the Lettische lang-gewünschte Postill of Georg Mancelius* (Wiesbaden: Harrassowitz, 1992).

[42] A good overview is provided by David P. Daniel, "Lutheranism in the Kingdom of Hungary," in Kolb, *Lutheran Ecclesiastical Culture*, 455–507.

producing a translation of Luther's Small Catechism into Tamil.[43] In 1730, German Lutherans were delighted that the Augsburg Confession had come to India.[44]

The world in which Lutheran theology attempted to guide and comfort people was, as every era is, a world filled with turbulence, a century of "crisis," according to some.[45] Theologians reacted to developments in their own intellectual environment, continuing old debates and opening up new ones regarding the essence of things, but they, like pastors and laity, also were being shaped by the rise of the absolutistic state, the Thirty Years' War and other conflicts, the advance of capitalistic practices, and other disjunctures that disrupted the lives of people. Preaching and catechesis reflected the turbulence of the time.[46]

CHURCH GOVERNANCE AND POLITY IN SEVENTEENTH-CENTURY LUTHERAN LANDS

Lutheran "Orthodoxy" involved more than just ideas and teachings. Its church life was governed and supervised by structures that grew out of the necessities of the breakdown of ecclesiastical authorities and their failure to provide good pastoral care in the early sixteenth century. Just as in medieval Europe, governing authorities exercised a good deal of power over the early modern churches.[47] The relationships between Lutheran

---

[43] Elof Haller, "Lappländische Mission," in *Realencyklopädie für protestantische Theologie und Kirche*, 3rd ed. (Leipzig: J. C. Hinrichs'sche Buchhandlung, 1896–1913), 11:281–83; Brijraj Singh, *The First Protestant Missionary to India: Bartholomaeus Ziegenbalg (1683–1719)* (Oxford: Oxford University Press, 1999); Daniel Jeyaraj, *Bartholomäus Ziegenbalg: The Father of Modern Protestant Mission* (New Delhi and Chennai: Indian SPCK and Gurukul Lutheran Theological College, 2006).

[44] Broadsheet in the Theodore Smithey Collection of Concordia Seminary library, St. Louis, MO.

[45] Geoffrey Parker and Lesley M. Smith, eds., *The General Crisis of the Seventeenth Century*, 2nd ed. (London: Routledge and Kegan Paul, 1997).

[46] E.g., see Alexander Bitzel, *Anfechtung und Trost bei Sigismund Scherertz: Ein lutherischer Theologe im Dreißigjährigen Krieg* (Göttingen: Vandenhoeck & Ruprecht, 2002); Dieter Wölfel, *Salomon Lentz, 1584–1647: Ein Beitrag zur Geschichte des orthodoxen Lutherums im Dreißigjährigen Krieg* (Gunzenhausen: Verein für bayerischen Kirchengeschichte, 1999).

[47] The independence of the church in the Middle Ages is largely a fictional myth; Pope Gregory VII (ca. 1020–85) may have had Emperor Heinrich IV (1050–1106) groveling before his doorstep in 1077, but his successor Calixt II (d. 1124) surrendered far-reaching powers to Heinrich's son, Emperor Heinrich V in the Concordat of Worms in 1122. Pope Innocent III (1160–1216) became lord of England through use of the interdict against King John "Lackland" (1166–1216) of England, but John exercised rule over the English. The

rulers and leaders of the church ranged over a wide spectrum from mutual respect to mutual suspicion, pious perceptions of church and world to cynical exploitation of the other institution.[48] In general, the patron's control of appointment to pastorates remained little changed apart from the disappearance of the rivalry of the bishop. Local nobles, town councils, regional counts, and dukes had the obligation of designating who would serve congregations. Smaller groups of congregations were led by superintendents, appointed by the prince who governed the territory and therefore its church. Yet the leaders of the church continually fought for the spiritual independence of the ecclesiastical leadership. Luther had admonished students to be assiduous in their God-given calling of admonishing rulers to repent and change when they were committing acts of injustice in governing. Some of his seventeenth-century heirs indeed stood up to their rulers who were practicing injustice against their subjects and particularly against the church.[49] Supterintendents exercised many of the functions of medieval bishops in oversight and encouragement, but their powers were practically limited by political forces on the territorial and local levels. Town councils often used Latin terms such as "consuls" and "senators" for their town council members. These leading citizens, from patrician and merchant families—rarely did artisans win places in these councils—demonstrated, like the princes, varying degrees of interest in and support for the church and its pastors and teachers.

Martin Luther aimed to create a culture in which God's Word permeated all elements of human life. He had no illusions about being able to fashion a perfect society, for he recognized that the ongoing eschatological battle between God and Satan would mean regress as well as progress in the dominance of God's truth. Nonetheless, he viewed striving for a society in which God's voice and his justice commanded public life as the calling of every believer. However, Luther also recognized that in what he called the "earthly realm," the horizontal dimension of life, consisting of situations in home and occupation, society, and congregation, human reason exercises God-given stewardship of all his created gifts. Reason, Luther insisted, is not the private possession of Christians but is shared to varying degrees by all people. Thus, Luther would not be surprised by the conclusion of proponents of "confessionalization" (a con-

---

"Pragmatic Sanction of Bourges" of 1438 placed the French bishops more under the power of the king than the pope.

[48] Robert von Friedeburg, "Church and State in Lutheran Lands, 1550–1675," in Kolb, *Lutheran Ecclesiastical Culture*, 361–410.

[49] Robert Kolb, "Luther on Peasants and Princes," *Lutheran Quarterly* 23 (2009): 125–46.

temporary framework for explaining early modern European developments) that in Roman Catholic, Lutheran, and Reformed commonwealths, many aspects of life show little or no impact of confessional differences.[50] Certainly, the Lutheran conviction (shared by followers of John Calvin [1509–1564] as well) that natural law governs daily life and that daily life is structured according to the framework of "callings" arose out of Luther's thinking, but it uses the medieval social theory of "estates" common to all Western Europeans of the time. So the pious people in Lutheran lands lived within social conditions that were perhaps marked by the faithfulness in earthly matters to which their trust in Christ, nourished by study of His Word, was cultivated. But few specific forms that can be labeled "Lutheran" appeared. In the formulation and administration of the legal systems for society, evidence of the impact of their faith on the work of Lutheran legal experts and governmental counselors, in both theory and practice, is quite clear.[51] In music, art, and architecture, in political structures and ethics, in relationships among the several levels of early modern society, Lutherans belonged to the wider culture of Europe of their time.[52]

The early modern period witnessed the height and beginning of the demise of absolute political power in Western Europe. Its denizens experienced the development of industry in revolutionary ways as the natural sciences, impelled in many cases by Christians seeking to exercise God-given dominion within creation, opened new insights and fields of investigation. Capitalism replaced feudalism as the dominant form of economic life. And Lutherans were there. To understand modern church developments, one must have some knowledge of this critical period in the processing and application of the Wittenberg theology as expressed in the Lutheran Confessions and the biblical interpretation and proclamation that flowed from them. Students today have more opportunities to read works from the period in English than ever before, but mastery of German, Latin, Greek, and Hebrew are necessary for deeper plumbing of the depths of the period. A command of other European languages—

---

[50] Thomas A. Brady, Jr., "Confessionalization: The Career of a Concept," in *Confessionalization in Europe, 1555–1700, Essays in Honor and Memory of Bodo Nischan,* ed. John M. Headley et al. (Aldershot, Hants, England/Burlinton, VT: Ashgate, 2004), 1–20.

[51] Luise Schorn-Schütte, *Gottes Wort und Menschenherrschaft: Politisch-Theologische Sprachen in Europa der Frühen Neuzeit* (Munich: Beck, 2015).

[52] Susan R. Boettcher, "The Social Impact of the Lutheran Reformation in Germany," in Kolb, *Lutheran Ecclesiastical Culture,* 305–59. On Calvinist attitudes and teaching on these matters, see David van Drunen, *Natural Law and the Two Kingdoms: A Study in the Development of Reformed Social Thought* (Grand Rapids: Eerdmans, 2010).

Nordic, Baltic, and Slavic—enables specialization in the several regions of Lutheran preaching and teaching in this era. To understand the texts of seventeenth-century theologians, one must also have some knowledge of the Latin and Greek pagan classics, particularly of Plato's and Aristotle's ways of thinking, and of the rules for logical analysis and effective rhetorical, literary communication, which governed the writing of seventeenth-century Lutherans.

This volume is offered as a means for familiarizing readers with a too-often neglected, if not maligned, period in the history of God's people and perhaps also to entice some into moving into the deeper waters just described. Taking these fellow believers as conversation partners cannot help but deepen and expand our knowledge of how the Christian faith has come to us as we experience it in our time.

Robert Kolb

AEGIDIUS HUNNIUS (1550–1603)

FATHER OF WITTENBERG LUTHERAN ORTHODOXY

by Roland Ziegler

LIFE

Aegidius Hunnius was born to Egdius und Apollonia Hunn in Winnenden (Duchy of Württemberg) on December 21, 1550. He came from a family of craftsmen (his father was a master dyer) that was by no means poor. After his mother had a dream that he would be a pillar of the church, she wanted him to become a pastor, and thus Hunnius went the usual educational route for a gifted, but not wealthy, student in Württemberg. He went through the preparatory boarding schools, some of which were monasteries that had been converted into schools during the reformation of Württemberg (namely, Adelberg and Maulbronn). Then Hunnius entered the University of Tübingen (in the "Foundation" [*Stift*], a pre-ministerial school) on a ducal scholarship on November 1, 1565. After he attained the degree of master, he became a graduate assistant (*repetent*). In 1574, he was called to serve as an associate pastor in Tübingen. In Tübingen, which has been called "the most important theological faculty of its time," he studied with Jakob Andreae (1528–90), Johannes Brenz (1499–1570), Theodor Schnepf (1525–86), and Jakob Heerbrand (1521–1600). He was especially close to the latter.[1] Hunnius married Eleonore Felder (1554–1620) on January 10, 1576. They had eight children, one of which, Nicolaus Hunnius (1585–1643), became a renowned theologian in his own right. Heerbrand recommended Aegidius Hunnius as a professor for the Philipp University in Marburg. He attained his doctorate of theology on July 16, 1576, and began his career as a professor of theology in August of the same year. Hunnius saw himself always as a proponent of the "Tübingen Theology," and was seen as such by his opponents.

The University of Marburg was jointly administered by the heirs of Landgrave Philip (1504–67), after Hesse was divided among his four sons. Hunnius soon entered the midst of theological struggles and controversy in Hesse. While Landgrave Ludwig IV of Hesse-Marburg (1537–1604) was sympathetic to Hunnius, even if Ludwig did not have a complete grasp of the theological issues, his brother Landgrave Wilhelm IV of Hesse-Kassel (1532–92) was opposed to what he saw as the innovative Christology of the Tübingen theologians and the Formula of Concord. The point of contention was the communication of attributes (*communicatio idiomatum*), especially the majestic genus (*genus maiestaticum*). Hunnius continued the tradition of Brenz, Andreae, and Heerbrand, which viewed the communication of attributes as the necessary implication of the personal union, not as something extrinsic to it, over and against an understanding of the personal union as the mere supposition of the human nature by the divine Word.[2] The potential for future conflict came to the surface shortly after the arrival of

---

[1] Markus Matthias, "Theologie und Konfession: Der Beitrag von Ägidius Hunnius (1550–1603) zur Entstehung einer lutherischen Religionskultur," *Leucorea-Studien zur Geschichte der Reformation und der Lutherischen Orthodoxie,* no. 4 (Leipzig: Evangelische Verlagsanstalt, 2004), 56. This is the only book-length monograph on Hunnius, though it only covers his life up to his move to Wittenberg. See also Theodor Mahlmann, "Hunnius, Aegidius," in *Theologische Realenzyklopädie* (Berlin and New York: Walter de Gruyter, 1977–2004), 15:703–7.

[2] Jörg Baur accuses Hunnius of deviating from Tübingen Christology and thus holding to the same teaching as his student Balthasar Mentzer I. See his "Auf dem Wege zur klassischen Tübinger Christologie," *Luther und seine klassischen Erben. Theologische Aufsätze und Erörterungen* (Tübingen: J. C. B. Mohr [Paul Siebeck], 1993), 218. In contrast, Matthias opposes Baur's interpretation. See his, *Theologie*, 178.

Hunnius in Marburg. Hunnius taught the omnipresence of Christ's human nature in his lectures on John, and at the General Synod of 1576, where the Torgau Book was discussed. He defended the Christology of articles VII and VIII on the Lord's Supper and person of Christ respectively, but he could not win over the majority of the General Synod.[3] Rather, the opinion of the Hessian church rejected the real communication of attributes. But even though the Hessian Church never adopted the Formula of Concord, a theological rift still opened between the different parts of Hesse. Hunnius influenced the church in Hesse-Marburg deeply and strengthened its Lutheran identity. Already in 1578, Landgrave Wilhelm IV demanded the dismissal of Hunnius as professor. Hunnius was asked to give an account of his theological position. (This *Confession on the Person of Christ* [1577], was later printed without his permission in Strassburg in 1590).[4] The Christological debates led to the publication of *Four Booklets on the Person of Christ and his Majesty, Sitting at the Right Hand of God* (1585).[5]

After the death of Elector Christian I of Saxony (1560–91), the overthrow of Chancellor Nikolaus Krell (1550–1601), and the end of Cryptocalvinism in Electoral Saxony, Friedrich Wilhelm I of Saxony-Weimar (1562–1602) became regent of the electorate. He called Hunnius to the University of Wittenberg in 1591 to restore the orthodoxy of the land. Hunnius became first theology professor (*professor primarius*) and provost (*Probst*) at the castle church. In 1595, he became superintendent of Wittenberg, as well. In this capacity, he authored the Saxon Visitation Articles (1595) to root out any residual Cryptocalvinism. From 1593 until 1597, Hunnius was also embroiled in a lengthy and significant debate with Samuel Huber (1547–1624) on predestination. Though Hunnius was called back to Tübingen in 1599 (after the death of his teacher Jakob Heerbrand), Elector Christian II of Saxony (1583–1611) retained his services. At the 1601 Regensburg colloquy between Lutherans and Roman

---

[3] The General Synod was an annual meeting of the six superintendents of the four Hessian landgraviates, select pastors, theological professors of the theological faculty of Marburg, and counselors.

[4] Aegidius Hunnius, *Ein kurtze / einfältige / vnd inn Gottes Wort gergründete Bekandtnuß. . . .* (Strassburg: Anton Betram, 1590). Matthias, *Theologie*, 334–402 gives a detailed bibliography of Hunnius's works. Henceforth Hunnius's writings will be referenced with abbreviated titles. In addition, their corresponding number from the complete bibliography of Hunnius's works found in Matthias, *Theologie*, 334–402, will be provided as follows (Matthias, no. 47).

[5] Aegidius Hunnius, *Libelli IIII De Persona Christi, Eivsqve Ad Dextram Dei Sedentis Divinae Maiestate* (Frankfurt a. M.: Johann Spies, 1585), (Matthias, no. 17).

Catholics, he was with Jacob Heilbrunner (1548–1618), the leader of the Lutheran delegation, defending the sufficiency and supreme authority of Scripture against the Roman position. Hunnius died in Wittenberg on April 4, 1603.

Hunnius's reputation was so great among Lutherans that Johann Schmidt in his funeral oration for Thomas Wegelin (1577–1629), one of Hunnius's students, said that Hunnius rightfully took by common consent the third place among theologians, after Luther and Martin Chemnitz.[6]

Hunnius was a prolific author in different genres. To give an overview, it may serve to list the content of his collected works. In his theological tracts, collected in the first volume of the *Latin Works* (*Opera Latina*), he gives an almost complete dogmatics. Volume two contains his polemical writings against Roman Catholics, Calvinists, and Samuel Huber. The third and fourth volumes encompass his exegetical writings and his treatise on homiletics.[7] The final, fifth volume contains disputations, orations, and three comedies: two on the patriarch Joseph, one on Ruth.[8] The treatise on Holy Scripture is one of the first extensive treatments of bibliology in Lutheran Orthodoxy.[9] His primary love was exegesis, and thus his exegetical contributions must be kept in mind when looking at the many theological controversies in which he was involved, to avoid the common caricature of him as zealot only

---

[6] Johann Schmidt, "Oratio parentalis . . . Dn. Thomae VVegelini," in *Memoriae theologorum nostri saeculi . . .*, ed. Henning Witte (Frankfurt a. M., 1685), 7:934. In contrast, Wilhelm Herbst, writes, "Seine hohe Bedeutung als Streittheologe, die außer aller Frage steht, drückt seinen Wert als Theologen überhaupt stark herab." See his *Das Regensburger Religionsgespräch von 1601 geschichtlich dargestellt und dogmengeschichtlich beleuchtet* (Gütersloh: Druck und Verlag von C. Bertelsmann, 1928), 114.

[7] Hunnius published commentaries on Genesis 1–12, Matthew, John, all of the Pauline epistles except 2 Timothy, Hebrews, and 1 John. This should be kept in mind because he is seen primarily as a polemical theologian.

[8] On the Latin comedies of the time in general, written for performance in schools, see Stefan Tilg, "Comedy," in *Oxford Handbook of Neo-Latin*, ed. Sarah Knight and Stefan Tilg (New York and London: Oxford University Press, 2015), 87–102. On Hunnius especially, see Detlef Metz, *Das protestantische Drama. Evangelisches geistliches Theater in der Reformationszeit und im konfessionellen Zeitalter* (Cologne, Weimar, and Vienna: Böhlau, 2013), 171–75. They are the only writings of Hunnius that were edited in modern times. See Eduard Schröder, ed. *Aegidii Hunnii comoediae Josephi* (Marburg: Friedrich, 1898); his, *Aegidii Hunnii comoediae Josephi pars posterior* (Marburg: Friedrich, 1899); and his, *Aegidii Hunnii comoediae Ruth* (Marburg: Friedrich, 1900).

[9] Aegidius Hunnius, *Tractatvs De Sacrosancta Maiestate Sacrae Scripturae. . . .* (Frankfurt a. M.: Johann Spies, 1590), (Mathias, no. 48).

concerned with obscure dogmatic minutiae.[10] The controversies in Hesse led Hunnius to formulate a thorough exposition of the communication of attributes and the polemical questions raised in this context: in what way does one counter the charge of monophysitism and how, then, does one understand the state of humiliation? Hunnius debated the omnipresence of Christ's human nature later also with Daniel Hoffmann (1538–1611), professor in Helmstedt, who held on to a Melanchthonian Christology.[11]

Hunnius published several writings against the Reformed theologian David Pareus (1548–1622), professor in Neustadt an der Haardt and Heidelberg.[12] He also publicized against the claim that the Reformed were following the Augsburg Confession, which was not only a theological question, but also a political one. According to the Augsburg Religious Peace of 1555, only the Church of Rome and the adherents of the Augsburg Confession were tolerated religions.[13] Hunnius was favoring a strict separation from the Reformed, so that even the impression of theological agreement was avoided. Thus, when he was accompanying Administrator Friedrich Wilhelm I of Saxony-Weimar to the 1594 Diet of Regensburg, Hunnius co-wrote an opinion that the duke should not join in a closer alliance with the Reformed Elector of the Palatinate.[14]

In his debate with Samuel Huber, Hunnius developed his thinking on predestination. On one hand, the Solid Declaration of the Formula of

---

[10] Hunnius's reputation was especially attacked by the prolific Hessian pro-union historian Heinrich Heppe. See his *Geschichte der Hessischen General-Synoden von 1568–1582*, 2 vols. (Kassel: Druck und Verlag von Th. Fischer, 1847), 184.

[11] Aegidius Hunnius, *Nothwendige Verantwortung des Christlichen Concordibuchs. ...* (Frankfurt a. M.: Johann Spies, 1597), 197 (Matthias, no. 125); Aegidius Hunnius, *Widerlegung der Vngegründeten Aufflagen Daniel Hoffmanns* (Frankfurt a. M.: Johann Spies, 1597), (Matthias, no. 126); Aegidius Hunnius, *Abtruck zweyer Schreiben. ...* (Lich: Erben, 1597), (Matthias, no. 130).

[12] Aegidius Hunnius, *Calvinvs Ivdaizans. ...* (Wittenberg: Matthias Welack, 1593), (Matthias, no. 76); Aegidius Hunnius, *Anti-Pareus. ...* (Frankfurt a. M.: Johann Spies, 1598), (Matthias, no. 131); Aegidius Hunnius, *AntiParevs alter. ...* (Frankfurt a. M.: Johann Spiess,1599), (Matthias, no. 131).

[13] Aegidius Hunnius, *Gründtliche Beweisung/ daß die Zwinglinaner vnnd Caluinisten der wahren Augspurgischen Confession niemals zugethan gewesen. ...* (Frankfurt a. M: Johann Spies, 1591), (Matthias, no. 55); Aegidius Hunnius, *Theses, Qvibvs Ostenditvr, Sacramentarios Calvinstas Avgvstanae Confessionsis Socios Non Esse* (Wittenberg: Matthias Welack Witwe, 1594), (Matthias, no. 99).

[14] Franz Dominicus Häberlin, *Neueste deutsche Reichs-Geschichte* (Halle: Johann Jacob Gebauer, 1774–86), 19:XVIII–XXII. Because of this attitude, Wilhelm Herbst had a rather negative view of Hunnius. See his *Das Regensburger*, 115.

Concord in Article XI rejected double predestination. On the other hand, it also rejected that man is the cause of his own election. It refused thus any symmetrical answer to the question, "Why are some elected and others are not?" This asymmetrical doctrine of election implied that election is particular (though the term was not used in the Solid Declaration), but God's will to save is universal.[15] Samuel Huber, originally a Calvinist from Switzerland, who later became a Lutheran Tübingen professor and then a colleague of Hunnius in Wittenberg, taught universal election in an effort to break completely with Calvinism, because any talk of a particular election implied that the cause of damnation lies with God. Hunnius maintained against Huber that election is particular (i.e., that it does not pertain to all men). In contrast, Hunnius stressed that there was no absolute decree of election, but that election is *ordinate*. This means that when God elects, this choosing includes God's grace, Christ's merit, and faith, the latter of which grasps both of the former.[16] If election is understood in this way, then it is obvious that there is no election outside of faith. Thus the discussion of faith is introduced into the disquisition on election, and this became standard in Lutheran Orthodoxy. Still, faith for Hunnius is not a meritorious cause (*causa meritoria*), but an instrumental cause (*causa instrumentalis*) of election. This change in the treatment of election had far-reaching repercussions, giving rise to the American Lutheran predestinarian controversy in the nineteenth century. At this time, the question of whether faith should be regarded in any way as a cause (*causa*) of election became alive again and Hunnius was blamed by C. F. W. Walther and Franz Pieper as the one who first deviated from the Formula of Concord into a synergistic direction.[17] Rune Söderlund gives a different interpretation of Hunnius's contribution. He does not see the talk of faith in election as synergistic, but rather in parallel to

---

[15] The term "asymmetrical" was coined by Rune Söderlund in his "Ex praevisa fide. Zum Verständnis der Prädestinationslehre in der lutherischen Orthodoxie," *Arbeiten zur Geschichte und Theologie des Luthertums*, Neue Folge, no. 3 (Hannover: Lutherisches Verlagshaus, 1983).

[16] Otto Ritschl, *Dogmengeschichte des Protestantismus* (Göttingen: Vandenhoeck & Ruprecht, 1908–27), 4:144.

[17] "Wie verschieden in unserer Kirche während des 17. Jahrhunderts von Aegidius Hunnius an über das Verhältniß des Glaubens zur Gnadenwahl von unseren besten Theologen geredet worden ist . . ." See [C. F. W.] W[alther], "Dogmengeschichtliches über die Lehre vom Verhältniß des Glaubens zur Gnadenwahl," *Lehre und Wehre* 26 (1880): 49; Franz Pieper, *Christian Dogmatics* (St. Louis: Concordia, 1950–53), 3:487. It did not help that the other side quoted Hunnius in their favor. See, e.g., Theo. Mees, *Dogmengeschichtlicher Beitrag zur Entwicklung der Lehre von der Gnadenwahl innerhalb der lutherischen Kirche von 1522 bis 1580* (Columbus: Lutherische Verlagshandlung, n.d.), 193–94.

justification, where faith is seen as instrumental. According to Söderlund, the inroad of synergism was not the teaching of election *ex praevisa fide* (on the basis of foreseen faith). Rather, it was the rationalization that sees in the different use of post-lapsarian freedom (in regard to the use of the Means of Grace) the answer of why some are saved and others are not.

Finally, we turn to his polemics against the Roman Church, the church of the "primary antichrist." Besides some disputations[18] and smaller writings,[19] Hunnius engaged Robert Bellarmine, one of the foremost Jesuit controversialists of the Roman Church in the late sixteenth century, whose Disputations on the Controversies of the Christian Faith were widely read and commented on, especially his first disputation on the doctrine of Scripture.[20] In connection with Hunnius's participation in the 1601 colloquy at Regensburg, he first published theses in preparation of the event.[21] The colloquy itself, which ended prematurely, spawned voluminous polemical literature. Hunnius co-authored with Johann Heilbrunner the "Anti-Tannerus" and gave an account of the colloquy.[22]

Hunnius's literary career ended with a posthumously published book: a collection of prayers he wrote during his final sickness, in which erudition, piety, and polemics are combined. This was a fitting summary of his work.[23]

---

[18] Aegidius Hunnius, *De Dvobvs Antichristis Primariis, Mahvmete & Romano Pontifice, Disputatio. . . .* (Marburg: Paul Egenolph, 1590), (Mathias, no. 50); Aegidius Hunnius, *De Purgatorio Pontificorum Dispvtatio. . . .* (Marburg: Paul Egenolph, 1591), (Mathias, no. 59); Aegidius Hunnius, *Labyrinthus Primus Papisticus. . . .* (Wittenberg: Georg Müller, 1601).

[19] Aegidius Hunnius, *Catholische vnd Christliche Abfertigung Der Vncatholischen vnnd vbel gegründten Thesium oder Schlußreden / D. Ioannis Pistorij Niddani, De Iustificatione. . . .* (Wittenberg: Matthias Welck [Widow], 1595); Aegidius Hunnius, *Nebelkap dem Bapst abgezogen. . . .* (Jena: Salomon Richtzenhahn, 1603), (Matthias, no. 173).

[20] Aegidius Hunnius, *De Indvlgentiis Et Ivbilaeo Romani Pontificis Tractatus. . . .* (Franktfurt a. M.: Johann Spies, 1599); Aegidius Hunnius, *Prima Convtroverisa Generalis, Roberti Bellarmini, Pontificiae Ecclesiae Cardinalis, de verbo Dei scripto. . . .* (Frankfurt a. M.: Johann Spies and Romanus Beatus [Erben], 1602), (Matthias, no. 161).

[21] Aegidius Hunnius, *De Colloqvio Cvm Pontificiis Ineundo. . . .* (Wittenberg: Paul Helwig, 1601), (Matthias, no. 153). For an account of the colloquy, see Wilhelm Herbst, *Das Regensburger.*

[22] Aegidius Hunnius, *Anti-Tannerus. . . .* (Frankfurt a. M.: Johann Spies und Romanus Beatus [Heirs], 1602), (Matthias, no. 166); Aegidius Hunnius, *Relatio Historica De Habito Ratisbonae Colloqvio. . . .* (Tübingen: Gruppenbach, 1602), (Matthias, no. 168).

[23] Aegidius Hunnius, *Passional-Gebet. . . .* (Wittenberg: Georg Müller, 1604), (Matthias, no. 176).

BIBLIOGRAPHY

Works of Hunnius in English Translation

A Clear Explanation of the Controversy Among the Wittenberg Theologians Concerning Regeneration and Election: With a Refutation of the Arguments that Dr. Samuel Huber has Thus Far Brought into the Midst of Dr. Aegidius Hunnius, Polycarp Leyser, Solomon Gesner, etc., in Defense of His Opinions. Translated by Paul Rydecki. Edited by Rachel Melvin. Malone, TX: Repristination Press, 2013.

The Christian Table of Duties: A Description of Various Estates and Orders of Christians: Teachers, Hearers, Rulers, Subjects, Spouses, Parents, Children, Menservants and Maidservants, Masters and Mistresses, Young People, Widows, and Then All Men in General—What Each One Ought to Do or Leave Undone in This Vocation and Estate. Arranged and Compiled in Twelve Different Sermons Now Published in a Second, Amended Edition. Translated by Paul Rydecki. Malone, TX: Repristination Press, 2013.

The Judaizing Calvin: That Is, Jewish Interpretations and Corruptions by which John Calvin Has, in Detestable Fashion, Shamelessly Corrupted the Clearest Passages and Testimonies of Holy Scripture Regarding the Glorious Trinity, the Deity of Christ and of the Holy Spirit, and Especially the Prophecies of the Prophets Regarding the Coming Messiah—His birth, Suffering, Resurrection, Ascension into Heaven and Session at the Right Hand of God. Translated by Paul Rydecki. Malone, TX: Repristination Press, 2012.

Theses Opposed to Huberianism. Translated by Paul Rydecki. Malone, TX: Repristination Press, 2012.

Theses on Repealing Exorcism: Composed by Dr. Aegidius Hunnius Shortly Before His Departure From This Life So That They Might Be Publically Discussed in the Academy of Wittenberg. Translated by Paul Rydecki. Edited by Rachel Melvin. Malone, TX: Repristination Press, 2013.

Select Works by Hunnius in German and Latin

Tomus Primus [-Quintus] Operum Latinorum D. Aegidii Hunnii, Celeberrimi August. Confeß. Theologi. Edited by Helwig Garth. Frankfurt a. M.: Porssius, 1607–9.

WRITING[24]

*Moreover, if one attribute (*idioma*) of the Word is not communicated to the humanity, then they say that certainly no [attributes] are communicated, because the deity is* ameristos *or indivisible. And truly infinity, eternity, being a spirit is not attributed to the flesh. Therefore, also the remaining attributes [are] not [attributed to the flesh].*

To begin with, I will answer that we in this mystery neither affirm nor defend anything beyond that which is prescribed by the divine Word. We have clear evidence that to Christ the man omnipotence, infinite wisdom, the power to make alive, and the presence until the end of the world are communicated. Because of these, we believe. On the other hand, since the Scripture nowhere says that the humanity of Christ exists from eternity, that it has been made infinite, etc., therefore neither do we assert it. Moreover, it does not follow that if eternity cannot be predicated of the humanity of Christ, that therefore neither other attributes, like omnipotence, omniscience, etc., should be predicated. The adversaries have not yet proven that what is said of one attribute is to be declared also of the remaining ones. Although, to be sure, all the attributes and properties of God in himself are the essence in the simplest way and clearly are one *adiaretôs* [without separation]; nevertheless, when considered in respect to the assumed nature, or as they work in creatures, there truly one discusses concerning them in a distinct manner, so that not every one is said or predicated of every one promiscuously. Thus we say that God saves us through his goodness. We do not say that he saves us or justifies us through his infinity or eternity. Thus we say that God condemns the ungodly through his righteousness. Therefore, should we say, according to the Zwinglian dialectics, that God condemns through his goodness, mercy, and love, which are in the same way God's attributes? This would be truly by far most absurd, if indeed it is possible that the reprobates experience and feel the righteousness of God; nevertheless, they are deeply excluded and put out from the experience of God's love and goodness. Moreover, since especially the human nature of Christ is neither infinite nor from eternity, nevertheless the power of majesty communicated to it is infinite and eternal, just as we read that to the Son of Man (Daniel 7) eternal power, and as Christ himself explains, all power in heaven and on earth is given. Concerning the manner, infinity and eternity are not in

---

[24] This is a translation of Aegidius Hunnius, *Libelli IIII De Persona Christi, Eivsqve Ad Dextram Dei Sedentis Divinae Maiestate* (Frankfurt a. M.: n. p. [Johann Spies, according to Matthias, no. 17], 1595), 56–62.

fact communicated immediately to the assumed flesh, but by means of the other *energêtikôs idiômasi* [operating attributes]. Additionally, although eternity cannot be predicated of the human nature in respect of origin, nevertheless, eternity is communicated to Christ the man in respect of the goal, because of the personal union.

If omnipotence, wisdom, etc. of the Word [John 1:1] are communicated to the flesh, does it follow that also the Father and the Holy Spirit are incarnate, since omnipotence is ousiôdôs *[essentially] common to the whole Trinity?*

If the Word communicated omnipotence, and the rest of his attributes to the humanity, insofar they are simply and absolutely common to the entire Trinity, then the argument would follow. But he truly does not communicate [them] in this way, but merely under his person and thus, insofar as they are considered and determined relatively, in the person of the Son. Just as omnipotence, wisdom, etc., when considered absolutely, is one essentially, so it is limited to the three persons, who are really distinct, in such a way that the Father is the begetting omnipotence, the Son the begotten omnipotence, the Spirit the proceeding omnipotence—numerically one omnipotence *ousiôdôs* [essentially], but three *hypostatikôs* [in regard to the persons]. These relations are not naked and empty, as Sabellius dreamt, but true and real, as God is one *ousiôdôs* [essentially], but threefold *hypostatikôs* [in regard to the persons]. Because of this real *hypostatikê* [personal] distinction, the omnipotence can essentially be communicated and common to the entire Trinity, but not essentially to the human nature, but *hypostatikôs* [in a personal manner] and thus be communicated under the one person of the Word, truly from the person of the Father and the Holy Spirit distinct. And so that the vanity of the argument itself may shine forth clearer by its own light, it helps to ask our adversaries if this consequence of the argument serves against the communication of attributes. If not, also the personal union itself could weaken its force, certainly in this way: The divinity of the Word is common to the entire Trinity and is indivisibly one *ousiôdôs* [essentially]. Therefore, the deity of the Son cannot be personally united to the humanity unless at the same time the divinity of the Father and Holy Spirit are united to the humanity (if in fact there is one inseparable divinity of all three persons of the Trinity), and in the same manner either also the Father and the Holy Spirit are incarnated, or the union of the divine and human nature is made to naught. But if the divine nature of the Son, even if essentially common to the Father and the Holy Spirit, nevertheless can be united to the human nature under the person of the Son alone, without the incarnation of the Father and the Spirit, why not in the same way can the same divinity of the Word communicate to the humanity under the sole person of the Word, so that in a similar way from this neither the incarnation of the Father nor of the Holy Spirit follows?

When has the Word communicated the majesty of omnipotence and his other attributes to the assumed flesh?

In the same union and in the first moment of the conception or incarnation.

How do you prove that?

It is obvious from this, because Scripture and the orthodox Church confess this way, that the majesty clearly depends on the union. The witness of the old church is treated at another time. Concerning Scripture, it presents[25] that the Word in the union had anointed through the infinite richness of his own Spirit without measure the assumed flesh, as the Baptist says [John 3:34]. Therefore, etc., Christ is chosen as his name.

But the Sacramentarians understand this anointing to be about those finite and created gifts?

This anointing can be understood in no way about only those finite gifts and graces, with which in itself the flesh of Christ is enriched, unless one rejects the testimony of the Baptist, who mentions that Christ has received the Spirit *without measure*. An excellent explanation is then added: "The Father loves the Son, and has given *everything* into his hand" [John 3:35; italics added]. And Peter does not restrict this to finite gifts, but he affirms that Christ has been anointed by the Spirit and the power (Acts 10[:38]). But through which power? That certainly through which he, travelling around, heals the ones oppressed by the devil in a miraculous way. This capacity of performing miracles is nothing but divine, according to this psalm: "You alone do miraculous things" [Psalm 72:18]. Hence we believe also that in Christ the man all treasures of wisdom and knowledge are hidden (Colossians 2[:3]), in as much as on the beautiful branch, blossoming forth from the root of Jesse, the Spirit of wisdom and knowledge rests without measure. Hence the apostle Paul asserts that in Christ all the fullness of the deity dwells "bodily" [*sômatikôs*] (Colossians 2[:9]). Hence also Christ Jesus, even at that time, was described as having been in the form of God, seeing that his flesh even at that time had been raised up in the person of the Word, who is himself the form and image of the visible God (Colossians 1[:15]). In the meantime, though, at the same moment in which he accepted that same majesty, he *ekenôsen*

[25] The text has "prohibit," which makes no sense. This translation follows the reading in Hunnius, *Opera Latina*, 1:170, which has "perhibit."

[emptied] himself of the full use of it, as the apostle says (Philippians 2[:7]).

If he has emptied himself, therefore he did not have it?

He had the majesty itself in respect to primary actuality [*actu primo*],[26] but according to secondary actuality [*actu secundo*],[27] that majesty, which he had and retained, he did not use at the time of the humiliation, except now and then merely in bringing about miracles, when the glory of God and the confirmation of the divine doctrine required it, as the apostles described this state of humiliation in Philippians 2.

But the adversaries put forth that this passage in Philippians is to be interpreted as speaking about Christ according to his deity?

The analogy of faith stands against it and the text itself refutes this interpretation that we refer this passage directly to the Word according to the deity. For Paul did not write in that passage at hand that the Son of God or the Word took on a human nature, but that Jesus Christ (who certainly was immediately God and man) has taken on the form of a servant. And it cannot be affirmed that the manhood of Christ is that form of a servant about which Paul is speaking. For he put off the form of the servant after the resurrection, but the manhood he kept. But if the form of a servant and the assumed manhood were simply one and the same, then Christ either, having put off the form of a servant, also laid aside the manhood; or, having kept the manhood, would have kept the form of a servant and would hitherto, in his glory at the right hand of God, be a servant, which opposes the clear words of Peter (Acts 2[:33–36]), who said: Jesus, crucified, exalted to the right hand of God, has been made LORD and Christ. Furthermore, neither does the Greek word *ekenôsen* [he emptied], through which this same state of humiliation is expressed, allow that this state is applied to the nature of the deity, which by its own reason exists without change, and cannot empty itself. But the Word rules heaven and earth at the same time with the Father and the Holy Spirit as he had emptied himself in regard to the humanity as Christ; said John 5[:17]: "My Father works hitherto and I am working." But according to the human nature [*ekenôsen heauton*], "He has emptied himself," not indeed because he stops being in the form of God, or that he has put away the same majesty given to him by the union, but because he has emptied himself of the full rule of the heaven and earth and, thus of the perfect use or *energeia* [working] of the received majesty, truly and not by some deception, so that he could suffer and die for us.

[26] "Primary actuality" refers to a power or potential that is not currently actualized.

[27] "Secondary actuality" refers to the actual operation of a thing.

Philipp Nicolai (1556–1608)

Mystic-Orthodox Polemicist

by Jonathan Mumme

Life

Introduction

Ten years after the death of Martin Luther (1483–1546), and four before the passing of Philipp Melanchthon (1497–1560), as Charles V (1500–1558) was abdicating as Holy Roman Emperor, a third son was born to the family of Dietrich Rafflenbeul of Mengeringhausen in Waldeck, Germany.[1] In a Lutheran parish and parsonage, Philipp Nicolai

[1] Philipp Nicolai was born on August 19, 1556. The family name was originally Rafflenbeul, but Dietrich also called himself "Nicolai" after his father, Nicolaus, which is the name that Philipp and his brothers then took as the family name. In all, the family came to have

grew with a teaching and practice of the Christian faith that was, according to the Religious Peace of Augsburg (1555), legal. Peace itself, however, was more elusive. The future pastor, theologian, polemicist, hymnwriter, and missiologist[2] was born into volatile times. The Western Church had recently been divided by multiple reform movements, whose appeals it could not, or would not, absorb as one. The Smalcald War (1547) and Princes' Revolt (1552) began an era of armed conflict that would culminate in the Thirty Years' War (1618–48). Meanwhile, Western Christians had begun to solidify the identities of their communities and confessions over against one another in a process now referred to as confessionalization,[3] which was often attended by no little written belligerence. And beyond clashes of arms and words, there was the sudden and sweeping confrontation with death, presented by the plague. This volatility and its wounds can be sensed in a 1599 hymn from Nicolai's pen:

---

five sons (one who died as a baby) and three daughters. Regarding the Nicolai family, a Lutheran ministerial dynasty, see Jacobus Pannekoek, "Das Pfarrgeschlecht Nicolai zu Mengeringhausen," *Geschichtsblätter für Waldeck* 76 (1988): 55–115.

[2] For Nicolai's missiological thought, which will not be further treated in this essay, see especially Willy Heß, *Das Missionsdenken bei Philipp Nicolai* (Hamburg: Wittig, 1962); Arthur Carl Piepkorn, "Philipp Nicolai (1556–1608): Theologian, Mystic, Hymn Writer, Polemicist, and Missiologist: A Biographical Survey," *Concordia Theological Monthly* 39, no. 7 (1968): 432–61, especially 453f. Nicolai's chief work in this regard was his *Commentarius de regno Christi* (Frankfurt am Main: Spies, 1596–97). Generally regarding Nicolai, in addition to specific sources cited below, see Walter Lacher, *Philipp Nicolai* (Leipzig and Hamburg: Schloeßmann, 1937); Martin Lindström, *Philipp Nicolais Verständnis des Christentums* (Gütersloh: Bertelsmann, 1939); Siegfried Schunke, *Philipp Nicolai: Ein Wächter der Kirche im Zeitalter der Orthodoxie* (Gelsenkirchen-Buer: Krämer & Banker, 1959).

[3] See Carter Lindberg, "Legacies of the Reformations," in *The European Reformations*, 2nd ed. (Chichester: Wiley-Blackwell, 2010), 347–79; Martin Friedrich, "Kirche und Gesellschaft im konfessionellen Zeitalter" in *Die Pest, der Tod, das Leben: Philipp Nicolai—Spuren der Zeit*, ed. Ev. Kirchengemeinde und Ev. Kirchenkreis Unna (Unna: Ev. Kirchengemeinde und Ev. Kirchenkreis Unna, 1997), 115–28; and Bodo Nischan, "Germany after 1550," in *The Reformation World*, ed. Andrew Pettegree (London: Routledge, 2000), 387–407. The process included, but was not limited to, confessional statements such as the Roman Catholic canons and decrees of the Council of Trent (1545–63); the Thirty-Nine Articles of the Church of England (1563); Reformed confessions such as the Second Helvetic Confession (1562), the Belgic Confession (1566), and the Canons of Dort (1619); and the Lutheran Formula of Concord (1577).

So to the world now do I say,
"Good night," and leave it perish;
If misery it yet should pay,
My God will keep and cherish.
I thought the world was naught but gold,
but now I know it other.[4]

Though keen to bid his very mortal plain adieu, Nicolai did not leave it without leaving upon it the theological, polemical, devotional, and musical mark of an avid theologian and earnest curate of souls.

Biographical Sketch

Nicolai's parents were keen to invest in a good education for their sons (boys destined also to be pastors), even if it could not be procured in one place. Philipp's pedagogical journey included legs in Rhoden, Kassel, Hildesheim, Dortmund (twice), Mühlhausen,[5] and Korbach before he began his university education in Erfurt in 1575. From there, he moved on to Wittenberg (1576–79) and then continued in private study, living with his brother Jeremias at the abandoned cloister of Volkhardinghausen.

In 1583, he was ordained and assumed his first parish at Herdecke in the County of Mark (modern North-Rhine Westphalia, near Dortmund), where his father had introduced the Reformation a generation earlier before being driven out for not accepting the Augsburg Interim. Philipp, too, would be forced to leave Herdecke, first temporarily in 1584 as Spanish troops penetrated the area, and later as he was pushed out under pressure from Roman Catholic circles, which saw to the cancellation of his salary (1586). For a short time thereafter, he served secretly among Lutherans in Cologne. In 1587, he was summoned to Nieder-Wildungen (today Bad Wildungen) and shortly thereafter to Alt-Wildungen by Countess Margaretha of Waldeck; there he served as parson, court

[4] Philipp Nicolai, "Der WeltAbdank," in *Frewden Spiegel deß ewigen Lebens* (Frankfurt am Main: Spies, 1599), 413–16. Hereafter *Freudenspiegel*. The translation of this first of twelve verses is by Jonathan Mumme. This, along with his better-known chorales, seems to have first been published in 1599, though Carl Bertheau's "Nicolai, Philipp," in *Allgemeine Deutsche Biographie* (München und Leipzig: Duncker & Humblot, 1875–1912), 23:607–11, mentions L. F. C. Curtze's *D. Philipp Nicolai's Leben und Lieder* (Halle: Fricke, 1859) presenting an earlier date for their composition. Most of the current scholarship seems to assume they were written at the same time as the *Freudenspiegel*.

[5] Among Nicolai's teachers here was the poet and hymnist Ludwig Hembold.

preacher, and tutor to her son, Wilhelm Ernst (d. 1598). In view of a 1586 anti-Calvinist writing,[6] Landgrave Wilhelm of Hesse-Kassel IV (1532–92) forbade Nicolai's being granted a doctorate by the University of Marburg (1590), so he followed Aegidius Hunnius (1550–1603) from Marburg to Wittenberg, where a doctorate was awarded him in 1594. In 1596, Nicolai left Wildungen, as he was summoned for the third time to Unna in the County of Mark, where the presence of a Lutheran clergyman able to defend against Calvinism was needed.[7] The five years in Unna proved the most difficult and trying, but perhaps also the most spiritually productive and subtly joyous period of his career: a flight from Spanish troops, a visitation of the plague, hefty exchange with Calvinist adversaries, and marriage[8] marked his time there. In 1601, he was called to the distinguished post of head pastor at St. Catherine's in Hamburg. Plague and polemics also punctuated his Hamburg years, but the lively protagonist of Lutheran Orthodoxy was also known for his collegiality and pastoral devotion. First and foremost, though, he was admired in the harbor city for his preaching—a "second Chrysostom."[9] Turning down professorships in both Greifswald and Wittenberg, he remained in Hamburg for the rest of his life but exercised extensive influence from there, as his letters and the dedications of his polemical works testify.[10] He died on October 26, 1608, at the age of fifty-two and was buried at St. Catherine's under the memorial plaque dedicated to Joachim Westphal (1510/11–74), his Gnesio-Lutheran predecessor and superintendent of Hamburg.

---

[6] Philipp Nicolai, *Fundamentorum Calvinianae Sectae ... detectio* (Tübingen: Gruppenbach, 1586). This "Disclosure of the Foundations of the Calvinist Sect Held in Common with the Ancient Arians and Nestorians" was made more prominent by the commendatory forward composed for it by the dean and professors of the theological faculty of Tübingen. See Martin Brecht, "Philipp Nicolai: Lutherische Orthodoxie und neue Frömmigeit" *Jahrbuch für westfälische Kirchengeschichte* 84 (1990): 159–83, especially 163. For a listing and translation of this and other titles, see Piepkorn.

[7] The area was experiencing an influx of Reformed immigrants from the Low Countries and East Frisia, who were challenging Lutheran preeminence there. See Brecht, "Philipp Nicolai," 160–69.

[8] On January 8, 1600, he wed Catherine von der Recke, a widowed mother of two from Dortmund.

[9] Piepkorn, "Philipp," 441. Although Nicolai's collected works were published by George Dedekenn in Hamburg (1617), little of his preaching survives.

[10] Brecht, "Philipp Nicolai," 162f.

Career and Theological Work and Profile

In 1599, *Mirror of the Evil Spirit that Moves in the Books of the Calvinists*[11] issued from Nicolai's pen as part of an escalating confrontation with Calvinists at home and abroad. In the same year, *Mirror of the Joys of Eternal Life*[12] came into print, from the same hand, though apparently from a quite different Nicolai. By necessarily examining him between such mirrors as these books, modern observers have struggled to get a clear profile of the city preacher of Unna.[13] How could acid polemics and ardent Jesus hymns spring from the same source?[14] A standard interpretation classifies Nicolai as part of a "Lutheran Orthodoxy" from which such polemics were typical, who then stumbles into a deeper, mystical, pre-Reformation spirituality by way of horrific encounter with the plague. Out of this encounter, historians maintain, comes Nicolai's most important work, in a way that would have surprised Nicolai himself:[15] his *Mirror of the Joys of Eternal Life* would take its place beside Johann Arndt's *True Christianity* as a preeminent piece of devotional literature. It would help to overcome the "crisis of piety"[16] in which Nicolai's orthodox *Luthertum* (Lutheranism)[17] found itself in the closing decades of the sixteenth century, thus preparing the way for Pietism.[18]

It would indeed be surprising if polemics were not part of the profile of a Lutheran preacher, parson, and doctor of theology in the late sixteenth and early seventeenth century. The Roman Catholic front, solidi-

---

[11] Philipp Nicolai, *Spiegel des bösen Geistes / der sich in den Calvinisten Büchern reget . . .* (Frankfurt am Main: Spies, 1599).

[12] See n. 4 above.

[13] The city preacher of Unna was its first pastor and so the parson; the city also had a second pastor. See Thomas Spohn, "Unna um 1600," in *Die Pest, der Tod, das Leben: Philipp Nicolai-Spuren der Zeit*, ed. Ev. Kirchengemeinde und Ev. Kirchenkreis Unna (Unna: Ev. Kirchengemeinde und Ev. Kirchenkreis Unna, 1997), 101–14, especially 110.

[14] For "Wake, Awake for Night is Flying" and "O Morning Star, How Fair and Bright" as "Jesus hymns," see Piepkorn, "Philipp," 450. Both were appended to the *Freudenspiegel*, 409–13.

[15] See, for example, the depiction by Martin Rößler, "Philipp Nicolai 1556–1608" in *Liedermacher im Gesangbuch* (Stuttgart: Calwer, 1990), 1:117–43, especially 132.

[16] Concerning this term, see especially Johannes Wallmann, "VI. Zur Frömmigkeitskrise des 17. Jahrhunderts," in *Pietismus-Studien: Gesammelte Aufsätze* (Tübingen: Mohr Siebeck, 2008), 2:118–31, about which there is more below.

[17] *Luthertum* points not just to a belief system, but the churchly, social, and political structures in which this particular practice of the Christian faith was at play.

[18] See, for example, Friedhelm Brusniak, "Nicolai, Philipp," in *Neue Deutsche Biographie* (Berlin: Duncker & Humblot, 1999), 19:206f.

fying during Nicolai's childhood with the latter sessions of the Council of Trent (1562–63), was present for him from the beginning. His earliest contests in Herdecke paralleled those of his father a generation before. Their efforts were toward the establishment of a teaching and practice of the Christian faith divested of the abuses defended by the papacy and its adherents. Though not the major front of Nicolai's career, anti-Romanist polemics remained a part of Nicolai's undertakings even in his later Hamburg years.[19]

His constant fencing came on the Calvinist front. Sensibilities for the threat posed by this second main stream of the Reformation were shaped and sharpened during his studies at the University of Wittenberg, for he arrived shortly after the fall of the Philippists in 1574 and was influenced by Polykarp Leyser I (1552–1610). Already during his time in Herdecke, Nicolai began to write against the Calvinists in what became a rather public fashion.[20] Contested undertakings of his Wildungen years were primarily directed against the Calvinist front,[21] and while there, he began taking written part in the ubiquitarian controversy.[22] If his former works had not fully established his reputation, his 1596 *Necessary and Entirely Complete Report on the Whole Calvininian Religion*[23] would do so. Thus, when the city of Unna was feeling the pressure of Calvinist influx, it sought out Nicolai as its city preacher precisely because he was a Lutheran with a proven anti-Calvinist reputation. In Unna, Nicolai had his hands full, as Calvinist and Lutheran antipathies played not only with pulpits, but also with the positions of mayors and members of the city council, and even in the valuable and burgeoning salt mining of the area.[24] Whether the exchanges were local or more remote, anti-Calvinist

---

[19] His controversy with the Jesuit Henricus Neverus (1560–1617) of nearby Altona was carried forward in the posthumous publication of his *Cum Lojolitanae Societate . . . conflictus* (Hamburg: Philipp von Ohr Erben, [ca. 1609]).

[20] See n. 6 above.

[21] These included his part in the removal of the sacramentarian clergymen Justus and Heinrich Crane, and the excommunication of a county councilor, Johannes Backbier, for his expressed understanding of the Lord's Supper.

[22] This began with a published letter to Daniel Hoffmann of the University of Helmstedt in 1590, which was followed by Nicolai's *Methodus controversiae de omnipraesentia Christi, secundum naturam eius humanam* (Frankfurt am Main: Spies, 1596). Nicolai published further works in this vein in 1599, 1602, and 1607; the controversy also accounted for part of the substance of his prolonged exchange with Urban Pierius (1546–1616).

[23] Philipp Nicolai, *Notwendiger und vollkommener Bericht von der ganzen Calvinischen Religion* (Frankfurt am Main: Spies, 1596).

[24] Spohn, "Unna"; See Piepkorn, "Philipp," 437–41.

writings, as well as answers to them by Calvinists, were rolling off the presses. With his *Short Report on the Calvinists' God and Their Religion,* his polemics reached their "sharpest tone,"[25] and found equally sharp answers from as far away as Zurich. Even with the more harmonious surroundings of his later Hamburg environs, Nicolai continued to publish readily against the Calvinists. His two-volume work on *The Most Sacred Mystery of the Omnipresence of Jesus Christ,*[26] which indicates "the salutary conversion on the part of Calvinists" as an aim in its very title, stands as Nicolai's most systematic work. The reference to Urban Pierius as a "Dull-Witted Mameluke" in the title to the final work published during his lifetime indicates that he had lost little of his bite in his last years.[27] These undertakings were not without fruit. In 1593, the clergy of Waldeck accepted the Formula of Concord, and Unna remained Lutheran.

Come, heav'nly Bridegroom, Light divine,
And deep within our hearts now shine;
There light a flame undying!
In Your one body let us be
As living branches of a tree,
Your life our lives supplying.[28]

That these rapturously sublime words, along with the music of what became known as "The Queen of Chorales," could spring from the anti-Calvinist crusader, always ready, with warning and scorning, for dull-witted Mamelukes, seems indeed to indicate a different side to Nicolai.

---

[25] Philipp Nicolai, *Kurtzer Bericht Vonn der Caluinisten Gott vnd jhrer Religion / Jn etliche Frag vnnd Antwort* (Frankfurt am Main: Spieß, 1597). The citation is from Brusnaik.

[26] Philipp Nicolai, *Sacrosanctum Omnipraesentiae Jesu Christi Mysterium* (Frankfurt am Main: Becker, 1602). See n. 23 above.

[27] Philipp Nicolai, *Von Gottes Gnaden Sieg und Freudentritt der Wahrheit christlicher Religion in den evangelischen und gut lutherischen Kirchen durch Sachsen . . . anmäulet* (Hamburg: Philipp von Ohr, 1608). The controversy with Pierius had a number of facets regarding the presence of Jesus Christ in the ministry. See Jörg Baur, "Das kirchliche Amt im Protestantismus," in *Das Amt im ökumenischen Kontext: Eine Studienarbeit des ökumenischen Ausschusses der Vereinigten Evangelisch-Lutherischen Kirche Deutschlands,* ed. Jörg Baur (Stuttgart: Calwer, 1980), 103–38, especially 122–26. See also Jonathan Mumme, *Die Präsenz Christi im Amt: Am Beispiel ausgewählter Predigten Martin Luthers, 1535–46* (Göttingen: Vandenhoeck & Ruprecht, 2015), 15–18, 356–64.

[28] This rather free translation is cited according to *LSB* 395:2; Nicolai, *Freudenspiegel,* 410, there the third verse.

He may have come to Unna to do battle with the Calvinists, but he was also there confronted with the common human enemy, death, in the form of the plague. From July of 1597 to January of 1598, more than fourteen hundred of Nicolai's parishioners succumbed to the Black Death.[29] Burying sometimes twenty or even thirty people on a single day, he wrote to his brother Jeremias that he was living in the cemetery.[30] Shaped by Luther's thoughts on "Whether One May Flee from a Deadly Plague" (1527),[31] the city preacher of Unna stayed the course, burying even his colleague Joachim Kersting.

In this time of sad partings, he also took his leave of all strife, instead "spending the time in prayer and laudable reflection on life eternal and on the state of the precious souls in the heavenly paradise prior to the last day."[32] The literary result was Nicolai's best-known work, *Mirror of the Joys of Eternal Life.*[33] In this two-part work, Nicolai sought to provide comfort for the sick and dying, but especially for those mourning, by first examining the joys of eternal life from several different aspects (including a presentation of six attributes of eternal life), and then by showing "from whom eternal life comes and how we are prepared for it."[34] The work can be seen as a part of the "old comforter" genre,[35] which had its place in the household medicine cabinet at a time when death could come very quickly.[36] Though popular as a whole for a time, its perpetual treasure has proven to be the first two chorales appended to the work: "O Morning Star, How Fair and Bright" and "Wake, Awake, for Night Is Flying."[37] So

---

[29] Nicolai, *Freudenspeigel*, "Vorrede," v.

[30] See Rößler, "Philipp," 1:124.

[31] Martin Luther, AE 43:119–38; WA 23:338–79.

[32] Rößler, "Philipp," 1:124; Nicolai, *Freudenspeigel*, title page.

[33] The translation below is taken from this work. See n. 4 above. A second confrontation with the plague in Hamburg between 1605 and 1606 led to the publication of a somewhat revised edition: Philipp Nicolai, *Theoria vitae aeternae, das ist: Historische Beschreibung dess gantzen Geheimnisses vom ewigen Leben* (Hamburg: Philipp von Ohr, 1606).

[34] Nicolai, *Freudenspeigel*, 168, 424.

[35] Wallmann, "VI. Zur Frömmigkeitskrise," 122.

[36] Brecht, "Philipp Nicolai," 170.

[37] Nicolai, *Freudenspeigel*, 409–11 and 412f respectively; *LSB* 395 and 516. Both have been standard fare in countless Lutheran hymnals and enjoy some reception in the hymnody of other Christian denominations. J. S. Bach worked both hymns into Choral-Cantatas; "O Morning Star" was (based on a certain misunderstanding) long a favorite at Lutheran weddings; "Wake, Awake" influenced the "Hallelujah Chorus" of G. F. Handel's *Messiah.*

rich and so agreeing with the rest of the work are these chorales that they may rightly be regarded as its quintessence.[38]

Though a mystical element at work in Nicolai's meditations on the joys of eternal life and the accompanying hymnody have led some to see in him a harbinger of a new or renewed spirituality that would help to overcome the "crisis of piety" into which a rather combative Lutheran Orthodoxy had run itself by the close of the sixteenth century, this typical construal of Nicolai's theology, piety, work, and legacy is deficient on several accounts. The diagnosis of a mystical strand strongly at play in *Mirror of the Joys* and elsewhere is, however, itself correct. The mystical union of Christ and believers (*unio mystica*), which may be seen as Nicolai's chief constructive theological contribution,[39] takes cues from the likes of Bernard of Clairvaux (1090–1153), Anselm of Canterbury (ca. 1033–1109), and Hugh of St. Victor (ca. 1096–1141), and Nicolai finds himself thereby in the company not only of Martin Luther, but also of Lutherans such as Andreas Musculus (1514–81), Martin Möller (1547–1606), Nikolaus Herman (1480–1561), Johann Arndt (1555–1621), Johann Gerhard (1582–1637), Johann Heermann (1585–1647), and Paul Gerhardt (1607–76).[40] There is indeed a strong internal, subjective aspect to Nicolai's thought and piety, which would grow with subsequent Lutherans of the seventeenth century. However, to identify him as a Lutheran overcoming the piety of a Lutheranism whose orthodoxy was just being defined during his lifetime by somehow reaching back into the pre-

---

[38] Brecht, "Freudenspeigel," 40. "O Morning Star," with more than thirty references to approximately fifteen different books of the Bible, evidences deep scriptural meditation combined with Christ-mysticism, similar to that of Bernard of Clairvaux, given voice in evocative language; most hymnals (German and English) reproduce it only with some degree of pious editing. See Brecht, "Philipp Nicolai," 172, 178–81; Piepkorn, "Philipp," 449–52 and 455; and Rößler, "Philipp," 1:132.

[39] Piepkorn, "Philipp," 457. Concerning the *unio mystica,* see Werner Elert, "Unio Mystica," in *The Structure of Lutheranism*, trans. Walter A. Hansen (St. Louis: Concordia, 1962), 154–76; Elert concludes that the mystical union evident in Nicolai's writing ties back to Luther and is a part of an unbroken Lutheran tradition that has its roots in the Middle Ages, albeit with some important differentiations to similar tendencies of that period. See also Johann Anselm Steiger, "5. Die Weiterentwicklung der Ästhetik der Realpräsenz durch Luthers Erben, a. Philipp Nicolai," in *Fünf Zentralthemen der Theologie Luther und seiner Erben: Communicatio, Imago, Figura, Maria, Exempla* (Leiden: Brill, 2002), 52–58; and Anne M. Steinmeier-Kleinhempel, "Von Gott kompt mir ein Frewdenschein" in *Die Einheit Gottes und des Menschen in Philipp Nicolais "FrewdenSpiegel deß ewigen Lebens"* (Frankfurt am Main: Peter Lang, 1990).

[40] See Piepkorn, "Philipp," 449f. Nicolai would have attributed Bernard's *Manuale*, Anselm's *Meditationes*, and Hugh's *Soliloquia* incorrectly, but commonly, to Augustine.

Reformation piety of the Middle Ages (as did Luther) is problematic. This view shoehorns an identifiable break with the piety of the Middle Ages, the solidifying of the Lutheran Reformation, the formation of a Lutheran Orthodoxy, its subsequent(?) crisis of piety, and the first inroads to this crisis's removal into the space of three generations.[41] Further, Nicolai's hand in overcoming the "crisis of piety" at the close of the sixteenth century is tenable only insofar as his *Mirror of the Joys of Eternal Life* is paired with Johann Arndt's *True Christianity*. But, as Johannes Wallmann has convincingly argued, there is more that separates these works than unites them.[42] More tenable than the rather

---

[41] This is the case, for example, with Martin Brecht's otherwise often insightful article "Philipp Nicolai." In an "act of pious ecumenism," he portrays Nicolai introducing "new ideas" that resulted in an "emotional vivifying of piety" (172) into Lutheranism/Protestantism in a form of piety "just emerging at the end of the sixteenth century" (171). An internal contradiction is evident in Brecht's own observation: "Since about the middle of the sixteenth century people in Protestantism began to reach back into medieval-mystical prayer literature" (172). In addition to the double problem of speaking of something that could be labeled "Protestantism" by the middle of the sixteenth century (Lutheranism alone first attained legal status in 1555!), for which the use of the mystical prayer literature of the Middle Ages would somehow constitute an act of ecumenism over against a supposedly equally identifiable (Roman) Catholicism (to whose purview the Middle Ages and its piety de facto belonged?), the fact that Luther too shows such elements in his piety points much more to the fact that such recourse never ceased. See Piepkorn, "Philipp," 449. "It must be stipulated that mysticism of the type described," i.e., one that "refers to theocentric and Christocentric mystical experience that consciously bases itself on the Word of God and on the Christian sacraments . . . is an indispensable part of the Catholic heritage that the Church of the Augsburg Confession shares with every century of the church that preceded the 16th."

[42] Wallmann, "Frömmigkeitskrise." The occasion for Nicolai's *Mirror of the Joys of Eternal Life* was the coming of the plague to Unna, a tangible situation of affliction and distress. This crisis needed no advertising, and Nicolai aimed in it to provide comfort and remove fear from the very real confrontation with death. Nicolai had no crisis with Lutheran Orthodoxy; rather, he is resourced by it to work scripturally, theologically, and not least eschatologically in a deeply devotional work that fluidly combines factors like the neo-scholastic use of Aristotelian categories of causality with the mysticism of Bernard of Clairvaux. Johann Arndt's crisis, on the other hand, was a construct. He perceived impenitence and security among his fellow Christians, whom his *True Christianity* meant to call to repentance. Rather than a life-and-death crisis, he was faced much more with opulence and abundance, and therein lay the crisis he wished to lay bare. Arndt's piety is not eschatological, but aimed at present change, and his mysticism falls more in the line of Tauler. In addition to these differences, Nicolai's work enjoyed immediate popularity, but then waned in use, whereas Arndt's grew in popularity after the Thirty Years' War, especially as subsequent editions began to overshadow its original objective by adding other devotional material between *True Christianity*'s covers. These devotional works may

strained attempts to explain Nicolai's thinking and legacy, which can only account for the *Freudenspiegel* and its chorales as a sort of plague-necessitated counterpoint to his other works, is to see the *Freudenspeigel* and the theology of mystical union with Christ at play there embedded in the very stuff that was at the heart of so much controversy with the Calvinists, namely the presence of the undivided Christ in the Word and Sacraments, chiefly in the Holy Supper.[43]

The cues for a proper profile of Nicolai are perhaps there right from the beginning, inscribed on the lintel above the door of the Mengeringhausen parsonage the construction of which his father oversaw. There an intertwined "VV" and "O," for the family motto, "*veritas vincit omnia*" ("truth overcomes all"), stood with Malachi 2:7 (in Latin): "The lips of the priest shall preserve knowledge."[44] Knowledge and truth were contested matters, given the fallout of the European reformations in the age of confessionalization. Contests of knowledge and truth resulted in blows of words and swords. The age itself was a crucible, and in it Philipp Nicolai was formed with the firm conviction that there was indeed knowable truth about the relationship between God and man that not only held but would, in fact, overcome all things, even death. Destined to be a clerical adherent of the Augsburg Confession from childhood on, he believed that it was his sacred duty to preserve the knowledge of such divine truth in preached and written word.[45] At times, the opponents of this divine

---

stand as two of the most significant writings among German Lutherans around 1600, but beyond this bare commonality, they share very little.

[43] The theme of mystical union at play in the *Freudenspiegel* and thus predictably in Nicolai's *Theoria vitae aeternae* is also developed in *Sacrosanctum omnipraesentiae Christi mysterium* (see n. 26 above). Even though the *Freudenspiegel* was not a polemical work, the mystical element at play in it cannot be understood apart from Nicolai's theological (and elsewhere polemically expressed) convictions about Christ's presence in the Holy Supper, by which Christ joins himself to the Christian. The Sacrament nourishes this union. Of "O Morning Star," Brecht, "Philipp Nicolai," 181, says that its venturesome portrayal boldly asserts "that the most unprecedented love story of all takes place in the distribution and reception of the Word and Sacraments."

[44] Peter Möbius, "Philipp Nicolai – Versuch einer Lebensbeschreibung aus der Sicht eines Künstlers," in *Die Pest, der Tod, das Leben: Philipp Nicolai–Spuren der Zeit*, ed. Ev. Kirchengemeinde und Ev. Kirchenkreis Unna (Unna: Ev. Kirchengemeinde und Ev. Kirchenkreis Unna, 1997), 81–100, especially 81.

[45] Even in the "Vorrede" of the Nicolai, *Freudenspiegel*, x, Nicolai mentions the Augsburg Confession and praises the pastors of Unna carrying out their office according to it, be it with sanction and warning against "all sectarian corruptions" or "with comforting instruction and bolstering of spiritually battered and downcast hearts at the time that the plague was raging." The confession and pastoral care were to him a piece of this.

truth were particular to the age—Calvinists and Romanists; and at other times, the opponents of the truth of God in Christ Jesus were its perennial enemies—the death, loss, and despair that rob human beings of the hope and confidence of God's goodness, presence, and love. With the conviction of a ministerial representative of Christ, who was present everywhere, present graciously and unifyingly in his Supper, and so present for Christians in victorious self-giving even in the face of death, Nicolai carried out his office with consistent character.

BIBLIOGRAPHY

Works by Nicolai in English Translation

"Nicolai: How Brightly Beams." In *Documents from the History of Lutheranism, 1517–1750*, edited and translated by Eric Lund, 271–72. Minneapolis: Fortress Press, 2002.

"Philipp Nicolai (1568–1608)." In *Seventeenth-Century Lutheran Meditations and Hymns*, edited and translated by Eric Lund, 277–80. New York: Paulist Press, 2011.

Select Works by Nicolai in German and Latin

Commentarius de regno Christi. Frankfurt am Main: Spies, 1596–97.

Cum Lojolitanae Societate . . . conflictus. Hamburg: Philipp von Ohr Erben, [ca. 1609].

Frewden Spiegel deß ewigen Lebens. Frankfurt am Main: Spies, 1599.

Fundamentorum Calvinianae Sectae . . . detectio. Tübingen: Gruppenbach, 1586.

Kurtzer Bericht Vonn der Caluinisten Gott vnd jhrer Religion/ Jn etliche Frag vnnd Antwort. Frankfurt am Main: Spieß, 1597.

Methodus controversiae de omnipraesentia Christi, secundum naturam eius humanam. Frankfurt am Main: Spies, 1596.

Notwendiger und vollkommener Bericht von der ganzen Calvinischen Religion. Frankfurt am Main: Spies, 1596.

Sacrosanctum Omnipraesentiae Jesu Christi Mysterium. Frankfurt am Main: Becker, 1602.

Spiegel des bösen Geistes / der sich in den Calvinisten Büchern reget. Frankfurt am Main: Spies, 1599

Theoria vitae aeternae, das ist: Historische Beschreibung dess gantzen Geheimnisses vom ewigen Leben. Hamburg: Philipp von Ohr, 1606.

Von Gottes Gnaden Sieg und Freudentritt der Wahrheit christlicher Religion in den evangelischen und gut lutherischen Kirchen durch Sachsen/ auf die faulstinkende Apologi/ damit der daummelwitzige Mammaluck zu Bremen D. Urbanus Pierius/ das wolbegründet Examen Examinis zu vergeblicher Beschirmung seines todtsüchtigen Calvinismi, feindlich anschnattert und anmäulet. Hamburg: Philipp von Ohr, 1608.

His collected works were published as the following:

Tomus Primus [-Secundus] Operum Latinorum. Edited by Georg Dedekenn. Hamburg: Michael Hering, 1617.

Erster [-Vierter] Theil, Aller Teutschen Schrifften. Edited by Georg Dedekenn. Hamburg: Michael Hering, 1617.

WRITING[46]

The Second Part of the *Mirror of Joys*, Wherein Is Treated How God Prepares Us for Eternal Life; The Six Mighty Benefactions of God, by which He Promotes Eternal Life in Us; The Third Benefaction of God regarding Our Rebirth to Eternal Life

A short description of what kind of mystery this rebirth is.

Now follows the third benefaction: our rebirth to eternal life. This rebirth is indeed a work of our God's ineffably great compassion and amicability toward human beings. This work consists in his calling, gathering, and enlightening sinners, as people who are spiritually dead, through the Word and Sacrament. God terrifies them through the preaching of the Law, and when they have been fully crushed and pulverized, he then comforts them with the Gospel, awakens faith, and reckons to them the righteousness, innocence, and victory of our Lord Christ through this faith. He graciously receives them, identifies them as his possession, gives them the Holy Spirit, and governs and leads them by his Word. He also holds them under the cross, so that the Old Adam may be put to death, their faith be tested, and they be moved to prayer and new obedience. And finally, he delivers them from this vale of tears to a home with him in the heavenly paradise and fatherland of eternal life. . . .

[46] This is a translation of Nicolai, *Freudenspiegel,* 232–44.

Examination of all the causes and factors of our rebirth.

Now here we must rightly consider the *causae* [*causas*], that is cause and conditions, of this precious mystery, namely: (1) Who, in fact, is the father and workman of this rebirth? (2) What moves him to this work? (3) Who might the mother or pregnant woman who is giving birth be? (4) What kind *uterus* [*uterum*] or womb does she have in which this work is brought about? (5) With what is this womb inseminated? (6) What kind of external instruments are involved in this process, spreading and propelling the holy, heavenly seed? . . .

I. Principal efficient cause [*Causa efficiens principalis*]. . . [47]

II. Motivating cause [*Causa impulsiua*] . . . [48]

III. Who the Spiritual Mother Is.

So, you say, if God himself is the Father and the one who causes this work to take place, begetting us again according to his will, what sort of wife does he have, who conceives by him, gives birth, and is a mother of the reborn children?

Secondary cause [*causa secundaria*], the spiritual mother is the Holy Christian Church.

Answer: The mother is the Holy Christian Church. Even if she indeed appears to the world to be a poor, little group and a barren woman, and also as a lonely and abandoned widow, nevertheless God Almighty impregnates her. Her Husband and heavenly Groom fecundates her at all times with his Word and Spirit, so that she is always giving birth and is never without children, and she will not cease to bear children until the last day. "Boast you barren one," says the Holy Spirit to her, "you, who do not bear children! Rejoice with boasting and exult, you who are not with child!"

Isaiah 54: The great fertility of the Holy Christian Church.

> "For the forlorn one has more children than she who has a husband," says the Lord. "Enlarge the place of your tent and spread out the curtains of your dwelling; do not hold back. Lengthen your cords, and make firm your stakes. For you will

[47] The father or author of this rebirth is God Almighty.

[48] The mercy and love of God move him to the work of rebirth.

> spread out to the right and to the left, and your hand[49] will inherit the nations and dwell in the desolate cities. Do not be afraid, for you will never be put to shame. Do not be confounded, for you will not be disgraced. Instead, you will forget the shame of your youth, and the disgrace of your widowhood you will remember no more. For he who made you is your husband; the Lord of Hosts is his name. And the Holy One of Israel is your redeemer, who is called God of all the earth. For the Lord left you to cry, so that you be as an abandoned woman, unhappy of heart, and as a young woman who is rejected," says your God. "I abandoned you for but an instant, but with great compassion I will gather you." (Isaiah 54[:1–7])

With the prophet Isaiah, the Christian Church is to be understood in [the figure of] the pregnant woman.

Here, through the pregnant and poor woman, the Christian Church is understood. This Church carries Christ spiritually in her heart, calls on him, publicly confesses him before the world, and continuously bears children through baptism and through the preaching of the Holy Gospel. This takes place, albeit, not without the cross and great pain, for she must at all times suffer fierce resistance, offense, and persecution at the hands of the devil and his bride, which is the world. For this reason, St. John in his Revelation (ch. 12) sees the Christian Church as a pregnant mother who is carrying a child in her body, is constantly in labor, and is being viciously attacked by the hellish dragon. Nevertheless, God the Almighty protects her and continually prepares a place for her in the desolate, wild world, where she is fed and rules in the midst of her enemies.

IV. What Is the Womb of the Christian Church, in which Conception and Birth Take Place?

Her womb, in which she becomes pregnant, is God's Word written in the prophetic and apostolic Scriptures of the Old and New Testaments, insofar as this Word always sounds in her ears and surges in her heart, along with the use of the Holy, Blessed Sacraments. For in the Word she finds the dear child Jesus Christ, as he himself says: "Search the Scriptures, for in them you think that you have eternal life, and they are that

[49] Hebrew, Greek, Latin, and Luther's 1545 German have "seed," to which "hand" is corrected in a 1854 edition of Nicolai's *Freudenspiegel* edited by Gustav Mühlmann (Halle: Mühlmann), 201.

which testifies of me" (John 5[:39]). All orthodox Christians and children of the light abide by these Scriptures and this Word as if wrapping themselves therein, lying hidden as in the womb, as David says: "In the words of your lips I protect myself from the works of men traveling the path of the violent" (Psalm 17[:4]).

Now given that the Christian Church is God's bride and her word as comprehended in Holy Scriptures is none other than God's Word, so is such Word also called God's *uterus*, God's uterus and womb, even as God says through Isaiah the prophet, "Listen to me, you of the house of Jacob and all who remain from the house of Israel, who are being carried by me in my body and lie in my womb" (Isaiah 46[:3]).

Faith (says Dr. Luther) makes them children of God who are thus born through the Word, which is the womb in which we are conceived, carried, born, and nurtured. Mathesius writes the same thing: "A child lives in the womb and is nourished there; day by day it grows and gains weight, even if lying beneath the mother's heart it is small and weak, doesn't move around easily, and rests. Thus we, too, are reborn in the Word; through the Word we begin to believe; in the Word we are nourished; and those who remain in Christ, the womb (Isaiah 46), and his Word, constantly grow and gain weight and live and move in it, as the verse says: 'We live in the Word, as an embryo enfolded in the womb.' "[50]

Holy Baptism is the door and entrance to the Holy Christian Church (John 3[:5]).

And here Holy Baptism (especially when young children are brought to Christ and incorporated into the Christian Church) is indeed the proper first door, portal, or entrance into the womb of the Holy Church. This is the case, as the Son of God openly testifies, because he who is not born anew of water and the Spirit will not enter into the kingdom of God. Contrariwise, it follows that children rightly enter through the Sacrament of Baptism by the power and working of the Holy Spirit. That is to say that in this way they have access and admission to the kingdom of God and become children of the Most High, members of the Christian Church, and co-heirs of eternal life in faith.

[50] Margin: "*Zeugnuß Lutheri Tom 1 VVitteb. Germ. fol. 220 Matthesius 21. Trinit.*" The last words, the verse, stand in Latin: "*Viuimus in verbo, velut embryo clausus in aluo.*"

V. How the Christian Church Is Inseminated.[51]

Accordingly, God's Word is not only the *uterus* or womb, in which we are spiritually conceived and born again. It is also the seed itself from which we have our beginning. "You have been reborn," says St. Peter, "not of perishable seed, but of imperishable, that is of the living Word of God, which remains forever" (1 Peter 1[:23]). St. James writes the same thing: "He begat us according to His will through the Word of Truth, that we be the first fruits of His creatures" (James 1[:18]). St. Paul testifying of Holy Baptism says, "According to his great mercy, he sanctifies us through the washing of rebirth and renewal of the Holy Spirit, whom he abundantly poured out on us through Jesus Christ our Savior" (Titus 3[:5–6]). . . .

VI. What God Uses as Physical Tools to Carry Out This Work of Rebirth.[52]

God, the Almighty, also uses physical tools in the spreading and propagation of this his heavenly seed, namely the preachers and servants of his Holy Word, so that they be as conveyors [*Traduces*], pipes, and physical means through which the Holy Spirit makes himself heard and sows and spreads the imperishable seed of the Gospel in the hearers.

Of this the Lord Christ testifies as he speaks to his disciples in most comforting fashion. . . .[53]

Godly preachers also bear the fame that gives new birth to their hearers.

Thus, if a preacher stands in the pulpit and preaches God's Word, sticks with the Scriptures, rightly implements them, and expounds the Gospel intelligibly so that it is heard with fear and grabs the heart—and similarly, when he administers the Holy, Blessed Sacraments, baptizes, and gives the Supper—then he is a true instrument of the Holy Trinity, lends the Holy Spirit his tongue, and receives the fame accorded in Holy Scripture, that he is a spiritual father who brings forth spiritual children, as St. Paul is not ashamed openly to write. "I admonish you," he says to

---

[51] Margin: "*Causa materialis.*"

[52] Margin: "*Causae administrae.*"

[53] Here follow a number of citations, first a conglomeration of parts of Matthew 10:19f.; Luke 21:15; Mark 13:11; and John 15:26f.; then parts of Jeremiah 1:7, 9; and finally Hosea 6:5 and 12:10.

the Corinthians, "as my dear children. For even if you should have ten thousand guardians in Christ, you have nonetheless not many fathers, for I begat you in Christ Jesus through the Gospel" (1 Corinthians 4[:15]). And to the Galatians, he says, "My dear children, with whom I again am in the anguish of birth, until Christ is formed in you" (Galatians 4[:19]).

Apostles/preachers and schoolmasters are fathers.

Luther explains this last citation with the following words:[54] "The apostles, all of them godly preachers and schoolmasters, are, in their own way, also our parents. For just as we, according to our natural birth, have the form of our bodies from our parents, so these assist in our heart and conscience taking right form in us. And the right form that a Christian heart should have is faith or confidence in the heart, through which we lay hold of Christ and him alone and cling to nothing else. So that heart which has such faith, that we are reckoned before God as righteous for the sake of Christ, has, according to Christ, its right form and is similar to him."

How the proper form of the begetting is brought about.

Such form is, however, prepared for it through the preaching office [*Predigtamt*], as St. Paul says in 1 Corinthians 4: "I have begotten you in Christ Jesus through the Gospel, so that you have known Christ and believed in him" [see 1 Corinthians 4:15]. Similarly 1 Corinthians 3: "You are a letter of Christ prepared by the preaching office and written by us, not with ink, but with the Spirit of the living God." For there the Word goes out of the apostle's mouth and touches the hearts of the hearers; there the Holy Spirit is also on the scene and sees to it that the Word takes hold in the heart, even as it is preached. In this way, every devout teacher is a father. For through the preaching office, he begets and prepares the right form of a Christian heart.

---

[54] Margin: "*Lutherus Tom 1. Vvitteb. Ger. fol. 239.*"

GEORG DEDEKENN (1564–1628)

PASTOR AND EDITOR

by Benjamin T. G. Mayes

LIFE

Most of the great names from the era of Lutheran Orthodoxy were professors of small theology faculties at universities such as Wittenberg, Jena, and Tübingen, where they touched the lives of many students and found ample time to write and publish books.[1] But other great names followed other paths. Georg Dedekenn certainly belongs among these great names, not as a professor but as a pastor, a casuist, and an editor. For these roles, too, are needed by the church.

Georg Dedekenn was born in 1564 in Lübeck, the only son of his father. His father died while Georg was young, and his mother took responsibility for his education. She omitted nothing that would contribute to the best education of her dear son. For this reason, besides sending him to school, she also put him under the instruction of private teachers in her home. These teachers filled young Georg with instruction in all the good arts, along with piety, and the boy showed himself ready to learn all that is good. At first, his mother wanted him to be a merchant, but as Georg advanced in his schooling, he came to realize how valuable it is to

---

[1] Dedekenn's biography is drawn from his statements about himself in his published works and in his autobiographical funeral sermon, which he wrote for himself shortly before his death in 1628, and which was summarized by Henning Witte, *Memoriae Theologorum Nostri Seculi Clarissimorum Renovata Centuria* (Frankfurt am Main: Martin Hallervord, 1685), 7:920–24. See also Hans Schröder, ed., "Dedeken, Georg," in *Lexikon der hamburgischen Schriftsteller bis zur Gegenwart* (Hamburg: Verein für hamburgische Geschichte, 1854), 2:19–22; Johannes Moller, *Cimbria Literata, Sive Scriptorum Ducatus Utriusque Slesvicensis Et Holsatici, Quibus Et Alii Vicini Quidam Accensentur, Historia Literaria Tripartita* (Copenhagen: G. F. Kisel, 1744), 1:132–34; Johann Heinrich Zedler and Carl Günther Ludovici, eds., *Grosses Vollständiges Universal-Lexikon* (Graz: Akademische Druck- u. Verlagsanstalt, 1961–64), s.v. "Dedekendus (Georgius)"; Carl Bertheau, "Dedeken, Georg," in *Allgemeine Deutsche Biographie* (Munich und Leipzig: Duncker & Humblot, 1875–1912), 5:11. The dating of Witte and Zedler is often incorrect and must be corrected by more recent biographers, such as Schröder.

be educated, especially for the purpose of teaching the Holy Word of God publicly to lead many souls to salvation. From an early age, therefore, he resolved to pursue this kind of life. He had to convince and persuade his mother to let him pursue this. At first she refused, since Georg was the only heir of his deceased father, but finally, conquered by her son's many requests, she consented. Georg's mother and grandmother thereafter contributed all that they could, and more, to his education.

Not all the names of the schools he attended are known, but at least by 1590 he was studying at the university in Frankfurt an der Oder. From there, around the festival of St. Michael (September 29) in 1590, he was called by the Duke of Mecklenburg to be a deacon or chaplain in Schönberg, in the diocese of Ratzeburg, about two miles from Lübeck, where his brother-in-law was a pastor. Here he worked hard to preach the Word of God purely and faithfully. As often happened for Lutheran pastors of the era, as soon as he had a stable position and income, but not before, he took a wife. The next year, on April 20, he married Anna Frerking of Lübeck. He would have been twenty-six or twenty-seven years old. Together the couple had three sons and nine daughters, and they lived together until Georg's death in 1628.

On July 25, 1594, Dedekenn advanced to the academic rank of master at Frankfurt an der Oder. For this promotion, the Duke of Mecklenburg paid for Dedekenn's costs. But the duke's favor did not last, since Dedekenn called his duke to repentance for having taken a mistress and living in concubinacy. In later years, Dedekenn reported that the early years of his ministry were difficult, presenting him with several cases of conscience, where he required the advice of professors of theology at the universities to give him instruction from God's Word so that he could choose the right course of action and put his conscience at peace. At this time, his actions led to conflict with his duke.

The next year, however, Dedekenn accepted a call to the pastorate of Neustadt in Holstein, four miles from Lübeck. His prince here was Johann Friedrich (1579–1634), the Evangelical prince-bishop of Bremen and Lübeck.[2] Here, too, he faced struggles. His consolation was the divine call to the ministry. In all his calls to ecclesiastical offices, Dedekenn relied only on God's fatherly leading. He never dared to use schemes or tricks to thrust himself upon a church. This is what supported his conscience in the many hard persecutions of bad men later in his life, and the considerable waves of evils that rose from different directions. When he

---

[2] Benjamin T. G. Mayes, *Counsel and Conscience: Lutheran Casuistry and Moral Reasoning after the Reformation* (Göttingen: Vandenhoeck & Ruprecht, 2011), 77–78.

was threatened and despised, he bore this in silence and disregarded their threats. Here he again labored strenuously in the vineyard of the Lord, for eleven and a half years, serving as pastor and director of the ecclesiastical consistory in Neustadt. Consistories served in part as adjudication committees, giving official rulings on matters of church discipline, and dealing with marriage and many other topics. In his service at Neustadt, therefore, Dedekenn started to collect the official doctrinal opinions and decisions of various authorities—theological faculties, famous theologians, letters of the reformers, excerpts from church orders, decisions of other consistories, and so on; these became the core of his greatest work, the *Treasury of Counsels and Decisions*, published in 1623. Here in Neustadt, Dedekenn again faced conflict, as he had to take action against an embezzling administrator of a welfare agency (*Hospital*) under his supervision.[3] At some time, Prince-Bishop Johann Friedrich, blocked from marrying by the local nobility for fear that the diocese would become a hereditary princely possession, took a series of concubines. It is not clear when this occurred, but if it happened during Dedekenn's pastorate, it would surely have led to conflict between him and his prince as well. Many of the counsels that Dedekenn later included in his *Treasury* asserted the right and duty of pastors to preach publicly and specifically against the public sins of princes, a course of action which would inevitably lead to conflict.

In 1606, Dedekenn publicly opposed another nobleman, Gabriel Grabau, who had fathered children with a woman who was not his wife. Dedekenn's admonitions did not bear fruit. In fact, Dedekenn was commanded to keep silent about the matter under threat of removal from office and harsh penalties. Therefore, from the pulpit, he publicly resigned from office, and soon thereafter was called to Hamburg. On September 9 of the same year, he was chosen by the Hamburg city council (which had the right to call pastors for the city) to be the assistant pastor to Dr. Philipp Nicolai (1556–1608) (i.e., as deacon or preacher at St. Catherine's Church in Hamburg). Dedekenn regarded this call as divine, submitted to it, and was installed at St. Catherine's on October 2. After only a few years, Nicolai died (in 1608), and Dedekenn preached the funeral sermon and had it published. In all, Dedekenn remained in office at St. Catherine's for nearly twenty-two years. (At some point during his tenure in Hamburg, he became a vicar of the cathedral church in Hamburg, holding this office concurrently with his office at St.

[3] Georg Dedekenn, *Thesauri Consiliorum Et Decisionum*, vol. 2 of *Politica continens. . . .* (Hamburg: Michael Hering, 1623), fol. a4v.

Catherine's.) In Hamburg, he flourished not only as a preacher but also as an author and editor.

His writings and publications can be placed into three groups. First, several of his writings opposed Calvinism. In 1608, he wrote about the general, gracious will of God (*Grund der h. Schrift von dem allgemeinen Gnadenwillen*), who wants all people to be saved, against the Reformed doctrine of God's absolute reprobation of the majority of humanity to damnation. Nicolai provided the foreword for this book. In 1611, Dedekenn wrote about the causes of sins (*Tractatus de peccatorum causis*), showing that the devil and the depraved human nature are at fault for sin and that God is not in any sense the author of sins. He wrote this against some Reformed writers who came close to this idea, due to their doctrine of predestination. In 1614, he wrote a book of questions and answers for laypeople to understand the difference between Lutheran and Reformed doctrine (*Fürnehmster Religionsstreit der Lutheraner und Calvinisten*). In 1622, he wrote against a treatise of the Reformed professor Johann Lampadius (c. 1569–1621) on predestination (*Christliche Beantwortung des Tractätleins M. Joh. Lampadii*).

This latter book leads to the second group: writings in defense and promotion of Philipp Nicolai. Lampadius's book on predestination had contained "horrible slander" against Dr. Philipp Nicolai.[4] Just as Luther had his supporters who promoted his works (such as Georg Rörer [1492–1557], Caspar Cruciger [1504–48], and Veit Dietrich [1506–49]), so Dedekenn was the promoter for Nicolai's works. Although they served together for only about two years, Dedekenn defended and promoted his former colleague until the end of his own life. For years, he edited all of Nicolai's writings, and he released them in 1617: two volumes of German works and four volumes of Latin works. Not even Martin Chemnitz and Johann Gerhard had followers who edited their "collected works." In 1619, Dedekenn wrote his *Practice of Life Eternal* (*Praxis vitae aeternae*), a sequel in five books to Nicolai's *Theory of Life Eternal.*

The final group of writings show Dedekenn's interest in the care of consciences and casuistry. Casuistry is the study of "cases of conscience," situations when the conscience is unsure about what is right and true. Reflecting his situation in the port city of Hamburg, he wrote a guidebook for the conduct and consolation of sailors and merchants (*Kleinod*

[4] See the subtitle of the aforementioned book: *Von der Gnadenwahl und ihren angehengten Fragen: Inwelchem zugleich / so wol desselben / als auch D. Davidis Paraei Heidelbergeschen Professorn / gar zu greifflich ertichtete / und von aller entschüldigung gantz befreihete erschreckliche Lästerung / wider den . . . Herrn D. Philippum Nicolai.*

der Seefahrenden) in 1608, and he strengthened the consciences of merchants with another book (*Der Kaufleute Schatzkammer*) in 1610. In 1612, he wrote his *Joyous Paradise of Grace* (*Frewden Paradeiß der Gnaden*) to console and strengthen "tempted, distressed, sad hearts." In 1614, he addressed sudden death, which many Christians feared (*Herzenstrost gegen plötzliche Todesfälle*). The same concern for consciences is shown in his 1616 work, *The Practice of Consciences* (*Praxis conscientiarum*). The "Summary Concept and Outline" (*Summarischer Begriff und Abris*) (1667) of the *Practice of Consciences* shows that Dedekenn addressed various trials in life that could lead one's conscience to despair of the grace of God, both spiritual trials and bodily trials that disturbed the consciences of Christians.

His chief accomplishment in this area was the *Treasury of Counsels and Decisions* (1623), in three large folio volumes with an appendix. While Dedekenn did not write most of the content of this work, he assembled and gathered a massive amount of official opinions, decisions, judgments, counsels, and statements on every situation a preacher or hearer might face in life. Organized according to the three estates of church, state, and household, Dedekenn gathered and published these materials, because in the thirty-four years of his ministry he suffered anxiety over important matters and cases such as these. In these cases, his goal was to keep his conscience uninjured. Therefore, rather than trusting his own judgment, he sought advice. Dedekenn knew that to keep one's conscience uninjured, one must determine the right thing to do, even in doubtful cases. This process of deciding is fraught with danger, because there are objective right and wrong choices, even in doubtful cases. This deciding, however, is the responsibility of the individual; one cannot simply rest secure in following another's counsel blindly.[5] This indicates the difference between Lutheran casuistry and Roman Catholic casuistry. Lutheran casuistry, demonstrated so abundantly by Dedekenn, does not have any independent authority apart from the Word of God and the principles and arguments drawn from it. It seeks to learn from the best, wisest men (contemporaries and historical figures) in order to guide uncertain consciences with reasoning, arguments, and testimonies drawn from God's Word.[6] Dedekenn's *Treasury* guided generations of Lutheran pastors and people, and was expanded and reissued in 1671 by Johann Ernst Gerhard (1621–68) and Christian Grübel (1642–1715).

[5] Dedekenn, *Thesauri Consiliorum Et Decisionum*, vol. 1, *Ecclesiastica continens. . . .* (Hamburg: Paul Langen, 1623), fol. [a5]v–[a6]r.

[6] Mayes, *Counsel and Conscience*, 11–50.

In 1628, Dedekenn barely survived a severe illness and knew that the end of his life was approaching. He prepared for himself, therefore, the inscription for his tombstone and even, singing like a swan, wrote a funeral sermon for himself, based on Revelation 7:13. On May 29, he died in Christ, and a memorial epitaph was erected in St. Catherine's Church. His wife, Anna, died in Christ three years later, in 1631.

BIBLIOGRAPHY

None of Dedekenn's writings have been translated.

Select Works by Dedekenn in Latin and German

Editor of Philipp Nicolai, *Erster [-Vierter] Theil, Aller Teutschen Schrifften.* Hamburg: Michael Hering, 1617.

Editor of Philipp Nicolai, *Tomus Primus [-Secundus] Operum Latinorum.* Hamburg: Michael Hering, 1617.

Editor of *Thesauri Consilorum Et Decisionum* (Treasury of Counsels and Decisions). 3 vols. Hamburg: Paul Lange, Michael Hering, Hans Mose, 1623.

Praxis Conscientiarum (Practice of Consciences). Hamburg: Michael Hering, 1616.

Tractatus De Peccatorum Caussis (Treatise on the Causes of Sins). Hamburg: Georg Frobenius, 1611.

WRITING

Opinion on the aforementioned case, where an outside, neighboring preacher accepts the other's unrepentant parishioner.[7]

Approved by the Honorable Ministerium of Hamburg.

Honorable and erudite dear lord and brother in Christ,

With astonishment, and indeed with great astonishment, I have understood from your letter that the blasphemer (who in bitter wrath while going to the Table of God screamed at a communicant with these horri-

[7] This is a translation of "Bedencken / wegen vorhergehenden Falles / da ein frembder benachbarter Prediger des andern unbußfertiges Pfarrkind auffgenommen" in *Thesauri Consiliorum Et Decisionum, vol. 1, Ecclesiastica Continens. . . .* edited by Georg Dedekenn and Johann Ernst Gerhard, 2nd ed. (Jena: Zacharias Hertel, 1671), 729.

ble words: "You villain! You are not worthy to be carried by the earth! Leave, and receive the devil!") in his unrepentance has been received by an outside, neighboring pastor, who had good knowledge of this man's malice, and was joined in marriage by him.

It is wrong for an outside preacher to accept someone else's unrepentant parishioner.

Now, I cannot judge for others, but for myself I hold in certainty that I could not with a good conscience marry such a crass blasphemer in that way, but would be sinning grievously by doing so, would be disturbing the Church extremely, and hence in this would be acting wrongly before God and men, for the reason that the crass delinquent belongs not in my parish but in yours.

For he is reaching into an office not his own.

Therefore, I would be reaching into an office not my own, which is not permitted according to God's Word [1 Peter 4:15]. St. Peter warns against this seriously in his first epistle (1 Peter 5:2): "Tend the flock of Christ which has been committed to you," as well as Paul in Acts 20:[28]: "Take heed to the flock among which the Holy Spirit has appointed you as bishops." Therefore, I would have been forgetful of my vocation and would have been opposing the aforecited command and will of God (besides the order of the Christian Church, in which all things, as the Apostle says in [1 Corinthians 14:40], should be done in an honorable and orderly manner) if I had strengthened the godless man in his godlessness and (what is horrible to think about, but even more horrible to do) had maintained him in his unrepentant sins, hindered his conversion, and thus made myself a grievous and indefensible participant in his sins.

He is making no distinction between godly and godless people.

I would have been disturbing the Church of God by not having made any distinction between holy and unholy (Ezekiel 22:26, 31), good and bad, godly and godless, but instead would have let them be just the same to me: a man without salvation (who, despising the venerable Sacrament, with an implacable and even fleshly heart toward God and men, entered the holy estate of marriage) and a saved, equipped Christian; indeed, an obedient and a disobedient parishioner, of whom the one remains "in the bosom of the church and the assembly of the pious," while the other, as a bad member, divides, separates, bans, and excommunicates (or, excludes) himself from his congregation.

He gives the parishioners an occasion for disobedience against their pastors.

I would have been giving a dangerous occasion for disobedience to the parishioners toward their parsons and ordinary pastors [*Seelsorger*], while the Holy Spirit commands them (Hebrews 13:17): "Obey your teachers and follow them," etc. Yes, I would have been giving many reasons for great slander on all sides against the holy ministry. In all of this and whatever else of this sort is connected with it, I would never be able to have a good conscience, but would certainly have to worry about the severe wrath and punishment of God.

A preacher should not separate from his synod.

Concerning your synod,[8] I give this well-intended advice: do not on your life separate from it, and do not cease to petition your dear government that in this matter they change, in a Christian way, their stated intention of excluding you from the synod. This sort of laudable church union is of great benefit in dangerous times—when the devil wants to stir up false doctrine and other unpleasantness—and may accomplish much in the Lord. If your church now were to be separated from the others, then in the future if an emergency occurred, it would stand alone and would perhaps also be reproached as rebellious, from which much evil could easily grow. Concerning this, your posterity might curse you who are now bringing this about. The things that moved your dear government to this intention—they can still hold these for themselves and, if it were necessary, make a protest concerning this. In that case you could seek the counsel and opinion of the synod.

How opinions of the theological faculties should be sought.

If someone also wanted to ask for instruction from one or two theological faculties at universities, it would be very good. But my advice would be that this not be done by you but by your government, since one would want to be on the good side of their authority, especially in this matter, whenever the instruction would be produced. But I do not want to take anything away from your government and from yourselves and others in your better counsel and opinion. Rather, it would not have been right for me, as a well-intentioned friend, to withhold just this from you at your request. Fervently commending you and your church to the most gracious protection of God! November 29, 1614.

---

[8] Synods at this time were conferences of pastors.

Christian instruction on the salvation of unbaptized infants, who die either in their mothers' bodies or suddenly and without our negligence, such that they cannot be baptized beforehand.

In the Lower Saxon Church Order, fol. 175b ff.[9]

Many a godfearing, motherly heart falls into great distress and sweat of fear over the fact that things went wrong while giving birth and in labor, in such a way that either the child comes from them into the world dead, or dies suddenly and unexpectedly, before they come with him to Baptism. On account of this, they fall into severe, sad thoughts about the salvation of their child. Therefore, we desire to give a brief instruction also about this, to console these troubled hearts.

Children who die in an emergency without Baptism must not be condemned.

These hearts should not plunge themselves in such thoughts, but should quietly hold God's gracious will and judgments, and should know that:

1. Example of the children in the Old Testament.

First, in the Old Testament doubtlessly many children died before the eighth day after their birth—on which, according to the Law of the LORD, they had to be circumcised, and not before (Genesis 17[:10–14])—and remained uncircumcised. Nevertheless, no one uttered any doubt about the salvation of these children. Since the children were deprived of circumcision not by their parents' fault or negligence, but God took them away, they committed these children to God's grace by their prayer, whenever they noticed the death, unto the coming Christ, and did not bear doubt about their salvation.

[9] This is a translation of "Christlicher Unterricht / Von der Seeligkeit der ungetaufften Kindlein / welche etwa in Mutterleibe / oder so plötzlich / und ohn unser Versäumnüβ eilend hinweg sterben / daβ man sie nicht zuvor täuffen tan" in *Thesauri Consiliorum Et Decisionum, vol. 1, Ecclesiastica Continens. . . .* edited by Georg Dedekenn and Johann Ernst Gerhard, 2nd ed. (Jena: Zacharias Hertel, 1671), 1:436–37; Herzog Franz II von Sachsen-Lauenburg, *Kirchen-Ordnung Unser von Gottes Gnaden Frantzen, hertzogen zu Sachsen, Engern und Westphalen* (Lübeck: Johan Balhorn, 1585), 175–79.

2. The Israelites in the desert.

Second, how many people died uncircumcised in the desert between Egypt and the land of Canaan in the forty years, since in their daily wandering they could not perform circumcision? And who will cut off salvation from all of these, since emergency prevented them from doing God's command concerning circumcision, without their will, in every way like such children who, without their parents' will, being born dead or suddenly taken away, do not and are unable to come to Baptism?

3. God is able to save even without the means of the sacraments.

Third, it is undeniable that the Holy Sacrament of Baptism is a means instituted by Christ by which he wants to give us rebirth and to save us, and this is what comes to the baptized. Nevertheless, it is also undeniable and certain that the divine Majesty has not absolutely bound himself with rebirth and salvation to Baptism and the Sacraments such that even he would be unable to give forgiveness of sins and salvation without Baptism to someone who, without his fault or intentional negligence, is unable to receive Baptism, since God did not grant him the time long enough to come to Baptism, but has brought his path to an end. This is certain and clear in the case of John the Baptist. Before he was born and circumcised, while he was still in his mother's body, was filled with the Holy Spirit and confessed his Creator (Luke 1[:43–44]).

4. The prayer of those present at the labor of childbirth.

Fourth, because Christ makes us certain with a powerful promise, saying (Matthew 18[:19]): "Again I say to you: if two or three of you agree on earth concerning anything that they want to ask, they will obtain it from my Father in heaven." As a result, women who are present with a mother in the labor of childbirth and notice that the infant is in danger should admonish each other to pray together and should thus call upon God in words similar to the following.

A prayer in the labor of childbirth.

We praise you, Lord God, heavenly Father, that you have blessed this woman with the fruit of the body, and we ask of your endless mercy that you would let her be commended to you, as a faithful Father, graciously unbind her of her maternal burden, and after her pains, give her the joy that your dear Son has promised and with whichh gives consolation. We also bring to you, dear Lord Jesus Christ, in our poor prayer, this unborn infant, at your word, as you speak, "Let the little children come to me"

[Matthew 19:14], and we pray from our hearts: Let him be yours. If then it happens that you give him into our hands, as have all our hope in you and as we certainly expect, then we desire to carry him to you physically, too, in the salutary Baptism, according to your command, who are the only Savior of all people, praised with your Father and the Holy Spirit, true God forever. Amen.

Such a prayer cannot remain unheard, but must result in the protection and benefit of the infant. Since we cannot bring such infants to Christ through Baptism, we bring them to him through our earnest prayer, knowing that he accepts them, as he says in John 6[:37]: "Whoever comes to me I will not cast away from myself."

5. The example of being deprived of the Holy Supper in an emergency situation.

Fifth, if one cannot have the Holy Supper, he should not be fearful about his salvation, but must and can comfort himself with his faith in Jesus Christ. Likewise, when one is not intentionally omitting Baptism, but due to a swift death is unable to partake of it, why should one not, in this same case, be comforted and cheered by this supplication of Christian people for a child like this, as was said?

And even though we could cite here more testimonies like this without any trouble, for the consolation of Christian hearts, at this time we will leave it at this. But whoever desires more instruction about this, we refer him to Dr. Johann Bugenhagen Pomeranus's book, *On the Unborn Children and on Those Children Whom We Cannot Baptize, Though We Wanted to Do So, Etc.*[10]

[10] Johannes Bugenhagen, *Von Den Vngeborn Kindern / Vnd von Den Kindern / Die Wir Nicht Teuffen Können / Vnd Wolten Doch Gern / Nach Christus Befehl / Vnd Sonst von Der Tauff / Etc.* (Wittenberg: Josef Klug, 1552).

Leonhard Hutter (1563–1616)

Redonatus Lutherus

by William R. Wangelin

Life

Leonhard Hutter (also Leonhart Hütter) was one of the most prominent Lutheran theologians at the opening of the seventeenth century. In the age of confessionalization, Hutter was the first professor (*professor primarius*) at the University of Wittenberg, holding the position that Martin Luther (1483–1546) held a few decades earlier. He was a staunch supporter of the Formula of Concord and the Gnesio-Lutherans, as well as a defender of the faith against Roman Catholic and Calvinist theologians. Because of the boldness of his apologetic, his prolific publications, and his evangelical focus, Hutter was given the name *Redonatus Lutherus* (Luther Given Again).[1] Although well known in his day, many of his

[1] Leonhard Hutter, *Compendium locorum theologicorum ex Scripturis Sacris et Libro Concordiae: Lateinisch, deutsch, englisch*, ed. Johann Anselm Steiger (Stuttgart-Bad Cannstatt: Frommann-Holzboog, 2006), 1:699–700. Some sources refer him as *redivivus*

works were incorporated into and overshadowed by later orthodox Lutheran fathers, such as Johann Gerhard (1582–1637) and Johann Andreas Quenstedt (1617–88). In addition, very few of his works have been translated into English. Hutter nevertheless serves as an important link between the Formula of Concord and the age of scholastic Lutheran Orthodoxy.

In January 1563, Hutter was born two miles from the city of Ulm in the village of Nellingen. Two years later, his family moved to Ulm where his father, also named Leonhard, served as the preacher at the main church until his death in 1601. Hutter attended the primary school in Ulm before going to study philology, philosophy, and theology in Strassburg, where he received his master's degree in 1583. He continued to lecture for the next eight years in Strassburg on the importance of determining the correct interpretation of the Scriptures. In 1591, he went to the University of Leipzig, and after two years he went to Jena, where he became a doctor of theology in 1594. After lecturing in Jena for two years, he was called as professor of theology at the University of Wittenberg.

When Hutter arrived in Wittenberg in 1596, he was responsible for taking up a lecture on Melanchthon's (1497–1560) *Commonplaces* (*Loci Communes*), which had been ongoing since 1577. Hutter's lectures were published posthumously by Nikolaus Hunnius (1585–1643) under the title *Theological Common Places* (*Loci Communes Theologici*) (1619). When these lectures concluded in 1602, the Wittenberg faculty asked Hutter to lecture on the Formula of Concord. These lectures, under the title *Christian Books of Concord* (*Libri Christianae Concordiae*), were published in 1608, 1609, and 1611. At Wittenberg, Hutter worked alongside fellow professors Aegidius Hunnius (1550–1603), Polykarp Leyser I (1552–1610), and Balthasar Meisner II (1587–1626). He expounded on the Formula of Concord, developed a more specific doctrine of verbal inspiration, and was the first to thoroughly treat the concept of the invisible Church.[2]

In 1599, Hutter married Barbara Manlich in Ulm. The two were married for sixteen years but never had children. Although Hutter displayed a very mild and peaceful spirit in person, he was a powerful

Lutherus (Luther Renewed). See *Allgemeines Gelehrten Lexicon*, s.v. "Hutter (Leonh)." Those that have *redonatus Lutherus* point out that it is an exact anagram of *Leonardus Hutterus*. See Leonhard Hutter, *Compendium Locorum Theologoricum*, ed. Wolfgang Trillhaas (Berlin: Verlag Walter De Druyter & Co., 1961).

[2] *Neue Deutsche Biographie*, s.v. "Hutter (Hütter), Leonhard."

writer and highly esteemed by his colleagues. When he was asked for a fourth time to serve as the rector of the university, he accepted. But soon he came down with a fever and died on October 23, 1616. He was buried in the Castle Church in Wittenberg, along with Luther, Melanchthon, and other notable Lutherans.[3] The sermon given at his funeral was delivered by his colleague, Friedrich Balduin (1575–1627). It serves as a primary source for biographical material on Hutter.[4]

Hutter's works can be divided into four categories. The first is his doctrinal works, such as his 1608 lectures on the Book of Concord, his *Compendium of Theology* (*Compendium Locorum Theologicorum*) (1610), and his *Theological Common Places*. The second category is his devotional works, such as his *Meditations on the Cross of Christ* (*Das Creutz Christi*) (1693) and *Biblical Handbook* (*Enchiridion Biblicum*) (1613).[5] The third category is his polemical works against the Roman Catholics, including his disputation against Robert Bellarmine (1542–1621) (*Contra Bellarmin*, 1610), a Jesuit polemicist and the chief spokesman for Tridentine Catholicism. The fourth category is his polemical works against the Calvinist theologians. When Swiss Reformed theologian Rudolph Hospinian (1547–1626) wrote a book called *Discordant Concord* (*Concordia Discors*) (1607), attacking the Formula of Concord, Hutter responded with his *Concordant Concord* (*Concordia Concors*) (1614). When Calvinists began asserting their influence in Holstein, Hutter wrote his *Calvinista Aulico-Politicus* (1609). He wrote a work with a similar title when the Elector of Brandenburg, Johann Sigismund (1572–1619/20), converted to Calvinism in 1613. The elector was reportedly so irate at Hutter's work that he banned the Formula of Concord in his lands and forbade his subjects from attending the University at Wittenberg.[6]

Countering the Counter-Reformation

The polemical works of Lutheran Orthodoxy must always be considered in their historical context, as they reflect the political, social, and

---

[3] His gravestone was moved after a fire and is now on the exterior of the Castle Church on the south side.

[4] Friedrich, Balduin, *Des Heiligen Propheten Eliae Himmelfahrt/Auß dem 2 Reg. 2. Bey Christlicher Leichbegängrüß . . . versetzet worden* (Wittenberg: Johann Gormon, 1617).

[5] A Danish edition of Hutter's Biblical Handbook was printed in Copenhagen in 1618. See Hutter, *Compendium*, 1:731.

[6] Leonhard Hutter, *Inbegriff der Glaubens-Artikel aus der heiligen Schrift und den symbolischen Bücher*, trans. Carl Emil Francke (Leipzig: Karl Franz Koehler, 1837), xii.

theological situations of their day. Leonhard Hutter's defense of Lutheranism and denouncement of Roman Catholicism often has a complicated background of interrelated events and persons. For example, the back story to Hutter's *Call and Ordination of Lutheran Preachers* (1608) reveals the religious and political tensions during this age. When Jesuits in Graz rewrote a mock edition of Luther's Small Catechism to support the Roman Catholic Church, the Lutheran theologian Jakob Heerbrand (1521–1600), professor of theology in Tübingen, replied to their mockery by engaging in a polemical exchange with the Archduke of Styria's confessor, the Jesuit Sigismund Ernhoffer of Graz (1547–97). An exchange of polemics soon occurred between Graz and Tübingen. Ernhoffer's chief tactic was to use Luther against Luther. From Graz, Ernhoffer anonymously published a collection of contradicting quotes of Luther to demonstrate his duplicity, calling him a "weather vane."[7] In 1589, he published his own re-write of the Small Catechism, citing only writings of Martin Luther from before 1517 that supported the Roman Catholic Church.[8] Ernhoffer died in 1597, and Heerbrand died three years later. Yet several of Ernhoffer's writings continued to circulate and still needed to be refuted by the Lutheran theologians.

One of those writings, *A Thorough Report on the Falsely-Named Succession*,[9] was Ernhoffer's attack of the Lutheran claim that it was a legitimate heir of the apostolic Church. In it, Ernhoffer argued that the Lutherans have no legitimate succession of teachers and are not connected to the ancient Catholic Church. Just as the noble lords of Austria must prove their hereditary titles with documentation of their noble lineage, so, too, the rightly called and ordained preachers of the Word must prove their ordination is sanctioned by the authorized bishops and ultimately by the pope. He pointed out the contradiction of Lutherans claiming ancient Church Fathers as their own by assembling twelve quotations of Luther himself that criticize and even partially

---

[7] [Sigismund Ernhoffer], *Der evangelische Wetterhahn, das ist: Ungleiche Reden Martini Lutheri von den fürnehmsten Artikeln christlicher Religion* ([Graz]: n.p., 1587).

[8] [Sigismund Ernhoffer], *Enchiridion; Das ist/ der kleine und raine Catechismus/ mit schönen newen Figuren/sampt einer Notwendigen Schutzred/für die Gemaine Pfarrherrn vnnd Prediger gemehrt vnd gebessert aus D. M. Lutheri Schrifften vnd Büchern* (n.p.: n.p., 1589).

[9] Sigismund Ernhoffer, *Gründtlicher Bericht von der falschgenannten Succession/ welche verschienes 89. Jahrs ein Fürnemer Lutheraner zusamen getragen/ und in Schrifften verfasset hat. Darauß starck erwiesen und dargethan wird/ daß die Lutherischen keine rechtglaubige Vorfahren unnd Uhrelter ihrer Lehr haben/ sonder daß ir Lehr ein pur lauterer newer Menschenrand ist* (Graz: Georg Widmanstetter, 1590).

condemn statements by the Fathers and councils. The conclusion of Ernhoffer's work condemns the Lutheran religion as a heretical and false church.

Ernhoffer's writing touched on an issue that had perennially been raised by the Jesuits: namely, the lack of any official sanction and ordination of the Lutheran preachers by Roman Catholic bishops. The Lutherans needed to find a way to legitimatize their preachers apart from the canons of the Roman Church. Although Ernhoffer's work was published eighteen years earlier, the matter of the call and ordination of Lutheran pastors had not yet been thoroughly addressed. Hutter took up this task eleven years after Ernhoffer's death in order to finally bury the Jesuit's claims once and for all.

Leonhard Hutter dedicated his work to the lords and knights of Lower and Upper Austria, although the booklet he was responding to was published in Graz, which was in Inner Austria (Styria). These regions of Austria were lands in which Lutheranism had spread among the knights and nobles, but which were controlled by the Roman Catholic Hapsburgs. By the last decades of the sixteenth century, nine out of ten Lower Austrian nobles had embraced Lutheranism, as had eighty-five percent of those in Upper Austria, where three-quarters of the urban population and half the peasants were Protestants.[10] For a time, religious concessions were granted to these Lutheran nobles, but in 1598 the bishop of Vienna, Melchior Klesl (1552–1630), began an intense program of Counter-Reformation, reinstating Catholic priests in Protestant parishes, often escorted by armed guards, and dismissing all Lutheran school teachers from Upper Austria. In Inner Austria, Lutheran teachers and pastors were forcefully deposed, church cemeteries exhumed, and in one town a Lutheran church was blown to pieces. These efforts led to the expulsion of eleven thousand Protestants from Inner Austria between 1598 and 1605. The Catholic revival was linked to the Hapsburg dynasty's attempt to reassert political authority, and the harsh policies to re-establish the Catholic Church were expanded in all Hapsburg territories.[11] In this light, the harsh polemics of the Lutherans against the Catholics seem less extreme, if not warranted.

The harsh and often inhumane tactics of the Hapsburgs did not go unchallenged. In the same year as Hutter's publication, "The Call and Ordination of Lutheran Preachers," 166 Upper and Lower Austrian

---

[10] Peter H. Wilson, *The Thirty Years War: Europe's Tragedy* (Cambridge: Belknap Press, 2009), 58–59.

[11] Wilson, *The Thirty Years War*, 111.

Protestant lords and knights gathered to form a confederation in October against the Archduke Matthias (1557–1619), and they appealed to other Protestant lands for assistance. This forced the archduke to acquiesce to their demands, and by March 1609, Matthias had halted Catholic reform. By 1612, however, Matthias was elected Emperor of the Holy Roman Empire, and he handed off the imperial administration to his trusted advisor, Bishop Klesl. The latter remained in the forefront of imperial politics and religious tensions up to the outbreak of the Thirty Years' War in 1618. Hutter's publication and dedication to the Austrian nobles was therefore timely, as it fostered Lutheran conviction and anti-Catholic sentiment in a pivotal year for the struggle between confessions in Austria. This shows the long reach of Wittenberg theologians, who were writing for the Protestant cause in many different lands.

Compendium

Hutter's most enduring and influential work was his *Compendium of Theology* (1610), which replaced Melanchthon's *Commonplaces* and *Body of Christian Doctrine* (*Corpus Doctrinae Christianae*) as the leading theology textbook for schools in Lutheran territories. In 1603, the Elector of Saxony, Christian II (1583–1611), conducted a visitation of schools and universities in Electoral Saxony. Hutter participated, visiting and evaluating the prince's schools (*Fürstenschulen*) in Meissen, Grimma, and Schulpforta. He reported three theological misunderstandings were evident in these schools, namely Christology, the communication of attributes in the two natures of Christ, and the related doctrine of the Lord's Supper. The elector then commissioned the Wittenberg Faculty in June 1603 to create a book of instruction based on the Formula of Concord that could be used in the schools and also for the examination of pastors. It was to preserve as much as possible the actual wording of the Book of Concord.[12]

The first attempt at such a work was made by Salomon Gesner (1559–1605), but this was unsatisfactory. Hutter, who had in the previous year begun lectures on the Formula of Concord, was given permission by the elector in December 1605 to make new attempt at creating such a manual. By the first week of January 1606, Hutter had completed a draft,

---

[12] For a thorough treatment of the *Compendium's* genesis, see Johann Steiger, "Leonhart Hütters Compendium Locorum Theologicorum Zu Entstehung und Wirkung eines lutherischen Lehrbuches" in *Compendium locorum theologicorum ex Scripturis Sacris et Libro Concordiae: Lateinisch - deutsch - englisch*, ed. Johann Anselm Steiger (Stuttgart-Bad Cannstatt: Frommann-Holzboog, 2006), 1:699–791.

which was sent to the Dresden Consistory for proofing. The consistory returned the draft with a number of improvements, including the placement of articles, use of contemporary terminology, and consistency with Melanchthon's method and ordering. [13] The revised draft was sent to the theological faculty at Leipzig for proofing in February 1606. The process of editing was far from over, however. Over a year and a half later (May 1608), a copy of the manuscript was sent to the three prince's schools in Meissen, Grimma, and Schulpforta for their opinions. They gave the elector very favorable reviews and added a few suggestions in August of that year. Finally, in May 1609, the elector commissioned the Wittenberg faculty to make the final edits for printing. Permission to publish was granted in November. Printing and binding commenced, and the first editions were sent to schools by the beginning of the new year.[14] There were so many requests that the *Compendium* was printed three more times that year and three times in the following year to keep up with demand. By the end of Hutter's lifetime, there were eighteen editions printed, and by the end of the seventeenth century, there were seventy-nine (until 1622, there was at least one edition printed each year). This work shaped students such as Paul Gerhardt (1607–76) and Johann Sebastian Bach (1685–1750). A German translation was printed in 1611. Later, editions were printed in Swedish (1618) and in Hungarian (1635). In the nineteenth century, an English translation appeared in North America (1868) and a Tamil edition in India (1881). Hutter's *Compendium* may rightly be called the "most widely used theological textbook of Lutheran orthodoxy,"[15] making it Hutter's most enduring contribution to the promotion and preservation of the Christian faith and Lutheran doctrine.

---

[13] While Hutter's *Compendium* replaced Philipp Melanchthon's *Loci Communes* as the primary theological textbook at Lutheran schools, this change was not done with a great amount of disdain or dismissal of Melanchthon. Hutter made extensive use of Melanchthon's *Loci* and *Examen Ordinandorum*, praising the author but also critiquing his writings. Excluding quotations from the Augsburg Confession and the Apology, Hutter quotes Melanchthon thirty-three times in the *Compendium*, Luther only fourteen times (excluding citations from the Small Catechism and Smalcald Articles).

[14] Leonhard Hutter, *Compendium Locorum Theologicorum: Ex Scripturis Sacris, & libro Concordiae* (Wittenberg: Paul Helwig, 1610).

[15] Hutter, *Compendium*, 732.

BIBLIOGRAPHY

Works by Hutter in English Translation

Compendium locorum theologicorum ex Scripturis Sacris et Libro Concordiae: Lateinisch - deutsch - englisch. Edited by Johann Anselm Steiger. 2 vols. Stuttgart-Bad Cannstatt: Frommann-Holzboog, 2006.

Compend of Lutheran Theology. Translated by H. E. Jacobs and G. F. Spieker. Philadelphia: The Lutheran Book Store, 1868.

"Leonard Hutter (1563–1616) On Why We Should Be Called Lutherans." Translated by William Wangelin. *Lutheran Quarterly* 25, no. 3 (2011): 326–31.

Select Works by Hutter in German and Latin

Calvinista Aulico-Politicus. Wittenberg: Paul Helwig, 1609.

Calvinista Aulico-Politicus Altar. Magdeburg: Joachim Böel, 1614.

Concordia Concors. Wittenberg: Clemens Berger, 1614.

Controversiae duae Theologicae: 1. De Verbo Dei scripto, & non scripto. 2. De persona Christi Jesu Servatoris nostri unici. Wittenberg: Johann Gormann, 1610.

Das Creutz Christi/ oder XXXVII Betrachtungen der gantzen Geschicht von dem heilsamen Leyden/ Sterben und Begräbüß unsers Herrn und Heylandes Jesu Christi. Wittenberg: Quenstedt, 1693.

Enchiridion Biblicum Oder Biblisches Handbüchlein. Wittemberg: Johann Gorman, 1620.

Gründlicher Bericht von Ordentlichen und recht Apostoliche Beruff Ordination, und kräfftigem Ampt. Wittenberg: Zacharias Schürer, 1608.

Libri Christianae Concordiae. Wittenberg: Zacharias Schürer, 1609.

Loci Communes Theologici: Ex Sacris Literis Diligenter Eruti, Veterum Patrum testimoniis paßim roborati. Wittenberg: Paul Helwig, 1619.

WRITING[16]

At this point we can, for our part, suffer both friend and foe to judge whether or not the call of a Lutheran preacher agrees with God's Word and the example of the apostle Matthias.

First, in our churches, no one is permitted to force himself into this holy office or assume this office himself without an orderly and proper call.

Second, when a church suffers a vacancy, the *Patronus* [patron] of the church begins with earnest prayer to seek a person fit for service, who is then presented to the *Presbyterio* [clergy].

Third, such a person is then also presented to the congregation so that it can publically hear one or more sermons. For today, God no longer calls new teachers and pastors in such a high manner through His own voice or by miraculous control of the casting of lots. Rather, He does this through the voice of his dear Church, which consists not only of the above-mentioned clergy, but also of the laity, just as at the calling of Matthias, not only the disciples but also the entire congregation of one hundred and twenty people was gathered.

Fourth, the congregation demands a *Judicium* [judgment] of the gifts and competence of a person, and if he is not considerably outstanding, either in life or in doctrine, then the confirmation is given to the church or the *Presbyterio* or the consistory.

Fifth, in order for such confirmation to be carried out, not only is a diligent inquiry made of the new preacher's life, but he is also given a thorough examination of the Holy Scriptures and most importantly of the chief articles of the Christian religion which they contain. This is to see if he, too, like Matthias, has spent time with the Lord; that is, if he has diligently studied the Bible and learned its theology, the goal of which is Christ, and that he is capable of teaching this to others.

And finally sixth, if he has sufficiently proved in these examinations his God-given gifts and abilities, then the confirmation is extended to him, which in many places happens through the *ordination*, or the public confirmation by the laying on of hands, more of which will be said later.

Now because the call of the Lutheran preacher completely agrees with God's Word, the *praxis Apostolica* [apostolic practice], and with the example of Matthias, we can easily conclude that this is to be considered

---

[16] This is a translation of Leonhard Hutter, *Gründtlicher Bericht von Ordentlichen und recht Apostolische Beruff Ordination, und kräfftigem Ampt* (Wittenberg: Zacharias Schürer, 1608), 26–30.

orderly and proper, and that their Ministerium and office is to be regarded as effective and salutary. And we are not at all at fault, as the Jesuits' attacks claim, as we will soon thoroughly demonstrate, once we have sufficiently reported on the second part, namely, the *ordination* or consecration of a new priest or preacher.

The Second Part

Of the *Ordination* or Consecration of the Lutheran Preachers.

Secondly now, it is asked by the Jesuits if the Lutheran preachers are ordained and consecrated according to the prescription of Holy Scripture and the common usage of the apostolic Church. To this, they answer with "no," and we answer with "yes!" And if our "yes" is to have sufficient basis, then we must first consider what is written in the Holy Scripture by the dear holy apostles regarding ordination or the consecration of new priests and what was faithfully commended and commanded by the Early Church. Second, we must diligently compare such apostolic practice regarding ordination with both that of the papists and that of our churches.

Now at this point it has already been sufficiently reported about how the ordination of Matthias was carried out; namely that after the apostles and the congregation were convinced of his gifts and capabilities and it was found through the casting of lots that this person had been set apart by God himself, so the text says, they ordained him and confirmed his office of apostle without the permission of a bishop, without the laying on of hands, without any chrism or oil, and without all other ceremonies. According to this practice, even today there are a few Lutheran churches of a certain sort that do not observe the ceremony of the laying on of hands at the consecration of a new preacher, but rather hold this to be an *adiaphoron*. On account of this, they cannot and should not be condemned, much less should the completed call be considered invalid or ineffective. The reasons for this are as follows:

When St. Paul instructed his disciple Timothy on how the ordination of the young preachers should be carried out, he wrote to him this instruction in 2 Timothy 2:2, "What you have heard from me in the presence of many witnesses, entrust to faithful men who will be able to teach others also." Regarding this, Dr. Luther rightly concluded:

> Here is neither chrism nor butter. It is the command [*Befehl*] of God's Word alone, and whoever has this, this one is considered by St. Paul to be a pastor, bishop, or pope. For everything depends on the Word of God, even to the highest office. This is

> in agreement with the *Formula Ordinationis* [formula of ordination], which Christ used as he sent out his disciples, saying, "Go into all the world and preach the Gospel. Make for me disciples of all nations and teach them to observe everything that I have commanded you." Here Christ also forgot the chrism! But what did he command the disciples at this ordination? Nothing else than to preach the Gospel, and in such preaching use the Holy Sacraments to convert all nations to Christ.[17]

We have now drawn out of the Holy Scripture the true and actual *substantiam* or the essence of Christian and proper ordination or consecration of priests, which is nothing else than the command [*Befehl*] of the office, and that a newly called preacher is presented and charged publically with the preaching office before the entire congregation, and at this time his office is solemnly recounted and finally, through prayer, our faithful God would be called upon over him.

Such a *Formula Ordinationis*, prescribed and practiced by Christ himself and the holy apostles, is strictly and faithfully retained to this very day at the ordination of the new preachers in the Evangelical Lutheran churches. Therefore, it cannot be doubted that among them is the proper apostolic ordination.

Regarding the ceremony of the laying on of hands, the New Testament Scriptures testify that the apostles laid their hands on the head of new, young preachers at their ordination. This was done in Acts 13 with Paul and Barnabas, though it was not only the apostles, but also the entire congregation that laid hands on them (see also Acts 6:6). Paul also writes of this in 1 Timothy 5:22, when he says, "Do not be hasty in the laying on of hands." Before this in 4:14, he says, "Do not neglect the gift you have, which was given you by prophecy when the council of elders laid their hands on you." Paul even testifies that he, too, did the same when he ordained Timothy (2 Timothy 1:6), "For this reason I remind you to fan into flame the gift of God, which is in you through the laying on of my hands."

Therefore, because such ceremonies (1) originated from the holy apostles and were customary in the first apostolic church, (2) according to the example of the holy patriarchs and prophets of the Old Testament, [these ceremonies] demonstrate how the newly called preacher is entirely set apart and at the same time wholly committed [*aufgeopffert*] to the

[17] Martin Luther, AE 38:212, "Tract on Private Mass and the Consecration of Priests" (1533), augmented by Hutter.

office and to the Church of God, and (3) since through such ceremonies both the *Ordinandi* [those being ordained] and the listeners are led to earnest prayer, such ceremonies are preserved to this day in our churches, and are useful in many ways.

[The churches] are also of the opinion that where such [ceremonies] are commonly in use, they should not be lightly abrogated or done away with. But they are not of the opinion that they are necessary in themselves or that they have any special power or effect of their own. On the contrary, they are used simply for the reasons which have already been presented.

Regarding this ceremony in and of itself, however, we hold it to be an *Adiaphoron* and "middle thing," which neither effects nor invalidates an orderly and proper call. Such a ceremony has no special promise from God. Rather, the benefit and strength that a new preacher experiences at ordination are to be attributed not to the ceremonies, but should and must [be attributed] solely and singularly to the prayer offered up during ordination over him.

As we consider these circumstances, it again becomes undeniably clear that the ordination of a Lutheran preacher completely agrees with the *praxi Apostolica*, since (1) the preaching office and that which it demands is publically commanded and entrusted in the presence of the congregation, (2) God is earnestly prayed to over them, and (3) through the external ceremony of the laying on of hands they are offered to both Christ and his Church.

And should all strength and might assert the contrary, as they repeatedly seek to prove regarding our preacher's call, then the refutation of their intended reasons and motives will soon be irresistibly set forth and demonstrated.

With regards, however, to the ordination of the papal priests, [their idolatrous ceremonies] will now be presented, of which the entire New Testament of Holy Scripture does not know of or teach a single letter.

Their ceremonies are described in the *Pontificale Romanum* page 16.[18] The sum and substance of this papal ordination rests on these two parts: First, in the anointing of the hands, when the bishop smears oil or chrism on the thumb of the right hand of the new priest and makes the sign of the cross on his hand with melted chrism. He then repeats this process from the thumb to the pinky finger of the right hand and the same for the left hand, until both hands are smeared and greased with oil.

---

[18] Hutter cites twenty-nine steps of the Roman Catholic ordination rite from the *Roman Pontifical* in Latin without translation.

The purpose of this is to give his hands the special power to bless, to consecrate, and to perform incantations over water, salt, wine, eggs, possessions, gold, silver, incense, etc.

After this, the ordination occurs, in which the new priest is given the power to sacrifice the body of Christ and hold mass for the living and the dead.

Now consider this and judge for yourselves what this papal consecration and ordination is all about. God's Word does not know anything in the least of such things. Neither did the apostles, as there is no example, no command, and no promise that has been given to such buffoonery. What kind of priests are they? What kind of office are they really carrying out? It is not God's, not Christ's, not that of the apostles either. Rather, it is of the devil and his cohorts in Rome—the pope. And if there were nothing else that could make a pious heart turn away from the papacy, this would be sufficient: What kind of power and effect, what kind of teaching, comfort, admonishment, absolution, and the like can be obtained through such an office and *Ministerio* [ministry], when it is completely not grounded in God's Word and even runs contrary to it?!

For when did Christ ever command his apostles, or when did the apostles themselves command those ordained by them to change bread and wine into the body and blood of Christ? When did they ever give the order that the Sacrament should be given in only one kind to the laity, contrary to the Lord's institution? When did they ever give the order to make the Sacrament into a sacrifice and offer up Christ all over again? When did they ever smear oil over the fingers of those they ordained? When have they ever commanded them to bless God's creation, as if it were full of devils? When did they ever use or institute the abovementioned ceremonies that are idolatrous, at times foolish, and even laughable?

Now whoever still does not want to see and understand what is behind their priestly consecration and office is deliberately blind and is lost forever. But woe—and eternal woe—to those who read, know, understand, even see with their eyes and grasp with their hands such things, and yet, on account of temporal honor and dignity or other bodily concerns, still give assent to the pope and his idolatry, or at least remain hypocrites and remain silent, lest they publically leave Babylon and give God more honor than men.

According to the testimony of Christ, this is how it will be for the servant who knows the Lord's will but doesn't do it: He will be struck down twice as hard, that is, he will suffer and be tormented much more than those who remained in the papacy due to ignorance.

VALERIUS HERBERGER (1562–1627)

JESUS-PREACHER

by Matthew Carver

LIFE

The author of the Lutheran hymn, "Valet will ich dir geben," translated by Catherine Winkworth (1827–78) as "Farewell I Gladly Bid Thee," could trace his love for Lutheran hymnody, and most likely his poetic skill, back to his father, Martin Herberger, a furrier and self-proclaimed "simple laborer." Of him, Herberger writes, "My blessed father Martinus Herbergerus was also a famous fencer and singer as well as a poet of German, many of whose meister-songs are still extant."[1] His

[1] K. F. Ledderhose, *Leben Valerius Herbergers, Predigers am Kripplein Christi* (Bielefeld: Verlag von Velhagen & Klasing, 1851), 3. While the first and best Herberger biography, from which all others are drawn, is Samuel Lauterbach, *Vita, Fama, Et Fata Valerii Herbergeri* (Leipzig: Gleditsch, 1708), Lauterbach's most popular interpreter and condenser in the nineteenth century was perhaps Ledderhose. Both are consulted here.

father earned awards in the singers' guild, and his own compositions, many of which focused on Christ and the crucifixion, were published in their own right. Martin Herberger was thus a God-fearing man, and a key citizen who participated in welcoming the Reformation to his native city of Fraustadt in 1552.

Frauenstadt (the old spelling), in Polish Wschowa, is a historically German town in western Poland that had its origin as a fortification in the borderland between German and Polish spheres of influence. By the time of Martin Herberger, it had, like some other cities of the region, long enjoyed rights of autonomy granted by Magdeburg law despite its politically Polish identity and the Polish culture that continued to grow in the surrounding regions. Frauenstadt means "city of (our) Lady," referring to Mary, the mother of Jesus; it was so named no doubt because of the altar dedicated to her in its fifteenth-century parish church. The town also boasted a small monastic community of Franciscans with a cloister and chapel (dedicated to St. Joseph) just outside town.

For some time, before the parish church's official conversion to the evangelical faith and adoption of the Augsburg Confession, a number of Fraustadt's parishioners made the trek to neighboring towns some ways away in order to hear the Gospel that Luther uncovered. It was through their agency, Martin Herberger no doubt among them, that the Reformation came to Fraustadt in 1552.

In 1558, Martin married devout Anna Hoffmann (born ca. 1538), with whom he would have five children. At about ten in the morning on April 21, 1562, the day of St. Fortunatus in the old calendar, Valerius Herberger was born. Two days later, little Valerius was baptized by his namesake, Valerius Gaunersdörffer (pastor from 1561 to 1567). His godparents were Mrs. Ubermann from the Bohemian Brethren community, the local magistrate Matthäus Ressel, and the school headmaster Martin Arnold.

Valerius was raised in the fear of God, in a pious household, listening to his father singing chorales like "By the Rivers of Babylon" (*An Wasserflüssen Babylon*) while working at his trade. The biographer Ledderhose notes an anecdote of the infant Valerius Herberger. When he was swaddled, he would raise the three fingers of his right hand in a way resembling paintings of the Savior. His father took this as a sign that he would become a preacher and bear witness to the Lord Jesus. With this in mind, Martin Herberger eventually taught Valerius to read and write, as

---

More recent work has been done by Ilse Buchholz, *Valerius Herberger: Prediger am "Kripplein Christi"* (Berlin: Evangelische Verlagsanstalt, 1965).

well as the rudiments of Latin; and when he could teach Valerius no more, he sent him to school.

In 1568, the first of three great plagues during Valerius's lifetime struck Fraustadt and claimed the lives of eleven hundred people. The boy was only six at the time, but he came out unscathed. By God's grace, he would survive many more troubles to come. The afflictions he experienced, however, were not restricted to physical maladies. Poland, unlike many neighboring German territories, was ruled by staunch Roman Catholics, whose religious monopoly, incited by the Jesuit order that came to Poland in 1564, grew increasingly hostile toward Protestants. In order to present a united front against the oppressive Catholic regime, the main Protestant groups, along with the Lutherans, met together in April 1570. The resulting Sandomierz Consensus, while not achieving the confessional unity between Protestants and Lutherans that some desired (the point of contention being the Lord's Supper), instead declared a mutual respect among the religious confessions to present a stronger front against the rising oppression of the Catholic Counter-Reformation. The increased hostility would eventually find greater force. Thus the precarious situation in the Kingdom of Poland (in which there was still hope for improvement but nevertheless fear of greater persecution) produced an irenic disposition in even the most avid supporters of the Augsburg Confession (especially with respect to the Lord's Supper). Such was the case with Valerius Herberger himself.

On February 8, 1571, after a time of sickness, Valerius's father, Martin, died. He was laid to rest by Rev. Johannes Pitiscus (pastor from 1568) on Septuagesima Sunday. Anna, Martin's widow, had lived happily with Martin for ten years and had given him five children, but now she was in distress and the family was without provision. In 1572, Anna's sister, Barbara, Valerius's aunt, who was married to a butcher by the name of Georg Wende and who had no children of her own, took the ten-year-old Valerius into her care. In this way, he was provided with all that he needed and his education continued until he left for Freystadt (now known as Kożuchów) in 1580. In 1573, Valerius's mother, Anna, married Johann Fengler, a shoemaker.

Georg and Barbara Wende provided the necessities for Valerius, but the greatest encouragement and inspiration to pursue his education came from Michael Vetter, a friend of his father, who noticed Valerius's talents and presented him with textbooks on dialectic and rhetoric, and also fed him at his table on occasion. At the Fraustadt school, Valerius's teachers included Valentinus Florianus (in ancient languages and sources) and the headmaster Kaspar Hoffmann. The former was eventually (in 1576) authorized by the town council to serve as a deacon of the parish church. By 1579, a seventeen-year-old Valerius, though excelling others at school, came to a turning point. He had decided to enter his stepfather Fengler's trade as an apprentice shoemaker. By God's grace, his godfather, Martin Arnold, now pastor of Fraustadt (after serving as headmaster of the school and deacon of the church), reminded him that his father hoped he would be a preacher and urged him to remember this and to study for the ministry. He was persuaded.

On Trinity Sunday 1579, Valerius Herberger left home for the famous school in the neighboring city of Freystadt, Silesia. Martin Arnold, his pastor and godfather, escorted him to town. There Valerius was introduced to the city clerk Petrus Scultetus (1536–89) with whom he found lodging, and he worked as a tutor for Petrus's two sons. Thus from 1579 to 1581, Herberger studied diligently at the Freystadt school, and especially came to favor the Hebrew language, as evident in his writings.

After three years of faithful study in Freystadt, Valerius received financial support from the mayor David Clos to study at the University of Frankfurt (Oder). He remained only a short time. On June 20, 1582, at the advice of his teacher Ludovicus, Valerius transferred to the University of Leipzig. There he lived and studied for two years on the stipendium established by Canon Dr. Lamprecht of Breslau. This stipendium required those receiving it to pray the seven psalms of repentance every Friday. Initially, Valerius had his residence in Our Lady's college (*Frauenkolleg*) with roommate Adam Curäus (who was later driven from Breslau for his Calvinistic view of the Lord's Supper). But in time, Valerius was able to procure some work and found bed and board as a domestic assistant to Dr. Michael Barth.

In 1584, Valerius Herberger received a call from the council of Fraustadt to the Latin school with duties that included teaching lower grades. On April 9, therefore, he appeared before the council of Fraustadt and received his authorization. He was inducted that afternoon into the school by headmaster Hoffmann. He continued in that position, attending to his school duties, for six years. Herberger exercised his piety no less diligently than he had studied. On the Feast of the Trinity that year, Herberger resolved that, in honor of God who had provided him with that call, he would dispense alms to the poor residents of the hospital annually on that day. During his time in this position, Herberger also enjoyed the trust and favor of Pastor Martin Arnold and Deacon Michael Gebhard. He even had the opportunity to practice his preaching abilities (which would be so famous later) in 1588, when the deacon suffered a prolonged illness and Valerius preached on three consecutive Sundays. In 1589, Herberger received two calls, one to the mining town of Goldberg (Polish: Złotoryja) at the instigation of his teacher Ludovicus, and another to Freystadt. He was offered responsibilities over the morning sermon as well as school duties, as well as civic positions such as notary and city clerk, but he rejected them all.

In 1589, Rev. Arnold was released from his service over a certain controversy, and Deacon Michael Gebhard left to take a call in his hometown Guhrau. Thus both positions were vacated simultaneously. The council called Pastor Paul Bernau (1553–1614) of Freystadt to fill Arnold's position, and Herberger was to take Gebhard's post. On January 22, 1590, then, Valerius Herberger was presented with the official call from the council through mayor Deutschländer. He subsequently departed for Liegnitz to be duly examined by Superintendent Leonhard Krenzheim (1532–98). On February 3, Herberger was ordained as deacon by five senior preachers. On the twenty-fifth of the same month, which was Septuagesima Sunday, he delivered his inaugural sermon on Luke 4:16–22 (see excerpt below). Many elements recognizable in his later writings were present already here: an ability to draw on a wide swath of history and anecdotes, a popular and heartfelt style, and an emphasis on Jesus as the center of all Scripture. Having officially relinquished his school duties, Herberger received the authorization of the church from Paul Bernau and was installed on March 21. Four days later he was engaged to Anna Rüdinger, daughter of Bartholomäus (a local jurist) and Dorothea Rüdinger. On October 8, Valerius and Anna were married. Their first son, Zacharias, came a year later on October 28, 1591.

Now in the neighboring Duchy of Liegnitz, an official visitation conducted by Aegidius Hunnius (1550–1603) and Wolfgang Mamphrasius (1557–1616) had been published in 1590, and Superintendent Krenzheim was charged with Calvinistic tendencies. On April 6, 1593, he was dismissed. After a year as a preacher in Rognitz (installed April 25, 1594), Bernau returned to Freystadt, and Krenzheim was called to the pastorate of Fraustadt. On August 20, Krenzheim gave his inaugural sermon in the parish church. From that point, an unlikely but fast friendship grew between him and Herberger.

In the same year, the Synod of Toruń met under King Sigismund III (1566–1632) with the purpose of confirming the Sendomierz Consensus. Few Lutheran preachers took part, however, and the Jesuits made advances. After this point, a marked shift occurred in Poland as church buildings long held by Protestants were lost to the Catholics. Eventually, most of the Reformed or Lutheran senators in the imperial council were removed.

On December 15, 1595, Herberger's second son, Valerianus, was born, taking his name both from the saint of the calendar day and from the fanciful combination of his parents' names. Suffering from an unspecified condition, he would die at a young age.

In 1598, the Second Sunday in Advent (December 6 that year), Valerius Herberger preached on the fire of judgment—a sermon that he afterward came to recognize as unwittingly prophetic. In keeping with the Gospel: "The bridegroom comes at midnight," fire broke out in Fraustadt at the stroke of midnight. Some sixty-eight or seventy houses were consumed by the flames. A few days later, on December 12, Krenzheim, who had been gravely ill already, died. The fire and the evacuation had taken their toll. At the funeral, the sermon was delivered by Herberger on Philippians 1:21: "Christ is my life and death my gain." Provision was quickly made to fill the post, and Herberger was called to the pastorate on Christmas Eve, 1598. His first sermon as pastor was given on January 1 "on the sweet name of Jesus." The diaconal post in the church, vacated by Herberger's promotion, was soon filled by Adam Crusius, who on March 10, 1600, was installed in the presence of the city council.

The following year, plague struck the people of Fraustadt again. The death toll was so great that authorities ordered all bodies to be buried without singing or music. But on September 26, another toll was felt in the Herberger household. Valerianus, Valerius's second son, died, and he was buried by his father three days later with great mourning.

Not long after this, a vacancy appeared in Oberpritschen when its Pastor Florianus died and was buried on the Fourth Sunday in Advent. Herberger's deacon, Adam Crusius, was called to fill that vacancy and left Fraustadt, being replaced by Deacon Johannes Timaeus. At this time, Herberger befriended and lodged the great hymnwriter Johann Heermann (1585–1647), whom he met through cantor Balthasar Thilo and employed for a brief but meaningful year as an amanuensis.

On the night of January 1, 1602, Valerius had a portentous dream. He was in the church and heard the hymn, "Grant Peace, We Pray, in Mercy, Lord" (*Verleih uns Frieden gnädiglich*) being sung. At once, however, he was shocked to behold the chancel filled with monks, and then he found himself transported to a beautiful house, entirely empty. Indeed, it was prophetic. Not long after this, the Catholics who in Fraustadt had since the Reformation been few in number and hardly filled the chapel of the Fransciscan cloister, began to demand the possession of the parish church. They were supported by the royal government. In October of 1603, a commission from the government arrived in Fraustadt to pursue the matter. Every attempt was made to prevent the tragedy. Herberger was very troubled, and in his sermon, in which he quoted from Psalm 83, "Be not silent, O God . . . ," he encouraged the congregation to meet whatever might come. The case was sent on to the royal court. On September 30, 1604, a royal decree demanded that the church, with its cemetery and incomes, be ceded to the Catholics. Only with great effort was permission obtained (on October 15) for a delay, effective until Christmas, in order to prepare a new place. Collections were taken, and two houses near the Polish Gate were purchased by the congregation. The houses were cleared, the adjoining wall knocked down, the upper floors opened up, and a relatively minimal but pleasing quantity of decoration was managed. On December 21 (St. Thomas's Day), Herberger preached his last sermon at the parish church; on Christmas Eve, 1604, he preached his first sermon in the new "house of God," suggesting that the church building be consecrated "Christ's Manger" (*Kripplein Christi*): even though Jesus might have no room in the inn (in this case, the parish church), He would have room in the manger (the new church building). On Christmas Day, which in the old calendar was the beginning of 1605, Herberger celebrated his first Mass in the new building.

On July 10, 1606, while the threat of Catholic oppression rose high in Fraustadt, Herberger received a call to Freystadt. Likewise, he also received a call to the superintendency of the Duchy of Liegnitz (from which Krenzheim was previously dismissed). He rejected both. It was Herberger's intention and privilege to keep his post in Fraustadt for the rest of his life.

In 1608, at the age of seventy, Valerius's mother died after a long affliction of gout. Her funeral sermon was preached by Deacon Johannes Timaeus. In 1610, Valerius accompanied his son Zacharias to enroll him at the University of Leipzig. On the way, however, they were persuaded by Johann Förster (1498–1556) to enroll him at Wittenberg.

In 1613, soon after Pentecost, severe plague struck a third time, and some two thousand men died. One man counted 1,505 men borne away, and 603 students and children too. Valerius's family was sent to neighboring Weigmansdorf and Oberpritschen. It was during this plague that Herberger, when not leading the carts of bodies to burial or visiting the sick, penned his famous hymn, "Farewell I Gladly Bid Thee." During this time also, Zacharias obtained his master's degree in Wittenberg. On

September 4, the family returned home to Fraustadt. The plague finally subsided.

On January 14, 1614, Deacon Johannes Timaeus died. This year also, Herberger's hymn was published in Leipzig. On Septuagesima Sunday, a festival of thanksgiving was held for the end of the plague. In place of Timaeus, Zacharias Herberger was called to the diaconate of Fraustadt. Further calls to Tropau and Breslau came and were duly rejected. Father and son were able to enjoy a decade of peace, serving together as ministers to Christ's Manger.

In 1623, on the evening before the Nineteenth Sunday after Trinity, Herberger suffered a stroke. On February 21, 1627, he suffered a second stroke on his left side while preaching. Still he went on to preach a funeral sermon he had planned. For twelve weeks, he lay in bed until at last he was brought gently into the retirement of blessed sleep on May 18, 1627, at the age of sixty-five. According to his wishes, he was laid to await the Lord's coming not in the stony floor of a church but in a cemetery plot among his faithful, slumbering sheep. Valentin Preibis, pastor in Glogau, gave the sermon on Luke 10:20: "Rejoice that your names are written in heaven," according to the instructions and outline that Valerius had drafted. His son, Zacharias, lived on a short while to continue Valerius's unfinished works and died in 1631 at the age of forty. Zacharias's son Valerius died in 1641. Thus the direct line of Valerius Herberger ceased.

Throughout Eastern Germany, Silesia, and the German-speaking areas of Poland, Valerius Herberger was known for his homiletic skill—mainly through his written sermons, which were printed often during his liftetime. The Lutheran Princess Anna of Sweden (1568–1625) was an ardent supporter and admirer of Herberger's works. One of the most popular and most exhaustive of these is the one that Herberger called *The Great Works of God* (*Magnalia Dei*), which is an ambitious edifice of devout meditations on the Scriptures as "those that bear witness about Christ." These he regarded rather like the linen cloths that wrapped the infant Jesus in the manger and traced his Lord in every little wrinkle. It is difficult to imagine how big this enormous tome would have been if finished; he only got as far as Ruth. Though Herberger was miraculously preserved by God's hand through multiple plagues, the cares and the labor of committing half a city to its earthly slumber meant there was little time left over for writing. Therefore, what we are left with is as astounding as it is edifying.

BIBLIOGRAPHY

Works by Herberger in English Translation

"Farewell I gladly bid Thee." In *The Chorale Book for England*, edited by C. Winkworth, no. 137. London: Longman, Green, etc., 1863. Winkworth's full translation of "Valet will ich dir geben" was taken into several hymnals, including *The Lutheran Hymnal*. St. Louis: Concordia, 1941. Further translations, such as that of A. T. Russell, "O World so vain, I leave thee" (*In Psalms & Hymns, Partly Original, Partly Selected for the Use of the Church of England*, edited by A. T. Russel, no. 248. [Cambridge: J. Deighton, 1851]) are mentioned in John Julian's *Dictionary of Hymnology* (London: John Murray, 1892). No published translation preserves the original acrostic of the author's name.

The Great Works of God. Translated by Matthew Carver. 4 Parts in 2 volumes. St. Louis: Concordia, 2010–11.

"6 July: Isaiah; 22 July: Mary Magdalene; 21 September: St. Matthew; 30 October: Matt. 20:1–16; 30 November: St. Andrew; 19 December: Adam and Eve; 26 December: St. Stephen; 24 January: St. Timothy; 23 February: St. Polycarp." In *Treasury of Daily Prayer*, edited by Scot A. Kinnaman and translated by Benjamin T. G. Mayes, 497–98, 548–49, 742–43, 864, 968, 1031, 1057, 1147–48, 1232 respectively. St. Louis: Concordia, 2008. These are selections from the *Heart-Postils of Valerius Herberger*.

Select Works by Herberger in German and Latin

Epistolische Hertz-Postilla Valerii Herbergers (Epistle heart-postils). Leipzig: Gleditsch, 1693. This is a collections of sermons on the epistle readings of the Church Year.

Erklärung des Haus- & Zucht-Buchs Jesus Sirach in 97 Predigten (Exposition of Ecclesiasticus, a book for domestic use and moral discipline, in 97 sermons). Hof: Leidenfrost, 1739.

Florilegium ex paradiso psalmorum. Paradies-Blümlein . . . / Paradieß-Psalter (Bouquet from the paradise of the Psalms). 4 parts. Leipzig: Schürer, 1611, 1625. This consists of meditations on Psalms 1–23:5 by Valerius Herberger and was extended from his notes to Psalm 28 by Zacharias Herberger.

Geistliche Hertzens-Lust und Freude für betende Christen (Spiritual heart-joy and gladness for praying Christians). Leipzig: Gleditsch, 1698. These are excerpts of devotional writings and prayers edited and arranged according to the Church Year for use as a prayer-book.

Geistliche Trawrbinden (Spiritual mourning-band). 6 parts. Leipzig: Schürer, 1611–21. It was revised and enlarged to seven parts (Leipzig, 1668). This is a collection of funeral sermons.

Hertz-Postilla Valerij Herbergeri (Heart-postils of Valerius Herberger). 2 parts. Leipzig: Schürer, 1613, 1625. This consists of sermons on the Gospel readings of the Church Year, the first part treating Sundays, the second part treating festivals.

Das Himmlische Jerusalem (Heavenly Jerusalem). Leipzig: Schürer, 1609. This is a set of sermons on the New Jerusalem from Revelation.

Horoscopia Passionis Domini. Passion-Zeiger (Timetable of the Passion). Leipzig: Schürer, 1606. This consists of meditations on the Passion arranged in chronological sequence.

Magnalia Dei: de Jesu scripturae nucleo et medulla. Die großen Thaten Gottes (The great works of God: of Jesus, the kernel and marrow of Scripture). 12 Parts. Leipzig: Schürer, 1601–18. This is an extensive, Christ-centered devotional commentary on the first eight books of the Bible.

Spicilegium Novi Testamenti Paralipomena. Geistreiche Stoppel-Postille (Spiritual gleaning-postils). Leipzig, J. F. Gleditsch und Sohn, 1715. This consists of postils on pericopes in the Gospels and Acts not treated in the Church Year.

WRITING[2]

Jesus Christ's first sermon in his fatherland of Nazareth: Valerius Herbeger's inaugural sermon in his fatherland, Fraustadt, 1590.

Dearest hearers and countrymen! I will cast out my net in the name of Jesus! When in Jesus' name and at His word the apostle Peter cast out his net, God granted him an exceedingly great catch of fish. Seeing then

[2] The translation is based on the German text in Dr. Karl Klaiber, ed., *Evangelische Volksbibliothek* (Stuttgart: Verlag von Carl Conradi, 1868), 2:452–63.

that I have, according to the will of God, been appointed a spiritual fisher of men, I, too, will cast out my net in the name of the Lord Jesus. May he enable me successfully to catch and snare many hearts and bring them to life everlasting.

Yet I know no better way to cast out my net in the name of Jesus than that, after the sincere invocation of his holy name, I should this day give my first sermon in my fatherland on that which he publicly taught long ago in his own dear fatherland. Then you will be the better able to consider my words. I bear toward my fatherland the same heart that Jesus had toward the town of Nazareth. My concern for this town shall from henceforth resemble that of the Lord Jesus for his. I, too, will bring no other teaching than that which the Lord Jesus propounded to his fatherland. I pledge to you that I shall not hereafter speak of anything save of the Lord Jesus' person, office, and benefits, and the manner in which you shall both lead a Christian life and die a blessed death in his benefits. . . .

. . . [A]ll the ancient books of the Church testify that this text [Luke 4:14–22] was long ago read on the Friday of this same week of Sexagesima. For there are many that hold that this story took place about this time of year; besides which we also have in this passage a proper example of what the Holy Gospel teaches. The heavenly Sower, Jesus, goes up to Nazareth. He scatters on the hearts of his countrymen the precious seed-grains of his Holy Gospel. Good soil is found (God be praised). Many wonder at the gracious words that went out of his mouth. But there are also tares, which, being quickly filled with wrath, drive Christ out of the city, bring him up a hill, and would cast him down thence, that he might break his neck. What rough roads, what rocks, what choking thorns these are! We also find occasion to ready ourselves for next Sunday, which bears its name from the fiftieth jubilee.[3] For in our text the Lord Jesus plainly relates the mystery of the jubilee to himself and his treasures of grace, concluding that Isaiah had prophesied of him and that he would preach the acceptable year of the Lord.

The five matters I will address in my sermon are: (1) Why and to what end the Lord Jesus went up to Nazareth of his native country immediately upon his ordination. (2) Where the path of his first journey to Nazareth tended: namely, to the synagogue. (3) What good he did there: namely, taught from the Word of God. (4) What the theme of his first sermon was. (5) How the Lord Jesus' sermon was received and honored. . . .

---

[3] Quinquagesima or the fiftieth day before Easter.

Christendom is our common spiritual fatherland, for just as we are born in our fatherland, so are we born again in the Christian Church. When Basil, wishing to praise a martyr, does not know his native country, he says, "He was a Christianite of Godland; that is, a citizen of Christendom." "To be the citizen of the Church is not the least praise," says Philipp. Come then, have a heart for this your spiritual fatherland, and fervently pray:

Lord Jesus Christ, Your power make known,
For You are Lord of Lords alone;
Your wretched Christian Church defend,
That she may praise You without end.[4]

. . . Finally, the true and best fatherland is in heaven. Let that one be most dear to you. Contemplate every hour and moment the fact that you not only have a room in your fatherland on earth, but will also come to possess a plot in the heavenly Fatherland. Many an only child is reckless and haughty, thinking he may do as he pleases. That will not work out. "Here have we no lasting city" (Hebrews 13:14). "Live in such a way that you may live," the empress Irene [d. 803] used to say: live in such a way on earth that you may live in heaven.

Therefore, if you want to know what has brought me to the office of preaching and to this pulpit, I will answer in keeping with this point that, next to God's immutable will, it was my affection for my fatherland and my love for the dear Church. May my Lord Jesus help me so to serve Him in my fatherland, that I may reap the benefit of it in the eternal Fatherland! . . .

. . . As the path of Christ's first journey was to the school [synagogue] where Moses, the Prophets, and the Psalms were read, direct the path of your dearest and first journey likewise to church each day to hear the Word of God, and let the custom of the Lord Jesus described in this passage be yours also. The Church is the great and common school of all God's children, where the Lord Jesus himself is headmaster, and the preachers his colleagues and assistants. Make sure to take many notes of doctrine and consolation on the slate-board of your memory. Students who forget their Latin are given no regard. Do not fear the rod of the preached Law. Think like Diogenes, who told his teacher, "Beat me as you will, only teach me what is needful." Do not play truant from your

[4] This is the second stanza of Martin Luther's hymn, "Lord, Keep Us Steadfast in Your Word" (1541).

dear Teacher, Christ; do not forsake your gathering (Hebrews 10:25). That might well result in your irreparable harm. "He who attends synagogue attends wisdom," say the rabbis. Long ago there was a saying: "A pig is not esteemed till it has rubbed its snout on the wall of a school."

Additionally, the Lord Jesus teaches by the path of his journey that every man is to help, as far as he may, to furnish and sustain the worship of God in his country. Christ adorned the worship of God in Nazareth with a comforting guest-sermon. Though you cannot all be preachers, you are able to help sing and to intercede for your ministers (so may a collapsing wall be propped up). Likewise, you can be of assistance, insofar as you have means, in supporting the Divine Service, as did the Israelites (Exodus 35:21); and David and Solomon; and the blessed Dr. Matthew Lamprecht, who was of considerable service to our church and to our country, and of whose benefaction I myself benefited in my studies. All that the poor are able to do, according to their means and with a good and willing heart, is dear to God. The two mites of the poor widow (Luke 21:2) have their eternal praise.

In the very same way, upon my being called from the college of electoral Leipzig by a most honorable council, the path of my first journey was to the school of my own fatherland, and there I taught your children for a good six years. Now, at the call of this Christian congregation, the path of my first journey is to that great school of the Church. God help me to find in you teachable students! God grant the Latin notebooks of your hearts to be filled to the margins with doctrine and consolation from the Word of God, that in prayer, cross, tribulation, and death you may always have the blessed ability to recite your Latin.

What good did the Lord Jesus preach in Nazareth? . . . Good preachers are recognized in the application. Therefore, do not wonder that I also have seen fit today to choose the first sermon of Christ in his fatherland for my own first proclamation in my fatherland. It is in that text that the jubilee is mentioned of which it will be necessary to speak eight days hence,[5] and it is there that we also have an example of our forebears. Do not think it strange that I apply each and every part of this text, making benefit of it for myself and reminding you of its proper use. It is my intent to pursue these things in the time to come, in accordance with Christ's example. . . .

Chiefly, however, [Christ] confines himself to the doctrine of the Messiah: what is to be thought of him, as the true Savior of the World, with respect to his person, office, and benefits. . . .

---

[5] Quinquagesima.

. . . [C]oncerning his benefits, he enumerates at length. "[He] sent me: (1) to make known the Gospel to the poor." I am rich toward all that call upon my name (Romans 10:12). My poverty obtains for them the rich inheritance of heaven (2 Corinthians 8:9). (2) "To heal the broken-hearted." I am the sure and spiritual Physician for all the repentant and contrite of heart that can so confess with David (Psalm 51:17). I am the blessed Samaritan, expert in the wounds of your heart (Luke 10); with the precious balm of my blood and Spirit I have the power to cure you of all your infirmities. (3) "To preach to the captives, that they shall be delivered." I am the Savior of all men (1 Timothy 4:10). Whoever believes in me need not fear the captivity of hell and eternal damnation. He will break through death to life. (4) "And sight to the blind." I am the Light of the world (John 8:12). "He who sees me sees the Father" (John 14:9). He who hears my words sees in a clear light in what manner he pleases the Lord his God, both now and forever. (5) "And to the oppressed, that they shall be freed and set at liberty." Those who in great tribulation, like Paul [2 Corinthians 12:7], are buffeted by the messenger of Satan, shall have protection in me. Those who are beaten by their own sorrowful imaginings, as it were with raging billows of the sea [Isaiah 51:15], shall find their consolation in me. (6) "And to preach the acceptable year of the LORD." Everything depicted in the Year of Jubilee (Leviticus 25) you shall have in shining truth from me. The jubilee was an acceptable year. By my merit, you shall be made children of heaven acceptable to my heavenly Father. The jubilee was a joyful year. From me, you shall receive everlasting joy, which no man shall take from you, and you shall frolic and sing and ring "Alleluia" forever. The jubilee was a free year. The whole land was required to rest; no man could labor in the field. With me you shall find true rest for your souls [Matthew 11:29]. In the jubilee, all conflicts were appeased. By my grace, all the contentious affairs of your conscience shall be pacified. In the jubilee, all servants were freed. By me, you shall come to the everlasting freedom of heaven. In the jubilee, the poor were returned again to their inheritances, which had been sold, displaced, or given on pledge. By me, you shall come again to the blessed and ancient heritage of paradise from which Adam and Even were exiled for their sin, and shall be heirs of the eternal inheritance. In the jubilee, all bills of debt were torn and all balances leveled. By my merit, your debt of guilt shall be paid to the last farthing. You shall have a spiritual jubilee in your heart as long as you live. Your joy shall be perfect [John 15:11] in prayer, cross, tribulation, and death. And after this life you shall at last have an acceptable and blissful jubilee in heaven, whenever my final trumpet shall sound (1 Thessalonians 4:16).

Do you see, dear Christians, what manner of teaching the Lord Jesus brought to the pulpit of His fatherland? Nothing other than the contents of our Christian Creed. He spoke of the three persons of the most blessed Trinity. He revealed the true knowledge of his person, office, and benefits, in which everlasting life consists (John 17:3). "He who does not honor the Son does not honor not the Father" (John 5:23). So has it always been with the people of God since the foundation of the world. It is he whom Adam heard in Paradise (Genesis 3:15). Of him David preached: "Kiss the Son . . . Blessed are all those who trust in him" (Psalm 2:12). It is his teaching that Isaiah speaks in chapters 7, 9, 43, 53, and 63. It is to this foundation that all the prophets bear witness (Acts 10:43). John the Baptizer points directly at the Lamb of God (John 1:29ff.); Peter knows of no other name (Acts 4:12); Paul knows no other Foundation (1 Corinthians 3:10); he patently refuses to know anything else (1 Corinthians 2:2). All the apostles are of this mind (Acts 15).

Therefore, since this book has (according to God's wisdom) been delivered to me in orderly manner[6] in my fatherland, I too affirm that I will not address, ought not discuss, and cannot speak of any other thing. "Far be it that I should boast, save only in the cross of our Lord Jesus Christ" (Galations 6:14). . . .

. . . In this passage it says that the people: (1) heard [Jesus] devoutly. "He that is of God hears God's Word" (John 8:47). And their hearts were mightily affected; for the Word of God is a piercing, double-edged sword (Hebrews 4:12). (2) "They all gave him witness," that is, that he spoke the truth. Let no man deny the truth. You should all hear preaching with such a heart that, when need requires, you may be able to give thorough witness to your ministers. The Lord Jesus himself appealed to the witness of his hearers before Caiaphas. (3) "They wondered at the gracious words that went out of his mouth," for Jesus is the Master with the learned tongue (Isaiah 50:4) and gracious lips (Psalm 45:2), the Magister sententiarum, the gallant Sigmond, Süßmund, Chrysostom, and Goldmund.[7] My dear countrymen, be content with this little yet good-hearted house,[8] for in so doing you shall have a good conscience, renown, and honor. If your ministers perform their office with groaning, it does you no good (Hebrews 13:17). Since Jerusalem always had occasion to trade Jeremiah and the apostles for the devil, the devil became her abbot. Therefore, I pray you, hear me with love and good will. Where there are

[6] By right ordination.

[7] Literally "Master of sentences, Victory-mouth, Sweet-mouth, Gold-mouth."

[8] The parish church of Fraustadt.

good relations between teachers and hearers, preaching is profitable and all is well. But where hearts are embittered, all is lost, even if a preacher should hatch eggs of gold. I will hope the best for you. May Jesus help me that my hope, grounded in his grace, may not be put to shame!

Thus have I decided to honor you at the first opportunity with the first sermon that the Lord Jesus gave in his fatherland. Accept my good heart, which thus apes the example of Christ. How can I do better than my teacher Jesus? As my Lord Jesus honored his countrymen, so also I honor you.

Likewise, I have decided to make my Lord Jesus, with his words and benefits, the foundation of every sermon henceforth until I die. Oh, blessed people you are, and wise, who remain on this foundation (Isaiah 28:16; Matthew 7:24f.)! Oh, accursed and reckless people you are if ever you should be led astray from this foundation! For Jesus alone is the gate to life (John 10:9). Jesus alone is our ladder to heaven (Genesis 28:12). Jesus alone is the true way to life everlasting [John 14:6]. Let us therefore take this way from sin to righteousness, from death to life, from every temporal affliction to the eternal jubilee of joy and blessedness, where with clear eyes we shall behold the Lord Jesus in the true and heavenly Fatherland, and with glorified tongues give him praise without ceasing. May God the Father, Son, and Holy Ghost, blessed forever, grant it to us! Amen. Amen.

Friedrich Balduin (1575–1627)

Exegete and Casuist

by Benjamin T. G. Mayes

Life

On November 17, 1575, a boy was born in Dresden, Germany, to Paul and Magdalena Baldwein, and the next day he was baptized and given the name "Friedrich."[1] His parents were working people in the fur business, not high in station. Early in life, his parents and teachers

[1] The biography of Balduin is told in the most detail in Erasmus Schmidt, *Oratio Funebris, Viri Reverendi & Optimi Friderici Balduini, SS. Theol. D. Et In Academia Wittebergensi Professoris Solertissimi, Eiusdemque Ecclesiae Pastoris, Et Vicinarum Superintendentis Supremi, longe dignissimi, Tou En Hagiois Memoriae* (Wittenberg: Johann Gormann, 1627). This is the basis for the present biography, too, with other sources indicated in the footnotes.

noticed his strong mind and hoped he would become a useful instrument for God's Church. From his earliest childhood, his parents spared no expense to give him a good education, both in the pursuit of piety and in good literature. He attended school in Dresden through age 14 and then attended the provincial school in Meissen for the next three years (1590–93), where he studied Latin and Greek. As a young person, he strove to avoid bad company and an intemperate, riotous lifestyle. Every day his goal was to advance in the pursuit of piety, in the knowledge of useful arts, and in mastering foreign languages. On September 29, 1593 (St. Michael's Day), he matriculated at the University of Wittenberg in the philosophical college. As the son of manual laborers, he relied on scholarships to fund his education, and he received these from the city counsel of Dresden at first, and then from a scholarship fund established by the Electors of Saxony for students at Wittenberg. At Wittenberg, he continued studying Latin and Greek and added Hebrew to these languages. There he also learned logic, metaphysics, physics, ethics, oratory, mathematics, history, and poetry. In this way, he left no part of philosophy untouched (as the field was then broadly understood). The course of study at a German university at that time included not just hearing lectures but also hearing and sometimes participating in disputations. These were debates on pre-determined topics that gave students the opportunity to research a topic in advance and then use their research in a carefully reasoned argument.[2] Balduin's disputations as a student at Wittenberg showed his mastery of logic and metaphysics. In his time as a student, he was known as having the makings of a good preacher and poet. (At age 24, in October of 1599, he was honored as a poet laureate by Nicolaus Reusner.) On March 15, 1597, he graduated as a master of philosophy, the first in a class of thirty-four. From that time on, he devoted himself wholly to the study of theology. For Balduin, this involved listening to public lectures, giving practice sermons, and participating in theological disputations. In 1601, he was chosen to serve as an adjunct instructor in the philosophical faculty.

At the end of October of that year, he accompanied Aegidius Hunnius (1550–1603) and David Runge (1564–1604) to the Colloquy of Regensburg, an ecumenical discussion and debate between the leading Lutherans and Roman Catholics of the day on the role of Holy Scripture as the source and norm of theology. As a young man, it was an honor for Balduin to be invited to attend. At the colloquy, his role was to take notes

---

[2] See Kenneth G. Appold, *Orthodoxie als Konsensbildung* (Tübingen: Mohr Siebeck, 2004).

from the debates, and many of his notes were included in the protocol of the colloquy.[3]

The next year, 1602, Balduin agreed to serve as a tutor for a Hungarian nobleman's son in Wittenberg, but the tutelage lasted only three months. Around Easter, Balduin was called to the diaconate (that is, a position as an assistant pastor, as the diaconate was understood by Lutherans of that era) of Freiberg, a town southwest of Dresden. Now he was a minister with an income and was in a position to marry, so at this time he began to look for a wife. In October of that year, he married Dorothea Meisner, the daughter of Balthasar Meisner Sr. (1556–1623), archdeacon of Dresden, and sister of Balthasar Meisner Jr. (1587–1626), the famous professor of theology at Wittenberg. Balduin was nearly twenty-seven years old at the time. The Lord blessed this union with ten boys, of whom four died young, and one daughter, who likewise died young.[4]

Balduin's time as a deacon in Freiberg was short. The next year, in 1603, Balduin was called to a pastoral position with more responsibility: the pastorate of Oelsnitz in the Vogtland (which is now near the border with the Czech Republic, south of Leipzig), along with supervision over the neighboring churches. After preaching a trial sermon, call documents were issued to him, and he began his office on October 30. However, the investiture (that is, the installation), was delayed until April 23 of the next year, when it was conducted by Polycarp Leyser I (1552–1610), the chief court preacher for the Elector of Saxony in Dresden.

Here, too, his time of service was short. On July 7, 1604, the Wittenberg theology professor David Runge died (whom Balduin had accompanied to the Colloquy of Regensburg three years previously). Balduin was chosen as Runge's successor. In October of 1604, he received call documents from Elector Christian II of Saxony (1583–1611) to the professorship in Wittenberg. As was usual for him, Balduin deliberated this call, prayed, and eventually consented. He moved to Wittenberg on February 5, 1605, and on February 28 began to lecture publicly on the penitential Psalms, followed by lectures on Haggai, Zechariah, and

---

[3] Kenneth G. Appold, "Abraham Calov on the 'Usefulness' of Doctrine," in *Hermeneutica Sacra: Studies of the Interpretation of Holy Scripture in the Sixteenth and Seventeeth Centuries*, ed. Torbjörn Johansson, Robert Kolb, and Johann Anselm Steiger (Berlin: De Gruyter, 2010), 295–312; Wilhelm Herbst, *Das Regensburger Religionsgespräch von 1601, geschichtlich dargestellt und dogmengeschichtlich beleuchtet* (Gütersloh: C. Bertelsmann, 1928).

[4] Henning Witte, *Memoriæ Theologorum Nostri Seculi Clarissimorum Renovatæ Decas Secunda* (Frankfurt am Main: Martin Hallervord, 1674), 272.

Malachi. Some of these lectures were eventually published as Bible commentaries. Previously, in 1603, Balduin had published a defense of Luther against the Jesuit Nicolaus Serarius (1558–1609).[5]

Therefore, when Balduin sought the doctoral degree later in 1604, nothing more seemed to have been required than to prepare for and successfully participate as the respondent in a theological disputation. The topic that was chosen for his disputation was "On the Will of God in Election." Leonhard Hutter (1563–1616) presided at this disputation and thus likely composed the theses, which Balduin successfully defended against the studied arguments of the other disputation participants. Sometime in the next year or two, Balduin held twenty-two disputations covering the Smalcald Articles; these disputations were published individually in 1606 and afterwards together as a commentary on this document of the Lutheran Book of Concord.[6]

On May 28, 1607, Balduin was nominated by Georg Mylius (1548–1607), the senior pastor in Wittenberg and Superintendent of Electoral Saxony, to be his successor. With the support of both the town council and the university senate, Elector Christian II consented to this nomination, as did Balduin himself. On January 10, 1608, Polycarp Leyser I preached and installed him at St. Mary's Church (the parish church) in Wittenberg, the very church where Luther had preached so often. Four days later, he was assigned the highest place in the ecclesiastical consistory, the governing board for the Church of Electoral Saxony.[7] Balduin continued, however, to be a professor of theology at the university as well. From this point on, Balduin was busy indeed. His duties included not only research and participating in academic disputations, but also preaching, ordaining new preachers, judging marriage cases, conducting visitations of churches, installing new pastors, and the like.

---

[5] Friedrich Balduin, *Hyperaspistes Lutheri, Adversus maledicam Orationem Nicolai. Serarii, Esauiticae factionis Monachi* (Leipzig: Michael Roth, 1603).

[6] Friedrich Balduin, *De Articulis Smalcaldicis: Quos ut commune Ecclesiarum orthodoxarum Symbolum Concilio exhibendos, Beatus Lutherus Anno Christiano 1537. conscripsit, Disputationes XXII. Habitae in Illustri Academia Wittebergensi. & nunc denuo in nonnullis locis correctiores editae* (Wittenberg: Johann Gormann, 1609).

[7] Erasmus Schmidt indicates that Balduin was called at this time not just to be the pastor of Wittenberg but also the "superintendent of the electoral diocese," and the "inspector of superintendents" (p. 23). A different source mentions his superintendency only over the town of Wittenberg and its vicinity. See Johann Heinrich Zedler, *Universal-Lexicon* (Halle & Leipzig: Zedler, 1731–54), s.v. "Balduinus, Fridericus" (www.zedler-lexikon.de).

As he did these things, his fame grew. His books also continued to be published. In 1608, Balduin's commentaries on the books of Hebrews, Ruth, and John came to market, and the next year his commentaries on the seven penitential Psalms and the Psalms of Ascent (Psalms 120–34) appeared. Then in 1610, his commentaries on Psalm 110, Haggai, Zechariah, and Malachi became available. Balduin also published polemical theology in these years, especially against the Jesuit Martin Becanus (1563–1624) on Communion in one kind (i.e., the Roman Catholic doctrine that in Holy Communion laypeople were not permitted to receive the blood of Christ in the consecrated wine).[8]

In 1610, Elector Christian II called Balduin to accompany him as his substitute court preacher for his journey to Prague for a congress (diet) of the Holy Roman Empire. The elector appreciated Balduin's service so much that he offered the prestigious position of court preacher to him, but Balduin declined.[9] He preferred to stay in Wittenberg as a pastor and professor. Regulations set by the Elector of Saxony required professors to lecture twice a week; Balduin usually lectured four times per week. He served as dean eleven times. (The position rotated among the faculty members.) When dean, he had the duty of editing and judging the writings of others, issuing official opinions and theological counsels on behalf of the faculty,[10] seeing to the well-being of the faculty and of the church, and participating in doctoral promotions.

The next years brought the publication of further books and commentaries on Scripture: Romans (1611), Latin sermon studies on the traditional Gospel and Epistle readings (*Hypomnemata*, 1612), funeral sermons (1612, 1617, 1623), sermons on Joshua (1613) and on Judges (1617), and a biblical prayer book (1616). In 1614, his *Typological Passion* was published, in which he expounded the entire Passion history

---

[8] *De Communione Sub Utraque Specie Disputatio Martini Becani, Jesuwiticae Theologicae Doctoris ac Professoris Moguntini: cum Notis Necessariis; Pro asserendo integro Sacramento Christi, una cum Confeßione constantißimi martyris Johannis Hussi de hoc articulo* (Wittenberg: Paul Helwig, 1610); Friedrich Balduin, *Epistola Apologetica: In qua respondetur ad Epistolam Martini Becani, S. Theol. Doctoris ac Professoris Moguntini, nuper editam, qua Notas de Communione sub utraque specie leviter perstringere conatus fuit* (Wittenberg: Johann Gormann, 1610).

[9] Zedler, "Balduinus, Fridericus."

[10] On the practice, see my *Counsel and Conscience, Lutheran Casuistry and Moral Reasoning After the Reformation* (Göttingen: Vandenhoeck & Ruprecht, 2011).

(Christ's suffering and death) from types (persons, things, and actions that were prophetic) of the Old Testament.[11]

In these years, Balduin also turned his attention to doctrinal disagreements with Calvinists. Against a Calvinist Reformed book criticizing Luther's doctrine of the Lord's Supper, he published a *Fundamental Decision on the Twelve Main Reasons of the Calvinists* (1614) and a defense of it two years later.[12] In response to the Heidelberg professor David Pareus's (1548–1612) supposedly peaceful call for a general council of Lutherans and Calvinists (that is, a call to agree that the Lutherans and Reformed were in agreement on fundamental doctrine, based on a shorter list of fundamentals than Lutherans could accept),[13] Balduin published a rebuttal about such a general council (1614).[14] His rebuttal prompted a critical response from Pareus, which Balduin promptly answered (in 1616).[15] Other writings against the Reformed include a polemical exchange with Christoph Pelargus (1565–1633) of Frankfurt an der Oder (1617).[16]

Balduin's ecclesiastical duties increased at the end of August 1617, when Elector Johann Georg I of Saxony (1585–1656) called him to

---

[11] Friedrich Balduin, *Passio Typica Seu Liber Unus Typorum Veteris Testamenti, Qui Passionem Ac Mortem Domini ac Salvatoris nostri Iesu Christi. . . exhibeat* (Wittenberg: Samuel Seelfisch & Paul Helwig, 1614). The second volume of this work followed in 1616.

[12] Friedrich Balduin, *Gründlicher Bescheidt Auff die Zwölff berühmte HauptUrsachen/ warumb die Reformirten, welche man sonst Calvinisten nennet/ mit Herrn D. Lutheri Außlegung der Wort Christi im Heiligen Abendmal nicht wollen eins seyn* (Wittenberg: Johann Gormann, 1614); Friedrich Balduin, *Nothwendige Antwort Auff das schendliche Lesterbuch eines Berlinischen Politici: Mit welchem Er seine vermeinte Zwölff Heuptursachen . . .bemühet hat* (Wittenberg: Samuel Seelfisch, 1616).

[13] David Pareus, *Irenicum sive de unione et synodo evangelicorum concilianda liber votivus paci ecclesiae & desiderijs pacificorum dicatus* (Heidelberg and Frankfurt am Main: Jonas Rosa and Johann Lancelot, 1614). On the controversy between Lutherans and Reformed in these years, see Hans Leube, *Kalvinismus und Luthertum im Zeitalter der Orthodoxie: Der Kampf um die Herrschaft im protestantischen Deutschland* (Aalen: Scientia Verlag, 1966).

[14] Friedrich Balduin, *Oratio Panegyrica De Synodo Evangelicorum Generali: Quam in componendis Controversiis Sacramentariis frustra urget D. Pareus in suo Irenico* (Wittenberg: Johann Gormann, 1614).

[15] Friedrich Balduin, *Rettung/ seiner Lateinischen Oration de Synodo generali Evangelicorum: in promotione Doctorali anno 1614. d. 19. Iul. gehalten/ Welche D. David Paraeus Professor zu Heidelberg in einer Teutschen Vorrede/ die er seinem Teutschen Irenico praefigiret, unlangst anzustechen sich hat gelüsten lassen* (Wittenberg: Paul Helwig, 1616).

[16] Christoph Pelargus, *Antitheses apologeticae . . . opposita thesibus censoriis vel examini Friderici Balduini* ([Frankfurt an der Oder]: Thymius, 1617); Friedrich Balduin, *Responsio Ad Antitheses Apologeticas Christophori Pelargi D.* (Wittenberg: Paul Helwig, 1617).

conduct annual visitations of the provincial schools. He continued to perform this supervisory duty until 1624.

In the first two decades of the seventeenth century, Lutherans faced a new challenge: the Unitarian theology that began to be published and disseminated from Raków, Poland (*Racovia* in Latin). In this Polish town, followers of Fausto Sozzini (1539–1604), such as Valentin Schmalz (1572–1622) and Christoph Ostorodt (d. 1611), established an upper school and a publishing house and were soon spreading their ideas throughout Europe. Their theology relied on human reason to interpret Scripture, which produced rank heresy. While the Racovian group considered the biblical miracles as not opposing reason, they rejected the doctrine of the Trinity, and especially the substitutionary atonement of Jesus Christ. The Lutheran Orthodox very often labeled them "Photinians," after the ancient heretic Photinus, who viewed Christ as a mere man and denied the personality of the Holy Spirit.[17] Among their many writings, the most influential was aimed at laypeople: The Racovian Catechism.[18] In 1613 and 1619, Balduin wrote in opposition to this neo-Photinianism.[19] He also held academic disputations refuting the Photinians' theology in the late 1610s.

The number of his published books continued to increase. In the 1620s, several commentaries came to market: 1 and 2 Corinthians (1620) and 1 Timothy (1621). His guidelines for biblical interpretation and preaching (1622) set forth rules for finding types of Christ and his Church in the Old Testament, and most of all, of drawing doctrine from the biblical text.[20] His German postil (model sermons for all the Sundays

---

[17] On the rise of neo-Photinianism and its development into full-scale biblical criticism, see Klaus Scholder, *The Birth of Modern Critical Theology: Origins and Problems of Biblical Criticism in the Seventeenth Century*, trans. John Bowden (London and Philadelphia: SCM Press and Trinity Press International, 1990).

[18] *Catechismus, Der Gemeine derer Leute / die da . . . affirmiren und bekennen / das niemand anders / den nur allein der Vatter unsers Herrn Jesu Christi / der einige Gott Jsrael sey* (Raków: [Sebastian Sternacki], 1608); *Racovian Catechism*, trans. Thomas Rees (London: Longman, Hurst, 1818); *Catechesis Ecclesiarum quæ in regno Poloniæ & magno ducato Lithuaniæ, & aliis ad istud regnum pertinentibus provinciis, affirmant* (Raków, 1651).

[19] Friedrich Balduin, *Assertio sanae doctrinae De Vera Deitate Domini Nostri Jesu Christi: Recentiorum Photinianorum blasphemijs opposita* (Wittenberg: Johann Gormann, 1613); Friedrich Balduin, *Außführliche unnd Gründliche Wiederlegung Des Deutzschen Arianischen Catechismi: Welcher zu Rackaw in Polen anno 1608. gedruckt . . .gesetzet ist* (Wittenberg: Paul Helwig, 1619).

[20] Benjamin T. G. Mayes, "Not Just Proof-Texting: Friedrich Balduin's Orthodox Lutheran Use of Exegesis for Doctrine," *Concordia Theological Quarterly* 79 (2015): 103–20.

and festivals of the Church Year) also came to light in 1624. In 1626, his largest work of polemical theology against the Roman Catholic Church was published, the *Morning-Star of True Catholicism*, directed especially against the writings of Péter Pázmány (1570–1637).[21]

In the 1620s, Balduin, by now one of Lutheran Germany's leading theologians, participated in a number of conventions of theologians: September 1621 in Jena, May 1624 in Dresden, June through August 1624 in Dresden, September 1624 in Dresden, December 1624 in Leipzig, and 1626 in "Dibena" (presumably Duben). In 1624, Elector Johann Georg I of Saxony ordered the Saxon theologians to resolve the controversy that had been stirring since 1618 between the theological faculties of Tübingen and Giessen regarding Christ's state of humiliation. The number and length of meetings that Balduin attended in 1624 attest to how difficult it was to resolve this controversy.[22]

On October 4, 1622, sorrow came upon Balduin's head as his wife, Dorothea, died from complications of a miscarriage. They had been married for twenty years. In the following months and years, the care of house and children proved too much for Balduin, and he sought out a wife to help with the domestic duties. His biographer mentions this several times as the reason he remarried. On January 20, 1624, he married Sophia Barwasser of Torgau, a virgin, the daughter of a merchant and city leader there. At the time of his second marriage, Balduin was forty-eight years old.

In his later years, Balduin suffered from gout in the feet and stones (lithiasis) due to his hard work. In 1625, Balduin was unable to carry out his annual visitation of schools due to poor health. The next year there was a plague in Saxony. As a result, he was unable to carry out his visitation that year as well. Finally, on May 1, 1627, the end of Balduin's earthly life had come.[23] Before his death, he requested the body and blood of his only Redeemer, Jesus Christ, and was communed by the Rev. Michael Blum, who at the time was deacon (assistant pastor) of the Wittenberg church. Balduin died at about 9:00 in the morning while

---

[21] Friedrich Balduin, *Phosphorus Veri Catholicismi: Devia Papatus, & viam regiam ad Ecclesiam vere Catholicam & Apostolicam fideliter monstrans, facemque praelucens legentibus Hodegum Petri Pazmanni* (Wittenberg: Kaspar Heyden, 1626).

[22] Erdmann Rudolph Fischer, *The Life of John Gerhard*, trans. Richard J. Dinda and Elmer Hohle (Malone, TX: Repristination Press, 2001), 108.

[23] Theodor Mahlmann seems to have erred in giving the date of Balduin's death as May 1, 1628. See his "Balduin, Friedrich," in *Religion Past & Present*, ed. Hans Dieter Betz et al., 4th ed. (Leiden and Boston: Brill, 2007–13), 1:559.

uttering prayers and sighs (*suspiria*, short phrases) to Christ. He was buried in the Wittenberg parish church on May 4.

In the time immediately after his death, Balduin was remembered as a great churchman and pastor of Wittenberg. In the centuries since then, however, he has been remembered for his other accomplishments. The year after his death, his *Cases of Conscience* (1628) was published, based on lectures he gave from 1622 to 1626, and this work could arguably be his most famous.[24] Balduin's service to church and academy gave him experience with casuistry. As pastor and superintendent of the entire "Electoral Saxon diocese,"[25] he had the highest seat in the ecclesiastical consistory and judged marriage cases. He was dean of the university eleven times, and his role here required him to issue official opinions and to prepare responses to requests for counsel in difficult situations. His commentaries on Scripture are full of difficult questions of right doctrine and practice with fitting answers. Therefore, he was well suited to write this work. His Wittenberg colleagues considered this book the first Lutheran work of casuistry—that is, the study of cases of conscience, in which moral principles are applied to difficult or ambiguous situations. In fact, it was not the first Lutheran work of casuistry; books answering cases of conscience were published by Lutherans ever since the end of Martin Luther's life. Indeed, five years before Balduin's casuistry, the monumental *Treasury of Counsels and Decisions* was published by the Hamburg pastor and editor Georg Dedekenn (1564–1628). But Balduin's posthumous work was the first Lutheran book to be given a title related specifically to casuistry, "On Cases of Conscience," and it was seen as more systematic than collections of official opinions. As a result, from that time on it was known as the first work of Lutheran casuistry, an aid to pastoral care and the advising of consciences in difficult situations.[26] The conclusion of the book's preface gives a summary of the purpose of Lutheran casuistry as set forth by Balduin: "We entreat God alone, that he might bestow on the afflicted church peace; on Christian magistrates,

---

[24] Friedrich Balduin, *Tractatus Luculentus, Posthumus . . . De materia rarissime ante hac enucleata, Casibus nimirum Conscientiae* (Wittenberg: Paul Helwig, 1628). See also Roderick Henry Martin, *The Reformation of Conscience: Rhetoric in the Lutheran Casuistry of Friedrich Balduin (1575–1627)* (PhD diss., University of Virginia, 2008); Wilhelm Loehe, *The Pastor: The Pastoral Theology of Wilhelm Loehe*, ed. Charles P. Schaum, trans. Wolf Dietrich Knappe and Charles P. Schaum (St. Louis: Concordia, 2015), 304.

[25] Schmidt, *Oratio funebris*, 23.

[26] See Mayes, *Counsel and Conscience*, 28–39; Hans Leube, *Die Reformideen in der deutschen lutherischen Kirche zur Zeit der Orthodoxie* (Leipzig: Dörfling & Franke, 1924), 46–47.

sound counsels; on consciences, liberty and integrity; on the afflicted, patience; finally, on us all, the rewards both of this and of the future life. Amen."[27] That is, avoiding superstition (God alone), the casuist's task is to give advice from God's Word, tested in experience (sound counsels), and thereby to console afflicted consciences (liberty, integrity, patience), with a view towards the good of the Church here below (peace) and in eternal life (rewards). Balduin's casuistry and the entire Lutheran casuistry literature is not just the resolution of moral problems. Rather, it is primarily an attempt to remove doubt and establish certainty of one's conscience. This doubt and certainty deals not just with questions of right behavior, but also with questions of right faith. Therefore, difficult doctrinal problems are handled in the Lutheran casuistry literature alongside moral matters.

Most of Balduin's publications were exegetical, written either in Latin as the result of university lectures and disputations, or written in German as the result of sermons in the Wittenberg parish church. The method Balduin followed in his commentaries was set forth explicitly in his *Way of Biblical Dispositions* (1622).[28] Here, Balduin teaches that the reader of Scripture should first pray. After the text has been explained and analyzed regarding its structure and philology, Balduin instructs his students to take another step and collect doctrines from the text. After that, the text along with the doctrines derived from it are to be applied to the spiritually "well" and "sick." Part two of the book is introductory to the various books of Scripture. Part three deals with how to interpret different kinds of biblical genres. This is also where allegories and types are discussed, along with how to preach. Balduin practiced his exegesis in a way that was very common among the Lutheran Orthodox. Not only did he aim to find out what the biblical text had to say, he also was looking for how it should be used and applied to the lives of Christians. In biblical exegesis, this meant that doctrines must be gathered from the biblical text after its literary structure had been recognized and it had been explained. This is because knowledge without use "puffs up" (1 Corinthians 8:1); our God "teaches us useful things" (Isaiah 48:17); all that has been written was "written for our teaching" (Romans 15:4); and Scripture is divinely inspired and useful for teaching (2 Timothy 3:16).[29]

---

[27] Balduin, *De casibus conscientiae*, fol. [IIII]4v.

[28] Friedrich Balduin, *Idea Dispositionum Biblicarum* (Wittenberg: Paul Helwig, 1622).

[29] Balduin, *Idea Dispositionum Biblicarum*, 31.

Balduin himself practiced this kind of "dogmatic exegesis" throughout his lengthy commentary on the epistles of St. Paul.[30]

Besides his casuistry and his exegesis, Balduin should also be remembered for his teaching on the Christian's union with Christ through faith. According to Theodor Mahlmann, Balduin was the "inaugurator" of this doctrine within Lutheran Orthodoxy, a doctrine that was later called the "mystical union."[31] Balduin's teaching on the mystical union could be seen as a response to the false mysticism of the time. Valentin Weigel's (1533–88) writings began to be printed in 1609, twenty-one years after his death. This was at the same time as writings of Paracelsus (1493/94–1541) were being printed, along with the fictitious Rosicrucian writings. Other Lutherans saw this "mystical theology" as being directed against the orthodox Lutheran churches and universities. Proponents of the heterodox mystical theology saw themselves as being essentially united to Christ and thereby as having the Holy Spirit indwelling in them substantially. What Balduin rejected in these writings was not the spiritual indwelling of Christ in believers, but the manner of this indwelling and union, which Valentin Weigel called "essential." This cannot take place, according to Balduin, since the substances are diverse and distinct. The fruit of Weigel's enthusiastic "essential union" is the despising of Scripture and the ecclesiastical ministry.[32] Therefore, Balduin, basing his teaching especially on the epistles of the New Testament, sought to teach clearly the substantial *nearness* of believers, not just with the gifts of Christ and with the Holy Spirit, but with Christ Himself, the God-man, mediated through the Church's ministry as it distributes Christ's Means of Grace.[33]

---

[30] Mayes, "Not Just Proof-Texting."

[31] Theodor Mahlmann, "Die Stellung der unio cum Christo in der lutherischen Theologie des 17. Jahrhunderts," in *Unio: Gott und Mensch in der nachreformatorischen Theologie,* ed. Matti Repo and Rainer Vinke (Helsinki: Suomalainen Teologinen Kirjallisuusseura, Luther-Agricola-Gesellschaft, 1996), 128. However, the doctrine has precedent in the Formula of Concord, FC SD III 6, 54, and in Luther himself: "Thus the true Spirit dwells in the believers not merely according to His gifts, but according to His own substance" (*Psalm 51*, 1538, AE 12:337).

[32] Mahlmann, "Die Stellung," 78–82.

[33] Friedrich Balduin, *Disputatio ordinaria De Communione Nostri Cum Christo. Opposita tum Calvinianorum, tum Fanaticorum quorundam erroribus, qui ex Theophrasti Paracelsi Philosophia novam plane de Christo & Christianis Theologiam comminiscuntur* (Wittenberg: Johann Matthäus, 1618).

BIBLIOGRAPHY

Works by Balduin in English Translation

None of Balduin's writings have been translated.

SELECT WORKS BY BALDUIN IN LATIN AND GERMAN

Commentarius In Omnes Epistolas Beati Apostoli Pauli (Commentary on All the Epistles of the Blessed Apostle Paul). Frankfurt: Balthasar Mevius, 1654.

Tractatus Luculentus, Posthumus . . . De materia rarissime ante hac enucleata, Casibus nimirum Conscientiae (Illustrious Treatise, Posthumous . . . On a Matter Very Rarely Hitherto Explained, Namely, Cases of Conscience). Wittenberg: Paul Helwig, 1628.

Idea Dispositionum Biblicarum (Way of Biblical Dispositions). Wittenberg: Paul Helwig, 1622.

WRITING[34]

Question VI. *Why is the dissolution of marriage granted on account of fornication, but not on account of unbelief (vv. 10 and 12), even though it is certain that unbelief is worse than fornication?*

Response. Here the sins are not being considered in themselves and by their nature, but with respect to marriage. There is no doubt that unbelief in itself and by its nature is a worse offense than fornication, since in the former case one is sinning against God directly, but in the latter case against man. However, in considering marriage, fornication is worse. You see, unbelief does not injure marriage so very much, as even among unbelievers there is marriage, and a believer is able to live together with an unbelieving spouse. Also, it is possible for one or the other spouse to fall into unbelief on account of ignorance, but one cannot fall into fornication except by deliberate evil behavior. Unbelief still leaves the two in one flesh, but fornication mixes in other people, and thus dissolves the conjugal union that was supposed to exist by the institution of God. . . .

Question VIII. *Does Paul contradict Christ, who says that fornication is the only cause of divorce (Matthew 5:32; 19:9), while the apostle*

[34] This is a select translation of Friedrich Balduin, *Commentarius in Omnes Epistolas Pauli* (Frankfurt: Balthasar Christoph Wust the Elder, 1692), 364–72, on 1 Corinthians 7.

concedes in this place that there can be a divorce on account of desertion (v. 11)?

Response. [Niels] Hemmingsen in his book *De Matrimon.* interprets the words of Christ as a synecdoche, so that under the word "adultery" there are included similar transgressions, such as: parricide, poisoning, treason, attempted murder, etc. This interpretation would be in order if this sort of inclusion of other crimes under "adultery" could be shown. Therefore, others reconcile these passages as follows: Christ is speaking about the cause which constitutes divorce. Paul is speaking about the cause on account of which it can be permitted with respect to the innocent. You see, [fleshly] mingling with a woman who is not one's own [wife] already dissolves the marriage bond by that very act, for they are no longer two, but several in one flesh, and even though there can be a reconciliation in that case, the deed cannot be undone; rather, the marriage has suffered a rupture. The situation is different in desertion, where a third person is not added, but one of the two has left, and where the innocent person does not so much make a divorce as allows it to happen by not following the deserter. Therefore, Christ is speaking about divorce, saying that by its nature it has already happened. Paul is speaking about the sort of case in which it is permitted. Or to say it more clearly: Christ is speaking about the cause for making a divorce, which is adultery, where the innocent party is able to send away the adulteress, or to depart from her. Paul is speaking about a divorce that has already been made, for he does not command that someone send away his spouse because of [her] hatred of religion, but if the unbelieving spouse has already left, and has refused to live together with the believing spouse, then the apostle judges that the deserted person is free from the law of marriage, and with good grace is able to be joined to a different spouse. And also, in this way, Christ does not disagree with His apostle, since there are different questions on each side.

The following can be added to this answer too. The Savior set his prohibition against the levity of the Pharisees, who would dissolve marriages for any trivial cause. Therefore, in the example, Christ wanted to show that divorce is not to be allowed unless those causes intervene for which the substance and end purpose of marriage is overturned, which is fornication especially. Now, there are similar causes, which are observed these days in ecclesiastical courts, which can be seen elsewhere (especially in Beust, *De Matrim.*, part 2, from chapters 8 to 17; and Monnerus, *De matrim.*, part 5, chapter 1), all of which overturn the substance of marriage either directly or indirectly, or impede its end purpose. First among these is malicious desertion, which makes the one who maliciously deserts suspected of adultery. Hence, together with adultery, it is considered the chief cause of divorces. Nevertheless, in all of these causes that are accepted by the civil laws, one should not proceed too quickly, but everything should be done legitimately and according to the procedure of law, especially in those causes that are not yet convicted by law, or those that do not directly overturn the substance and end purpose of marriage. Indeed, even in a case of admitted adultery, one spouse cannot depart from the other unless the case has been examined before the competent judge. For one spouse can indeed be the legitimate accuser of the other, but cannot be his own judge. Therefore, it is necessary that even this case be examined in [a court of] judgment, and that [the judge] make the divorce by his sentence. However, in this matter it must be observed that it would be far better and much to be desired that the law about killing adulterers (Leviticus 20:10; Deuteronomy 22:22) would be put into effect in these days. In this way, there would be no need for a question about divorces with regard to this cause.

As for the other causes that are usually enumerated, it must be noted that they are not valid by divine right, but belong only to the [secular] forum and have been established by pious emperors for just causes. Therefore, the distinction must always be left between those causes and the one that Christ cited. It is certain that there can be no cause by which the substance of marriage—that is, conjugal unity—is overturned so directly as adultery. . . .

Question XII. *What should be judged, if an unbelieving or heretical person, after marriage has been contracted, not only remains in his unbelief or heresy tenaciously but also tries to seduce the believing spouse into his error and impiety in such a way that the believer fears she will be conquered due to her weakness? In this case is it permissible for the faithful person to seek freedom from such a great peril by means of divorce?*

Response. There are some who think that in this case, after a certain time, divorce can be sought and can be granted by a judge through his sentence. For if the unbelieving person did not promise security to the believer, there would be no place for a remarriage. They argue in this way: If because of attempted murder it is permissible to separate from a violent husband, it will be much more permissible to leave one who tries to destroy the soul; the pious ought to care about this much more than about their fortunes and bodies. However, the apostolic text ([1 Corinthians 7:]10–11) seems very much to stand in the way of this opinion. There he [Paul] simply does not want the faithful person to initiate the departing; but if the unbeliever departs, then and only then does he free the innocent person from her bond. Also, the example about attempted murder is invalid here. You see, making an examination concerning these [cases] belongs not only to theologians but also to the political magistrate, who will punish this crime as it deserves, either with the punishment of prison or in another way; for separation is not granted easily even in that case.

Therefore, even though that answer may seem too harsh, I think that it can satisfy the question that was proposed, as long as a distinction is used: Either the wife compels the husband toward heresy, or the husband compels the wife. First, if the wife compels the husband, there cannot, of course, be any violent coercion since she is subject to the man, who can fend off that power by lawful means. But if she tries to do anything through flattery, the husband will think she is not extending conjugal love to him in order that he might become guilty of something that the spouse holds against faith in Christ given in grace. Hence, if he is pious and loves the Christian truth, he will easily be able to decline those enticements by his own authority. But if the husband should fear persecution from an unbelieving or heretical magistrate, then he, as the head of the family, should move his family elsewhere. If the wife refuses to follow, then he is not to be considered the deserter, but she, since she did not render faithfulness and subjection to her husband. And thus the husband's conscience has been looked after, as long as Christian moderation is used, that he may not hasten too quickly in so serious a matter, and that nothing may be done against the genuineness of conjugal love.

Second, if the peril of seduction and coercion is on the part of the unbelieving or heretical husband, the situation is a little different. The wife, mindful of subjection to the husband, should not omit anything in beseeching and imploring that the husband not allow her to become guilty of anything against her conscience. But if the husband persists harshly in such a way that she must either risk her life or do something against the true religion, then of course on both sides there is the greatest peril. In order that this might be avoided by a faithful person, pious people and circumspect theologians judge that it is just as if someone is maliciously deserting his wife, or driving her away from himself with threats or violence. Therefore, if all means of reconciliation have been tried and nothing has been obtained from the harsh husband, then they think that the husband indeed should be considered a deserter, so that the wife can leave and go to a safer place, as though deserted by her husband, yet she is not permitted to remarry unless quite a long time has passed. In the meantime, nothing at all should be omitted that could lead to obtaining reconciliation and retaining freedom of conscience. But if, in the meantime, the believing wife would have to fear persecution from an unbelieving or heretical magistrate (as often happens in the Spanish Inquisition), then if the heretical husband seriously and genuinely loves his spouse, he will doubtlessly provide for a safer place, and thus there would be no place for divorce. But if he neglects her, or even is about to bring her before her persecutors, then there is no doubt that she should avoid dwelling with him, as a deserter, since, as much as is in him, he has already divided the marriage bond by his betrayal. For what else is throwing one's spouse before the most present peril than maliciously deserting her? Indeed, "if anyone does not provide for his own, and especially for those of his own house, he has denied the faith, and is worse than an unbeliever" (1 Timothy 5:8). . . .

Theological Aphorisms from this Part of the Chapter

. . . 4. The end purpose of marriage is double. One is primary, namely, the procreation of offspring, from which comes the preservation and spread of the family, republic, and Church. The other is secondary, namely, the avoidance of fornication. Here, the apostle Paul touches on this end purpose in verse 2. Therefore, what some of the more recent papists write is false, that in this passage the apostle has made a concession to the Corinthians against the true end of marriage for the sake of satiating lust. You see, it is not a concession but a command of Paul that they marry wives if they are unable to be continent, lest they pollute themselves with lusts. From this, Clement of Alexandria (*Strômat.*, book 3) rightly concluded that intercourse in marriage, even if it is not for procreation but to avoid burning, might be undertaken like fornication, yet is not to be condemned. And Paphnutius in the Council of Nicea said that there is chastity in marriage, too, when people resist inordinate lusts. . . .

15. Marriage is the indissolvable bond of man and woman, which must not be broken for a light reason. Therefore, the apostle commands that a woman must not depart from a husband who is morose, harsh, or who strikes her, etc., and a man must not send away or cast out a wife who is ugly, foolish, or quarrelsome. Instead, these troublesome features must be remedied either with patience or with other means. For here this saying of Christ must always be kept in our minds: "What God has joined together, let man not separate" [Matthew 19:6].

CONRAD DIETERICH (1575–1639)

TEACHING THE CHRISTIAN FAITH AND LIFE

by Gerhard Bode

LIFE

Conrad Dieterich (1575–1639) was a Lutheran educator and pastor in the German lands during the early period of Orthodoxy. He was director of the *Paedagogium,* or university preparatory school, and professor of practical philosophy at the University of Giessen before receiving a call to serve as *Superintendent* and *Münsterprediger* in Ulm. He is perhaps best known for several catechetical writings, all of which were based on Luther's Small Catechism. His *Institutiones catecheticae* (Catechetical Instructions) (1613) was one of the most important and popular textbooks on Lutheran catechesis in the seventeenth century.[1] For younger students, Dieterich also wrote the *Epitome Catechetica* (Catechetical

[1] Conrad Dieterich, *Institutiones Catecheticae, è B. Lutheri Catechesi Depromptæ, variisque notis Logicis & Theologicis, in usum Juventutis Scholasticae illustratae, a Cunrado Dieterico Practicae Philos. Professore publ. & Paedagogiarcha. Cum praefatione & approbatione Venerandi Collegii Theologici* (Giessen: Casparus Chemlinus, 1613).

Summary) (1614) that was widely used in Latin schools.[2] In addition, Dieterich prepared *Der Kleine Catechismus D. Martin Luthers* (The Small Catechism of Dr. Martin Luther) (1616), a German catechism based on Luther's Small Catechism for use in the churches and schools in Ulm.[3] Although known for his educational writings, hundreds of Dieterich's sermons were published during and after his lifetime. His sermons reveal a preacher whose messages were biblical and doctrinal as well as engaging. Perhaps most significantly, the sermons show that Dieterich remained a teacher in the pulpit. His sermons were often instructional lessons in the words of Scripture, and in the Christian faith and life. It is clear that Dieterich considered his role as preacher, in part, to convey information and instruction in the Christian faith, as well as to proclaim the Word of God to his hearers. In the classroom, the pulpit, or in his many written works, Dieterich was a Lutheran educator.

Early Life

Conrad Dieterich was born on January 9, 1575, in Gemünden an der Wohra, Hesse.[4] He was the fourth of six children born to Nikolaus Dieterich and his wife, Elisabeth. His father had served as a soldier in the army of Ludwig IV (1537–1604), Landgrave of Hesse-Marburg, and was severely injured in the Smalcaldic War (1546–47).

After early education in Latin schools in Treysa and Marburg, Conrad matriculated at the University of Marburg in 1590.[5] Dieterich studied philosophy and the liberal arts, learning under Rudolph Goclenius (1547–1628) and Aegidius Hunnius (1550–1603). In 1593, he received his

---

[2] Conrad Dieterich, *Epitome Catechetica, Autore Cunrado Dieterico SS Th. D. antehac Practicæ Philosophiæ Professore & Pædagogiarcha Gissæ, nunc Pastore ac Superintendente Ulmensi*. Editio nova, recognita & elimata (Giessen: Casparus Chemlinus, 1617).

[3] Conrad Dieterich, *Der Kleine Catechismus D. Martin Luthers/ beneben den Fragen deß Summarischen begriffs der sechs Hauptstucken Christlicher Lehr/ &c. Mit Angehengetem Christlicher Unterricht/ für Junge vnd einfältige Leut/ welche begehren zum Heyligen Abendmal zugehen/ Auch etliche Kinder vnd Schulgebettlein/ Für Vlmische Kirchen vnnd Schulen in Statt vnd Land* (Ulm: Jonas Saur, 1629).

[4] Conrad Dieterich's name appears in various forms. His philosophical writings published before 1614 appeared under the name "Cunradus Theodoricus," while afterwards they were published under the name "Cunradus Dietericus." Other spellings of his name appear in different sources. Some versions of his catechisms printed in the nineteenth century bore the name "Johann Conrad Dieterich," although he never went by that name; he did, however, have a nephew with that name who also was a theologian.

[5] Philipp I the Magnanimous, Landgrave of Hesse, had founded the university as a Lutheran institution in 1527.

bachelor and master of arts degrees. He began studies in theology at the university, chiefly with professors Balthasar Mentzer (1565–1627) and Johannes Winckelmann (1551–1626), as well as David Arcularius (d. 1596). His teachers had a formative and lasting influence on him. As a student of Hunnius, Winckelmann, and Arcularius, Dieterich was instructed by some of the original subscribers and defenders of the Formula of Concord. From these men, he learned how to articulate and defend the Lutheran faith and its teaching.

Pastor Dieterich

In 1599, Dieterich was called by Johann Georg, Count of Solms-Laubach (1547–1600), to serve as preacher and private tutor in Laubach. He left the university and was ordained and installed in his pastorate in February 1599. Within a few months his role changed when Johann Georg's son, Georg Philipp, asked Dieterich to serve as a *Feldprediger*, or military chaplain, on a campaign against Spanish troops in the Netherlands. After Georg Philipp died from wounds received in battle, the campaign ended and Dieterich returned to Laubach. He requested a leave of his duties from Count Johann Georg, which was granted, and he returned to Marburg, where he was called to serve as *Archdiakon*, or assistant pastor, of the churches of Marburg. He was installed in November 1599 and served in this position until 1605.

In January 1601, Dieterich married Margarethe Lüncker, the daughter of a landowner and member of the Marburg city council. The marriage produced two daughters and three sons.

In 1604, Ludwig IV, Landgrave of Hesse-Marburg, died childless, and a territorial dispute over Marburg and its university followed. Marburg became the property of Moritz the Learned (1572–1632), Landgrave of Hesse-Kassel, an ardent Calvinist. Moritz quickly took steps to introduce Reformed teaching and practice into the churches and university in Marburg. The Lutheran Superintendent, Heinrich Leuchter (1558–1623), and Archdeacon Conrad Dieterich, along with professors Balthasar Mentzer and Johannes Winckelman, contended that they were obligated to uphold the Hessian Church Ordinance of 1574, which provided for a Lutheran church and university. Moritz demanded that the four theologians comply with his order, but they refused and were removed from their offices. Eventually, Moritz would remove a total of sixty Lutheran pastors and professors from his territory.

Teacher Dieterich

In the summer of 1605, Dieterich found a new position in nearby Giessen. Ludwig V (1577–1626), Count of Hesse-Darmstadt, founded a new university there and named Dieterich the director of the *Paedagogium,* or preparatory school. Dieterich taught dialectic, rhetoric, oratory, and catechetics in the school, and over the next few years, published textbooks in all four fields.[6] When the University of Giessen opened in 1607, Dieterich held the post of professor of practical philosophy, or ethics. He also served as dean (*Dekan*) of the university in 1607 and as prorector in 1609.

Dieterich's catechetical writings were published toward the end of his tenure at Giessen, yet it is likely that he had been teaching the catechism since the beginning of his time there.[7] He had a significant influence on both the content and the methods of catechetical instruction at the school. From the start, Dieterich had used Luther's Small Catechism as the basis for all religious instruction at the *Paedagogium,* a change from the practice at Marburg, where other catechisms had been used. In Giessen, Dieterich's *Institutiones Catecheticae* (1613) was intended for use by the most advanced students in the school, while his *Epitome Catechetica* (1614) was aimed at the lower classes. Both books by Dieterich were used in Hesse for nearly one hundred years.[8]

His nine years of work in Giessen gained Dieterich recognition as a scholar, educator, and administrator, and this reputation drew the attention of the Ulm city council in 1614. The position of superintendent and *Münsterprediger,* or chief preacher, in the city's largest church was vacant, and the council hoped that one appointed to the post could also reorganize the city's *Gymnasium*, or academy. After a visit to Ulm in May 1614, Dieterich was called to the position. That summer, at the request of

[6] Dieterich's books were based on the courses he taught at the *Paedagogium*: *Institutiones Dialecticae* (1609), *Institutiones Catecheticae* (1613), *Institutiones Oratoriae* (1613), and *Institutitiones Rhetoricae* (1613). These books were frequently reprinted and were used in Latin schools across the German lands for much of the seventeenth century.

[7] In the dedicatory epistle of the *Institutiones Catecheticae* (1613), Dieterich states that he wrote his catechetical instruction for the use of his students in the *Paedagogium* in Giessen.

[8] Wilhelm Diehl, "Das Gießener Pädagog in den Jahren 1605–1623," in *Monumenta Germaniae Paedagogica*, vol. 28, *Die Schulordnungen des Grossherzogtums Hessen*, ed. Karl Kehrbach (Berlin: Hofmann, 1903), 2:21–22.

the city, he held his doctoral disputation at the University of Giessen and received his doctor of theology degree.[9]

Dieterich in Ulm

Situated on the Danube River, Ulm was an important trading center in the southern German lands. It was a free imperial city with a large territory and a population of approximately twenty thousand inhabitants. Officially, Ulm had joined the Reformation in 1530 and joined the Smalcaldic League. Although beginning with a Swiss orientation, the city soon embraced Lutheranism and accepted the Augsburg Confession in 1532. Like other Lutheran cities in the German lands, Ulm's confessional stance was shaken during the time of the Augsburg Interim. However, by the beginning of the seventeenth century, it had become a Lutheran stronghold.

As *Münsterprediger* in Ulm, Dieterich was given specific responsibilities for preaching. He was to preach in the main worship services in the main church (*Münster*) on Sundays and on festivals, and also on Thursdays. In fulfilling this role, Dieterich preached hundreds of sermons, many of which were published during his lifetime, and hundreds more of which were published by his family after his death.

The body of Dieterich's published sermons is great and includes homilies on a wide range of topics for many different occasions. The collection lists a large number of expository sermons on biblical texts, as well as entire books of the Bible. Other collections include sermons for special occasions, on themes in the life of the church, or on topics such as civil authority, natural phenomena (the appearance of a comet in 1618), war (to address the trials and tribulations produced by the Thirty Years' War [1618–48]), and other subjects. Other sermons take up the topic of education, the nurturing and training up of children in the Christian faith, and the importance of teaching the catechism.

During his early years in Ulm, Dieterich worked to reorganize the city's churches and schools. He improved the religious instruction of people in the congregation and took measures to provide them with materials that would educate them in the Christian faith as well as form them for Christian life. In 1617, he produced a new hymn book and

[9] Dieterich's disputation, on the Wittenberg Formula of Concord (1536), was later published as *Discursus Theologicus De Formula Concordiae Wittenbergae Anno 1536 . . .* (Giessen: Nicolaus Hampel, 1614).

prayer book, along with a new church agenda for the church in Ulm.[10] The new agenda established Luther's Small Catechism as the catechetical text for public reading in worship services and set the practice for the *Katechismusgottesdienst,* or catechetical instruction service in the church. In addition to producing a new edition of Luther's Small Catechism for Ulm in 1616, Dieterich also published instructional books for use in homes and schools. In the same year, he issued the *Spruchbüchlein* (passage booklet), which was a book of biblical texts for memorization and included sections from the catechism and prayers.[11] His *Zuchtbüchlein* (discipline booklet), also published in 1616, was a book of Christian discipline intended for young people. It included verses on the Christian life, prayers, and other educational and devotional material.[12]

Dieterich's *Catechismus Predigt* (Catechism sermon)

On January 8, 1626, the church in Ulm announced a new order (*Ordnung*) for catechetical practice. This order was proposed by Dieterich and the other clergy in Ulm and approved by the city council. Published simultaneously as a general order for compulsory school attendance in Ulm, the rules for catechetical instruction required the participation of all young people in catechetical services in the churches held every second Sunday. In this way, the city's young people were to learn the catechism and be examined in it prior to the first reception of the Lord's Supper and prior to marriage.

---

[10] The first editions of these books have been lost, but the printings from 1620 and 1621 survive. The new hymnal appeared as *Christliche Kirchengesänge von Außerlesenen Psalmen und Geistlichen Liedern ...* (Ulm: Johann Meder, 1620). The new prayer book appeared as *Christliche Kirchengebet ...* (Ulm: Johann Meder, 1621). The new *Kirchenagende* for Ulm was first published in 1617. However, the earliest text does not survive. It appeared as *Form, Verrichtung: 1. Der Heyligen Tauffe, 2. Deß Heil. Abendmahls, 3. Der Ehe-Einsegnung, 4. Der Ordination dero newen Kirchendiener, 5. Der Sonn- und Wochentägliche Kirchen-Gebet: Wie die in denen Ulmischen Kirchen, ihren ublichen Christlichen Ceremonien nach gebrauchet werden* (Ulm: Johann Meder, 1622).

[11] *Biblisches Spruchbuechlein/ darinn vnterschiedene vornehme Sprueche der Heil. Schrifft/ zu Erbaw vnd Fortpflantzung der Gottseligkeit bey der SchulJugend zusammen getragen/ Fuer die Vlmische Teutsche Schulen/ in der Stadt vnd auff dem Land* (Ulm: Balthasar Kuehnen, 1656). This book was printed first in Ulm in 1616, but the earliest texts have been lost.

[12] *Christliches Zuchtbuechlein/ Allerhand feiner Sitten und Tugenden/ deren sich junge Leuth in Gottseligem Wesen und Geberden/ bey sich selbst und gegen maenniglich befleißigen sollen ...* (Ulm: Christian Balthasar Kuehnen, 1674). This was first issued in 1616; earlier editions of the book have not survived.

In his *Catechismus Predigt*, which Dieterich preached as part of the effort to introduce this practice, he addressed parents concerning their role and responsibility in the training up of children in the Christian faith and life. Dieterich's expectations of parents and of the progression of instruction is clear. He explained at length the reasons why parents must educate their children. First, in his Word, God exhorts parents in great seriousness to teach his Word to their children. Moreover, Dieterich observed that God gives children to parents with the purpose that they bring them up in the fear and knowledge of God. For this reason, parents are stewards of their children and they are expected to train up their children in the faith. But parents were not alone in this work of teaching. These catechetical lessons were to be reinforced with the learning received in worship services and later in schools.

In addition to the scriptural mandate, Dieterich reminded parents of the practice of handing down the faith from the time of the first Christians. This teaching was preserved in the catechism and brought to light again by Luther. Aside from pointing out the origins of the traditional practice of catechetical instruction, Dieterich recalled that such teaching had been the primary means of communicating the message of salvation to children throughout the Church's history. For Dieterich, the training of children is also done for the sake of their salvation. Implicit in the course of instruction is the activity of the Holy Spirit, working through the Word of God. It is taken for granted that the Spirit and Word are active in catechetical instruction.

Dieterich emphasized that faith is necessary for understanding Absolution and the Lord's Supper, and this is especially important as young people grow up and mature. An absence of faith could lead to a person receiving the Lord's Supper to his or her condemnation. In the same way, instruction in the faith is important for marriage and a couple's relationship with God. Once again, even more important within the family is that parents make sure their children are brought up in the fear of God and in his teaching.

As parents, elders, and adults foster catechetical training, Dieterich urged that they should also be examples for young people to follow. If parents themselves are not instructed in the Christian faith or do not live the Christian life and know nothing of God and His Word, how will they teach their own children these things? In the same way, Dieterich encouraged the leaders in the church and the community to maintain a good example for young people.

In his sermon on the catechism, Dieterich emphasized the role of parents in catechetical instruction of children in the home. This instruction was to move from the most basic elements to the more advanced, and included teaching children prayers, Bible passages, the simple text of the catechism (first without explanations), then Luther's Small Catechism with explanations. Memorization of the parts lays a solid foundation and allows children to move on to a greater mastery and understanding of the material. Dieterich's expectations regarding the role of parents in teaching the catechism and the nature of this instruction are clear. This teaching is essential, and, after all, "the most necessary thing in this world."[13]

Conclusion

Dieterich began to suffer the effects of asthma, and his health began to decline. He died on March 22, 1639, with his wife, children, and grandchildren around him. He was buried in the church cemetery next to the Münster in Ulm. Johannes Greiner, the historian of the schools in Ulm, wrote of Dieterich: "He is uncontestedly the most significant figure in the history of the church and school in Ulm. His reforms gave the entire following period its character."[14]

Conrad Dieterich was a leading figure in the Lutheran churches and schools of Ulm for a quarter of a century. His skills as a pastor, educator, and administrator were greatly beneficial to the city and its people during a difficult time in its history. His dedication to Christian education and formation among the heirs of the Lutheran Reformation would help train up believers in the Church and serve as a lasting legacy for generations to come.

BIBLIOGRAPHY

None of Dieterich's writings have been translated.

Select Works by Dieterich in Latin and German

"Catechismus Predigt. Darin von fleissiger Ubung des Catechismi in denen Häuptstücken Christlicher Lehr gehandlet/ und Ursachen außgeführet werden/ warumb dieselbig unter gemeinen Leuten fleissig zu treiben seye. Gehalten zu Ulm am Sontag nach der H. drey Könige Tag den 8. Januarii Anno 1626. Als daselbsten eine newe Ordnung mit der Praxi des

[13] Dieterich, *Catechismus Predigt* (1626), (Schleusingen: Zacharias Schürer, Matthias Götz, 1634), 116.

[14] Johannes Greiner, "Geschichte der Ulmer Schule," in *Geschichte des Humanistischen Schulwesens in Württemberg. Ulm, Oberschwaben*: 20 (Stuttgart: Kohlhammer, 1914), 43.

Catechismi publiciert worden." In *D. Cunrad Dieterichs/ Ulmischer Kirchen Superintendenten, Sonderbarer Predigten/So von unterschiedenen Materien/ Hiebevor zu Ulm im Münster gehalten/ deren theils schon allbereit in offenen Truck außgegangen/ theils jetzo von newem darinn verfertiget worden/ Vierdter Theil. Darinnen die Sontägliche Evangelische Text=Predigten begrieffen werden. Auff sonderbar Begehren zusammen gedruckt*, 110–21. Schleusingen: Zacharias Schürer, Matthias Götz, 1634.

Der Kleine Catechismus D. Martin Luthers/ beneben den Fragen deß Summarischen begriffs der sechs Hauptstucken Christlicher Lehr/ &c. Mit Angehengetem Christlicher Unterricht/ für Junge vnd einfältige Leut/ welche begehren zum Heyligen Abendmal zugehen/ Auch etliche Kinder- vnd Schulgebettlein/ Für Vlmische Kirchen vnnd Schulen in Statt vnd Land. Ulm: Jonas Saur, 1629.

Epitome Catechetica, Autore Cunrado Dieterico SS Th. D. antehac Practicæ Philosophiæ Professore & Pædagogiarcha Gissæ, nunc Pastore ac Superintendente Ulmensi. Editio nova, recognita & elimata. Giessen: Casparus Chemlinus, 1617.

Institutiones Catecheticae, è B. Lutheri Catechesi Depromptæ, variisque notis Logicis & Theologicis, in usum Juventutis Scholasticae illustratae, a Cunrado Dieterico Practicae Philos. Professore publ. & Paedagogiarcha. Cum praefatione & approbatione Venerandi Collegii Theologici. Giessen: Casparus Chemlinus, 1613.

Institutiones Dialecticae; ex probatissimis Aristotelis et Rami Interpretibus Studiose conscriptae, variisque exemplis in usum Illustris Paedagogii Giesseni Illustratae, à Cunrado Theodorico, Philosophiae Moralis Professore & Paedagogiarcha. Giessen: Nikolaus Hampel, 1609.

WRITING[15]

Wise counsel on remedying the problem of ignorance of the catechism and of the teachings of the Christian faith:

As soon as children are born into this world, bring them to God and His Church in Holy Baptism, so that through the same, as the bath of rebirth and renewal of the Holy Spirit, they are born anew, cleansed, and washed from sin, which they received in their mother's womb and in which they were born (Psalm 51:[5]; Titus 3:5; Ephesians 5:[1–]2). They are incorporated into the Church of God, thereby become children of God, and put on Christ with all of His blessings and benefits (Galatians 3:27).

When the children receive these things at the same time as their mother's milk, and when they begin to babble, they are brought to faith and knowledge of God, to prayer and fear of the Lord, in order that they crave the wise, pure milk (the Word of God) as newborn infants, so that they grow up through the same Word (1 Peter 2:2).

When they arrive at the age of discretion, send them to school so that there they may be instructed in their catechism—the foundation of faith—Christian discipline and virtue. In this way, they learn the Holy Scripture from their earliest childhood (2 Timothy 3:15).

Take your children to church, so that in the Divine Service with the hearing of God's Word, they take part in prayer, singing, praise, and thanksgiving.

Urge them to attend catechetical instruction, so that there they remember not only what they have learned from God's Word and their catechism in school and church through frequent repetition, but also that their knowledge increase and be strengthened day by day and year by year.

---

[15] This a select translation of Conrad Dietrich's "Catechismus Predigt. Darin von fleissiger Ubung des Catechismi in denen Häuptstücken Christlicher Lehr gehandlet/und Ursachen außgeführet werden/warumb dieselbig unter gemeinen Leuten fleissig zu treiben seye. Gehalten zu Ulm am Sontag nach der H. drey Könige Tag den 8. Januarii Anno 1626. Als daselbsten eine newe Ordnung mit der Praxi des Catechismi publiciert worden. Luc. 2. 41. Und seine Eltern giengen all Jahr gen Jerusalem/auff das Osterfest. 42. Und da er (Jesus) zwölff Jahr alt war/giengen sie hinauff gen Jerusalem nach Gewonheit des Festes/etc.," which was based on Luke 2:41 and preached on January 8, 1626. The sermon can be found in his *D. Cunrad Dieterichs/Ulmischer Kirchen Superintendenten, Sonderbarer Predigten/So von unterschiedenen Materien/Hiebevor zu Ulm im Münster gehalten/deren theils schon allbereit in offenen Truck außgegangen/theils jetzo von newem darinn verfertiget worden/ Vierdter Theil. Darinnen die Sontägliche Evangelische Text-Predigten begrieffen werden. Auff sonderbar Begehren zusammen gedruckt* (Schleusingen: Schürer, 1632), 110–21.

As they begin to grow older, when the foundation of the Christian faith has been laid, grasped, and understood, they will go to the Lord's Supper, which is the Paschal Lamb of evangelical Christians (1 Corinthians 5:7), and partake of it alongside other Christians in the congregation of God.

Finally, when children have been brought up under the fatherly discipline in the fear and admonition of the Lord, they will grow not only in age, but increase chiefly in wisdom and grace before God and human beings.

God commands all parents to teach their children the Word of the Lord at home and to strengthen it in their memory (Deuteronomy 6:7). Likewise, parents should bring up their children in the fear and admonition of the Lord (Ephesians 6:4) and bring them along to church . . . (Exodus 12:24) . . .

For this reason, children are born into this world and given to parents so that they will be given back to God, who created them; that they be instructed in his knowledge; improved; and brought up in true religion and the fear of God, that they will recognize and follow him alone. . . .

Children are reborn in Holy Baptism and washed of their sins, so that they not only put on Christ and are registered in the rolls of the churches as citizens of the Church, but also because we are cleansed in no other way than by faith in our hearts; even Christ dwells nowhere else than by faith in our hearts (Ephesians 3:17). Children are also instructed in the knowledge of faith, so that in this way Christ may dwell in their hearts; similarly that they may serve him in holiness and righteousness as believing citizens and members of the Church. . . .

It is necessary for Christianity and for our evangelical faith, since we are called Christians, to be able to give a faithful answer. What kind of Christian is it who knows nothing of Christ and Christian doctrine? . . . Our faith is not a Word faith [*ein Wort Glaub*], but rather *scientia*, a proper knowledge [*scio cui credidi*], "I know in whom I have believed," says the apostle Paul (2 Timothy 1:12). . . .

Instruction in the faith is necessary for the sake of the salvation of children, since by nature we are all children of unbelief (Ephesians 2:3). The natural person perceives nothing of the Spirit of God—it is foolishness to him and he cannot recognize it (1 Corinthians 2:14). Our understanding is obscured . . . we flee from the knowledge and fear of God, we do not strive for faith and salvation, but rather we must be instructed in them and thus be educated. When you have a child and let him grow up without discipline or education; you do not teach him to pray; do not send him to school, to church, and catechetical instruction, with the result that he does not learn his catechism and other necessary elements of salvation, how will he know God? How will he believe? How will he be saved? . . . If you wish your child to be saved, then he must be instructed in the knowledge of God, of faith and salvation. . . .

Therefore, the method through which we have the catechism memorized is the drilling of it at home, and then in public catechetical instruction, in which it is repeated, reiterated, and emphasized. But when you parents do not send your children to catechetical instruction, and do not drill the catechism at home yourselves, how will your children retain it in their memories? . . .

How will parents, when God blesses them with children, educate them in the fear of the Lord and teach them to pray, how will they teach little Nicholas when they themselves are not able to pray, and know nothing of the fear of God and of his teaching? For this reason, the instruction and knowledge of the catechism and of the articles of faith is the most necessary thing in this world. . . .

Through the instruction of Christian teaching and the training up in the fear of God, children are snatched from the devil as if from the jaws of death; they are brought up in faith to salvation. From the Creed they know God as Father, Son, and Holy Spirit. From the Ten Commandments children learn to love God and their neighbors, and which vices they should flee from and avoid. From the Lord's Prayer they learn how to pray and how they should call upon God their heavenly Father. From the Sacraments they learn how their faith may be strengthened and how in the Sacraments they may be assured of the gracious forgiveness of their sins, the attainment of God's kindness, grace, and blessing in temporal and eternal prosperity. . . .

When each Christian child and adult correctly believes and lives the Christian life in proper godliness and discipline (Titus 2:12), in this way they will be edified in the faith and blessed in all their activities and purposes. Then God gives them prosperity; they know to thank him for it in a Christian manner and not to be self-boastful about it. When God sends them this or that cross or affliction, they know how to deal with it all the better and to bear it with patience. God blesses parents with children; they know how to bring them up in a Christian and godly manner, as they were brought up by their own dear parents, and in all things they have all the more happiness, blessing, and prosperity. . . .

Tell me, then, Christian *Haußvater* [father of the household] and Christian *Haußmutter* [mother of the household], tell me what kind of splendid ornament for home and church do you have, when your little children stand around the table in your home like young olive branches, saying their prayers to their heavenly Father with folded hands and Christian humility? What kind of splendid ornament for home and church do you have, when they stand in school, in church, and in catechetical instruction, like tender little church seedlings, reciting their faith-statements from the catechism and their fine Bible passages? I know of no greater honor, glory, or praise that fathers and mothers can have because of their children than this, and indeed [this] should fill their eyes with tears of joy. Tell me, boys and girls, young men and women, tell me, what can be more praiseworthy and honorable for you than this, that you have correctly laid the foundation of your salvation from God's Word, been able to give account of your faith from your catechism, and have given it publicly in church, in catechetical instruction and in the confession of sins, and also to others, and have led a Christian life according to God's Word? When such a child is heard praying, everyone says: "Whose boy is this? Whose girl is this? This is a pious little son, a fine little daughter who can pray so well; God preserve this child! He will grow up to be a fine man, she a fine woman!" I know no more noble and beautiful adornment for young people than this; when I see such a young person, my heart rejoices . . .

For what can be more harmful to a person than to know or understand nothing of God, of Christ, of the catechism, of the Sacraments, of prayer, Creed, religion, and the fear of God, but rather from earliest childhood to weary old age to live in the world only like dumb brutes. When they come to church or to school and receive the Holy Sacraments, does it improve one hair on their heads? . . .

It is also disgraceful, shameful, and dishonorable when people know nothing of God, Creed, catechism, Commandments, and salvation. For indeed, what is a greater disgrace, shame, and dishonor than when not only children and young people, but even robust grown-ups who have reached adulthood, and have lived sixteen, seventeen, eighteen, twenty, even thirty more or less years, and cannot properly pray the Lord's Prayer, have not been sent to school, church, and catechetical instruction, have not been brought up in the fear of God and Christian discipline, but rather go out as the herds in the streets, leaping and kicking around like wild cattle (Job 20:11–12), causing all kinds of mischief, are insolent, lewd, and shameless; you know how they are carrying on in prostitution and fornication, how they curse, swear, and utter dreadful blasphemies, yet during their entire lives have never entered a school, never learned the catechism. O eternal God, it is to fathers and mothers, to a very honorable gathering of friends, to an entire city and congregation, indeed, to the whole Gospel and Christianity an everlasting disgrace and shame for God and for humanity!

That and other things the dear ancient Christians considered well and in a Christian manner, and for this reason saw to it, above other things, that the true religion, the foundation of the Christian faith and piety, would be imparted above all to the youth, from their childhood days on, both by the parents and by their specially appointed pedagogues and masters, as occurred even in the times of the apostles. . . . And although under the papacy such instruction disappeared, nevertheless the three chief parts were preserved by the special providence of God: the Ten Commandments, the Apostolic Creed, and the Lord's Prayer, which the blessed Dr. Luther used to call the perfect threesome [*das Trinum perfectum*], until finally Dr. Luther brought forth the golden jewel of this catechism, and thereby instructed many thousands of souls to eternal life.

I implore, beg, and exhort parents in Christ Jesus, that each acts in accordance with their responsibility, to bring their children and household servants, be they small, young, or grown-up, with the child Jesus to Jerusalem for the Passover festival. Every father and mother, be they rich or poor, wants to send their child to school to be instructed in writing, reading, in the catechism and fear of God. Every father and mother, be they rich or poor, wants to send their children and servants to catechetical instruction, so that there they may learn the foundation of their faith and salvation. Every father and mother, be they rich or poor, wants to be home teachers themselves, to teach their children the catechism, or to teach others and have them repeat the catechism with them. Every father and mother, be they rich or poor, wants their grown-up children to go to the Lord's Supper, and so they do not go like the sow to the trough, without knowledge of God, of Christ, of faith, and of training in the catechism. They send them to the choir on Thursdays for confession, examination in the catechism, and to receive absolution so they can go properly to the Lord's Supper, and not play the idle fellow at home, and receive judgment on themselves.

JOHANN HEERMANN (1585–1647)

THE SILESIAN JOB

by Jon D. Vieker

LIFE

Johann Heermann[1] (1585–1647) was the most important and prolific German hymnwriter between the time of Martin Luther (1483–1546) and Paul Gerhardt (1607–76). Heermann flourished during the period of Lutheran Orthodoxy and the Thirty Years' War (1618–48), and his life's

[1] The sources consulted for this essay are as follows: John Flood, *Poets Laureate in the Holy Roman Empire: A Bio-bibliographical Handbook*, 2 vols. (Berlin: Walter de Gruyter, 2006); Wolfgang Herbst, ed., *Wer ist wer im Gesangbuch* (Göttingen: Vandenhoeck & Ruprecht, 2001); Bernhard Liess, *Johann Heermann (1585–1647): Prediger in Schlesien zur Zeit des Dreißigjährigen Krieges* (Münster: LIT, 2003); Christian Möller, ed., *Kirchenlied und Gesangbuch: Quellen zu ihre Geschichte,* Mainzer Hymnologische Studien, no. 1 (Tübingen: A. Francke Verlag, 2000); Martin Rößler, *Liedermacher im Gesangbuch: Liedgeschichte in Lebensbildern* (Stuttgart: Calwer Verlag, 2001); *The Canterbury Dictionary of Hymnology*, s.v. "German Hymnody," accessed October 14, 2015, www.hymnology.co.uk/g/german-hymnody; *The Canterbury Dictionary of Hymnology*, s.v. "Johann Heermann," accessed October 14, 2015, www.hymnology.co.uk/j/johann-heermann.

course and hymn texts reflect both the bane and blessing of his times. Dubbed “The Silesian Job” by his contemporary Andreas Gryphius (1616–64), much of Heermann’s life traversed unspeakable sorrow, sickness, and anguish. His hymn texts, therefore, reflect on human suffering in light of Jesus’s suffering and death and thereby proclaim comfort and hope.

Heermann exhibited a weak and sickly constitution from birth. Born in Raudten (between Breslau and Glogau in Lower Silesia) to Johann and Anna on October 11, 1585, Heermann’s four previous siblings had been stillborn. Heermann’s mother was so thankful to finally have a son that she vowed that he would receive a formal education in spite of the family’s impoverished circumstances. At age 12, Heermann attended Latin school in Wohlau and quickly distinguished himself in composing Latin poetry, but shortly thereafter he contracted malaria and was confined to his home for nearly a year. At seventeen, Heermann began to study in Fraustadt under the famous pastor and theologian, Valerius Herberger (1562–1627), for whom he served as a writing assistant in preparing manuscripts, and by whom he was deeply influenced in both piety and theological thought. In 1603, Heermann attended *Gymnasium* (an advanced secondary school emphasizing Latin, biblical languages, philosophy, and other subjects to prepare students for university study) in Brieg, where he further distinguished himself, and in 1608, at the age of twenty-three, was crowned Latin poet laureate by Emperor Rudolf II (1552–1612). In 1609, he attended university in Strassburg, but the following year he was forced to return home and take a break in studies due to serious illness.

By 1611, Heermann began service as a vicar in Köben and within a year was ordained a pastor. He soon became a popular pastoral preacher. In 1612, he married Dorothea née Fiege, and their first year of marriage was joyful and invigorating. From 1613 onward, however, Heermann began to experience unspeakable suffering and sicknesses, which would follow him the rest of his life. A devastating plague struck all of Silesia in 1613. In 1616, most of Köben was destroyed by fire. In 1617, Dorothea died childless, and a year later, Heermann was remarried to Anna née Teichmann, with whom he would have four children.

The Thirty Years’ War was not kind to Köben, as the town was plundered four times by armed forces. Each time, Heermann fled his home and lost all of his possessions. The plague returned to Silesia in 1631 and killed more than five hundred people in Köben—nearly half of Heermann’s parishioners. By 1634, Heermann’s health had deteriorated to such an extent that his assistant had to read his sermons to the congregation. In 1638, Heermann retired to Lissa (in Poland) with his wife, who cared for him there until his death on February 17, 1647.

In 1640, their son Samuel converted to Roman Catholicism under the influence of nearby Jesuits. Heermann wrote his son a heartfelt letter titled "Treuherzige Abmahnungsschrift" (Heartfelt Letter of Warning), filled with fatherly love and a Lutheran confession of the faith. Samuel eventually returned to Lutheranism, only to die shortly thereafter in 1643. It was thought that the Jesuits had poisoned him. Heermann was too weak to attend the graveside service. He wrote: "Das auge tränet stets, das Herze weinet Blut" (The eye constantly weeps, the heart cries blood).

Heermann's numerous writings consisted mostly of religious poetry and hymnody. His earliest published work was *Flores ex odorifero annuorum Evangeliorum vireto ad fontes Israelis* (1609) (Flowers from the Fragrant Pasture of the Annual Gospels by the Founts of Israel), a collection of Latin poems on passages from the Sunday Gospels. Another early collection of poems was *Andächtige Kirch-Seufzer oder Evangelische Schliess-Glöcklin, in welche den Saft und Kern aller gewöhnlichen Sonntags- und Vornehmsten Fest-Evangelien . . . reimweise gegossen* (1616) (Devotional Church-Sighs, or Evangelical Closing Bell, in which the Heart and Core of the Gospels of All Customary Sundays and Chief Festivals Are Cast in Rhyme), which contained summaries of the preaching texts for all Sundays of the Church Year in Latin and German in short mnemonic rhymes or meditative poems that could be prayed. He also published a collection of sermons titled, *Labores Sacri: Geistliche Kirch-arbeit In Erklerunge aller gewönlichen Sonntags- undt Vornembsten Fest-Evangelien* (1624) (Sacred Labors: Spiritual Church Work in the Form of Explanations of the Gospels of All the Customary Sundays and Chief Festivals).

Heermann's most significant publications were his hymn collections. The most important of these was *Devoti Musica Cordis. Hauss- und Hertz-Musica* (1630) (Music for a Devout Heart), which contained metrical paraphrases of prayers and other devotional writings from the Church Fathers (e.g., Augustine, Bernard, and Tauler). Also significant were *Exercitium Pietatis. Übung in der Gottseligkeit* (1630) (An Exercise in Piety: An Exercise in Godliness) and *Sontags- und Fest-Evangelia* (1636) (Sunday and Festival Gospels). Both collections of hymns were based on the Sunday Gospels and festivals of the Church Year.

Among his poetic writings, Heermann was a particularly prolific hymnwriter, with some four hundred hymns to his name. Following the publication of Martin Opitz's *Buch von der deutschen Poeterey* (1624) (Book on German Poetry), Heermann became a champion of his fellow

Silesian's literary reforms. With his background and skill in Latin poetry, he brought his considerable craft to bear in showing how Opitz's reforms could be implemented with both elegance and brilliance.

Thematically and theologically, Heermann was influenced, as were many hymnwriters and theologians from this period, by the proto-pietist writings of Johann Arndt (1555–1621) and Martin Moller (1547–1606). Not as cosmopolitan and urbane as Johann Rist (1607–67), Heermann's hymnody stood almost entirely in the service of his calling as a pastor, both as preacher and as the caretaker of souls. In the tradition of hymnwriters Nikolaus Herman (1480–1561), Bartolomäus Ringwaldt (1530/1531–99), and Ludwig Helmbold (1532–98), a great number of Heermann's hymns served to catechize and reinforce the themes of Sunday's preaching texts for devotional use throughout the week. Other prominent themes in Heermann's hymn texts include everyday piety and vocation (e.g., "O God, My Faithful God," *LSB* 696); Christian persecution and suffering (e.g., "O Lord, Our Father, Shall We Be Confounded," *TLH* 269); and the passion and suffering of Christ (e.g., "O Dearest Jesus, What Law Hast Thou Broken," *LSB* 439).

A number of Heermann's hymns are in common usage today among American Lutherans and German Protestants. Nine are included in the German hymnal, *Evangelisches Gesangbuch* (1993); six in *Christian Worship* (1993); ten in *Evangelical Lutheran Hymnary* (1995); two in *Evangelical Lutheran Worship* (2006); and six in *Lutheran Service Book* (2006).

BIBLIOGRAPHY

Works by Heermann in English Translation

"Heermann: O Holy Jesus." In *Documents from the History of Lutheranism, 1517–1750*, edited and translated by Eric Lund, 272–73. Minneapolis: Fortress Press, 2002.

"Johann Heermann (1585–1647)." In *Seventeenth-Century Lutheran Meditations and Hymns*, edited and translated by Eric Lund, 281–89. New York: Paulist Press, 2011.

Select Works by Heermann in German and Latin

Devoti musica cordis: Haus- vnd Hertz- Musica, das ist, Allerley geistliche Lieder. . . . Breslau, 1630.

Exercitium Pietatis, Ubung in der Gottseligkeit. Das ist: inbrünstige Seuffzer, und andächtige Lehr- und Trostsprüchlein, für die . . . Jugend . . . aufs newe . . . übersehen und gemehret. Leipzig, 1636.

Flores ex odorifero annuorum Evangeliorum vireto ad fontes Israëlis . . . excerpti, et . . . filo poëtico contexti. Olsnae Silesiorum, 1609.

Sonntags- und Fest-Evangelia/ Durchs gantze Jahr. Breslau, 1644.

WRITING[2]

To the most noble, stern, and lord high-official,
David von Schweinitz[3]
Sitting heir of Seyfersdorff:
Ruler of Leignitz, Chief Counselor, and
To my most favorable, highly honored lord,
patron, and faithful supporter.

Here is what I have drafted for my devotion,
and often in times of sorrow my heart has delighted in it:
this also many a pious Christian has desired to have.
So then, let it now be granted that which he wants.

Whoever lets the speaker's splendor enliven everything,
he will find nothing here for himself. Here he must only practice
devotion. Here is the way of words [with] adornment and art.
Here I seek [to be] with God in humility, grace, and affection.
Whoever desires to speak with God and to obtain his favor,
he dare not parade before Him merely with high speech.
The heart beholds God. It is only good and right,
[that] words be gently pleasing to it.

But to whom, then, should I show these hymns
That he should be their protector? I know that from time to time
there are many who, like Momus,[4] can do nothing but criticize:
And when such a one dares, he attacks straightaway

---

[2] This is a translation of Johann Heermann, dedication to *Devoti Musica Cordis. Hauß- und Hertz-Musica* (Leipzig: Johann Albrecht Mintzeln, 1630), iii–iv.

[3] David von Schweinitz (1600–67) was duke of Leignitz, Silesia and was a German jurist and author of devotional writings.

[4] In Greek mythology, Momus is the god of poets and writers and represents the personification of satire and mockery.

what God himself has made. What God has indeed built,
has been built so well that when one rightly contemplates it,
one should contemplate it as nothing other than art and sheer marvel,
as wisdom and understanding, as omnipotence, power and strength.

You, O worthy champion, are born from noble stock,
and I am merely predestined [to serve] my patron and protector.
You are one who loves art and godliness,
and who yourself also has it very much in you at all times.
One knows where the sun, on its beautiful path,
brings with joy the bright and gentle day.
One knows it from its place, as it flees from here to there,
and with its luster crawls deep into the sea.

You are not like those who only dine with words,
those pious folk: what their mouth has spoken,
they render nothing in deed. With you, mouth and heart agree.
With you, the throng of muses have no fear of being fooled.
So take this now from me, what I here express,
and let me be your [subject] until my life's end.
I know that you will act. Through your gracious eyes,
I can see into your heart, and know that you do not deceive.

In heaven, [the] proper confidence.

JOHANNES RUDBECKIUS (1581–1646)

SWEDISH EDUCATOR AND BISHOP

by Otfried Czaika

LIFE

Johannes Rudbeckius was born on April 3, 1581, in Örebro, a city in the province of Närke in central Sweden. His parents were Johan Pederson Rudbeck (the town clerk) and Christina Pedersdotter Bosse.[1] In 1588, he entered the trivial school in his hometown. Rudbeckius continued his education at the trivial school of Strängnäs, the bishop's see for the provinces of Södermanland and Närke, in 1595. In 1599, he matriculated at Uppsala University, which had been restored in conjunction with the Diet and Synod of Uppsala in 1593. The acceptance of the Augsburg Confession at the Diet and Synod of Uppsala (1593) was a milestone on the Church of Sweden's way into the confessional age. Since Uppsala University was still small and quite unimportant, many Swedish students like Johannes Rudbeckius made academic peregrinations or visits to other universities. Together with his brother Petrus Rudbeckius (1578–1629), he enrolled at the University of Wittenberg on July 10, 1601. There he was promoted to master on April 12, 1603. During the winter semester of 1603–04, he continued his studies at Jena University.[2] According to Rudbeckius, Altdorf University offered him a professorship, but he chose instead to return to Sweden.

After returning home, Rudbeckius started an academic career as a teacher at Uppsala University. In 1604, he was appointed professor for mathematics in Uppsala. Between 1607 and 1609, he returned to Wittenberg for further study. He became a professor of Hebrew in Uppsala in

---

[1] *Svenskt biografiskt lexikon*, s.v. "Rudbeck (Rudbeckius, Rudebeck, von Rudbeck), släkt," accessed March 3, 2016, sok.riksarkivet.se/sbl/artikel/6973.

[2] Christian Callmer, *Svenska studenter i Wittenberg,* Personhistorisk tidskrift, no. 72 (Stockholm: Personhistoriska samfundet, 1976), 48–49; Hans Cnattingius, *Johannes Rudbeckius och hans europeiska bakgrund: En kyrkorättshistorisk studie*, Uppsala universitetets årsskrift, no. 8 (Uppsala: Lundequistska bokhandeln, 1946).

1609. Two years later, he became a professor of theology. On October 24, 1617, he was promoted to doctor of theology at the University of Uppsala.

Already in 1613, he had been appointed chaplain at the royal court. For this reason, Rudbeckius followed King Gustavus Adolphus II (1594–1632) on his Livonian campaign (1614–15) against Russia. In March of 1615, Gustavus Adolphus II named him leader of his Bible commission. In this capacity, Rudbeckius profoundly shaped the so-called *Gustav II Adolfs Bibel* (1618), which is a revised version of the first Swedish Bible, the Gustav Vasa Bible (1541).

At Linköping's cathedral, Rudbeckius was consecrated bishop of Västerås on January 28, 1619, and he started his work in this diocese in September of that same year. During the late 1620s, Rudbeckius was a part of the commission working with financial, juridical, and educational reforms in Estonia, which belonged to the Swedish Empire since 1561.[3] On August 8, 1646, Bishop Rudbeckius died and was buried in the Cathedral of Västerås. He lived to be sixty-five years old.

Rudbeckius was married twice. His first marriage (1610–18) to Christina Stiernman, the daughter of the Swedish Archbishop Nicolaus Olai Bothniensis (1550–1600, archbishop 1599–1600), was childless. His second marriage to Magdalena Hising (1602–49), a daughter of the Rural Dean Carl Hising (1572–1642), was blessed with eleven children. His son Olof Rudbeck the Elder (1630–1702) was one of the most important Swedish scientists in the seventeenth century. Petrus Rudbeckius (1625–1701) became professor of theology at Uppsala University (1660–92) and later bishop in the Swedish diocese of Skara (1692–1701). Nicolaus Rudbeckius (1622–76) became his father's successor as bishop in the diocese of Västerås (1670–76).[4]

Protestant theologians in the Swedish Empire during the century of Reformation cannot be described as original thinkers. The bishops during the age of Reformation promoted Lutheran doctrine through administration and practical theological work in their dioceses. Even the Swedish reformer Olaus Petri (1493–1552) and the Finnish reformer Mikael

---

[3] Titus Christiani, "Bischof Dr. Johannes Rudbeckius und die erste estländische Provinzialsynode," *Baltische Monatsschrift* 34 (1887): 549–87, 637–68; *Svenskt biografiskt lexikon*, s.v. "Johannes Rudbeckius," accessed March 3, 2016, sok.riksarkivet.se/sbl/artikel/6999; Hjalmar Holmquist, *Svenska kyrkan under Gustav II Adolf 1611–1632*, Svenska kyrkans historia, no. 4 (Stockholm: Svenska kyrkans diakonistyrelses bokförlag, 1938), 164–66.

[4] Gunnar Eriksson, *Rudbeck 1630–1702. Liv, lärdom, dröm i barockens Sverige* (Stockholm: Atlantis, 2002), 17–33ff.

Agricola (1507–57) can be described as eclectic theologians. They adopted ideas from the centers of the Reformation, especially Wittenberg but also from Upper Germany, and merged them into a unique Swedish model for Lutheran Reformation. The religious texts produced by the Swedish and Finnish reformers can, therefore, be described as practical. They include translations of the Bible; catechetical writings; church orders; and even tractates on marriage, the Lord's Supper, or monastery life; all of which breathe this practical orientation. In this regard, it should also be remembered that the Swedish Church adopted the three ancient confessions of the Church and the unaltered Augsburg Confession in 1593 and did not produce an original confession of its own like other Protestant churches of that time.

From approximately 1515 until the end of the century, Uppsala University was closed; all attempts to revive the university during the 1560s and 1570s failed. Therefore, the sixteenth century Lutheran theology in Sweden was highly dependent on the universities, theologians, and theological writings of Protestant Germany. Things slowly changed around 1600, after the re-establishment of Uppsala University. During the entire seventeenth century, the number of Swedish theologians who contributed to the discourse on theology grew steadily. Johannes Rudbeckius's contemporary Laurentius Paulinus Gothus (1565–1646), professor at Uppsala University from 1593 to 1606, bishop in Skara from 1608 to 1609, bishop in Strängnäs from 1609 to 1637, and Swedish archbishop from 1637 to 1646, published his magnum opus, *Christian Ethics* (*Ethica christiana*) between 1617 and 1630, which comprised seven volumes and approximately 3,700 pages.[5] However, Rudbeckius did not belong to the Swedish theologians of the seventeenth century who added substantial dogmatic works to the discourse of theology. He could probably best be described as a typical representative for a church and society in transition. On the one hand, his thinking was receptive and eclectic. In this respect, he continued the work of the Swedish reformers and bishops during the sixteenth century. His main interest was practical: education of the students at Uppsala University, the priests in his bishopric, the students at the *Gymnasium* in Västerås (the first one in the entire Swedish Empire, founded by Rudbeckius in 1623), and the catechetical education of the common man. Rudbeckius's lifelong and sustainable commitment to educational questions reveals, on the other hand, that his re-

---

[5] Herman Lundström, *Laurentius Paulinus Gothus. Hans lif och verksamhet* (Uppsala: Almqvist & Wiksell, 1893–98); *Svenskt biografiskt lexikon*, s.v. "Laurentius Paulinus Gothus," accessed March 2, 2016, sok.riksarkivet.se/sbl/artikel/1107.

ceptive and eclectic tendencies were future-oriented and secured him a place among the most important theologians (if not as the most important) in Sweden during the first half of the seventeenth century.

Both the sixteenth and seventeenth centuries fomented the struggle between throne (*imperium*) and the altar (*sacerdotium*), but with slightly different ingredients than during the Middle Ages. In Sweden, this struggle formed the decades after 1600, when Sweden rose to the hegemonic power in Northeastern Europe. In the center of this fight for the church's freedom from state control (*libertas ecclesiae*) was Johannes Rudbeckius and his dedication to science, theology, and the church. The Swedish Kings Charles IX (1550–1611) and Gustavus Adolphus II tried to govern the church's affairs. This happened partly through efforts to implement studies in politics at Uppsala University, partly through attempts to replace Laurentius Petri's (1499–1573) church order (1571) with a new church law, and last but not least, through the establishment of a general consistory (*Consistorium generale*) between 1623 and 1625, which should "place the external power of the church [*potestas ecclesiastica externa*] ... into the hands of the worldly authorities."[6] However, Swedish churchmen like Laurentius Paulinus Gothus and Johannes Rudbeckius hindered the king's direct attempts to increase its control over the church. The consistory did not become reality, and a new church law, which made the king the leader of the Swedish Church, was issued as late as 1686.

Until the Swedish historian of ideas and worldviews, Erland Sellberg, published his pivotal study in 2010 on the early modern church and state,[7] research had primarily treated the discussions of Aristotelianism and Ramism in Sweden and the struggle of power between church and state as two different things. Sellberg, however, has shown that these two spheres are interconnected. On the surface, there is struggle between Johannes Messenius (1579–1636), professor of law, and Jonas Magni (1583–1651), professor of ethics, on one side, and their colleagues Laurentius Paulinus Gothus and Johannes Rudbeckius on the other. Arguing from a Melanchthonian and Ramistic point of view, Gothus and Rudbeckius attacked the Lutheran Scholasticism and Aristotelianism of their colleagues Messenius and Magni. King Charles IX had appointed

[6] Sven Lindegård, *Consistorium regni och frågan om kyrklig överstyrelse: En studie i den svenska kyrkoförfattningens teori och praxis 1571–1686* (Lund: Gleerups, 1957), 267. This is the author's translation of Lindegård's German summary. Hans Cnattingius, *Den centrala kyrkostyrelsen i Sverige 1611–1636* (Uppsala: Almqvist & Wiksell, 1939), 152–59, 241–58ff.

[7] Erland Sellberg, *Kyrkan och den tidigmoderna staten. En konflikt om Aristoteles, utbildning och makt* (Stockholm: Carlssons, 2010).

Johannes Messenius as a professor in law at Uppsala University in 1609. With this appointment, Rudbeckius and his colleagues feared, however, that the king disregarded the privileges of the university. In addition, Rudbeckius accused Messenius (who had studied at the Jesuit college in Braunsberg from 1595 until 1603) of being a Crypto-Catholic. From Rudbeckius's speech at his accession to the professorship at Uppsala in 1604 (*Oratio de litterarum et scholarum utilitate ac necessitate*, 1604), it is evident that he had been highly influenced by philosophical studies, Aristotelianism, and Scholasticism. But just five years later he took a totally different position,[8] namely that the Scholastic tradition—personified in his counterpart Messenius—ultimately leads back to the Roman Church and pope as Antichrist (*Oratio de servitude pontifica*, 1609 [printed 1610]). The conflict between Messenius and Rudbeckius lasted until 1613 and did not come to a satisfactory conclusion. The king appointed Messenius as head of the royal archive and assessor at the Svea Court of Appeal in Stockholm. He removed Rudbeckius from the university, albeit naming him Royal Chaplain. As soon as Jonas Magni was appointed by the king as professor in ethics and the successor of Messenius in Uppsala, the old fight flamed up again, and Laurentius Paulinus Gothus started to attack Magni. According to Gothus, ethics (which included both theology and politics) should not be part of the university's curriculum. Magni was a scholar especially interested in Aristotle's philosophy. According to Laurentius Paulinus Gothus, this made him unsuitable to serve as professor. Behind Rudbeckius's and later Gothus's criticism against Messenius and Magni are only partly scholarly and philosophical differences. These conflicts must especially be understood as a bulwark against the king's attempts to take over control of educational and ecclesiastical matters. They are only at the surface a scholarly conflict between newer Lutheran Scholasticism (Aristotelianism) on the one hand, and the older Melanchthonian (Ramistic) way of thinking on the other.[9]

Even Rudbeckius's sermon, given on July 30, 1615, for the Swedish army at the campaign against Russia[10] reveals his critical potential against the authorities. In this sermon, he reminds the king and the nobility,

---

[8] Sellberg, *Kyrkan och den tidigmoderna staten*, 114.

[9] See Erland Sellberg, *Filosofin och nyttan*, vol. 1, *Petrus Ramus och ramismen* (Göteborg: Acta Universitatis Gothoburgensis, 1979).

[10] Johannes Rudbeckius, *Krigz predikan hållin vthi Ryszland, twå mijl när Pletscho, j thet swenska läghret, then 30. julij anno Christi 1615. Aff . . . Johanne Rudbeckio Nericio. på hwilken dagh then swenske krigzmachten strax effter predikan, intoghade för stadhen och honom sedhan beläghrade* (Våsterås: Olof Olofsson Helsing, 1626).

among others, that they are human beings and no better than ordinary people, via an exposition of Psalm 146:3–4. Furthermore, he reminds his listeners that negotiations are better than battles and accuses the officers of the army of being cowards for sending the commoners into the fire and not fighting side by side with them. In contrast, Rudbeckius underlines the greatness of God.[11]

The allocation of rights and duties between church and state was even addressed by Rudbeckius in his inaugurational speech as bishop of Västerås diocese in 1619.[12] Despite the fact that the king had given Rudbeckius a letter of confirmation, Rudbeckius explains that the right of patronage (*ius patronatus*) under no circumstances confines the judgement and consensus of the church and its ministers. In conjunction with the discussions about the general consistory in the 1620s, Rudbeckius developed his ecclesiology and understanding of the ministry. Rudbeckius did not deny the priesthood of all believers. But for him, the ministry has a divine foundation, and the worldly and heavenly kingdoms are less mixed than the Swedish kings or later Axel Oxenstierna (1583–1654), the Lord High Chancellor of Sweden after the death of Gustavus Adolphus II and de facto regent of the Swedish Empire, supposed. According to Rudbeckius, a vital part of the priestly tasks is to judge and punish. In 1636, Rudbeckius published a collection of texts (*Privilegia quædam doctorum*), derived from both the ancient Church and the Middle Ages, that proved the privileges of the clergy. This book was harshly criticized both by Johan Skytte (1577–1645), the chancellor of Uppsala University, and Axel Oxenstierna. The latter claimed that Rudbeckius followed the papists who requested worldly power for the Church. The book was banned by the Council of the Realm; Rudbeckius had to recall it. However, the most severe consequence for Rudbeckius was that after this affair he could no longer be an appropriate candidate for the post of Archbishop of Sweden.[13]

For his entire life, Rudbeckius was dedicated to educational questions. In 1606, he revised the statues of Uppsala University, and he certainly wrote the first draft of the school plan of 1611.[14] Both from his

---

[11] See Holmquist, *Svenska*, 146–48.

[12] Johannes Rudbeckius, *Oratio de legitima vocatione ministrorum ecclesiæ. Habita Arosiæ in synodo anniversaria 5. Septembris a. 1619. . . .* (Stockholm: Ignatius Meurer, 1621).

[13] *Svenskt biografiskt lexikon*, s.v. "Johannes Rudbeckius," accessed March 3, 2016, sok.riksarkivet.se/sbl/artikel/6999.

[14] These statues were not officially approved but were used in practice until new statues were issued by Johan Skytte and Axel Oxenstierna in 1626. See Jenny Ingemarsdotter,

time as a professor in Uppsala and as bishop of the Västerås diocese, many scholarly texts, such as disputations (*in eius private collegio*), are preserved. Between 1611 and 1613, students at Uppsala recorded his lectures on theological articles of the faith (*loci theologici*).[15] From these notes, we learn that his theology is marked by conformity to the orthodox, especially the Wittenberg, theology of his time. For example, his lectures follow Matthias Hafenreffer's (1561–1619) *Compendium of Heavenly Doctrine* (*Compendium doctrinae coelestis*) (which was used as part of the curriculum at Uppsala)[16] and Johann Gerhard's (1582–1637) *Theological Commonplaces* (*Loci theologici*) (1610–11).[17] Other contemporary Lutheran authors who contributed to Rudbeckius's thinking are Aegidius Hunnius (1550–1603), Leonhard Hutter (1563–1616), David Runge (1564–1604), and Salomon Gessner (1559–1605), all of whom were his teachers in Wittenberg, as well as Martin Chemnitz (1522–86). The influence of the Magdeburg Centuries (which were initiated by Matthias Flacius Illyricus [1520–75]) can also be traced in Rudbeckius's works.[18]

The foundation of the academic *Gymnasium* in Västerås is probably Rudbeckius's most important deed. The academic *Gymnasium* was his answer to the authorities' attempts to control the church and education in Sweden. Higher education was thus decentralized and diversified as academic *Gymnasiums* were founded in most Swedish and Finnish dioceses during the seventeenth century.

Rudbeckius was not only committed to higher education in his diocese. In 1622, Västerås was the first diocese in the Swedish Empire to issue instructions to record both the catechetical examinations (*husförhör*) of all parishioners and to keep accounts of the people living in the dioceses through parish registers that listed events such as births, marriages,

---

Ramism, Rhetoric and Reform: An Intellectual Biography of Johan Skytte (1577–1645) (Uppsala: Uppsala universitet, 2011), 222–25.

[15] Johannes Rudbeckius, *Loci theologici. Föreläsningar vid Uppsala universitet 1611–1613*, ed. Bengt Hägglund, Acta Regiae Societatis Humaniorum Litterarum Lundensis, no. 83 (Stockholm: Almqvist & Wiksell International, 2001).

[16] Matthias Hafenreffer, *Compendium doctrinae coelestis*, ed. Bengt Hägglund (Skara: Skara stiftshistoriska sällskap, 2010).

[17] Bengt Hägglund, "Wittenberger Orthodoxie in Uppsala am Anfang des 17. Jahrhunderts zu Johannes Rudbeckius' Loci Theologici (1611–1613)," in *Chemnitz - Gerhard - Arndt - Rudbeckius. Aufsätze zum Studium der altlutherischen Theologie*, ed. Alexander Bitzel & Johann Anselm Steiger (Waltrop: Hartmut Spenner, 2003), 185–95.

[18] *Svenskt biografiskt lexikon*, s.v. "Johannes Rudbeckius," accessed March 3, 2016, sok.riksarkivet.se/sbl/artikel/6999.

and deaths.[19] Rudbeckius's interest in catechization is found not only in these administrative acts, but also in practical religious texts that addressed the people.[20] In 1627, he published guidelines for "simple questions and answers" that believers should know at catechetical examinations (*Eenfalligha frågor och spörsmål om wår christendoms stycker, som eenfallight folk bredhe widh catechismo Lutheri i visitatione förehållas plägha*). In addition, Rudbeckius made sure that his diocesan publishing house printed copies of his brother's 1620 Swedish hymnal (*Enchiridion eller then swenska psalmboken sampt andra små wanligha handböker*) for use in his jurisdiction.[21] Many editions of the hymnal were issued in Västerås during the 1620s and 1630s.

Some of Rudbeckius's sermons were printed and are therefore preserved. His sermons were thoroughly formulated and drafted according to Latin rhetoric standards (albeit they were delivered in Swedish). However, they were easily understandable, analytical paraphrases of the biblical texts and thus followed the homiletic standards of the sixteenth century rather than the more complicated orthodox preaching style.[22] Furthermore, Rudbeckius belongs to the first generation of Swedish theologians who published funeral sermons; thus, he both popularized and developed the Lutheran understanding of the art of dying (*ars moriendi*). Funeral sermons were preached already during the sixteenth century in Sweden, but the publication of funeral sermons in Sweden started first in the decades after 1600 (probably due to better printing facilities in the Swedish Empire). Funeral sermons became a popular genre in Sweden. Already around 1650, funeral sermons were the most common religious texts printed in Sweden.[23]

---

[19] "Den svenska folkbokföringens historia under tre sekler," Skatteverket, accessed March 10, 2016, www.skatteverket.se/privat/folkbokforing/attvarafolkbokford/folkbokforingenshistoria/densvenskafolkbokforingenshistoriaundertresekler.4.18e1b10334ebe8bc80004141.html#Nr1.

[20] Holmquist, *Svenska*, 327–80.

[21] Johannes Rudbeckius, *Enchiridion eller then swenska psalmboken sampt andra små wanligha handböker: flitigt öfwersedt och corrigerat, såsom ock medh några nödtorfftiga stycker forbättrat och förmerat. Aff M. Petro Joh Rudbeckio N. studio suo & sumptibus capituli* (Stockholm: n.p., 1630).

[22] *Svenskt biografiskt lexikon*, s.v. "Johannes Rudbeckius," accessed March 3, 2016, sok.riksarkivet.se/sbl/artikel/6999.

[23] Otfried Czaika, "Andlighet och genealogi: den tryckta likpredikan i Sverige," *Släkt och hävd* 1 (2004): 29–60.

Rudbeckius's contribution to the confessional culture of early modern Sweden cannot be overestimated. Even though he was eclectic[24] in his theology, his administrative skills as a bishop and his dedication to educational issues, especially the foundation of the *Gymnasium* in Västerås and his commitment to catechetical learning, had long-term effects that shaped the culture and history of early modern Sweden and Finland. Thanks to the catechetical education of the believers, Sweden had an extraordinarily high amount of literate inhabitants already by the eighteenth century. What is often only described in terms of social discipline during the dark age of Lutheran Orthodoxy was—at least in its effects—an effective tool of modernization for the modern and postmodern history of Sweden. Thus Rudbeckius's efforts had a significant impact both on the religious awakening movements in Sweden and Finland during the eighteenth and nineteenth centuries, as well as on the development of the postmodern welfare state. The parish registers established by Rudbeckius were adopted by the registration office of the secular state and still serve, in 2016, as the central unit for registration. Today a person born in Sweden still does not have his birthplace on his passport, but rather the name of the home parish, regardless of if he or she belongs to the former Lutheran State Church.

BIBLIOGRAPHY

None of Rudbeckius's writings have been translated.

Select Works by Rudbeckius in Latin and Swedish

Biblia: thet är: all then helgha scrifft, på swensko: effter förre bibliens text, oförandrat: medh förspråk på the böker ther förr inge woro, medh summarier för capitelen, marginalier, flere concordantier, samt nyttighe förklaringar och register, etc. förmerat. . . . Edited by Johannes Rudbeckius. Stockholm: Oloff Oloffson, 1618.

Een Christeligh Lijkpredikan, Hållin vthi S. Claræ Kyrkia i Stockholm, Vthi Then Edle och Wälborne . . . F. Anna Oxenstiernes Begraffning. . . . Then 17. Septemb. . . . 1618. Stockolm: Prælo Reusneriano, n.d.

Een Christeligh Lijk Predikan, hållin vthi Storekyrckian j Stockholm vthi . . . Her Hindrich Horns . . . Begraffning . . . Then 21. Iunij Åår effter Christi börd 1618. Stockholm: Oloff Oloffson, 1621.

---

[24] *Svenskt biografiskt lexikon*, s.v. "Johannes Rudbeckius," accessed March 3, 2016, sok.riksarkivet.se/sbl/artikel/6999.

Dagbok. Edited by Rud B. Hall. Stockholm: Svenska kyrkans diakonistyrelses förlag, 1938.

Eenfalligha frågor och spörsmål om wår christendoms stycker, som eenfallight folk bredhe widh catechismo Lutheri i visitatione förehållas plägha. Våsterås: Olof Olofsson Helsing, 1627.

Jordeferdz eller uthförelse predikan öffuer . . . fru Catharinæ: boren konunga dotters til Swerie, etc. . . . Tå thet vthaff Wästerås Slott i Wesmanneland medh tilbörlig wyrdning och process fördes til . . . Stregnäs Doomkyrkia i Södermanland, nemliga then 2. Febr. A. 1639. Västerås: Peder Wald, 1539.

Krigz predikan hållin vthi Ryszland, twå mijl när Pletscho, j thet swenska läghret, then 30. julij anno Christi 1615. Aff . . . Johanne Rudbeckio Nericio. på hwilken dagh then swenske krigzmachten strax effter predikan, intoghade för stadhen och honom sedhan beläghrade. Våsterås: Olof Olofsson Helsing, 1626.

Loci theologici. Föreläsningar vid Uppsala universitet 1611–1613. Edited by Bengt Hägglund. *Acta Regiae Societatis Humaniorum Litterarum Lundensis*, no. 83. Stockholm: Almqvist & Wiksell International, 2001.

Logica ex optimis et præstantissimis autoribus collecta & conscripta, A M. Johanne Rudbeckio . . . ac primum ibidem discipulis privatis communicata, & 20. disputationibus privatis examinata. Deinde recognita, et multis locis emendata, ab eodem Wittebergæ, & vicissim Ubsaliæ aliquoties aliis atqque aliis similiter prælecta & ventilate. Västerås: Olof Olofsson Helsing, 1625.

Oratio de legitima vocatione ministrorum ecclesiæ. Habita Arosiæ in synodo anniversaria 5. Septembris a. 1619. . . . Stockholm: Ignatius Meurer, 1621.

Oratio de lingvae hebreae præstantia & dignitate habita in . . . academia Vbsaliensi . . . Anno Christi 1610. 23. Januarii . . . et iterum . . . in . . . celebri gymnasio Arosiensi anno 162. . . . Västerås: n.p., 1625.

Oratio de literarvm et scholarum utilitate simul ac necessitate, habita in illvstri academia Ubsaliensi . . . anno, 1604. 12. Septembris. . . . Västerås: Olof Olofsson Helsing, 1624.

Oratio De servitvte pontificia, qvadiu satis oppressi eramus, et miranda liberatione per singularem Dei virum b. Lutherum facta. Qvam Vbsaliæ habuit M. Iohannis Rvdbeckivs . . . anno 1609. 11. Decembris. . . . Stockholm: typis Anundianis, 1610.

Privilegia quædam doctorum, magistrorum, baccalaureorum, studiosorum et scholarium omniu.... Västerås: Peder Wald, 1536.

WRITING

Oration on the Legitimate Calling of Ministers of the Church[25]

It is called a mediate call when God himself calls and sends, but through other people to whom he has granted this power. In this manner the ordinary priests in the Old Testament and the bishops and presbyters in the New Testament were called.

Aaron and his sons, at God's command, were called through Moses and anointed as priests. Their calling was considered valid by God. The apostles chose and established the first bishops and presbyters in the cities, and then these chose and established others in turn, as is indicated in Acts 14[:23] and 1 Timothy 4[:6; Titus 1:5].

The latter calling was no less divine than the former, since concerning those called mediately, Scripture also testifies that they were called by God, as may be seen concerning the presbyters at Ephesus who were called by Paul and Timothy (Acts 20[:28]).

Here, another question arises. What are those means through which God in this manner calls ministers in his Church? Or to say the same thing with other words, to whom has God committed the right and power of calling ministers of the Church ordinarily?

---

[25] Johannes Rudbeckius, *Oratio de legitima vocatione ministrorum ecclesiæ. Habita Arosiæ in synodo anniversaria 5. Septembris a. 1619 ...* (Stockholm: Ignatius Meurer, 1621), fol. C2v–D1r, translated by Benjamin T. G. Mayes. This is a selection from Bishop Rudbeckius's Latin address on September 5, 1619, at the annual synod (pastors' conference) at Västerås, over which he was bishop. In this selection, he argues that the right to call ministers of the church belongs not to the king or princes alone, but to the entire church, which he defines as consisting of three estates: ministers of the church, hearers, and the civil magistrate. He stresses that the latter is entitled to participation in the call process only if he is a Christian and thus a member of the church. This tripartite division of the members of the church can be seen also in Johann Gerhard's theological commonplace on the ecclesiastical ministry, published in 1619 (Johann Gerhard, *On the Ministry Part One*, Theological Commonplaces XXVI/1 [St. Louis: Concordia, 2011], § 128, p. 194; *On the Ministry Part Two*, Theological Commonplaces XXVI/2 [St. Louis: Concordia, 2012]). Whereas Gerhard argues especially against the Roman Catholic claim that only bishops in communion with the pope can call ministers, Rudbeckius here especially argues against attempts by the civil magistrate to arrogate to himself alone the right to choose ministers of the church.

In the papacy, the Roman pontiff with his bishops and prelates arrogates this power to himself, completely excluding the civil magistrate and the church from suffrage. Among the Anabaptists, it is attributed to the people or the indiscriminate multitude. Elsewhere the civil magistrate is believed to have this right. None of these is found agreeing with the truth.

Therefore, we, having followed the leading of the divine Word and having followed the above report[26] that we sought from there, shall attempt to trace out what is utterly true. First, therefore, we distinguish the times, and we say that in the Old Testament from the creation of the world to the times of Moses, neither the magistrate, nor the people, nor the ecclesiastical ministry possessed the appointing of teachers of the Church. Rather, by hereditary law the duty of teaching belonged to the firstborn [sons]. Indeed, the ecclesiastical and civil magistracy were conjoined duties and referred to the same man. Then, from that time until the coming of Christ, there still was no choosing. Instead, this duty belonged only to the tribe of Levi. All these things were revealed, likewise, by the above, undoubted report.

In the New Testament, I say, first, this right does not belong to this or that estate specifically, but to the whole church, whether it consists of one estate or several.

First, Christ in Matthew 18[:18] gives the keys of the kingdom of the heavens to the Church, and soon adds, "If two of you agree on earth concerning anything that they ask, it will be done for them by My Father who is in the heavens" [v. 19]. Now add: If the keys of the Church—that is, the spiritual governance, which is what is understood by "keys"—have been given to the Church, then assuredly to the Church belongs the choosing and appointing of teachers and governors for herself, as is clear from the forms of republics. Second, God entrusted the Word and Sacraments to the Church, as is clear from Romans 3:[2–]3 [cf. v. 1]. From this it follows that establishing ministers of the Word and Sacraments belongs to the Church. Third, Paul proves this more clearly in 1 Corinthians 3[:21–22], when he says, "All things are yours, whether Paul or Apollos or Cephas," etc. If ministers belong to the Church, then assuredly the choosing of ministers belongs to her.

Now we shall prove that this right belongs in part to each estate in the Church, but not to any of them alone, unless one of them alone is what constitutes the Church. First, this right belongs to the ecclesiastical estate, as is proved from this: Even though the keys—that is, the govern-

[26] Rudbeckius refers to an earlier part of the address, where he had described the immediate call of God and the call of ecclesiastical ministers in the Old Testament.

ance of the Church—were given to the whole Church, nevertheless specifically and in particular they were given to the teachers and ministers of the Church, as is obvious from Matthew 16[:18–19], where the keys are given to Peter and the other apostles. Hence, for the same reason by which we proved that this right belongs to the Church, the consequence is that it belongs also to the teachers of the Church themselves. Indeed, since the teachers of the Church have greater experience with this matter than the others, and they understand better what people are suitable for this duty, reason itself dictates that they should not be excluded from the choosing of others. This right belongs to them so certainly that they alone, wherever there are not other members of the Church, can choose teachers and send them to teach. Therefore, at the beginning of the Church of the New Testament, when there was no civil magistrate of any eminence that had converted to the Christian faith, and there were few people, the Church had not yet been constituted of these three estates. Rather, the apostles and disciples alone with a few of the common people who belonged to the Church took this right to themselves alone, as the apostolic history testifies clearly. After Christ's ascension to the heavens, the apostles with the rest of the faithful soon gathered in Jerusalem and, without consulting Herod or Pilate, chose Matthias to take the place of the traitor, Judas. This was also shown above from Acts 14 in the choosing of others. The apostles imparted this very same right to their disciples, the bishops, and pastors, as is evident from Paul, Titus 1[:5]. "For this reason," he says to Titus, "I left you in Crete, that you should correct the things that are lacking and appoint presbyters in every city just as I commanded you."

On account of this, too, whenever a minister of the Word was to be sent to a place where there was not yet any Church, but all the people were still devoted to heathen religion, he was sent by the apostles or their successors, the bishops and other presbyters, without waiting for the choosing or asking or suffrage of the pagans. On the contrary, instead of the suffrage of the heathen people or magistrate being required, much rather, even against their will, [the ministers] taught with extreme peril of life in their cities and countryside. As a result, too, many of them were either not accepted, or again cast out, or were afflicted with death. From these things, no one is so stupid that he would not understand that this right belongs to the ecclesiastical estate.

Next, I say, where the people or a part of it have been converted to the Gospel, and thus a Church has been gathered to Christ, there the teachers of the Church ought to be chosen with the suffrage and consent of the Church—that is, of the hearers and the domestic estate—

something that reason itself first teaches. Indeed, since the teachers of the Church do not constitute the whole Church, nor are they the lords of the Church—as is clear from 1 Peter 5[:3]; rather, they are named "ministers" and "stewards" as in 1 Corinthians 4[:1]—neither should they attempt anything in these matters without the consent of the Church.

Next, the practice of the apostles and of the Early Church proves the same thing. The apostles, even though the Church was very small at that time, soon began to require its suffrage in the choosing of teachers, as we heard above, in the choosing of Matthias in place of Judas, from Acts 1. This can be seen also in the choosing of the seven deacons, from Acts 6. Yes, indeed, in Acts 14[:23] it is reported with clear words that Paul and Barnabas appointed presbyters in the cities through suffrages [*per suffragia*].[27] By whose suffrages were they carried out, I ask, but those of the hearers? If the apostles, whose authority was so great, refused to appoint presbyters without the consent of the hearers, how much less should this be done by us, who are not to be compared with them in authority? From this, again, I think it is plain that the right to call ministers of the Church belongs also in part to the hearers and the domestic estate.

Third, finally, we also assert this, that where the political estate—that is, the magistrate—is Christian and consents with the other estates in faith and religion, to it also this right belongs in part. If the suffrage of the Church in this choosing is required, excluding no member, then certainly the consent of political magistrates, too, as chief members, should be added. This is the case all the more, since the magistrate is the foster father of the Church and ought to have the chief care of her, as is evident in Isaiah 49:[23]. To him the care and custody of both tablets [of the Decalogue, Exodus 20:1–17] have been committed. Therefore, if the teachers of the Church forget their office, neglect to provide suitable pastors for the Churches, or [if] the hearers themselves do not greatly desire pastors, it belongs to the political magistrate to aid his subjects in this matter with his care and providing. Therefore, not only the godly kings in the Old Testament used this right, as far as it was permissible by the laws—David, Solomon, Hezekiah, Josaphat, Josiah, as we see from their history—but

---

[27] Theodore Beza's (1519–1605) Latin translation of the New Testament at Acts 14:23 reads *Quumque ipsis per suffragia creassent per singulas Ecclesias presbyteros* [And when through suffrages they had created for them presbyters in each city]. *Per suffragia creassent* translates the Greek χειροτονήσαντες, which is normally translated "appointed" or "ordained" in English Bibles. See Theodore Beza, trans., *Iesv Christi D. N. Nouum testamentum, Gr. & Lat. Theodoro Beza interprete* (s.l.: Henricus Stephanus, 1567). The translation by Desiderius Erasmus (1466–1536) is similar: *cum suffragiis creassent*. See Desiderius Erasmus, trans., *Novum Testamentum Omne* (Basel: Joannes Frobenius, 1519).

also Christian princes and emperors in the New Testament, as the *Church History* [*hist. Eccl.*] testifies.

By the way, here this principle must, nevertheless, be maintained: this right does not in any way pertain to the political rights of the magistrate, which are called "royal [rights]" [*Regalia*]. Rather, it belongs to the magistrate only insofar as he is a member of the Church. There are two distinct empires: spiritual, which is of the Church; and worldly, which is of the kings and princes of this world. In the secular empires of kings and princes, one may govern his subjects according to the laws and statutes of the empire, and appoint governors and judges subordinate to himself. Here, the teachers of the Word are subjects and are bound to render to them their obedience. In the spiritual empire, which is of the Church, Christ alone is King and Lord. The teachers of the Word are apostles or legates, ministers and stewards, through whom he rules and manages his Church. Kings and princes, however, as well as their subjects, are the subjects of Christ and citizens of his kingdom, and owe obedience to his ministers, and to this extent also they have suffrage in electing ministers of the Church.

From all of these things, I believe firmly that it is evident that the entire Church—not a part or estate of it in particular or alone—possesses the right to call ministers, unless a part by itself constitutes the Church, or the others are neglecting their office in this matter. For, to repeat, just as the teachers of the Church are not its lords, but are ministers and stewards, and therefore should not arrogate to themselves alone this power, so also the civil magistrate is not its lord, but is only a member. Therefore, for this reason, he should not claim this for himself alone. Much less, finally, is there either democracy or anarchy in the church, as happens when this is conceded to the people while the teachers and magistrate are neglected.

JESPER RASMUSSEN BROCHMAND (1585–1652)

THE PROTECTOR OF DANISH LUTHERANISM

by Jason D. Lane

LIFE

Jesper Rasmussen Brochmand (Casparus Erasmus Brochmandus), Danish theologian and bishop of Zealand (Sjæland), could arguably be the most influential theologian in Danish history. Peder Palladius (1503–60) guided the Reformation in Denmark as its first bishop. Niels Hemmingsen (1513–1600) made a name for the University of Copenhagen beyond the Danish borders. Denmark's great philosopher was Søren Kierkegaard (1813–55), and N. F. S. Grundtvig (1783–1872) was perhaps its most influential author, poet, and social reformer. But Brochmand will be remembered in the annals of history as Denmark's pastor and theologian. As bishop of Zealand (1639–1652), he reformed the Danish liturgy, and as Denmark's leading theologian, he aligned the church's doctrine with orthodox Lutheranism against Roman Catholic and Crypto-Calvinistic pressures. Yet for all his scholarly and dogmatic work, it was his collected sermons, or house postils, *A Religious Reflection and Short*

Explanation of All Gospels and Epistles (*Sabbati Sanctification, det er gudelig Betænklning og kort Forklaring over alle Evangeliger og Epistler*) (1635–38) that left the deepest impression on the Danish people. His sermons went through twenty-four editions until their last printing in 1862. They served as popular devotional material for Danish homes, and the practical theology they contained shaped the piety of generations of Lutherans in Denmark.[1] According to Werner Elert, few theologians could compare to Brochmand. In fact, Elert claimed that no German Lutheran of the seventeenth century could rival him in the combination of dogmatic ability, ethical activism, and episcopal generosity.[2] Robert Preus called Brochmand "the giant among the Scandinavian theologians during the period of Lutheran orthodoxy"[3] and put his great dogmatic text, *A System of Universal Theology* (*Universae Theologiae Systema*, 1633) on par with Johann Gerhard's *Loci Theologici*. Though Brochmand did not incorporate the same exegetical thoroughness as Gerhard, his inclusion of a lengthy discussion of casuistry and practical application of the articles of faith marked a new development in the tradition of Lutheran dogmatic texts, giving Brochmand's work a unique place in the church.[4] In his preface, he listed those who had influenced him theologically. Besides Luther (1483–1546), he mentioned Martin Chemnitz (1522–86), Aegidius Hunnius (1550–1603), Nikolaus Hunnius (1585–1643), and Johann Gerhard (1582–1637); Melanchthon (1497–1560) he omitted.[5] His lengthy commentary on the Epistle of James (1640) that Brochmand would later include in his *Systema* is, according to Preus, "one of the finest commentaries written during the period of orthodoxy."[6] Throughout every page of the commentary, Brochmand demonstrates that Christian doctrine is altogether practical. In short,

---

[1] Jens Chr. v. Johansen, "Preacher and Audience: Scandinavia," in *Preachers and People in the Reformations and Early Modern Period*, ed. Larrisa Taylor (Leiden: Brill, 2001), 297–326, especially 318. See also F. Nielsen, "Brochmand, Jesper Rasmussen," in *The New Schaff-Herzog Encyclopedia of Religious Knowledge*, vol. 2, *Basilica-Chambers* (New York and London: Funk and Wagnalls, 1908), 272–73; Jørgen Stenbæk, "Brochmand, Jesper Rasmussen," in *Theologische Realenzyklopädie*, ed. Gerhard Krause and Gerhard Müller (Berlin: De Gruyter, 1977–2004), 7:192–94.

[2] Werner Elert, *Morphologie des Luthertums*, 3rd ed. (Munich: C. H. Beck'sche Verlagsbuchhandlung, 1961), 2:232.

[3] Robert Preus, *The Theology of Post-Reformation Lutheranism*, vol. 1, *A Study of Theological Prolegomena* (St. Louis: Concordia, 1970), 54.

[4] Preus, *Post-Reformation Lutheranism*, 1:54.

[5] Sternbæk, "Brochmand, Jesper Rasmussen," 7:193.

[6] Preus, *Post-Reformation Lutheranism*, 1:55.

Brochmand possessed a rare combination of intellect, piety, and doctrinal fortitude. His prominence as bishop of Zealand and the support he had from the crown allowed him to put his rare gifts to use for the church in ways that Lutherans in Germany could not. The time is perhaps ripe for this relatively obscure theologian of Lutheran Orthodoxy to emerge from the gloomy north and shine on Lutherans to the south and west.

Brochmand was born in Køge on the island of Zealand, Denmark on August 5, 1585, to the mayor of Køge, Rasmus Sørensen Brochmand (1537–99), and his wife, Bodil Jacobsdatter Truelsen (1561–1619). He died while serving as bishop of Zealand on April 19, 1652. Due to his father's prominence, Brochmand had a privileged childhood and was afforded the very best opportunities to study. He received his early education at the prestigious Latin school, Herlufsholm Academy, in Copenhagen. He continued his studies at the age of sixteen in Greek and philosophy at the University of Copenhagen, and later the Dutch Universities of Leiden and Franeker, where he must have had great success, since he was called back to Herlufsholm in 1608 to be its rector. In 1610, he joined the faculty of Copenhagen as professor of pedagogics, and three years later he became professor of Greek as well as dean of the faculty of philosophy. While teaching Greek, he finished his doctorate in theology from Franeker and joined the theology faculty of Copenhagen in 1615, the same year that the leader of Lutheran Orthodoxy at the time, Hans Poulsen Resen (1561–1638), was ordained as bishop of Zealand. He took a brief hiatus from the university (1617–20) to serve as a private tutor for the son of King Christian IV of Denmark (1577–1648). The close connections to Christian IV, who had always desired a strongly Lutheran Denmark, would prove invaluable for Brochmand's later reform efforts as bishop. Brochmand succeeded Hans Poulsen Resen as bishop of Zealand in 1639 and served productively in office until his death in 1652.

Like many orthodox Lutherans of his day, Brochmand was a staunch defender of the faith against Roman Catholic and Reformed teachings. One biographer suggests that he cannot be classified as an "original theologian."[7] Yet this is an oversimplification of a complex man. To understand Brochmand, one must have an appreciation for the Danish political and theological culture in which he developed as a theologian and especially give attention to the many personalities and conflicts that caused him to stand ever more firmly in the doctrine confessed in the Book of

[7] Stenbæk, "Brochmand," 7:194.

Concord, a book that Brochmand ardently defended, though the Danish Church never formally accepted.

When Brochmand first came to the University of Copenhagen in 1610, the theological faculty consisted of many Philippists who, on the one hand, were swayed by Calvinistic teachings concerning the Lord's Supper, and on the other, were receptive to the philosophy, cosmology, and medicinal theory of the enigmatic sixteenth-century theosopher Paracelsus (1493–1541).[8] Both Crypto-Calvinist theology and Paracelsian cosmology were accommodated under the irenic guidance of Niels Hemmingsen and continued to influence the university after Hemmingsen's death. Yet when threats of Crypto-Calvinism escalated at the university around 1615 and King Christian IV insisted that the university stamp out the Philippist heresy, Brochmand, in a decisive moment of his career, sided with Bishop Hans Poulsen Resen[9] against the Philippists and defended the orthodox position of the Formula of Concord. It was thereafter that Brochmand was regarded as the spiritual heir of Resen.

Brochmand's theological convictions grew firmer during the 1620s as he responded to Roman Catholic publications, especially those of Robert Bellarmine (1542–1621). Brochmand's great dogmatic work for which he is most well-known outside of Denmark, his *Systema*, was in large part the fruit of his classroom lectures and early publications. Of special importance is the 1628 publication *De Pontifice Romano*. Robert Preus considered it "one of the most searching analyses of the Roman papacy ever made."[10] It was later included in his *Systema*, but it would not be his last response to Roman Catholics. In 1633, Margrave Christian Wilhelm

[8] Paracelsus [Philip Bombast von Hohenheim] (1493/4–1541) was the most popular and most controversial figure of medicine in sixteenth- and seventeenth-century Europe. His influence was especially powerful in Denmark. See Hartmut Rudolph's "Paracelsus," in *Theologische Realenzyklopädie*, ed. Gerhard Krause and Gerhard Müller (Berlin: De Gruyter, 1977–2004), 25:699–705 for a summary of Parcelsus's life, work, and influence. For a collection of helpful essays on Paracelsus in English, see Ole Peter Grell, ed. *Paracelsus: The Man and His Reputation, His Ideas and Their Transformation* (Leiden: Brill, 1998), particularly Grell's article: "The Acceptable Face of Paralesianism," 245–67. See as a response to Grell's work: Jole Shackelford, "Paracelsianism and the Orthodox Lutheran Rejection of Vital Philosophy in Early Seventeenth-Century Denmark," *Early Science and Medicine* 8, no. 3 (2003): 210–52, who argues that the resurgence of Lutheran Orthodoxy under Resen and Brochmand eventually made Paracelsianism untenable on religious and philosophical grounds.

[9] Resen joined the theology faculty of Copenhagen in 1597 and served as bishop of Zealand from 1615 to his death in 1638. Brochmand took his place in office in 1639.

[10] Preus, *The Theology of the Post-Reformation*, 1:55.

from Brandenburg (1587–1665), King Christian IV's brother-in-law, scandalously converted to Catholicism and defended his conversion in writing (*Mirror of Truth* [*Speculum Veritatis*, 1633]). At the king's request, Brochmand wrote *The Lamp of the Prophetic Word* (*Lychnos logou prophetikou*, 1634), a formal response written in Latin in which he argued point by point against the margrave. It was one of the most popular Lutheran defenses against Roman Catholicism in the sixteenth century and had influence beyond the Danish borders. Clearly his work found readership among the German laity, as evident by the several editions that were translated into German. Not only this, but many of Brochmand's Danish works were translated and published in Germany. His Latin works, especially the *Systema*, were reprinted and read liberally in German circles.

A looming question for understanding Brochmand and his strides toward orthodoxy was his relationship with his mentor, friend, and influential political ally Holger Rosenkranz (1574–1642), an originally orthodox-Lutheran-leaning nobleman and prominent member of the Danish Council who had studied theology in Wittenberg and Rostock but had become increasingly disenchanted with orthodox Lutheranism. It seems that Rosenkranz had something of a spiritual crisis around 1600 that caused him to slowly abandon his orthodoxy.[11] Convinced that doctrinal sterility could not lead to true piety, Rosenkranz turned to Johann Arndt's (1555–1621) mystical program of spiritual reform and sought to implement Arndtian piety in Denmark. The accommodation of Paracelsian medicine at the university and the Danes' interest in true piety may have made the subtleties of emphases difficult to detect, even for Brochmand. Rosenkranz's shift from orthodoxy to heterodoxy, therefore, must have been gradual and private, because when he joined the Danish Council in 1617, he aligned himself publicly with Bishop Resen and was highly respected among the orthodox theologians, including Brochmand, until he stepped down from the Council in 1627, to Christian IV's displeasure, and began to publish his heterodox ideas.

The case of Rosenkranz and his close relationship with Brochmand points to a larger truth about Danish churchmen. It seems that in Denmark, at least from 1614 to 1627, many orthodox Lutherans were unalarmed by certain aspects of the Parcelsianism that they had received

---

[11] Thorkild Lyby and Ole Peter Grell, "The Consolidation of Lutheranism in Denmark and Norway" in *The Scandinavian Reformation: From Evangelical Movement to Institutionalisation of Reform*, ed. Ole Peter Grell (Cambridge: Cambridge University Press, 1995), 114–43, especially 138.

through Johann Arndt's writings. Although Arndt maintained that he was a faithful supporter of orthodoxy and the Book of Concord, it is a matter of fact that Arndt's fourth book from his *Four Books of True Christianity* (*Vier Bücher des Wahren Christentums*, 1610), was translated into Danish because of the Danes' interest in Paracelsianism.[12] However, as the theological consequences of Paracelsianism emerged in Denmark, namely, its metaphysical suppositions that favored a Calvinistic Christology, the Lutherans flatly rejected Paracelsian theory.[13] In other words, Brochmand and others made use of Arndt's piety but rejected the metaphysical implications of his anthropology and Christology that were drawn from Paracelsus.

Rosenkranz's journey away from orthodoxy mirrors in many ways Brochmand's journey to orthodoxy. Brochmand had admired Rosenkranz as a professor and never wavered in their mutual commitment to pious Christianity. Yet Rosenkranz's emphasis of piety over doctrine led Brochmand to more tenaciously defend the doctrine. A distinct feature of Rosenkranz's theology that Brochmand would reject was his teaching of double justification. He taught that a person is first justified before God by faith and then justified before God by works, and that both justifications are necessary. In other words, the works that are a consequence of faith are reckoned as righteousness.[14] When Rosenkranz's views were made known to Christian IV, he demanded that Rosenkranz revoke his opinions. But Rosenkranz defended them. In response, the theology faculty in Copenhagen issued a response condemning his doctrine as "Socianian," and it appears that Brochmand was the responder.[15] Brochmand made his final reply to Rosenkranz in his commentary on James by distinguishing between the justification before God by faith (Paul) and the declaration that faith is living before the world (James).[16]

---

[12] Begnt Arvidsson, "Wissenschaft und Frömmigkeit. Johann Arndt in der dänischen Geistengeschichte der ersten Hälfte des 17. Jahrhunderts," in *Johann Arndt — Rezeption und Reaktion im Nordisch-Baltischen Raum*, ed. Anders Jarlert (Lund: Lund University Press, 1999), 27–33. The translation was done by Resen's protégé, Peder Gjelstrup, *Liber Naturae eller Naturspeyel* (Copenhagen, 1618). See also Schackelford, "Paracelsianism," 236n69.

[13] Shackelford, "Paracelsianism," 236–37.

[14] Lyby and Grell, *The Scandinavian Reformation*, 139.

[15] Lyby and Grell, *The Scandinavian Reformation*, 139.

[16] Jesper Brochmand, *In Canonicam et Catholicam Jacobi Epistolam Commentarius* (Copenhagen: Molken, 1641), 153–55.

Brochmand's commentary on the Epistle of James deserves special attention because it is his first major publication as bishop of Zealand and because it is programmatic for his theological leadership of the church. Brochmand regarded James as a pastoral letter that is intended to guard the doctrine and life of the pastors and thus the church. In his preface, Brochmand urges his fellow pastors to give attention to James, who forcefully reminds them about the duties of their office and urges them to profess the faith in times of suffering.[17]

By the time Brochmand ascended to the office of bishop, he had become the uncontested leader of the Danish Church. His massive *Systema* combined his most important writings into one place and was widely studied. But because of its size, Brochmand edited an abridged *Systema* for students, which remained the doctrinal standard at the University of Copenhagen until the Enlightenment. As mentioned earlier, his sermons were common devotional material in Denmark until the nineteenth century, and his devotional works were read long after his death.[18] As concerns doctrine and piety in Denmark, no one has matched Jesper Brochmand's influence. There is, however, still much work to be done to fully appreciate the many contributions that Brochmand made to Lutheran theology.

Two criticisms of Brochmand tend to surface among scholars, and both will need further study to confirm their general suspicions. The first has to do with Brochmand's piety, his relationship to Arndt's spiritual reform, and his teaching concerning repentance. Some scholars suggest that Brochmand placed too much emphasis on a sinner's preparation to receive forgiveness.[19] The evidence for this is found in Brochmand's *Systema*, where he distinguishes between the will's freedom to do outward acts (such as hear God's Word, read it, meditate on it, and go frequently to the gathering of the church) and the will's bondage as regards internal holiness. This distinction between the externally free will and the internally bound will allowed Brochmand to establish legislation for church attendance and ecclesiastical bans for those who rejected God's pure Word, including Catholics, Calvinists, Jews, and Turks.[20] He is sometimes criticized for placing too much emphasis on church discipline and for resembling the church polity of John Calvin. However, any criticism

[17] Brochmand, *Jacobi Commentarius*, Preface.

[18] Stenbæk, "Brochmand," 7:194.

[19] Stenbæk, "Brochmand," 7:194.

[20] Martin Schwarz Lausten, *The Jews and Christians in Denmark: From the Middle Ages to Recent Times ca. 1100–1948*, trans. Margaret Ryan Hellman (Leiden: Brill, 2015), 36–37.

of Lutheran church discipline must also take into consideration how Lutherans understood the Office of the Keys. Brochmand and the Danish Church excommunicated the unrepentant not in order to settle who was elect and who was reprobate, but rather to carry out the duties of the pastoral office for the salvation of souls, which included both the preaching of repentance and the forgiveness of sins. The goal in Lutheran theology was to bring sinners to Christ's forgiveness and save their souls, as the selected text from Brochmand's works below will demonstrate.

The second criticism of Brochmand stems from the first, namely, that Brochmand was merely a puppet of the king, legislating political reform at the expense of the church's proclamation of the Gospel. The criticism is partly unjust, because the relationship between the bishop and the crown was built into the church structure set up by Johannes Bugenhagen in 1539. Rather than a pure episcopal system as the Lutherans in Sweden had, Bugenhagen structured Denmark's episcopacy after the German territorial churches. The latter had temporarily loaned episcopal authority to the princes and land owners—an old medieval custom that Luther and Melanchthon advised be implemented as a stopgap measure, in hopes that a church council of Western Christendom would resolve the ambiguity of ecclesiastical authority. Sadly, the council that Luther and others had hoped for never happened, and the states continued (for better or for worse) to exercise great influence over the churches. The episcopal authority in Denmark therefore belonged to the king, and the bishops were seen as an extension of his authority over church.[21] As an example of the king's involvement, Christian IV established in 1617 a biennial synod of the church in Jutland to promote ongoing pastoral education, visitation, and theological unity.[22] The fact that Christian IV and Brochmand largely agreed about matters of the church was downright felicitous. It would have been a very different history if the king had opposed Lutheran Orthodoxy. If one were to write a history from the perspective of the Philippists or the Catholics in seventeenth-century Denmark, one could suppose that the relationship between the king and the bishop would hardly be viewed so favorably. But as the history stands for the Lutheran Church in Denmark, Brochmand made

---

[21] Elert, *Morphologie*, 2:228.

[22] Troels Dahlerup, "Sin, Crime, Punishment and Absolution: The Disciplinary System of the Danish Church in the Reformation Century," in *Die dänische Reformation vor ihrem internationalen Hintergrund. The Danish Refromation against its International Background*, ed. Leif Grane and Kai Hørby (Göttingen: Vanderhoeck & Ruprecht, 1990), 277–87, especially 282.

the very most of his opportunity as bishop under a Lutheran king and guided by a Lutheran church order. He is remembered as a pious bishop and "the champion of Orthodoxy."[23] And his influence may reach farther still.

BIBLIOGRAPHY

None of Brochmand's writings have been translated.

Select Works by Brochmand in Latin, German, and Danish

Commentarius In Epistolam Ad Hebraeos: Opus Posthumum ex Authoris autographo nunc primum editum. Copenhagen: Hieronymus Christian Pauli and Nikolaus Spiering, 1706. This was published posthumously.

Evangelisch Liecht und Recht, deß vesten Prophetischen Worts / das da scheinet in einem duncklen Orth. Nuremburg: Endters, 1638. This is a German translation of *Lychnos* (1634).

In Canonicam & Catholicam Jacobi Epistolam Commentarius. Copenhagen: Joachim Moltken, 1641.

Lychnos logu prophētiku, phainon en auchmero topo: Oppositus Veritatis Pontificiæ Speculo Hoc est: Succincta, sed solida, causarum, quibus inductus Illustrissimus Dux Christianus Wilhelmus, Marchio Brandenburgensis etc., â Lutheranâ Ecclesia defecit, et se Ecclesiæ Pontificiae mancipavit, refutatio. Copenhagen: Moltken Martzan, 1634.

Sabbati Sanctificatio: Huus-Postil. Copenhagen: Moltken, 1635–38.

Universae Theologiae Systema. 3 vols. Ulm: Görlinus, 1658–64.

[23] Eric Lund, "Nordic and Baltic Lutheranism," in *Lutheran Ecclesiastical Culture. 1550–1675*, ed. Robert Kolb (Leiden: Brill, 2008), 411–54, especially 427.

WRITING[24]

Concerning the Ecclesiastical Ministry

Chapter I: In which the true understanding of the ecclesiastical ministry is briefly explained.

In order to communicate clearly the article of the Christian religion concerning the ecclesiastical ministry, we will consider the following: (1) The various voices in Sacred Scripture that set forth the common teaching of the ecclesiastical ministry will be briefly presented and explained. (2) The definition of the ecclesiastical ministry will be articulated, and each and every cause of this ministry will be examined. (3) What constitutes a legitimate call for ministers of the Word will be considered. (4) The office of the ministry of God will be set forth. (5) The life of the ministry of the divine Word will be described. (6) The wages of faithful ministers of the divine Word and its counterpart, the wages of those who eat the bread of idleness, will be weighed. (7) Finally, the distinctive orders and degrees of divine ministers will be considered. This article of the Christian Religion is, however, not confined to these parts only.

Section One: Concerning the Terminology of the Holy Ministry as it is set forth in the Sacred Scripture.

Although we commonly call it the ecclesiastical ministry, the Holy Spirit in Sacred Scripture sometimes gives it the title *diakonia*, other times *leiturgia*.

As concerns the former, *diakonia*, its use in the Sacred Books of Divine History can be taken in its broadest sense, in its strict sense, and in its strictest sense. In its broadest sense, *diakonia* refers to any ministry, whether ecclesiastical, political, or domestic, whether carried out in a sacred or in a secular office. Thus, Luke 10:40, "But Martha was distracted with much *diakonia*." In Hebrews 1:14, the angels are sent for *diakonia* to serve the elect. And in Romans 13:4, political magistrates are called *deacons* of God. The original word lends itself to this meaning,

[24] The brief selection from Brochmand's *Universae Theologiae Systema* on the ecclesiastical ministry (Volume II, *De Ministerio Ecclesiastico*, Article XXX, Chapters I, Sections 1–2, pp. 877–83) may not be altogether new to those who have read Johann Gerhard's *Theological Commonplaces: On the Ministry*. However, it offers clarity concerning the holy office from the perspective of an episcopal Lutheran. Brochmand demonstrates with doctrinal clarity and pious intentions that the holy office is God's gift to his Church for her salvation.

since it comes from the word *koneô*, which according to Hesychius [of Meletus] means, I rush, run, or toil,[25] and its derivatives, *konis* or *konia*, mean dust. Hence *diakonia* indicates any kind of servile duty that is prepared with effort and haste, and not without some sweat and dust.

In its strict sense, the word *diakonia* designates the ecclesiastical ministry or sacred office that is carried out by the ministers of God in God's Church. Thus Judas was put forth as one who received his lot in the *diakonia*, that is, the apostolic office (Acts 1:17). And in Acts 6:4, the apostles say to assign others to the *diakonia* of serving tables. "But we will devote ourselves to prayer and to the *diakonia* of the Word." We call this the ministry of the Word. Although the apostle calls it here *diakonia* of the Word, it is elsewhere called simply *diakonia* (Acts 21:19; Romans 11:13; 2 Corinthians 6:3; 1 Timothy 1:12; and other passages).

In the strictest sense, the word *diakonia* is used for a certain aspect of the holy ministry, such as caring for the poor. Thus, in Acts 6:1 it says that a complaint arose from the Greeks against the Jews, that their widows were being overlooked in the daily *diakonia*, that is, in the administration of alms that were given to the poor and daily apportioned to those in need from the common treasury. In this context, however, it is proper to add to *diakonia* the holy ministry that is concerned with the preaching of the Word and the administration of the Sacraments.

Concerning the second term, *leiturgia*, we accept the typical designation that refers to the holy ministry. The term has three senses. First, it is used for any kind of office or ministry, whether sacred or secular. See, for example, Philippians 2:25.[26] Epaphorditus is said to have supplied what was lacking in Paul for the Philippian *leiturgia*. Furthermore, civil magistrates are called *leiturgoi theou* (liturgists of God) in Romans 13:6. Yet among the Greek authors, Plato, Artistotle, and others, as Casaubon remind us in *Exercitationes XVI* (number 16), "to serve [*leiturgein*] is properly to perform a work publicly" and "*leiturgia* is a public office."[27] The use of *leiturgia* remains consistent. It is a public office or public work, that is, any kind of service or business rendered. Thus in Romans 16:17, Paul says that some serve (*leiturgein*) for the things of the flesh.[28]

---

[25] Literally, according to Liddell and Scott, "to raise dust."

[26] The original has Phillippians 2:20.

[27] Isaac Casaubon, *De Rebus Sacris et Ecclesiasticis Exercitationes XVI* (Frankfurt: Ioannes Bring, 1615).

[28] Brochmand may be summarizing Romans 16:17–18. But St. Paul refers to those who serve their own bellies. The term used in Romans 16 for "serve" is not *leiturgeô*, as Brochmand suggests, but *douleuô*.

For as it is said in Book IV of Artistotle's *Politics,* those who serve should be compensated.

Second, *leiturgia* is strictly used for the holy ministry, because it is carried out by preachers of the divine Word in God's house. Therefore, the priestly office that Zacharias performed in the temple is called *leiturgia* (Luke 1:23). And in Hebrews 10:11, it says that every priest stands daily at his *leiturgōn*, that is, administering his priestly office. And in Romans 15:16, Paul calls himself the *leiturgos* of Jesus Christ.

Third, the term *leiturgia* is used to mean the care of the poor. This is the sense of its use in 2 Corinthians 9:12. In this article, it is clear that the meaning of *leiturgia* refers to that ministry which is performed by the preachers of the divine Word in God's house.

Section Two: In which the Definition of the Ecclesiastical Ministry is articulated and expounded, and the causes of the Ecclesiastical Ministry—Efficient, Material, Formal, and Final—are presented, explained, and articulated.

The ecclesiastical ministry is an office [*munus*] that is (1) holy, (2) public, (3) instituted by God, (4) and is carried out by apt men, (5) who are placed into the office by a legitimate call, so that, having been equipped with the peculiar power [of the office], they teach the Word of God, administer the Sacraments, intercede before God on behalf of the gathered flock, and exercise discipline as prescribed by the divine Word. In this way, (6) the glory of God and the eternal salvation of mankind is increased.

The individual parts of this definition will be explained and expounded. (1) We say that the ecclesiastical ministry is a holy office [*munus*]. Thus, it is distinguished from the political ministry or office. In what way the political and the ecclesiastical governments are distinguished according to their material, formal, and final causes, we have discussed and demonstrated in the article *Concerning the Church*, chapter I, section 3, where readers can inquire about those things belonging to each realm.

(2) We say that the ecclesiastical ministry is a public office. For although the Spirit of God calls each and every Christian a priest (1 Peter 2:9; Revelation 1:6), and lays on all Christians the priestly duty to incite one and another with exhortations to piety and works of charity (Hebrews 3:13; 10:25–26), to be ready to respond to anyone who asks for the reason of the hope that is in them, and to offer up to God sacrifices of prayer and a holy life (1 Peter 3:15; Romans 12:1), nevertheless there are

certain men who by means of a public authority [*publica auctoritate*] draw others to Christ, just as Paul says in Ephesians 4:11–12: "Christ gave some to be apostles, others to be prophets, evangelists, pastors and teachers, for joining together the saints, for the work of the ministry, for the edification of the body of Christ."

(3) The efficient cause of the ecclesiastical ministry is God the Father, the Son, and the Holy Spirit. To the Father, the institution and preservation of the ecclesiastical ministry are ascribed in these passages: Hebrews 1:1; Matthew 9:37–38; and Galatians 1:16.[29] To the Son, however, the Scriptures attribute the institution and preservation of the ecclesiastical ministry in the following witnesses: Matthew 10:1; Luke 9:1; Matthew 28:19; Mark 16:15; Ephesians 4:11; 1 Corinthians 12:18f.; John 20:21; and 1 Corinthians 1:17. And finally, it is ascribed to the Holy Spirit in the following passages, the office to call men to carry out sacred functions [*functiones sacras*]: Acts 20:28; 1 Corinthians 12:4–6; and 2 Peter 1:21. The ecclesiastical ministry is, therefore, entirely the work of the Most Holy Trinity.

(4) To the material cause of the ecclesiastical ministry belong fit persons and a legitimate call. When we say fit persons, we consider both a person's gender and gifts. When we say that fit persons are required for the ecclesiastical office, we certainly consider their sex, for only men should be admitted to this office. The instructions of St. Paul in 1 Corinthians 14:33–34 and 1 Timothy 2:11 are well known. We want this to be understood, however, according to the ordinary office [*munere*] of teaching. For we are not ignorant of Huldah, Deborah, and other women in the Old Testament with the gift of prophesy. In fact, Paul calls Priscilla a co-worker in the Lord in Romans 16:3. If it were a matter of the gifts that one possesses, which are required for the office, then any person could be said to be fit and could seize the ecclesiastical ministry. Nevertheless, we confess that this office is so majestic and lofty that scarcely anyone could invent it. Who can be said to be equipped with sufficient gifts for this office? Just as Paul says in 2 Corinthians 2:16, "Who is sufficient for these things?"[30] Chiefly, three things must be in place before one thinks himself worthy of the ecclesiastical office and ministry. First, it is required that he be orthodox or true concerning God and concerning divine matters or the meaning of the articles of the faith. We urge the following words of the Holy Spirit: Malachi 2:7; Matthew

---

[29] Brochmand gives the full citation for many of the passages in this section. Since they are uncommented biblical citations, only the Bible reference is given.

[30] Brochmand mistakenly cites 2 Corinthians 3:16.

13:52; 28:20; 2 Timothy 1:13 and 3:14–17. Second, for a person to be deemed worthy of the ecclesiastical office, he must be apt to teach the truth, to refute his adversaries, and to speak with boldness. To that end, we submit these testimonies from the Sacred Scriptures: 1 Timothy 3:2; 2 Timothy 2:24; Titus 1:9; Acts 4:29; and 2 Timothy 4:2. Third, for someone to be considered a person apt to be chosen for the ministry of the divine Word, it is necessary that they possess integrity of life. The Sacred Scriptures bear witness: 1 Timothy 3:2, 7; 4:12; Titus 1:7; 1 Peter 5:3; and 2 Thessalonians 3:9.

Consequently, these three qualifications, which have now been enumerated, are by necessity required before anyone can be considered a fit person, to whom the sacred ministry is committed.

(5) The formal cause of the ecclesiastical ministry also consists of three parts, namely, a legitimate call, holy ordination, and the administration of the holy office of teaching. First, belonging to the formal cause of the ecclesiastical ministry, is the call [*vocatio*]. Its necessity is confirmed by the testimonies of the Sacred Writings: Hebrews 5:4; Jeremiah 23:21; and Romans 10:15. Second, ordination is surely required for the ecclesiastical office. So it was for those seven deacons on whom hands were laid, as mentioned in Acts 6:6. And Paul was clearly called immediately by God, but was placed into the sacred office by the laying on of hands through Ananias (Acts 9:17). Timothy also is directed not to neglect the gift that he received through prophecy and by the laying on of hands (1 Timothy 4:14; 2 Timothy 1:6), and who is warned in 1 Timothy 5:22 not to lay hands on anyone quickly, lest you partake in someone else's sin. Third, it is required above all and is fitting of the sacred office that its administration be endowed with a peculiar and public authority, which can be comprehended in four ways: without doubt in the preaching of the divine Word (Matthew 28:19; 18:18;[31] Ephesians 2:20–21), in the right administration of the Sacraments in conformity with God's Word (Matthew 28:19–20; 1 Corinthians 11:23), in devoted intercession for the flock (Leviticus 5:6; 9:7; 12:7; James 5:14), and in the right use of ecclesiastical discipline (Matthew 18:17; John 20:23; 1 Corinthians 5:1–13).

(6) The final cause of the ecclesiastical ministry is, then, the glory of God and the salvation of man, as the Spirit of God teaches (Romans 1:16; 1 Corinthians 1:23–24; 2:6–16; James 1:18; 1 Peter 1:2–3). And thus we have explained, illustrated, and provided a strict definition of the ecclesiastical ministry.

---

[31] Brochmand has Matthew 15:15.

JOHANN GERHARD (1582–1637)

MORNING STAR AND ARCH-THEOLOGIAN OF LUTHERANISM

by Steven R. J. Parks

LIFE

Johann Gerhard[1] was born on October 17, 1582,[2] in the city of Quedlinburg, Germany. Recalling the idyllic setting of his childhood, Gerhard wrote:

---

[1] The majority of this biography is summarized from Erdmann Rudolph Fischer, *Vita Ioannis Gerhardi* (Leipzig: Coerner, 1723). Fischer carefully utilized Gerhard's own handwritten diary, as well as other early works on the life of Gerhard (e.g., those by Theophilus Spizel, Antony Reiser, Paul Freher, Johann Zeumer, Johann Wendler, et al.). Virtually all later biographies of Gerhard credit Fischer as their primary source (e.g., Carl Julius Böttcher, *Das Leben Dr. Johann Gerhard* [Leipzig and Dresden: Naumann, 1858], 1). More recent studies likewise acknowledge their reliance upon Fischer (e.g., Robert P.

> [Quedlinburg] is situated for the most part in the plains at the foot of the Harz Forest, and is watered by that most fertile and clear river called the Bode, whose spring is about four miles from the city. The climate in the neighborhood of the mountains and forest is also beneficial for a wholesome temperature, the ground is fertile for raising produce, hence it is impossible for the inhabitants to lack an abundance of wood, corn, fish, or any other supplies necessary for the upkeep of life.[3]

Johann's father, Bartholomäus, was the prefect of the senatorial treasury of the city.[4] His mother, Margareta (d. 1624), was the daughter of an aide of the municipality of Halberstadt.[5] Shortly before Johann was born, Bartholomäus ordered a servant to load his wagon with wood. However, the servant had been drinking and refused. Angered at his defiance, Bartholomäus hurled a wooden club at the servant. Despite his intoxication, he dodged the cudgel. Unfortunately, the weapon struck Margareta in the abdomen. Those who witnessed the event expected Johann to be born with severe defects. However, he was later born healthy and without incident. Bartholomäus and Margareta eventually had six other children: a son, Andreas, and five daughters, Catherine, Dorothea,[6] Salome, Anna, and Margareta.

Johann was baptized at just four days old with witnesses,[7] including the Consuls of Quedlinburg and Halberstadt. As Johann grew, his parents decided not to educate him in the home, as was often the custom of the time. Instead, they sent him to the public school of Quedlinburg. While all of the subjects that Gerhard studied as a young man have not been noted, he clearly excelled at both linguistics and biblical studies, even going so far as to produce a history of the life, death, and resurrec-

---

Scharlemann, *Thomas Aquinas and John Gerhard* [New Haven and London: Yale University Press, 1964], 16).

[2] Johann Gerhard, "Epistola Dedicatoria," in *Loci Theologici Cum Pro Adstruenda Veritate Tum Pro Destruenda Quorumvis Contradicentium Falsitate Per Theses Nervose Solide Et Copiose Explicati*, ed. Preuss (Berlin: Gust. Schlawitz, 1863–75), 1:xiv.

[3] Gerhard, *Loci*, 1:xiv–xv.

[4] Gerhard, *Loci*, 1:xiv–xv.

[5] Gerhard, *Loci*, 1:xiv–xv.

[6] Dorothea gave birth to Johann Andreas Quenstedt, making Gerhard the uncle of another of Lutheranism's greatest theologians (Johann Andreas Quenstedt, "Praefatio Ad Benignum Et Candidum Lectorem," in *Theologia Didactico-Polemica, Sive Systema Theologicum* [Leipzig: Fritsch, 1715], 5).

[7] It would appear that these were his godparents. Fischer refers to them both as "witnesses" as well as "sponsors." See Fischer, *Vita*, I, § 5, 8.

tion of Christ in both Greek and Latin verse between the ages of thirteen and fourteen.[8]

At the age of fifteen, Gerhard became deathly ill with tuberculosis and edema, which led to an extreme depression and a prolonged spiritual malaise.[9] Confined to his bed for a year, Gerhard rarely spoke, seldom slept, and ate only on occasion. In the midst of his illness, Gerhard penned the first of many devotional works—a small prayer book, which he regularly used and frequently soaked with his own tears.[10] "During this time Gerhard, as Luther before him, experienced deep pangs of conscience and desired the assurance of the forgiveness of sins and fellowship with God in Christ."[11] In his distress, Gerhard was visited by his family's pastor, Johann Arndt (1555–1621), whose aid and counsel delivered Gerhard from spiritual despair.[12] During his visits, Arndt frequently encouraged Gerhard to dedicate himself to the study of theology, which Johann vowed to do if God would grant him recovery.

While Gerhard did recover, the following year sickness once again laid hold of him. In 1598, a severe plague swept through the city of Quedlinburg, killing three thousand in just three weeks.[13] Gerhard contracted the disease and soon became very ill. Out of concern for her son, Margareta called for a doctor and gave Johann the maximum dose of the only medicine known to help those afflicted with the plague. Upon arriving, the doctor—who did not know that Gerhard's mother had already given her son medicine—administered a second dose. For several hours, Gerhard perspired a thick, yellow fluid, after which he showed major signs of recovery.

Though just seventeen years old, Gerhard enrolled at the famed University of Wittenberg in 1599. His instructors included the noted theologian Leonhard Hutter (1563–1616).[14] His studies would eventually take

---

[8] Fischer, *Vita,* II, § 5, 16.

[9] Fischer, *Vita,* II, § 5, 12–13.

[10] Fischer, *Vita,* II, § 2, q, 13.

[11] Gaylin R. Schmeling, "Johann Gerhard: Theologian and Pastor," in Johann Gerhard, *Sacred Meditations*, trans. Wade R. Johnston (Saginaw, MI: Magdeburg Press, 2008), 216.

[12] Throughout the remainder of his life, Gerhard maintained a close friendship and fatherly affection for Arndt, a fact which made him suspect in the eyes of some who severely criticized Arndt's *Von wahrem Christenthumb* for its mystical content. See Daniel R. van Voorhis, "A Prophet of Interior Lutheranism: The Correspondence of Johann Arndt" (PhD diss., University of St. Andrews, 2008), 30–31.

[13] Fischer, *Vita,* II, § 3, 14.

[14] Fischer, *Vita,* III, § 1, 18–19.

him to the universities of Marburg[15] and Jena. In these centers of learning, he studied such varied subjects as history, logic, ethics, mathematics, physics, anthropology, and medicine. In addition to these, he especially excelled in the study of philosophy and theology.

In the midst of these studies, on Christmas Day in 1603, Gerhard once again took ill. The sickness became so severe that within days he believed he would soon die. Thus, he began making preparations to depart this life, penning what he believed would be his final confession of faith along with his last will and testament. The confession demonstrates a keen awareness of Lutheran doctrine and carefully traces his beliefs regarding Scripture as the sole infallible rule of faith, the Trinity, creation *ex nihilo*, angels, demons, mankind's fall into sin, the two natures of Christ, the atonement, predestination, the proper distinction between Law and Gospel, divine monergism, justification through faith alone, Holy Baptism, the Lord's Supper, the resurrection of the dead, and the divine institutions of family, government, and the church.[16] He closes his confession by asking for forgiveness for ever having unintentionally engaged in flights of philosophical fancy or having unknowingly advocated heterodox doctrine.[17]

During this bout of sickness, Gerhard wrote what would eventually become the sixth in his series of *Sacred Meditations*, which reads, in part:

> It is Jesus himself, the very same who is my Judge, and in whose hands I am trembling with fear. Take courage then, O my soul, and despair not. Hope thou in him whom thou dost fear; flee thou to him for refuge, from whom thou hast fled in fear. O Jesus Christ, for thy name's sake, deal with me according to thy name. Mercifully regard me, a miserable sinner, as I

---

[15] In Marburg, he studied under such renowned Lutheran theologians as Johann Winckelmann, Balthasar Mentzer, and Johann Scholl. See Fischer, *Vita*, III, § 7, 38–39. Gerhard was ultimately forced to leave Marburg when the Landgrave of Hesse converted to Reformed Protestantism and replaced the theology faculty there with Reformed theologians. See Joachim Whaley, *Germany and the Holy Roman Empire* (Oxford: Oxford University Press, 2012), 1:459–60.

[16] Steiger notes that his "Testament" is a precursor both of his *Theological Commonplaces* (dogmatics) and of his many devotional writings, and that it is really a dogmatic theology "in a nutshell." See Johann Anselm Steiger, "Pastoral Care according to Johann Gerhard," *Lutheran Quarterly* 10, no. 3 (Autumn 1996): 322.

[17] For a complete reproduction of Gerhard's last will and testament, along with an excellent analysis thereof, see Johann Anselm Steiger, *Johann Gerhard (1582—1637): Studien zu Theologie und Frömmigkeit des Kirchenvaters der lutherischen Orthodoxie* (Stuttgart-Bad Cannstatt: Frommann-Holzboog Verlag, 1997), 159–227.

> call upon thy name. If thou shouldst admit me within the capacious bosom of thy compassion, it will not be the more straitened on my account. True is it, O Lord, that my participation in sin merits condemnation, and my penitence can never satisfy thee; but certain is it also that thy mercy exceeds all my offense. In thee, O Lord, do I put my trust, let me not be confounded forever.[18]

Gerhard labored under this sickness where nothing is said to have helped him except bloodletting.[19] After three weeks, he finally recovered.

By 1606, Gerhard had gained a sterling reputation among academics and clergy alike. In June, he was summoned to Coburg by the chancellor. Upon arrival, Gerhard was tasked with preaching a sermon before the royal court.[20] At the completion of his sermon, Gerhard was offered the office of bishop of Heldburg in the name of Duke Johann Casimir of Saxony-Coburg (1564–1633). Though Gerhard did not desire the office, the duke applied considerable pressure to Gerhard, leaving him little choice.[21] Thus, Gerhard reluctantly accepted the position and was ordained on August 24, 1606. His installation and investiture occurred on September 6, 1606.[22] He immediately returned to Jena to complete his dissertation and undergo examination by the faculty of theology. On November 11, 1606, Gerhard was awarded the degree of doctor of theology.

By all accounts, Gerhard administered the office of bishop faithfully. In addition to his regular ecclesiastical duties, he was charged with delivering monthly theological discourses at the Coburg *Gymnasium*. Over the course of the next three years, Gerhard's lectures covered virtually every major locus of Christian doctrine. While he had already made a beginning of writing, it was during his time as bishop that Gerhard authored a number of works, which would receive wide circulation and renown, including dogmatic works such as the first volumes of his *Theo-*

---

[18] Johann Gerhard, *Gerhard's Sacred Meditations*, trans. C. W. Heisler (Philadelphia: Lutheran Publication Society, 1896), 39. Cf. Johann Gerhard, "Sacred Meditations (1606)" in *Seventeenth-Century Lutheran Meditations and Hymns*, ed. Eric Lund (Mahwah, NJ: Paulist Press, 2011), 57.

[19] Fischer, *Vita,* III, § 6, 39.

[20] This was a testament to Gerhard's reputation, inasmuch as he had preached fewer than six sermons up until this point. Gerhard later urged students of theology to defer preaching until they had received at least four years of advanced theological study. See Johann Gerhard, *Methodus Studii Theologici* (Leipzig: Fuhrmann: 1654), III, § 4, 2, 200–201.

[21] Fischer, *Vita,* IV, § 1, 48–52.

[22] Fischer, *Vita,* IV, § 3, 54–56.

logical Commonplaces[23] and *A Comprehensive Explanation of Holy Baptism and the Lord's Supper*, exegetical works such as *An Explanation of the History of the Suffering and Death of our Lord Jesus Christ*, and materials of a more devotional nature, such as his *Handbook of Consolations for the Fears and Trials That Oppress Us in the Struggle with Death* and *The Daily Exercise of Piety*.

As part of his duties as bishop of Heldburg, and later of Coburg,[24] Gerhard regularly visited the congregations in his jurisdiction throughout the duchy in order to appraise their overall well-being. He also regularly visited the sick and infirm, even dispensing medical advice based upon his previous academic training. In addition to these visitations, Duke Johann Casimir frequently requested that Gerhard accompany him as ecclesiastical councilor during his diplomatic journeys. This, in particular, greatly taxed Gerhard's fragile health.[25]

In 1608, Gerhard made the decision to take a wife. While acquaintances offered to introduce him to suitable candidates, Gerhard preferred a young woman named Barbara Neumeier of Weimar. The two were engaged on April 29, 1608, and later married on September 19 that same year. Pondering the blessed union into which he was entering, Gerhard prayed: "Lord Jesus, who instituted marriage in the garden, who was present at the wedding at Cana, and who still today engages the hearts of spouses with the bond of chaste love, bless this my institution and grant a calm, durable, and fruitful marriage. Amen."[26]

On December 24, 1610, Johann and Barbara welcomed a son, Johann Georg. Sadly, the child took ill and died at just seventeen days old. Barbara became sick with tuberculosis almost immediately afterwards, though many believed she had simply lost her will to live after her son's death. She joined Johann Georg in death on May 30, 1611, leaving Gerhard bereft of wife and child alike. These were difficult times for Gerhard but were nevertheless instrumental in forming and shaping his faith in Christ. During this period, Gerhard penned his *Handbook of Consolations for the Fears and Trials That Oppress Us in the Struggle with Death*, a work which was no doubt beneficial to him as he struggled with

---

[23] The completion of which would ultimately earn Gerhard the title of "the founder of systematic dogmatics." See Adolf Hoenecke, *Evangelical Lutheran Dogmatics*, trans. James Langebartels and Heinrich Vogel (Milwaukee: Northwestern, 1999–2009), 1:12.

[24] On January 7, 1615, at the age of thirty-two, Gerhard was made bishop of Coburg.

[25] He already suffered with asthma, arthritis, fever, laryngitis, kidney trouble, and chronic fatigue. See Fischer, *Vita*, V, § 1–2, 68–79.

[26] Fischer, *Vita*, XIV, § 2, 252.

difficult questions, but which would also help countless other pastors in their ministry to the sick and dying. Gerhard wrote:

> Moreover, death recently made a very grievous visit to my house, and there are many other reasons why I should fear that my own life will not be long. Therefore, it is an appropriate time for me to strengthen and prepare my soul for that final contest . . . and when I saw that my meditations could perhaps be of some value to others, I did not oppose making them available to the public.[27]

The whole of the work is a contemplation of death—both Jesus' death and the Christian's own. Gerhard provided his rationale as follows:

> Indeed, the death of Christ and his suffering is the essence of Christianity. . . . By Christ's death our sins have been expiated, Satan's power destroyed, the New Covenant confirmed, and the fears we associate with our own death lessened. Contemplation of the death of Christ, therefore, ought never to recede from our memory. Nor should our own death be forgotten at any time during our own life. As death awaits us every day, let us likewise expect it every day.[28]

Several years later, on July 13, 1614, Gerhard would happily marry again, this time to Maria Mattenberg of Gotha. Theirs was a long and fruitful marriage, yielding ten children: Georg Sigismund, Margareta, Elisabeth, Johann Ernst, Johann, Maria, Polycarp, Johann Friedrich, Johann Andreas, and Anna Christina.

As early as 1611, the University of Jena had sought to call Gerhard to serve as professor of theology. Duke Casimir, however, continually thwarted their attempts.[29] Nevertheless, in October of 1615, Gerhard was once again called to serve in the University of Jena, this time at the behest of Elector Johann George of Saxony. Reluctantly, Duke Casimir agreed to release Gerhard from his episcopal duties on January 31, 1616, giving Gerhard enough time to complete his final round of visitations and name a suitable successor.

---

[27] Johann Gerhard, *Handbook of Consolations for the Fears and Trials That Oppress Us in the Struggle with Death*, trans. Carl L. Beckwith (Eugene: Wipf and Stock, 2009), 5. Used by permission of Wipf and Stock Publishers. www.wipfandstock.com.

[28] Gerhard, *Handbook of Consolations*, 3. Used by permission of Wipf and Stock Publishers. www.wipfandstock.com.

[29] Duke Casimir argued that it was immoral to "enrich and adorn one altar by plundering another." See Fischer, *Vita,* V, § 4, 84–85.

Gerhard began teaching in Jena as professor of theology in 1616. During his tenure as professor, Gerhard proved to be an extremely influential professor,[30] teaching theology, polemics, exegesis, and ethics, among other subjects.[31] While there were many who excelled at one of the theological disciplines, Gerhard was highly regarded in every field as a man of unparalleled skill and erudition. Summing up the popular impression of Gerhard's contemporaries, Matthias Hoë von Hoenegg (1580–1645), Electoral Saxon chief court preacher, regularly addressed his letters to the theologian as follows:

> The most worthy and deserved arch-theologian, standard-bearer of the theologians, light and support of the Christian republic, the primary theologian of our age, theologian concerning whom this world has no peer, leader of theologians, morning star of theologians, adornment of theologians.[32]

With such accolades from colleagues,[33] it is no wonder that Gerhard was a highly sought-after professor who received no fewer than twenty-four other calls to the various universities of Europe during his lifetime.[34] His popularity was such that Johann Michael Dilherr (1604–99), a fellow professor at Jena, observed: "In the European world, there is no Protestant academy, no church of any famed city which has not sought the illumination of this lamp of Thuringia and which has not called to itself this principal name of Europe with the offer of a liberal salary."[35] This admiration of Gerhard, however, was not peculiar to theologians of the Augsburg Confession. Fischer noted: "Johann Gerhard, the Evangelical Lutheran theologian, is so well known to teachers of the things of God, both those initiated into our sacred rites as well as those inducted into others, that

---

[30] His students included such luminaries as Michael Walther, Salomon Glassius, Johann Konrad Dannhauer, and Balthasar Mentzer II. See Fischer, *Vita,* VII, § 5, 117–19.

[31] Fischer offers a complete list of the courses Gerhard taught from 1616 until his death in 1637. See Fischer, *Vita,* VI, § 3, 100–103.

[32] Fischer, *Vita,* XVIII, § 2, 356.

[33] Fischer dedicates an entire chapter to the accolades heaped upon Gerhard from his Lutheran contemporaries. See Fischer, *Vita,* XIII, §§ 1–25, 184–250.

[34] Gerhard received dozens of invitations to serve in both ecclesiastical and academic positions throughout his lifetime, including calls to the Universities of Giessen, Prague, Altdorf, Wittenberg, Helmstedt, Leipzig, Strassburg, Uppsala, and Marburg. See Fischer, *Vita,* XIII, § 1, 184–85.

[35] Fischer, *Vita,* XIII, § 6, 184.

neither party places anyone ahead of him, and there are few thought his equal."[36]

This claim was no empty boast.[37] The radical pietist Gottfried Arnold (1666–1714), who criticized Gerhard for his insistence upon pure doctrine as well as his persistent polemics, nevertheless conceded that Gerhard was rightly prized for his "great erudition and sharp intellect,"[38] making him "the principal Lutheran theologian."[39] The eminent Roman Catholic bishop and theologian Jacques-Bénige Bossuet (1627–1704) referred to Gerhard as "the third man of the Reformation after Luther and Chemnitz."[40] For these and other reasons, Fischer places Gerhard second in influence only to Luther, even before Chemnitz in some respects.[41]

Gerhard's reputation as the preeminent Lutheran theologian, however, came at great cost. He toiled with such fervor: "He broke himself with these so that, when he was mature at that age when others are most vigorous, his physical strength had already become scarce."[42] On August 12, 1637, Gerhard contracted a fever. In a matter of days, his capacity to speak diminished, his eyesight dimmed, his hearing faded, and his breathing became labored. On August 17, 1637, Gerhard uttered his final words, "Come, come, Lord,"[43] before dying at three in the afternoon. Reflecting upon the death of such a beloved figure, Dilherr lamented: "the academy has not lost a doctor, but the doctors have lost the academy."[44]

Gerhard was survived by his second wife, Maria, and six of their ten children. His funeral text was 2 Corinthians 12:9, a text from which Gerhard had drawn significant encouragement: "But he said to me, 'My grace is sufficient for you, for my power is made perfect in weakness.' Therefore, I will boast all the more gladly of my weaknesses, so that the power of Christ may rest upon me" (ESV). Johann Gerhard, the morning

---

[36] Fischer, *Vita,* I, § 1, 1–3.

[37] Fischer devoted an entire chapter to praises heaped upon Gerhard from his theological adversaries. See Fischer, *Vita,* XVIII, §§ 1–4, 355–71.

[38] Fischer, *Vita,* XVI, § 3, 307.

[39] Fischer, *Vita,* XVI, § 3, 307.

[40] Fischer, *Vita,* XVIII, § 4, 370. This is, perhaps, the origin of the Lutheran adage: "Gerhard is the third in that series of Lutheran theologians (Luther, Chemnitz, and Gerhard) in which there is no fourth." See Heinrich Schmid, *The Doctrinal Theology of the Evangelical Lutheran Church*, trans. Charles Hay and Henry Jacobs (Philadelphia: Lutheran Publication Society, 1876), 675.

[41] Fischer, *Vita,* VII, § 2, 113.

[42] Fischer, *Vita,* XVII, § 1, 355.

[43] Fischer, *Vita,* XVII, § 8, 350.

[44] Fischer, *Vita,* VI, § 2, 99.

star and arch-theologian of Lutheranism, whose work is said to "tower above the whole galaxy of theologians who have appeared in Lutheranism since the Reformation,"[45] was laid to rest at St. Michael's Church in Jena on August 20, 1637; his epitaph read: "Here lies Piety, Honesty, Sincerity and Johann Gerhard. Such praise befits him, and that is enough."[46]

BIBLIOGRAPHY

Works by Gerhard in English Translation

A Christian Mans Weekes Worke. Or The Dayly Watch of the Soule. Translated by Richard Bruch. London: Snodham, 1611.

A Comprehensive Explanation of Holy Baptism and the Lord's Supper (1610). Translated by Elmer Hohle. Edited by David Berger. Malone, TX: Repristination Press, 2000.

A Golden Chaine of Divine Aphorisms. Translated by Ralph Winterton. Cambridge: Buck and Daniel, 1632.

A Handbook of Consolations for the Fears and Trials That Oppress Us in the Struggle with Death. Translated by Carl L. Beckwith. Eugene, OR: Wipf & Stock, 2009.

An Explanation of the History of the Suffering and Death of our Lord Jesus Christ. Translated by Elmer M. Hohle. Malone, TX: Repristination Press, 1999.

Annotations on the First Six Chapters of St. Paul's Epistle to the Romans. Translated by Paul A. Rydecki. Malone, TX: Repristination Press, 2014.

Annotations on the Revelation of St. John the Theologian. Translated by Paul A. Rydecki. Bynum, TX: Repristination Press, 2016.

Gerhard's Meditations and Prayers. Translated by Ralph Winterton. Cambridge: University of Cambridge, 1627.

Meditations on Divine Mercy: A Classic Treasury of Devotional Prayers. Translated by Matthew C. Harrison. St. Louis: Concordia, 2003.

---

[45] Herman A. Preus and Edmund Smits, eds., *The Doctrine of Man in the Writings of Martin Chemnitz and Johann Gerhard*, trans. Mario Colacci, Lowell Satre, J. A. O. Preus Jr., Otto Stahlke, and Bert H. Narveson (St. Louis: Concordia, 2005), vi.

[46] Fischer, *Vita*, XVII, § 9, 351.

On the Legitimate Interpretation of Holy Scripture. Translated by Richard J. Dinda. Malone, TX: Repristination Press, 2015.

Postilla: An Explanation of the Sunday and Most Important Festival Gospels of the Whole Year. Translated by Elmer M. Hohle and O. Marc Tanger. Edited by Heidi D. Sias. 4 vols. Malone, TX and Fort Wayne, IN: The Center for the Study of Lutheran Orthodoxy, Repristination Press, and Lutheran Legacy, 2003–12.

Sacred Meditations. Translated by C. W. Heisler. Philadelphia, PA: Lutheran Publication Society, 1896.

Sacred Meditations. Translated by Wade R. Johnston. Saginaw, MI: Magdeburg Press, 2008.

"Sacred Meditations (1606)." In *Seventeenth-Century Lutheran Meditations and Hymns*, edited and translated by Eric Lund, 39–179. New York: Paulist Press, 2011.

Schola Pietatis. Translated by Elmer M. Hohle. Edited by Rachel Melvin. 3 vols. Malone, TX: Repristination Press, 2006–15.

"School of Piety or the Practice of Godliness (1622)." In *Seventeenth-Century Lutheran Meditations and Hymns*, edited and translated by Eric Lund, 180–206. New York: Paulist Press, 2011.

The Christian's Support Under All Afflictions: Being the Divine Meditations of John Gerhard. Translated by Thomas Rowell. London: Curll and Sanger, 1709.

The Daily Exercise of Piety. Translated by Matthew C. Harrison. Malone, TX: Repristination Press, 1998.

The Soules Watch: or, A Day-Booke for the Deuout Soule. Translated by Richard Bruch. London: Purslowe, 1621.

The Summe of Christian Doctrine. Translated by Ralph Winterton. Cambridge: Daniel, 1640.

Theological Commonplaces: Exegesis, or A More Copious Explanation of Certain Articles of the Christian Religion (1625) On the Nature of God and On the Most Holy Mystery of the Trinity. Translated by Richard J. Dinda. Edited by Benjamin T. G. Mayes. St. Louis: Concordia, 2007.

Theological Commonplaces: Exegesis, or A More Copious Explanation of Certain Articles of the Christian Religion (1625) On the Nature of

Theology and On Scripture. Translated by Richard J. Dinda. Edited by Benjamin T. G. Mayes. St. Louis: Concordia, 2009.

Theological Commonplaces: Exegesis, or A More Copious Explanation of Certain Articles of the Christian Religion (1625) On the Person and Office of Christ. Translated by Richard J. Dinda. Edited by Benjamin T. G. Mayes. St. Louis: Concordia, 2009.

Theological Commonplaces: On Creation and Angels, On Providence, On Election and Reprobation, and on the Image of God in Man before the Fall. Translated by Richard J. Dinda. Edited by Benjamin T. G. Mayes and Joshua J. Hayes. St. Louis: Concordia, 2010.

Theological Commonplaces: On Original Sin, On Actual Sins, and On Free Choice. Translated by Richard J. Dinda. Edited by Benjamin T. G. Mayes and Heath R. Curtis. St. Louis: Concordia, 2014.

Theological Commonplaces: On the Church. Translated by Richard J. Dinda. Edited by Benjamin T. G. Mayes. St. Louis: Concordia, 2010.

Theological Commonplaces: On the Ecclesiastical Ministry, Part One. Translated by Richard J. Dinda. Edited by Benjamin T. G. Mayes. St. Louis: Concordia, 2011.

Theological Commonplaces: On the Ecclesiastical Ministry, Part Two. Translated by Richard J. Dinda. Edited by Benjamin T. G. Mayes and Heath R. Curtis. St. Louis: Concordia, 2012.

Theological Commonplaces: On the Law of God, On the Ceremonial and Forensic Laws. Translated by Richard J. Dinda. Edited by Benjamin T. G. Mayes and Joshua J. Hayes. St. Louis: Concordia, 2015.

Theological Commonplaces: On the Nature of Theology and Scripture. Second Edition. Translated by Richard J. Dinda. Edited by Benjamin T. G. Mayes. St. Louis: Concordia, 2009.

Select Works by Gerhard in German and Latin

Ausführliche schriftmässige Erklärung der beiden Artikel von der heiligen Taufe und dem heiligen Abendmahl. Jena: Steinmann, 1610.

Enchiridion Consolatorium Morti ac Tentionibus in Agone Mortis Opponendum. Jena: Steinmann, 1611.

Erklaerung der Historien des Leidens und Strebens unsers Herrn Iesu Christi. Jena: Steinmann, 1611.

Exegesis sive Uberior Explicatio Articulorum de Scriptura Sacra, de Deo et de Persona Christi. Jena: Steinmann, 1625.

Exercitium Pietatis Quotidianum Quadripartitum. Coburg: Hauck, 1612.

In Harmoniam Historiae Euangelicae de Passione, Crucifixione, Morte et Sepultura Christi Saluatoris Nostri, ex Quatuor Euangelistis Contextam. Jena: Steinmann, 1617.

Confessio Catholica: In Qua Doctrina Catholica et Evangelica, Quam Ecclesiæ Augustanæ Confessioni Addictæ Profitentur, ex Romano-Catholicorum Scriptorum Suffragiis Confirmatur. Jena: Steinmann, 1634–37.

Loci Theologici. Jena: Steinmann, 1610–22.

Meditationes Sacrae. Leipzig, 1606.

Methodus Studii Theologici. Jena: Steinmann, 1620.

Postilla, das ist, Erklaerung der Sonntaeglichen und Führnehmsten Fest-Evangelien das gantze Jahr. Jena: Steinmann, 1613.

Schola Pietatis. Jena: Steinmann, 1622–23.

Tractatus de Legitima Interpretation Scripturae Sacrae. Jena: Steinmann, 1610.

WRITING[47]

To the most serene and most high prince and lord Lord Christian II, elector and arch-marshall of the Holy Roman Empire, duke of Saxony, Jülich, Kleve, and Berg; landgrave of Thuringia; marquis of Meissen; burgrave of Magdeburg; count in Mark and Ravensberg; lord in Ravenstein; to my most clement elector and lord, I pray the perpetual grace of God, perennial tranquility of rule, eternal health of body and soul.

Most serene elector, most high prince, most clement lord! Cassian famously writes (*De Incarnat.*, bk. 1), "When sickness is resurgent, never should the medicine be delayed, but the greater the illness, just so much more steadfastly is the cure sought after." Doubtless, the mystical Body of Christ once struggled with the grave illness of various heresies. The Church, I say, was most severely oppressed in earlier centuries by Arians, Photinians, Nestorians, Eutychians, and other monsters of the same sort,

[47] Johann Gerhard, "Dedicatory Epistle to Christian II of Saxony," in *On the Nature of Theology and on Scripture,* translated by H. R. Curtis, edited by Benjamin T. G. Mayes (St. Louis: Concordia, 2009), 1–6.

but when a cure was provided by the Chief Shepherd and Doctor through the patronage of very devout rulers and faithfully teaching doctors—especially Athanasius, Cyril, Augustine, Vigilius, and other ministers—then the Church, freed from these infections and with her health secured, obtained strength.

But, indeed, that same sickness is resurgent today; the infernal dragon breathes out the same infectious virus, even today, from his own throat. Indeed, how I could obscure differences [in doctrine] in a cloud of silence! Nevertheless, these differences are all erroneous opinions. By means of [such obscuring clouds] a great many proclaimed that Nestorianism and Eutychianism themselves were united in the Church by way of reconciliation. But do those more recent [heretics] not threaten a great infection, whether they be Samosatenes or Photinians (whom the public calls Neo-Arians)? [Indeed,] the former are worse and more pestilent by far than the latter! Shall the healing hand stop here? Shall we stand by in silence and watch a great many members of the Church be snatched up by this wild infection and given over to eternal death? . . .

Therefore, let us continue. When the subsistence[48] of the Son of God with the Father from eternity is denied, at once his divine nature is denied; when the divine nature of the Son is denied, the mystery of the most holy Trinity is denied; denied also is the eternal person of the Holy Spirit, co-essential with both Father and Son. Furthermore, when the divine nature of Christ is denied, the entire mystery of our redemption and satisfaction supplied through Christ is denied. For the Passion and death of a mere man could not have been a sufficient ransom for the sins of the world; the obedience of a mere man could not have promised justification and salvation to the others; the blood of a mere man could not have extinguished the fire of the divine wrath. "If our sins," says Dr. Luther in *De conc. et eccles.*, German Jena Edition, volume 7, p. 264, "and the wrath of God owed against our sins were stacked on one pan [of a scale] and in another were placed the death of only a human nature, or if only a man had suffered for our sins, then the first pan would sink us down to the lowest hell. But if, indeed, in the opposite pan the Passion of God were placed, the death of God, God's blood, or were God to suffer and die for us, then this pan would become heavier and more weighty than all our sins and the entire wrath of God."

Furthermore, when the satisfaction for our sins supplied by Christ is denied, all that remains is to hope to achieve salvation through the merits of our own works, for no other way of salvation exists. When the merit of

[48] That is, *hypostasis*, person.

our works is set forth, the perfect and in all particulars absolute completion of the divine Law is established. When the perfect completion of the Law by ourselves is set forth, the article concerning gratuitous justification through faith in Christ is overturned. "For if it is by works, then it is no longer by grace" (Romans 11:6). When the foundation of gratuitous justification is undermined and, on the other hand, the merits of our works and the perfect completion of the Law are established, the powers of the free will are claimed to be whole and complete in every way. When the well-being of free will is established, original sin and the propagation of the same in the descendants of Adam is denied; when original sin is denied, the power of Baptism is denied, and this sacred washing is transformed into a mere external rite devoid of any spiritual efficacy. Finally, when the divine nature of Christ is denied, denied also is the true communion of his own saving body and blood in the Holy Supper, nor could the flesh of a mere man be eaten except in a Capernaitic gnawing, much less could the flesh be life-giving. But the flesh of Christ is life-giving because of this: "Because it is the Word's own flesh, having power to vivify all things," as the Council of Ephesus, [anathema] 11, rightly declared.

Yet when the satisfaction for our sins that is provided through Christ is denied, when the merit of Christ is denied, when the gratuitous justification through faith in Christ is denied, when the efficaciousness of Baptism is denied, when the presence of Christ's body and blood in the Supper is denied, what of hope (I ask), what of consolation, indeed, what of salvation is left for us miserable people? Nevertheless all those Photinians baldly and without any euphemism or whitewash propose, spread, and defend in public writings these monstrous ravings—for they are ravings more than errors—that completely overturn the very foundation of salvation. They recently have arrived at such a state of audacity and impudence that they were not afraid to dedicate a certain catechism published at Racovia to the illustrious academy at Wittenberg and to send and commend the same to the most high Senate of Gotha.

Here and now the bars of that religious silence that orthodox teachers, not without reason, have used up till now must be burst. Here and now, with all force, we must stand in the way of their raving. Here and now, the healing hand must be applied, and with as much zeal as is possible that poisonous crop must be crushed underfoot at the first weed.

Although others might be aware of my inadequacy, I am just as conscious of it. Nor does it escape me that other theologians with whom I ought not be compared in any way in matters of erudition, authority, and experience train in this palaestra and, indeed, will continue training further. Nevertheless I, too, wish to bestow my own little contribution for the use of the Church. Therefore, offering a series of disputations in this first volume, I intend to argue widely against the Photinians and, indeed, against their first lie, with which they attack the eternal generation of the Word from the Father and His personal subsistence. That reverend and most celebrated man, Lord Friedrich Baldwin, the exceptional doctor of theology, professor of the same at the Academy of Wittenberg, and superintendent of the church there, my lord and singularly honorable friend, kindly added the following words of public judgment concerning my little scribbles in his own writings and spurred me on to this task not a little: "In your most holy work you neglect nothing worth examining in the Racovian Catechism concerning the teaching of others; so continue and bring this treatise to public light as quickly as possible, and you will make a work pleasing to God and useful to the Church of Christ, moreover one that is honorable for yourself and salutary for those who either hear or read you." So far his words. I wanted to place these words, which appear in his own hand on the frontispiece shield of this writing, before all disparagers. . . .

Take up, therefore, Most Serene Elector, Most Clement Lord, this writing, which I present as a small gift, and open it, so that some light might be procured for this little work from the splendor of the name that has been current among all men for a long time now because of the proven zeal for heavenly truth, the singular specimens of magnificent munificence in the churches and schools, the provident conservation of public peace, the sincere administration of justice, and the other heroic virtues worthy for the Elector, Your Most Serene Highness. [Take it up also] that even more men may be incited to unfurl its scroll.

May our God, who is mightily exalted among the shields of the earth (Psalm 47:[9]), give to Your Most Serene Highness long life, secure rule, a safe home, powerful armies, a faithful senate, an upright populace, a peaceful world, and whatever things constitute the wishes of a man and prince (with which words they were accustomed to supplicate God for the health of the emperors in the Early Church, as Tertullian bears witness, *Apolog.*, c. 30).

Written at Heldburg on the first of April, 1610,
to Your Most Serene Highness,
from your most humble subject,
Johann Gerhard, doctor

SALOMON GLASS (1593–1656)

A LEARNED PHILOLOGIST IN THE EPISCOPAL OFFICE

by Armin Wenz

LIFE

Gottlieb Theophil Spitzel (1639–91) in his *Templum Honoris*, a collection of biographies of theologians from the age of Lutheran Orthodoxy, calls Salomon Glass a *sacer philologus* (sacred philologist).[1] This nicely summarizes Glass's theological approach. For theological reasons,

[1] Gottlieb Theophil Spitzel, *Templum Honoris* (Augsburg: Gottlieb Goebel, 1673), 218. For more biographical details, see: Christoph Brumhorst, "Lebens-Lauff," printed after the funeral sermon delivered for Glass on July 29, 1656, and included in the *Selecta Scripturae Divinae Mosaicae Süsser Kern und Außzug Oder Geistreiche und Heylsame Betrachtung der vornehmsten Lehr-reichen Geschichten/ Dinge und Sprüche in den Büchern Mosis begriffen* (Nuremberg: Endter, 1657), 32–48 of the appendix; Michael Walther, "Oratio parentalis," a memorial lecture in Latin, which was delivered in Celle by the Superintendent of Celle and Lüneburg on September 12, 1656 (pages 49–73 of the appendix of the *Selecta Mosaicae*); Spitzel, *Templum Honoris*, 218–26.

every minister of the Gospel of Christ necessarily has to be a philologist, someone in love with the Word of God,[2] both in its written form, which is the foundation of his ministry, and in its oral form, which is the focus of his ministry. This love includes and shapes the love of the pastor for his flock; the husband and father for his family; the theological teacher for his students; and the husband, pastor, and professor for the pious rulers of his home territory. Glass, in fulfilling his duties in these orders, produced outstanding literary fruits without ever losing his deep humility, which was formed by the very Word of God that was his constant comfort in the temptations he suffered.

Glass was born in the town of Sondershausen in Thuringia on Rogate Sunday, May 20, 1593. His grandparents, Georg and Barbara Glass, were pious people of humble origins. His father, Balthasar Glass, served as secretary for the counts of Schwarzburg-Sondershausen. His mother, Anna Maria, was born in Eisleben. She was the daughter of Heinrich Müller, councilor for the principality of Braunschweig, and his wife, Anna née Milwitz. Salomon was baptized one day after his birth. Salomon Blattner, the chancellor of Schwarzburg-Sondershausen, served as his godfather. Young Salomon was homeschooled by his parents and later by a home tutor who taught him the fundamentals of Latin and Greek. From 1608 to 1610, Glass attended school in Arnstadt, where he studied under the principal Martin Coco. In 1610, his father sent him to the Gotha *Gymnasium*. Two years later, the rector, Andreas Wilk, recommended sending Salomon to the university. His school certificate attests to Salomon's outstanding literacy in the languages, in the rhetorical art of disputation and declamation, his piety, manners, humility, diligence, and loyalty.

Glass enrolled at the University of Jena on April 27, 1612, and studied under the guidance of Professor Wolfgang Heider, who was a relative of his father. Heider (1588–1626), Thomas Sagitarrius (1577–1621), and Michael Wolff (1584–1623) were his philosophy professors. Johannes Gryphiander (1580–1652) gave him private lectures "in Politicis" (politics) because Glass had desired to study law for a period of time. Daniel Stahl (1589–1654) was his professor of logic, metaphysics, and physics. In May 1615, Glass continued his studies in Wittenberg, but now with a clear theological focus. His teachers, Leonhard Hütter (1563–1616), Friedrich Balduin (1575–1627), Wolfgang Franz (1564–1628), and Balthasar Meisner II (1587–1626), were among the most famous Lutheran theologians of those days. During this time, Glass delivered his first

[2] See Armin Wenz, "The Doctrine of the Ministry in Salomon Glassius," *Concordia Theological Quarterly* 78, no. 1 (2014): 319–46.

sermon in a village near Wittenberg, reportedly with a frail appearance and a weak voice. His weak voice remained a source of temptation. Salomon wondered whether he really should become a pastor. The situation grew worse when he suffered from a fever for almost half a year. Only after his return to Jena in April 1616 did he recover and was able to continue his studies.

Upon the recommendation of Count Anton Heinrich of Schwarzburg (1571–1638), Glass was received into the household of Johann Gerhard (1582–1637) together with Polycarp Leyser's I (1552–1610) sons, Friedrich (1590–1645) and Wilhelm (1592–1649). For a period of five years, he shared his life with his famous teacher, attended his public and private lectures, and conducted eight academic disputations under him. For two years, Salomon had the privilege of using Gerhard's study and enjoyed conversations with his teacher as well as the use of his immense library. On the occasion of the hundredth anniversary of the Reformation in 1617, Glass earned the first academic place among thirty masters of theology and became an adjunct teacher at the philosophy department in May 1619. Besides holding public disputations, his main task was to teach Hebrew. He earned his theological licentiate with a lecture on Isaiah 63 and a public disputation on John 17 in 1621 over which Professor Johann Major (1564–1654) presided. From 1621 to 1625, Glass served as professor of Hebrew and Greek, succeeding Balthasar Walther (1586–1640) who was called to be superintendent in Gotha. In 1625, Bartholomäus Bermel (1579–1625), the superintendent of Glass's home territory of Sondershausen, passed away. After so many years of support from his home duchy, Glass felt obliged to follow the call to serve as superintendent of Sondershausen. He was installed on November 17, 1625, and served in this episcopal office until 1638. Nevertheless, he earned his academic merits in January 1626, when he was promoted to a *Doctor Theologiae* (doctor of theology) under Johann Himmel (1581–1642), the rector of the university, and Johann Gerhard, the dean of the faculty. In the same process, his brother Balthasar (1596–1666) received his promotion as a medical doctor and became the court's head physician.

The next change in Glass's career took place when Johann Gerhard passed away in 1637. It was Gerhard's desire that Glass should become his successor as professor of theology in Jena. Since Duke Ernst the Pious of Sachsen-Gotha (1601–75) already had observed Glass's academic excellence in his work on the Electors' Bible, he was willing to follow Gerhard's last will. Thus for a very short period of two and a half years, Glass again joined the academic realm and became professor at Jena in

March 1638. He presided over sixty disputations and lectured on the epistles to the Romans and to the Corinthians. In addition, he served as dean of the faculty and as rector of the university during this period. Only two years later, in October 1640, Glass took a second, and this time definite, leave from the university. Duke Ernst had called him to be general superintendent at Gotha in order to restore ecclesial life in his duchy after the turmoil of the Thirty Years' War (1618–48).[3] Glass remained in this episcopal office until his death on July 27, 1656.

Glass's main focus during this last period of his life was the support of the liturgical life of the parishes and the improvement of the school system, which was considered fundamental for the well-being of the church and the state. To facilitate this end, Glass conducted three general visitations of the whole duchy and a visitation of the University of Jena in 1644. He also presided over a synod in 1645. Whereas his groundbreaking theological hermeneutics *Sacred Philology* (*Philologia Sacra*) was published already before 1640, Glass was able to publish many more theological works at his last position in Gotha. Most of these focus on homiletical, catechetical, and pastoral aspects of theology.

Glass's first wife, Elisabeth, was the daughter of one of Germany's most famous publishers, Tobias Steinmann from Jena. Steinmann had edited works by Martin Luther and Johann Gerhard. The wedding took place in Jena on November 19, 1621. The young couple was blessed with the birth of three boys and three girls. Johann Tobias passed away at the age of eleven, Johann Salomon at the age of twelve, Anton Heinrich at the age of two. Only the daughters lived into adulthood. Barbara was married twice and gave birth to three girls from her first husband and one boy from her second husband. Glass's second daughter, Clara Elisabeth, married Johann Hattenbach who served as pastor in Unterneubronn and Goldbach. Four more grandchildren resulted from this marriage. Glass's third daughter, Anna Maria, remained unmarried and took care of her father at the end of his life. In September 1638, Glass's first wife, Elisabeth, passed away after seventeen blessed years of matrimony. Two years later and only one month after his installation in Gotha, in November 1640, Glass married Catharina Maria, widow of the ducal court lawyer, Georg Mylius. Another daughter, Elisabeth Sophia, was born. After less than three years, Catharina Maria died in July 1643, leaving behind a

---

[3] See Veronika Albrecht-Birkner, *Reformation des Lebens: Die Reformen Herzog Ernsts des Frommen von Sachsen-Gotha und ihre Auswirkungen auf Frömmigkeit, Schule und Alltag im ländlichen Raum (1640–1675)*, Leucorea-Studien zur Geschichte der Reformation und der lutherischen Orthodoxie, no. 1 (Leipzig: Evangelische Verlagsanstalt, 2002).

devastated two-time widower. After a period of solitude, Glass married his third wife, Maria née Klein, from Eisenach in August 1647, who had been a two-time widow herself and who would survive her third husband, Salomon. Having had health problems throughout his life, the situation worsened in 1649. Glass was not able to preach anymore due to his lung problems. Nevertheless, he never stopped writing. He passed away while working on a commentary on the Psalms. The last verse he wrote upon when he died was Psalm 34:22: "The Lord redeems the life of his servants; none of those who take refuge in him will be condemned."

When we turn to Glass's theological works, an important aspect of his disposition has to be mentioned. This aspect, which shaped Glass as a theologian, is his relationship to Johann Gerhard. Even after Gerhard's death, Glass never stopped venerating his friend as his most eminent teacher und mentor. This became most visible at the beginning and at the end of his short period as member of the theological faculty of Jena, both in his inaugural address from April 1638 and in his farewell address from October 1640. In his inaugural lecture on Psalm 110 (published under the title: *Davidic Christology* [*Christologia Davidica*]), he praised Gerhard as the Augustine of the orthodox Lutheran Church.[4] Moreover, he praised him as his personal Augustine, identifying himself with Augustine's favorite student, Eradius.[5] Glass saw himself as the one who was to fulfill the theological legacy of Johann Gerhard. This consciousness was a constant motif throughout his career. It started with the cooperation of the two theologians on the Weimar Electors' Bible, to which thirty theologians contributed verse-by-verse commentaries on the biblical books. Gerhard served as organizing editor and as main theological proofreader until his death in 1637, when this task was also laid into the hands of Glass. Glass's preface to this Bible, which is a basic exposition of the Lutheran doctrine of Scripture and hermeneutics, was dated the hundred and tenth anniversary of the Augsburg Confession.[6] This is another reminder regarding the intimate connection between the scriptural principle and the confessional obligation, which for Gerhard, Glass, and the

---

[4] "GERHARDUS mihi, imo toti Academiae, imo Ecclesiae orthodoxae universae, AUGUSTINUS est." See *Christologia Davidica, ex Ps. CX. conscripta* (Jena: Steinmann 1678), 78.

[5] "Est igitur Gerhardus mihi Augustinus: sim ego ipsi, sim & vobis, auditores honoratissimi, Eradius." See *Christologia Davidica, ex Ps. CX. conscripta*, 79.

[6] For an exposition of this preface, including details on the renaissance of the Weimar Bible in the nineteenth-century LCMS and C. F. W. Walther's reception of the preface, see: Armin Wenz, "Biblische Hermeneutik im Spiegel der Vorreden der 'Weimarer Kurfürstenbibel' aus drei Jahrhunderten," *Lutherische Beiträge* 20, no. 1 (2015): 26–50.

territory of Sachsen-Gotha, also included the Formula of Concord. Furthermore, it can be shown that Glass, with his five-volume hermeneutical text, *Philologia Sacra*, brought the hermeneutical thinking of his teacher Gerhard, along with his predecessors like Luther (1483–1546), Melanchthon (1497–1560), Chemnitz (1522–86), Flacius (1520–75), and others into systematic completion. It was Glass who finally succeeded in elaborating a concise clarification of the complex relationship between the *sensus literalis* (literal sense) and the *sensus spiritualis seu figuralis* (spiritual or figural sense) of the Scriptures.[7] After having laid the systematic foundation of his hermeneutics early in his life in the *Philologia Sacra*, his main goal was to apply these insights in the field of practical theology for the church. Not only his commentaries on the Psalms and the Solomonic books (especially the Song of Songs) in the Weimar Bible served this purpose, but also his edifying book *Tree of Life* (*Arbor Vitae*)[8] and his four-volume *Prophetic Utterance-Postil* (*Prophetische Spruch=Postill*).[9]

The latter was published between 1642 and 1654. It was based on sermons Glass preached in Gotha. Glass refrained from the customary practice of preaching on the Gospels in order to preach on prophetic texts. Still, he did not ignore the Gospels of the respective holy days, but rather compared both texts with each other and applied them for the benefit of his hearers. For most Sundays and holy days, Glass presented two sermons on two different prophetic texts. These postils show how Glass's hermeneutical insights into the figurative dimensions of the biblical texts—especially of the Old Testament—helped him to preach the Gospel truth not only clearly, but also gracefully, not only addressing the intellect of his hearers, but also their senses and their emotions.

Glass was a universal theological talent. He started out as a teacher of Hebrew and as an expert of biblical grammar and rhetoric. Later on, he systematically expounded the Lutheran doctrine of the Scriptures both for the academic realm in his disputations on the Augsburg Confession

---

[7] See Johann Anselm Steiger, "Salomon Glassius' Hermeneutik des *sensus mysticus*. Dargestellt anhand seiner Predigten über die Jona-Erzählung," in *Hebraistik – Hermeneutik – Homiletik. Die 'Philologia Sacra' im frühneuzeitlichen Bibelstudium*, ed. Christoph Bultmann and Lutz Danneberg, Historia Hermeneutica: Series Studia, no. 10 (Berlin: De Gruyter 2011), 383–412.

[8] See Ernst Koch, "*Arbor vitae*. Salomon Glass als Erbauungsschriftsteller," in *Hebraistik – Hermeneutik – Homiletik. Die 'Philologia Sacra' im frühneuzeitlichen Bibelstudium*, ed. Christoph Bultmann and Lutz Danneberg, Historia Hermeneutica: Series Studia, no. 10 (Berlin: De Gruyter 2011), 373–82.

[9] For a short introduction into both major practical works, see Wenz, "The Doctrine of the Ministry."

and in his *Foundation of Faith* (*Glaubensgrund*) and for the pastoral realm in the preface to the Weimar Bible and in the four prefaces for the *Spruch=Postill*. In his contributions to the Weimar Bible, his *Spruch=Postill*, as well as his posthumously published commentaries on the Mosaic books and on the Psalms, he laid open the manifold Christological, ecclesiological, and eschatological riches of the Old Testament testimony to Christ, to the Church Militant, and to the Church Triumphant. He was able to discover these riches in an unsurpassing depth with the help of his elaborate hermeneutics. This can be observed especially in his interpretations of the many figurative passages of Holy Scripture and the way Glass applied his knowledge and theological understanding of the grammatical and rhetorical phenomena of the Old and New Testaments.

BIBLIOGRAPHY

None of Glass's writings have been translated.

Select Works by Glass in Latin and German

Arbor vitae. Der Baum des Lebens / Jesus Christus / Aus göttlicher Schrifft durch die Gnade des heiligen Geistes vorgestellet / Und zu tröstlicher Betrachtung / unnd nöthiger Lebenserbawung In fünff Büchlein verfasset. Jena: Steinmann, 1629.

Biblia. Das ist die gantze Heilige Schrift Deutsch. D. Mart. Luth. Nuremberg: Endter, 1641–.

Christlicher Glaubens-Grund. Das ist / Deutliche Ausführung / daß allein die H. Schrifft der Christlichen Lehr / Glaubens und Lebens / waares principium, vester Grund / sichere Regel / und unbetriegliche Richtschnur; Hingegen aber / was dißfals von des Papsts und desselben Kirchen autorität / item von traditionen / Kirchenbräuchen / Vätern / Concilien etc. von alten und neuen Päpstischen Scribenten / vorgegeben wird / falsch / irrig und verführerisch sey. Nuremberg: Endter, 1654.

Christologia Davidica, ex Ps. CX. Conscripta. Jena: Steinmann, 1678.

Christologia Mosaica, ex prioribus Capitibus Geneseos. Jena: Steinmann, 1678.

Dissertationum Super Augustanam Confessionem, ejusq(ue) Apologiam, Prima. Prooemialis: De Scriptura Sacra. Gotha: Peter Schmidt, 1641.

Evangelicorum Et Epistolicorum Textuum, Qui Dominicis & festis diebus in Ecclesia tractari solent. Nuremberg: Endter, 1664.

Onomatologia Messiae Prophetica. Jena: Johannes Beithmann, 1624.

Philologia Sacra. Jena: Steinmann, 1623–36.

Prophetische Spruch-Postill. 4 vols. Jena and Nuremberg: Endter, 1642–54.

"Salomon Glassius' Vorrede zum Nürnberger Bibelwerk (1640). Kommentierte Edition." In *Philologia Sacra, Zur Exegese der Heiligen Schrift im Protestantismus des 16. bis 18. Jahrhunderts*, edited by Johann Anselm Steiger, 155–226. Biblisch-Theologische Studien, no. 117. Neukirchen-Vluyn: Neukirchener Verlag, 2011.

Selecta Scripturae Divinae Davidicae. Davidische Schrifft-Kern oder Geistreiche und Heilsame Betrachtungen. Etliche Trost und Lehrreiche Psalmen und Sprüche deß königlichen Propheten Davids. Nuremberg: Endter, 1658.

Selecta Scripturae Divinae Mosaicae. Süsser Kern und Außzug Oder Geistreiche und Heylsame Betrachtung der vornehmsten Lehr-reichen Geschichten / Dinge und Sprüche in den Büchern Mosis begriffen. Nuremberg: Endter, 1657.

WRITING[10]

Sermon for the Fifth Sunday after Epiphany

"For as the rain and the snow come down from heaven and do not return there but water the earth, making it fruitful and letting things grow, giving seed to sow and bread to eat, so shall the Word be that goes out from my mouth as well: It shall not return to me empty, but it shall accomplish that which pleases me, and shall succeed in the thing for which I sent it" (Isaiah 55:10–11).

Today's Gospel [Matthew 13:24–30] speaks about the Christian church here on earth in the manner of a parable: As long as the world exists, there are good and bad [people] with and among each other in the

[10] This is a select translation of Salomon Glass's "Am fünfften Sontage nach Epiphania / Evang. Matth. 13," which was based on Matthew 13 and Isaiah 55:10–11. The sermon can be found in his *Prophetischer Spruch=Postill ander Theil* (Nuremberg: Endter, 1647), 2:321–23, 337–44. The numbers of the pages differ in the different editions of Glass's works. The page numbers here are according the copy that is available in the Rare Book Room of Concordia Seminary, St. Louis (# 101-056315-7).

church, and the perfect separation between them will take place first on the Last Day in the resurrection of the dead. Then the faithful will be admitted to the heavenly kingdom and to eternal life, whereas the wicked will be turned away into the fire of hell.

The Lord Jesus Christ, then, presents this doctrine in the form of a parable that is taken from the realm of farming: He compares the faithful and pious to the good seed, which grows in the soil, greens, blossoms, and brings forth fruit, and finally will be brought into the barn for safekeeping. The unfaithful and wicked, however, he compares to the weeds, which also grow together with and among the good seed and are impossible to be completely rooted out and weeded out because they grow together. Therefore, the weeds remain and also bear fruit, which, however, is not beneficial but very harmful, until finally, at the time of the harvest, they are separated from the good seed, bound together, and thrown into the fiery furnace.

In today's sermon, we want to reflect further on the good seed in God's field. Concerning its beginning and origin, Christ the Lord says the following: "The kingdom of heaven may be compared to a man who sowed good seed in his field" (Matthew 13:24). Thereafter, he also explains this to his disciples, saying (vv. 37–38): "The one who sows the good seed is the Son of Man. The field is the world, and the good seed is the sons of the kingdom."

It is necessary for the sprouting, the growth, and the fruit-bringing of the seed that "the Lord will open to you his good treasury, the heavens, to give the rain to your land in its season," as Moses says in Deuteronomy 28:12, "by giving you rains from heaven and fruitful seasons," according to St. Paul's words in Acts 14:17. In the same way, the spiritual seed that the Gospel talks about cannot proceed, grow, increase, green, bloom, and bring forth fruit, unless rain and fruitful seasons are given from above. That is to say, it is impossible for man to come to the true saving faith and to be preserved in it for life eternal except solely by the heavenly rain and the blessed means, which the Lord God has ordained for the sake of man's conversion and salvation. This means is his holy revealed Word, which in the prophetic saying at hand is pleasantly compared to the rain and the snow.

How this takes place shall be examined further and in greater detail in three points of comparison:

I. The quality of the origin (*Ortus qualitas;* 323ff.)

II. The dignity of the fruit (*Fructus dignitas;* 329ff.)

III. The pleasant diversity (*Jucunda diversitas;* 337ff.)

The third point of comparison consists in the simultaneous mentioning of the rain and the snow and in that the Word of God is compared to both. This certainly has not been done without a specific reason. Let us here ponder nature a little in order to awaken in us pleasant thoughts concerning the divine Word. Rain and snow are but one and the same matter, for both are water. The difference is that in the one, namely, the snow, we find freezing, that is, the cold has transformed the water into fluffy fine wool, as it were. In the same way, the Word of God is but one and the same thing. Nevertheless—as far as the form of revelation is concerned—there is a difference in that it is not only proclaimed orally but it is also put into writing. The dear prophets and apostles first proclaimed it orally; later they also put it down in writings. These writings are called the Bible. By God's grace, this Bible is still available for us. It is now also preached and explained and usefully applied in the church. This difference between the preached and the written Word of God is now gently pointed out to us in the parable taken from the rain and the snow.

The rain, which falls down drop by drop can fittingly be compared to the preached divine Word. This can be seen in Moses' speech in Deuteronomy 32:2: "May my teaching drop as the rain, my speech distill as the dew, like gentle rain upon the tender grass, and like showers upon the herb."...

But snow, which falls down to the earth in a much gentler, imperceptible manner, and does so in the form of flakes, can very fittingly be compared to the written Word of God or the Holy Scripture.

1. When snow has fallen repeatedly on the ground in winter, it does not quickly vanish again as the rain, but remains there for a while and covers the soil of the earth. The written Word of God remains with and in the Christian Church here on earth, not only for a short time, but until the end of the world. For the Church is the "pillar and buttress of the truth" (1 Timothy 3:15), namely, of the divine truth in His holy written Word, which it preserves, presents, and puts forth in order to help men attain salvation. For this is one of the reasons why the Church of Christ is compared to Mount Lebanon in Isaiah 35:2. Due to the great height, snow has supposedly always been found there (accordingly, in Jeremiah 18:14 the snow of Lebanon is mentioned, and the name "Lebanon" is derived from the color white).

2. Snow is not heard with our ears like rain, but is only seen with our eyes as it falls down to the earth and remains there for a while. It is seen and touched; it does not disappear into the ground as quickly as the rain.

So it is with Holy Scripture, which by eyesight is recognized and read. It is mentally perceived and memorized. Scripture is impressed upon our hearts, pondered, and kept therein. It is transformed into life.

3. Since snow is totally white and light, the highest degree of purity and beauty is compared to it (Psalm 51:7; Isaiah 1:18; Mark 9:3). Accordingly, Holy Scripture is free from all error and falsehood, totally clear and undefiled: "The Words of the LORD are pure words, like silver refined in a furnace on the ground, purified seven times" (Psalm 12:6).

4. Snow, in order to become beneficial to the ground through its moisture, finally has to melt and become liquid. In the same manner, Holy Scripture has to be learned, presented, explained, and, as it were, poured into the heart, if it is to have its benefit for the enlightenment and sanctification of men. The melting of the snow in spring usually takes place very gently and slowly. In the same manner, it is impossible to exhaust Scripture and to be finished with learning it at once. But, in a manner of speaking, it keeps on melting in the Christian Church for as long as the Church lasts on earth. By the assistance and enlightenment of God's Spirit, there is found always one person after another who presents and usefully explains the mysteries that are hidden in the written Word. However, unlike the melting snow, Holy Scripture miraculously never vanishes, but remains the same in its perfection in each age.

5. Among its other benefits, snow also has this one that it covers the seed and the plants of the earth and protects them against the cold and from freezing in winter. In the same manner, it is, as it were, winter for as long as the world exists. Here the written Word of the Lord covers his dear Christendom as the spiritual field of God and protects the plants of the Lord, so that they may not be conquered and destroyed by the coldness of unbelief and godless wickedness. Yet when the Last Day will break in and the resurrection of the dead will take place, it will not be winter anymore, but the beginning of the eternal summer of heavenly, unspeakable joy. So it is prophesied in Isaiah 66:14: "You shall see, and your heart shall rejoice; your bones shall flourish like the grass." Then the written Word of God also will not be needed anymore, but its complete fulfillment will be experienced and seen with gladness and joy in eternity.

6. Snow has the appearance of pure fine wool, as David says in Psalm 147:16: "He gives snow like wool." When just in the verse before, the Word of God is mentioned: "He sends out His command to the earth; His Word runs swiftly." At the same time, our spiritual snow, that is, the Word of Scripture, is the beautiful white wool of the most precious "Lamb of God, who takes away the sin of the world" (John 1:29). Spun and made from this wool are "the robe of righteousness" and "the gar-

ments of salvation" (Isaiah 61:10) by which we are clothed and adorned through faith in Christ. In the Psalm just mentioned, follows in verse 18: "He sends out His Word, and melts them [i.e. snow and ice]; He makes His wind blow and the waters flow." And again the Word of God is mentioned in the next verse 19: "He declares His Word to Jacob, His statutes and rules to Israel." So when God lets His wind of grace blow, that is, when He sends and gives the Holy Spirit, He melts and pours into the hearts of men the Word of Holy Scripture, makes them moist and fruitful, and refreshes them with heavenly comfort, as has been further explained above.

7. Yet there is one more thing to note: Rain and snow are identical as far as their efficient, material, formal, and final causes are concerned ("ratione causarum, efficientis, materialis, formalis, & finalis"). This is also how it is with the Word of God, as it was first preached by the prophets and the apostles and was later written down: it is but one and the same Word. No difference concerning the matter and the perfection of doctrine can be found between the two. The papists err on this topic, as we have expounded in other places. Irenaeus, *Against Heresies*, book 3, chapter 1[, writes]:

> We have learned from no one else the plan of our salvation, than from those through whom the Gospel has come down to us, which they did at one time proclaim in public, and, at a later period, by the will of God, handed down to us in the Scriptures, to be the ground and pillar of our faith.

[In] Nicephorus, *Church History*, book 2, chapter 34[, we read]:

> The very things which Paul in his presence plainly taught in his sermons, he being absent set them down in epistles as a summary recalling them into [his] memory.

[And] Augustine, Treatise 49 on John[, states]:

> The Lord Jesus having done many things, not all of them were written, as the holy evangelist [St. John] testifies, that the Lord Christ said and did many things that are not written, but those were chosen for writing, which appeared to be sufficient for the salvation of those who should believe.

Balthasar Meisner (1587–1626)

"Blessed Are the Meek"

by David R. Preus

Life

Balthasar Meisner, a pious and gifted Wittenberg theologian, belonged to a privileged circle of highborn Lutheran ecclesiastics and statesmen. He was born on February 3, 1587, in Dresden, the capital city of Electoral Saxony, where seven years earlier the Book of Concord was first printed "with the privilege of his electoral grace of Saxony."[1] His father, also named Balthasar Meisner (1556–1623), was head pastor of the famous Frauenkirche (Church of our Lady) in Dresden and held this position for forty years (1583–1623). His mother, Anna, was the daughter of

[1] *Concordia. Christliche Widerholete einmütige Bekentnüs nachbenanter Churfürsten, Fürsten und Stende Augspurgischer Confession* (Dresden: n.p., 1580), cover page.

Franziskus Crantz, a court minister and intimate friend of Elector Christian II (1583–1611). Throughout his life, Meisner associated with the most influential people in Germany, not least of whom was Matthias Hoë von Hoënegg (1580–1645), the court preacher and trusted advisor to Elector Johann Georg I (1585–1656). His privileged sphere extended as well to his happy marriage with Magdalena, the daughter of Ludwig Person, professor of law at Wittenberg and prominent member of the Electoral Saxon council. These connections, combined with close friendships with the most important theologians of his day, and the extraordinary industry and genius with which he adorned the University of Wittenberg during his short life, distinguish Meisner as a theologian particularly suited for his time.[2]

Meisner's parents immediately recognized their son's native talent and mustered the means to provide him with a first-rate education. They enrolled him at the reputable city school in Dresden and supplemented his schooling with a private tutor at home. From early on, he "burned with the greatest passion for knowledge" and was "anxiously occupied with good books."[3] The boy possessed such a gentle soul and singular genius that, when the other boys his age were still learning to read Vergil's *Aeneid* and had only begun to form their Latin sentences with due elegance, Balthasar Meisner was well on his way to the university to sharpen his wits on the subtler arts of philosophy.[4]

In the fall of 1602, fifteen-year-old Meisner matriculated at the University of Wittenberg. Supported by an electoral stipend, he boarded in the home of Aegidius Hunnius (1550–1603), who may be regarded as the father of Wittenberg orthodoxy for his successful role in reestablishing

---

[2] Jakob Martini, *Christlicher Leichsermon Uber den schönen Spruch S. Pauli 2. Timoth. 4. Ich hab einen guten Kampff gekämpffet etc.* (Wittenberg: Solomon Auerbachs S. Erben, 1627). Eulogies are appended to Martini's funeral sermon (1–32) by Jakob Martini (33–48), Georg Wecker (49–58), and August Buchner (59–61). See also Gottlieb Spitzel, *Templum Honoris Reseratum* (Augsburg: Gottlieb Göbel and Jakob Koppmayer, 1673): 60–67; August Tholuck, *Der Geist der lutherischen Theologen Wittenbergs im Verlaufe des 17. Jahrhunderts* (Hamburg and Gotha: Friedrich und Andreas Parther, 1852), 14–37; August Tholuck, *Lebenszeugen der lutherischen Kirche aus allen Ständen vor und während der Zeit des dreißigjährigen Krieges* (Berlin: Verlag von Wiegandt & Grieben, 1859), 202–9. The only monograph to date that is dedicated to Balthasar Meisner is Walter Sparn, *Wiederkehr der Metaphysik: Die ontologische Frage in der Theologie des frühen 17. Jahrhunderts* (Stuttgart: Calwer Verlag, 1976).

[3] Spitzel, *Templum*, 61.

[4] George Wecker, *Programma in funere Magnifici Academiae huius Rectoris, Viri, Plur. Reverendi, Clarissimi & Excellentissimi, Domini, Balthasari Meisneri, SS. Theol. Doctoris & Profess. eximii, de Ecclesia Christi optime meriti* (Wittenberg, 1627), 52.

the Formula of Concord as the doctrinal standard in Saxony. During that first year, Hunnius was Meisner's mentor and main theological influence. Besides attending theological lectures, Meisner studied philosophy under Jakob Martini (1570–1647), who had assumed the chair of logic that same year. In two years, Meisner completed his studies in the liberal arts, and on March 27, 1604, he graduated with a master's degree in philosophy. Over the next few years, Meisner would make a name for himself both as a philosophical lecturer and as a respondent to theological disputations of Leonhard Hutter (1563–1616) and Friedrich Balduin (1575–1627). On May 1, 1608, he was made adjunct of the philosophical faculty and retained the right to lecture on every philosophical discipline at the university.[5]

The following year, Meisner embarked on his academic journey to three of the most important Lutheran universities in Germany.[6] During those years, Meisner's reputation grew among his professors and comrades because of his theological insight and homiletical skills. Supported by an electoral stipend of ninety guldens, Meisner left Wittenberg on March 23, 1609, and arrived at the University of Strassburg on April 11. There he participated in theological disputations under the respected theologian John Pappus (1549–1610), whose vigorous adherence to the Formula of Concord a generation earlier had won the University of Strassburg to the cause of Lutheran Orthodoxy.[7] In October of that same year, Meisner proceeded to Basel and then to Tübingen, the latter of which was a "volcano" of polemical-dogmatic theology at that time.[8] There he gained the acquaintance of the practical-minded Matthias Haffenreffer (1561–1619). From Tübingen he went on to Giessen and came under the influence of his life-long friend and confidant, "the reverend and most excellent man," Balthasar Mentzer (1565–1627).[9]

Upon the untimely death of Heinrich Velsten (d. 1611), and by the influence of his father and Hoë von Hoënegg, Meisner was recalled to

---

[5] Heinz Kathe, *Die Wittenberger Philosophische Fakultät 1501–1817* (Cologne: Böhlau, 2002), 217–18; 455–70.

[6] Tholuck, *Geist*, 17. In those days, it was common for students to branch out and attend foreign universities.

[7] Richard Otto Zoepffel, "Pappus, Johannes," in *Allgemeine Deutsche Biographie* (Leipzig: Duncker and Humbolt, 1875–1912), 25:163–64.

[8] Tholuck, *Geist*, 50.

[9] See Wecker, *Programma*, 53. According to Wecker, the young scholar so captivated his older friend by his brilliance—the two were virtually inseparable for the duration of Meisner's seven-month visit—that, had Meisner decided to stay at Giessen, Mentzer would have permitted it.

Wittenberg to assume the chair of ethics and politics. The intention was not for him to remain on the philosophical faculty, however. He was already slated to teach theology, and to that end, on November 22, 1611, he was awarded the degree of licentiate (*licentia docendi*), which authorized him to hold public disputations in theology. This provision made it perfectly clear that his appointment to the ethics chair was meant as a transitional post en route to the higher faculty. On January 21, 1612, Meisner was promoted to doctor of theology and, again, through the influence of his wealthy friend Hoë von Hoënegg, he assumed the theological professorship vacated by Johann Förster II (1576–1613) in 1613.[10]

Meisner's swift promotion to the theological faculty, despite the fact that his senior Jakob Martini was also being primed for that position, was to be expected. Not only did his interest lie from the very beginning chiefly in the controversial theological issues of the day, but he also had already achieved international fame as a first rate theologian through the publication of his 1611 *Sober Philosophy* (*Philosophia Sobria*), which he developed from a series of disputations in Giessen. In this meticulously composed work, Meisner takes up the question of how philosophy ought to be used in theological discourse. He exposes the tendency of Reformed philosophers to reduce Lutheran theological assertions to their philosophical parts and press them *ad absurdum* to their logical conclusions. According to Meisner, the Reformed misuse philosophy; their wine is mixed with water (Isaiah 1:22).[11] By contrast, he endorses a "sober philosophy" and indicates a universal foundation upon which each philosophical discipline—logic, ethics, physics, and metaphysics—may thrive in its own respective sphere without intruding on the substance of theology.[12]

With his *Sober Philosophy*, Meisner had begun to accomplish in literary form what would become his practical objective: namely, to bring the structure of the university into the service of Lutheran Orthodox theology.[13] His administrative duties included serving as dean of the theological

---

[10] Kathe, *Die Wittenberger*, 217.

[11] Balthasar Meisner, *Philosophia Sobria, Hoc est: Pia Consideratio Quaestionum Philosophicarum in Controversiis Theologicis, quas Calviniani moverunt Orthodoxis, subinde occurrentium* (Wittenberg: Johann Mannstadt, 1655), 1:44.

[12] Sparn, *Wiederkehr*, 19. Spanning nearly his entire career at Wittenberg, Meisner expanded his *magnum opus* to include three volumes (1611, 1615, and 1623), highlighting the most pressing philosophical issues and coming to solutions that would be decisive for generations to come. Meisner's *Philosophia Sobria* was published and used as a textbook well into the eighteenth century.

[13] Kathe, *Die Wittenberger*, 251–52.

faculty seven times, as rector of the university three winter terms (1614, 1620, 1626), and as member of the Wittenberg consistory in 1624. For Meisner, all theology was *pastoral* theology, and the training of pastors took precedence over all other academic concerns. In opposition to the Reformed philosopher Bartholemew Keckermann (ca. 1571–1608), who envisioned theology as a "religious prudence" for *coming* to salvation, Meisner defined theology in terms of a "God-given practical aptitude," analogous to the practice of medicine, for *leading others* to salvation.[14] In order to facilitate the theologian's competence in carrying out this task, Meisner revamped the old disputation method. The pastor-in-training must learn to *demonstrate* the truth of the Bible, and thus build assent and understanding of the subject, so that he might re-examine it and explain it further. Rather than producing theological commonplaces (*loci theologici*) in the tradition of Philipp Melanchthon (1497–1560), Martin Chemnitz (1522–86), and Johann Gerhard (1582–1637), Meisner dedicated most of his energy to writing over two hundred theological disputations.[15] In addition to disputations, he lectured on various books of the Bible, trained his students in homiletics, and assumed the post of Latin preacher to foreign students.[16]

Meisner would not have owned the label of polemicist. Nonetheless, as a theologian tasked with defending the legal boundaries of Lutheranism, recognized by the Peace of Augsburg in 1555 and defined by the Book of Concord of 1580, he was naturally involved in the arena of public controversy. While he published a good deal of tracts against the traditional Catholic foe,[17] the greater threat to Lutheran religion during the first two decades of the seventeenth century was posed by the Calvinists, who had successfully planted their "second reformation" in the Palatinate

---

[14] Meisner, *Philosophia Sobria*, 3:137–206. See also Kenneth Appold, *Orthodoxie als Konsensbildung: Das theologische Disputationswesen an der Universität Wittenberg zwischen 1570 und 1710* (Tübingen: Mohr Siebeck, 2004), 64–66; Marcel Nieden, *Die Erfindung des Theologen: Wittenberger Anweisungen zum Theologiestudium im Zeitalter von Reformation und Konfessionalisierung* (Tübingen: Mohr Siebeck, 2006), 189–216.

[15] Meisner's most important disputations over the course of his fifteen years as a Wittenberg professor dealt with the subjects of anthropology (1612–15), sacraments (1620), Christology (1624), Scripture (1623–25), prolegomena (1625), and religion (1625–26). See Appold, *Orthodoxie*, 72–98.

[16] Tholuck, *Geist*, 32.

[17] See, for instance, Balthasar Meisner, *A Catholic Answer to the Heretical Question of the Society Against Jesus (The Jesuits): "Where were the True Religion and Church before the Time of Luther?"* trans. Steven Matthews (Decatur, IL: The Johann Gerhard Institute: 1997).

(1560), Hesse-Kassel (1605), and Brandenburg (1613). Despite the conversion of Elector Johann Sigismund of Brandenburg (1572–1620) to Calvinism, his wife, Anna of Prussia (1576–1625), and the vast majority of his subjects remained faithful to Lutheranism. In January of 1620, at Anna's behest, Meisner journeyed to the electoral palace of Brandenburg where he preached a series of sermons highlighting the distinct comfort of the Lutheran doctrine of grace.[18] Meisner's most influential tract against Calvinism appeared in 1615 under the title, *A Christian Instruction to Guard against the Calvinist Doctrine.* Therein he advises his German readers that Calvinist teachings build on the uncertain foundation of reason rather than Scripture.[19] He also disputed against the Socinians, who rejected the mysteries of the Trinity and the deity of Christ on rational grounds.

One of Meisner's most significant controversies involved the Lutheran Helmstedt philosopher Cornelius Martini (1568–1621) over the necessity of the syllogism in theological disputations. In the first volume of his *Sober Philosophy*, Meisner had argued (against the Calvinists) that, despite its usefulness, the syllogism was not necessary because Scripture nowhere requires it. In 1621, Martini issued a malicious attack against Meisner, arguing that unless a theological disputation adheres to the perfect form of a syllogism, it cannot prove anything. On the other hand, he maintained, where logic is mastered, the Bible can be grasped in an instant.[20] Meisner did not wish to enter into the debate, but was prevailed upon by Heinrich Julius Strube (1586–1629), Martini's colleague at Helmstedt and father confessor (!), who admonished Meisner of his duty to "stuff the mouth of the Cyclops."[21] Meisner acquiesced, but proceeded with remarkable restraint throughout the dispute.

Meisner was widely respected for his extreme moderation in controversy. Johann Schmidt, a professor in Strasbourg, intimated in a letter to Heinrich Höpfner (1582–1642) of the University of Leipzig, "If the unholy theological controversies of this time should be lifted, there would be no better man to do it than Meisner."[22] His personality was epitomized

---

[18] Balthasar Meisner, *Sieben Predigten uber unterschiedene biblische Text* (Wittenberg: Kaspar Heyden,1620).

[19] Balthasar Meisner, *Ein Christlicher Unterricht, Das man sich vor Calvinischen Lehre hüten solle, . . . erbawet ist* (Wittenberg: Johann Gormann, 1615).

[20] Cornelius Martini, *Responsio ad primam & miserabilem vexatam quaestionem Balthasari Meisneri* (Helmstedt: Zacharias Rabe, 1621).

[21] Tholuck, *Geist*, 59.

[22] Tholuck, *Geist*, 26–27.

by Jesus' words in Matthew 5:5: "Blessed are the meek" (*Beati Mites*), which correspond to the initials of his name. He was celebrated, even during his life, as a paragon of piety and prudence. According to one biographer, Gottlieb Spitzel (1639–91), "There was no place for anger or hatred in his heart; neither his face, nor his expression, nor his color, nor his words, nor his hands, nor his step ever showed a hint of feelings of anger."[23] He was also known for his outstanding industry. Throughout his life, he worked harder than everyone around him. He excelled in every task, even holding disputations on Sundays.[24] While serving his third term as *rector magnificus*, a thirty-nine-year-old Meisner died on December 29, 1626, a victim of his own work ethic. He left behind his wife of fifteen years, Magdalena, who was currently with child, and their four surviving children. Jakob Martini preached his funeral sermon on January 2, 1627, on the text of 2 Timothy 4: "I have fought the good fight."

Shortly before he died, Meisner dictated to those gathered around his bed the chief concerns that rested on his heart. He perceived many defects in church and society and called on pastors and princes alike to reform their respective domains. Among "theoretical defects," he stressed the lack of a correct Latin translation of Scripture, the need for an annotated commentary on every book of the Bible, and too much intensity and acrimony in theological controversies. Among "practical defects," he cited the impious and scandalous lives of many clergymen, too many financial cares, a lack of conventicles, the neglect of the mutual conversation of Christians, and a lack of missionary zeal. He also called on the magistrates to give their attention to various "political defects," including too much taxation, too much pomp and lavish living among the nobility, monopolies, and lack of schools. In 1679, Philipp Jakob Spener (1635–1705) attached his own dedication to Meisner's last words and had them published under the title *Pia Desideria: Expressed and Delineated Shortly Before His Blessed Death.*[25] The fact that he should have uttered such "pious desires" in the dismal hour of his death stands as a lasting testimony to the kind of dedication that characterized his entire life.

Meisner bequeathed a two-pronged, yet singular, legacy on the church. He was an imposing theologian and a pious Christian man. He was a sophisticated university professor and a prudent churchman. His influence on the latter half of the seventeenth century remained with rep-

---

[23] Spitzel, *Templum*, 63.

[24] Tholuck, *Geist*, 18.

[25] Balthasar Meisner, *Balthasari Meisneri Pia Desideria, Paulo ante beatum obitum . . . tollendis*, ed. Gottfried Wegner (Frankfurt am Main: Johann Zunner, 1679).

resentatives of Orthodoxy and Pietism alike. From the very beginning, he gave his attention to both theoretical and practical concerns. Perhaps his greatest contribution to theology was this: rather than choosing one or the other, he embodied a genuinely practical orthodoxy by investing the theory of doctrine in the practice of life. His success on that score is borne out in his speech, "On the Excellence and Dignity of a Christian."[26] Meisner delivered this speech on November 5, 1622, at the graduation of Andreas Grosshenning, pastor at Loburg. In 1709, the Hamburg preacher Hermann Gerhard Weland came across a printing of this speech and, becoming convinced that it merited a greater audience than the academy, translated it into German. In it, Meisner illustrates how the lofty doctrine of the two natures in Christ has parallels with the spiritual (mystical) union between Christ and the Christian and ensures practical consequences for the Christian life.

BIBLIOGRAPHY

Works by Meisner in English Translation

A Catholic Answer to the Heretical Question of the Society Against Jesus (The Jesuits): "Where were the True Religion and Church before the Time of Luther?" Translated by Steven Matthews. Decatur, IL: The Johann Gerhard Institute: 1997.

Select Works by Meisner in German and Latin

Anthropologias sacrae. 3 vols. Wittenberg: Johann Gormann, 1612–15.

Balthasari Meisneri Pia Desideria, Paulo ante beatum obitum ab ipso manifestata et delineata, acinsimul Consilia Theologica, de quibusdam Defectibus in & ab Ecclesiis Evangelicorum tollendis. Frankfurt am Main: Johann Zunner, 1679.

Brevis admonitio de Magistri Cornelii Martini, logices in Acad. Helmstadiana Prof. publ. maledicentia, iniquitate et in logicis suis legibus observandis negligentia, quam in iterata ventilatione quaestionis, An semper syllogistice de rebus theologicis disputandum sit? Wittenberg: Kaspar Heyden, 1621.

[26] Balthasar Meisner, *Geistreiche Bedanken von der Vortreflichkeit und Würde Eines Christen/ als welcher das herzlichtse und heiligste Geschöpf Gottes . . . Theologi*, trans. Hermann Gerhard Weland (Hamburg: Philip Ludwig Stromer, 1709).

Brevis consideratio Theologiae photinianae, prout eam Faustus Socinus descripsit in libello suasorio, cui titulus: Quod Evangelici omnio deberent se illorum coetui adjungere, qui falso Ariani atque Ebionitae vocentur. Wittenberg: Kaspar Heyden, 1619.

Christologia sacra disputationes L. Wittenberg: Johann Gormann, 1620–24.

Collegii adiaphoristici Calvinianis oppositi. Wittenberg: Johann Gormann, 1620.

De religione et eius articulis generatim consideratis. Wittenberg: Johann Gormann, 1625–26.

Disputatio Inauguralis De Fidei Iustificatintis: 1. Appelationibus. 2. Partibus. 3. Causa efficiente. 4. Objecto. & 5. Subjecto: Photinianorum & Pontificiorum erroribus opposita. Wittenberg: Johann Gormann, 1613

Dissertatio de legibus: in quatuor libellos distributa, quorum primus agit de lege in genere; secundus de lege aeterna; tertius de lege naturae; quartus de legibus humanis, tum politicis, tum ecclesiasticis. Wittenberg: Bechtold Rab, 1616.

Ein Christlicher Unterricht, Das man sich vor Calvinischen Lehre hüten solle, weil sie auff einen ungewissen Grundt, nemlich, auff der blinden Vernunfft Sinnen und Gedancken erbawet ist. Wittenberg: Johann Gormann, 1615.

Eines seeligen Menschens dreyfacher Schatz, der Herr Christus, Christi heiliges Wort, auss dem Wort geschöpffte Busse, von welchem allen im Neunzehenden Psälmlein Davids gehandelt wird. Wittenberg: Johann Gormann, 1614.

Geistreiche Bedanken von der Vortreflichkeit und Würde Eines Christen/ als welcher das herzlichtse und heiligste Geschöpf Gottes/ aller Göttlichen Wunder und Geschöpffe Schauplatz/ Spiegel/ Siegel/ Mittel-Punkt und kurtzer Begriff ist/ Auf Begehren eines wohlbekandten Theologi, translated by Hermann Gerhard Weland. Hamburg: Philip Ludwig Stromer, 1709.

Philosophia Sobria, Hoc Est: Pia Consideratio Quaestionum Philosophicarum, In Controversiis Theologicis, quas Calviniani moverunt Orthodoxis, subinde occurrentium. 3 vols. Giessen and Wittenberg: Martin Henckel et al., 1611–23.

Praecognitorum theologicorum disputationes. Wittenberg: Johann Gormann, 1625.

Quaestiones vexatae, I. An semper syllogistice de rebus Theologicis disputandum sit? II. An Christus tempore mortis verus homo fuerit? III. An Christus pro finali etiam impoenitentia satisfecerit? IV. An peccatum originis formaliter sit aliquid positivi? Wittenberg: Johann Gormann, 1620.

Sieben Predigten uber unterschiedene biblische Text. Wittenberg: Kaspar Heyden, 1620.

WRITING[27]

Spiritual Meditations on the Excellence and Dignity of a Christian

Whenever you hear a Christian speak, you do not hear him, but Christ speaking from him. When you see a Christian work, you do not see him, but Christ who works in and through him. When you see a Christian fight and win, you do not see him, but Christ fighting and winning in and through the Christian. For it is not so much the Christian as Christ who speaks, works, and wins inside of him. A Christian can do everything, but not by himself, since he is the weakest of all; but in Christ, who gives him strength and through whom he becomes the strongest of all, he can do everything.

We are by nature wretched and wild olive trees. In our natural state, we lie, as it were, dead and cast away; but when we become Christians, behold, we are just as soon raised on high and grafted into the good olive tree, and we acquire a new and divine nature. . . .

As a man, a Christian is a person subsisting in and for himself; but as a Christian, he subsists not in himself, but in Christ alone from whom he receives his life and spiritual abode.

A Christian is not something whole, but a member with respect to the Church; and yet he is something whole with respect to himself and Christ with whom he becomes united in such a way that the two become one. . . .

This, then, is the divine manner in which a Christian has his life and abode—not existing in himself, but in Christ—as a limb on a tree, a branch on a vine, and as a wild shoot is grafted onto an olive tree. He

---

[27] This is a select translation of Balthasar Meisner, *Geistreiche Bedanken von der Vortreflichkeit und Würde Eines Christen*, trans. Hermann Gerhard Weland (Hamburg: Philip Ludwig Stromer, 1709), 44–57, 61–62.

receives his life, movement, power, and light from Christ as a limb from the body, the body from the soul, the iron from the fire. Such grafting and spiritual unification (from which stems this unique manner of life) leads us further to elaborate a fourfold communion that exists between Christ and the Christian.

The first is a communion of essence or nature, and we have already made reference to it above. Accordingly, Christ partakes of our human nature, and we partake of Christ's divine nature—albeit, in a different way. For he himself has assumed our flesh and thus united it to his essence in such a way that he is true man and like us in every way, except for sin. From this special union and likeness with us flows a perfect communion of power and good works. Hence, the Church Fathers were accustomed to saying, "Whatever has not been assumed has also not been cured."[28] For even as a branch could not draw sap apart from the vine, unless it shared the same nature as the vine, it was necessary for our Mediator to be true man in order that we might draw sap from him and be grafted into him alive.

Now, just as Christ has become a partaker of our nature through the incarnation, a Christian has been made a partaker of the divine nature through the union of grace, and consequently there exists a communion of the latter with the former and the former with the latter. However, these communions differ with respect to their manner: the first one is personal, but the second one is spiritual and gracious. In the case of Christ, the union and communion are so solid that the two natures cannot ever be separated from each other. In the case of Christians, however, while the same union is indeed firm and insoluble, it can be separated and abolished by us if we sin. But if we flee from sin, we may exclaim with St. Paul: "Who can separate us from the love of Christ? . . . I am certain that neither death nor life, nor things present nor things to come, nor height nor depth, nor any other creature may separate us from the love of God, which is in Christ Jesus our Lord (Romans 8:35, 38–39.)

The second communion pertains to suffering. For on account of this spiritual union, it comes about that Christ's suffering and satisfaction are our suffering and satisfaction, and God regards Christ's satisfaction as though we ourselves had suffered and died for our sins. For this reason, we are called saints[29] through his wounds (Isaiah 53:5). Moreover, Christ's suffering becomes our suffering through faith, even as our suffering becomes Christ's suffering because he so claims it as his own and

---

[28] Gregory of Naziansus, *Epistle 101*.

[29] German: "*Geheiligten*," "saints," or "those who are healed."

appropriates all of the suffering of believers to himself, as though such suffering were being inflicted on himself and his person. Thus, in the Old Testament he calls out from heaven: "Whoever touches you touches the apple of my eye" (Zechariah 2:8), and in the New Testament: "Saul, Saul, why are you persecuting me?" (Acts 9:4). Rejoice, therefore, dear Christians! Your sins will not weigh you down to hell, for Christ's suffering, whereby satisfaction has been made for sin, is yours through the apprehension of faith. Rejoice, dear cross bearers! You are not being afflicted alone, for the suffering that encompasses you in the world is Christ's suffering—and by means of a real appropriation, Christ suffers in you. The apple of his eye is being touched. He is feeling it, and he will rise up and take vengeance for it. Why, then, are you so afraid of the cross? It has not been laid upon you as much as upon Christ, whose shoulders are strong enough. He will help you carry it. He will requite it and fill you with joy forever.

The third communion pertains to morals and good works. For Christ's righteousness, holiness, and good name become the possession of Christians in general and are traced from him to us as from the body to its members, with the consequence that we all take everything from his fullness (John 1:16). He has become our wisdom through his prophetic office, our righteousness through his priestly office, and our sanctification and redemption through his kingly office (1 Corinthians 1:30). Everything Christ can do or has, we Christians can do and have as well—although in a lesser degree. We are wise through his wisdom, righteous through his righteousness, holy through his holiness, mighty through His might, and joyful through his joy. He has risen from the grave—indeed! In him then we, too, have been raised. He has ascended into heaven, and we with him. He sits at the right hand of his Father, and so does our flesh through him. Therefore, rejoice, dear Christians, and exult in your victory! We are everything inasmuch as he is everything. We can do everything inasmuch as he can do everything. Although presently we still cling to the earth, we have indeed been raised to heaven. "Be assured, dear human flesh and blood, that you have taken hold of heaven and the kingdom of God!" So says Tertullian in Book 1 of *De Resurrectione*, chapter 51. Consider what great things have happened to your flesh! In the man, Christ, exists a part of every one of us, even our flesh and blood. Hence, where my part reigns, there I believe that I reign also; where my flesh is exalted, I acknowledge that I am exalted in the same place; where my blood rules, there, indeed, I perceive that I rule. This is how Maximus explains it in his sermon on the resurrection. Although I remain a sinner, I do not doubt this communion of grace. Should my sin deny it to me, my essence now requires it. Though my transgressions would exclude me, the communion of nature does not repel me, as the blessed Church Father Augustine states it so beautifully in his *Meditations*, chapter 15.

The fourth communion pertains to the office, which is threefold: the prophetic, the priestly, and the kingly. Indeed, these offices remain Christ's unique property in view of their most noble performance and the manner in which they are exercised. Nevertheless, they belong to Christians in a certain sense because they are united to Christ and live in Christ.

For we are prophets in that we confess the teaching of the Gospel and instruct our brothers in the same.

We are priests in that we sanctify our dear God completely (Romans 12:1; 1 Peter 2:5) and offer to him the sacrifice of our prayer (Psalm 141; Revelation 5:8), the offering of praise (Psalm 50:14; Hosea 14:[2–]3; Hebrews 13:15), the offering of alms (Philippians 4:8), the sacrifice of penance (Psalm 51:19), and the offering of departure from this world and the martyr's crown (2 Timothy 4:6[–8]).

We are kings in that we have dominion over our enemies—over our flesh, which would infect us; over the world, which seeks to deceive us; and over the devil, who would murder us. We have overcome these enemies by the sword of the Spirit and faith; likewise, we have power and authority over all creatures to use them in a legitimate manner.

Initially, at the creation, these offices were indeed entrusted to all men, but they were all lost through the fall. Christ has restored these offices to believers. In particular, he has given them every good thing, and now that power and dominion over creation have been regained as well, they may with good conscience use food and drink without distinction. But whenever the godless eat or drink, they commit robbery and become manifest thieves, and that is why their food and property are seldom consecrated so that they might become beneficial to themselves or their children. Indeed, since they are outside of Christ, who has restored the lost right, they use the creation with such violence that they cannot so much as take a small kernel of corn, or even a small drop of wine (apart from what God's goodness grants them through no right of their own) without committing theft or larceny. You, who are unrepentant and godless: whenever you eat or drink anything, you do so in an ungodly manner, without any right at all, but as impetuous thieves. As far as it depends on you, your eating and drinking is an act of public robbery. But since our Savior has restored all things to us, everything belongs to us, and hence we are free to eat all kinds of food, which were formerly forbidden to the Jews. Through Christ and in Christ, we have been made lords of all creation so that nothing we receive with thanksgiving is objectionable (1 Timothy 4:4).

And when we take this fourfold communion of spiritual union and our abode in Christ into consideration, we may further compare it with the unity of the Word and the substance of the flesh with respect to its effects and consequences.

For just as the divine nature partakes of the human nature and the human nature partakes of the divine as a result of the communication of the natures, even so the Word is in the flesh and the flesh is in the Word, in such a way that the Word is rightly called the man and the man is rightly called the Word. Hence, from this spiritual union flows a communication of our nature and the divine nature because we live in Christ and Christ in us. Likewise, we do not only come together with Christ in a separate (or human) nature, considered separately, but Christ joins our indivisible nature to himself, making us in turn partakers of his divine nature. In this manner, the finite is capable of the infinite, not through some mental abstraction, but through an intimate association. A Christian is thus a living and moving temple of the entire blessed Trinity around which the heavenly legions are gathered. For when we are united with the Son of God and are taken into the society of the divine nature, we are at the same time graciously united with the Father and the Holy Spirit, who are one with the Son—and many thousands of angels are standing there continually and serving in the presence of God. We can have no doubt that they will attend us, and looking through the eyes of your soul, you can see in one and the same person of a Christian not one but all three persons of the Godhead and the entire heavenly host. Wherever a true Christian lives and goes, there lives and goes the entire blessed Trinity with his entire host of angels.

Furthermore, just as three kinds of communication of attributes come about through this real and effective unity—the appropriation of the attributes [*idiopoia*], the communion of the offices [*koinopoia*], and the communication of infinite gifts revealed in the assumed flesh [*metapoia*]—likewise, our spiritual union with Christ produces: the *appropriation* inasmuch as our Savior reckons to us his doing and suffering and, conversely, reckons to himself our doing and suffering; the *communion of offices* inasmuch as we, too, are all made into prophets, priests, and kings and rulers of the world; and finally, the *communication of divine gifts*, which include wisdom, righteousness, holiness, the power to perform miracles, to convert others and regenerate them. When we take all of these things to heart in the fear of God, they hold out a pleasant foretaste of eternal life and give us solid comfort.

What blissful joy! What joyful bliss! To be Christians—to be with Christ and in Christ! Indeed, this we will be if we walk in his ways. For whoever keeps the commandments remains in Christ and Christ in him (1 John 3:24). Let us therefore keep them in faith and love, and he will keep his promise and share with us the reward of everlasting life. There we will remain united with him forever, and we will see him face to face. We will see him and love him. We will love him and praise him. With the Church, we will say the words of Song of Solomon 2:4: "My king has led me into his wine cellar and his banner over me is love."

You, O King of all kings, Jesus Christ, from whom we receive your name, through whom we are born again, and in whom we live—we praise You alone above all things. Let your name be praised, for you have given us a precious name. Your praise grows and is being born in our mouths because you were born for our sakes in time and are still being born in us in a spiritual manner. We will be and remain in the perpetual praise of your divine majesty, for we live in you alone and draw our life and spiritual impulse from you alone. You alone are worthy to receive strength and honor and glory and praise (Revelation 5:12). Therefore, to you alone be given praise and glory, to you be honor and power forever—from everlasting to everlasting. Amen.

JOHANN CONRAD DANNHAUER (1603–66)

PROCLAMATION, POLEMICS, AND THE CHRISTIAN LIFE

by Timothy Dost

LIFE

Dr. Johann Conrad Dannhauer was born on March 24, 1603, in the city of Strassburg. He was baptized on March 27 of the same year. The precocious and prodigious young Dannhauer grew up in a pastor's household. Having imbibed his father's teaching, his serious studies of Christ and theology began at age 7.[1]

---

[1] Wilhelm Horning, *Der Strassburger Universitäts-Professor, Münsterprediger und Präsident des Kirchenkonvents Dr. Johann Conrad Dannhauer* (Strassburg: Bomhoff, 1883); see also Johann Wallmann, "Straβburger lutherischen Orthodoxie im 17. Jahrhunderts. Johann Conrad Dannhauer. Versuch einer Annährung," *Revue d' Histoire et de Philosophie Religieuses* 68 (1988): 55–71.

At Strassburg's famous Renaissance humanist-based *Gymnasium*, his studies were molded toward positive influences. By the age of fourteen, he was already enrolled in the preaching seminary. His first three years of college studies were primarily geared to the cultivation of a fine rhetorical style, as well as the science of speaking, the content of philosophy, and the nuance of poetical expression. These studies were carried out in both Latin and German, leading to his bachelor's degree in 1619 and his master's degree in 1621. Apparently he was talented, as he won first prize in a poetry contest and was made a laureate in 1622.[2] He continued his studies, embellishing his master's degree with a lecturing credential in 1622 and various honors by 1624.[3]

Dannhauer next pursued theological studies at Marburg University under Balthasar Mentzer I (1565–1627), Johannes Winkelmann (1551–1626), Justus Feuerborn (1587–1656), and Johann Steuber (1590–1643).[4] In 1626, he enrolled at the University of Altdorf near Nuremburg until Professor Georg König died in 1626. The next year he moved to Jena University, which was once the Gnesio-Lutheran successor to the University of Wittenberg. Here he had the opportunity to sit at the feet of both Johann Gerhard (1582–1637) and Johann Major (1564–1654).

By 1629, he was called as a professor of rhetoric at the University of Strassburg. He was named a Strassburg theology professor in 1633 and minted a doctor of theology in February of 1634. His teaching duties included dogmatics and ethics, classes that communicated the faith through both doctrine and practice. Dannhauer's learned execution of these tasks ranks with that of Leonhard Hutter (1563–1616), Johann Gerhard, Nikolaus Hunnius (1585–1643), Johann Hülsemann (1602–61), Abraham Calov (1612–86), Johann Andreas Quenstedt (1617–88), Johann Wilhelm Baier (1647–95), and David Hollaz I (1648–1713).[5] Furthermore, he was expected to defend the faith against the errors of both the Papists and the Calvinists. In 1649, he published the first edition of his *The Christian Path of Wisdom or Positive Theology* (*Hodosophia Christiana seu Theologia Positiva*), which was 1,507 octavo pages in length.[6] In the first part, he taught the Holy Scriptures as the light of that way. Continuing the metaphor, the second part discussed the Church as

---

[2] John Flood, *Poets Laureate in the Holy Roman Empire: A Bio-bibliographical Handbook* (Berlin: Walter de Gruyter, 2006), 2:417–28.

[3] Horning, *Der Strassburger*, 4.

[4] Horning, *Der Strassburger*, 5.

[5] Horning, *Der Strassburger*, 12.

[6] Horning, *Der Strassburger*, 13.

the candlestick bearing that light, and the final part focused on the goal of the faith (the Holy Trinity).

Teaching was a primary focus of Dannhauer's life and work. In the vein of the *The Christian Path of Wisdom or Positive Theology*, he sought to equip his students so that they might help others stay on the Christian path of wisdom. Some other books that he wrote in pursuit of this goal include: *Opened Book of Conscience or Theology of Conscience* (*Liber Conscientiae Apertus, sive Theologia Conscientia*), *Wisdom of Christ* (*Christosophia*), *School of the Decalogue* (*Collegium Decalogicum*), *Wisdom of the Antichrist* (*Antichristsophia*), *Wisdom of the Sacramental Mysteries* (*Mysteriosophia*), *Wisdom of Polemics* (*Polemosophia*), *Sacred Hermeneutics* (*Hermeneutica Sacra*), *Use of Pre-Adamic Fables* (*Praeadamita Utis*), and *Temptations and Obstacles to Peace in the Holy Church* (*Illex et Obex Pacis Ecclesiarum Sanctae*).[7] He even wrote a history of the Christian Church, depicted as a holy drama in which the Church Militant arose from Christ, seated on his heavenly throne. The Church was divided into historical periods, stretching from Constantine to the Holy Roman Emperor Charles V. In addition to the writings of Luther and his colleagues, his teaching drew on the writing of Johannes Brenz I (1499–1570), Martin Chemnitz (1522–86), Aegidius Hunnius (1550–1603), Friedrich Balduin (1575–1627), John Calvin (1509–64), Theodore Beza (1519–1605), Jakob Arminius (1560–1609), and other well-known evangelicals. His colleagues found his theology to be both rational and clear, and he was seen to be free from Pietistic tendencies.

Dannhauer's concerns for reform were not purely academic, as he was also concerned about the piety of his students and the reform of university life.[8] Here he followed Luther in teaching that both Christian authority and Christ as the cornerstone were the foundations of a true education. He saw that the schools had been frequently turned to the purpose of the prince, rather than what Luther originally saw as their central Christ-based purpose. Warnings about money, a stress on adherence to the Word, strong moral teachings about marriage and godly living, the education of nobles in mathematics (so they could better pursue battle [when it was required] and assist with the placement of artillery), the building of fortifications and use of explosives, as well as many other interesting topics were included in Dannhauer's ideal of a well-rounded education.[9] Academics were to serve both the sacred and

---

[7] Horning, *Der Strassburger*, 14–15.

[8] Horning, *Der Strassburger*, 20.

[9] Horning, *Der Strassburger*, 22.

the secular professions. In pursuit of these goals, he recruited exemplary professors, administrators, and reformers.

As to his lectures, they were peppered with examples from both the Old and New Testaments, designed to establish a dogmatic point, while drawing out practical applications for the lives of clergy and laity alike. His most influential student, Philipp Jakob Spener (1635–1705), worked tirelessly to restore the Christian faith. While Dannhauer influenced Spener, the former did not always completely approve of the latter's writings.[10]

Dannhauer saw the Lutheran Confessions as a heavenly way of life and a locus of battle with the enemies of the faith. In defending these teachings, he engaged three main adversaries: the Papacy, Calvinism, and syncretism.

Following the death of Luther, the Papacy had renewed its attack on the Reformation via a Counter-Reformation. Of special note was the work of the Jesuit order, which served as a kind of band of papal shock troops. They worked with more subtlety than the Dominicans had to undermine the Lutheran teachings, particularly in the area of pastoral care. In Germany, the Jesuits had expanded rapidly from Vienna, through Cologne and Ingolstadt, into the Tyrol and Swabia, and even to the Rhineland, Hungary, and Bohemia.[11] They succeeded in changing the debate at many universities and even managed to educate some prominent Protestant children at their schools. This led to concerns among the Lutherans about sound catechetical instruction. Jesuits frequently challenged the evangelical teaching of the Gospel, and opposed celebrations of the centennial of the Reformation. By contrast, the Jesuits celebrated their own centennial in 1640 with much fanfare. The papal influence on the Thirty Years' War, which ended in 1648, placed further pressure on the Lutherans.

Dannhauer opposed these papal moves by describing the reasons the Papacy was properly titled antichrist, for the pope represented a physical manifestation of the bloodguilt and sins of Rome with its satanic and worldly kingdom. Dannhauer attacked the Papacy for its lack of piety and for taking up the mantle of Babylon rather than bringing people to

---

[10] Horst Scheunemann, "Religion und Sittlichkeit bei Dannhauer, dem Lehrer Speners, nebst einem Ausblick auf die Gestaltung bei Spener" (diss., theol., Universität Kiel, 1929); Horst Scheunemann, *Der Heiligungsbegriff in der theologischen Gedenkwelt Dannhauers* (Breklum, 1929); Karl-Heinz Möckel, "Die Eigenart des Straβburger orthodoxen Lutherthums in seiner Ethik, dargestellt an Johann Conrad Dannhauer" (diss., theol., Universität Greifswald, 1952).

[11] Horning, *Der Strassburger*, 28.

the physician of their souls, Jesus Christ, through the study of God's Word. The Roman Church was one of death rather than life, and therefore Dannhauer confronted this problem using Scripture and directly confuting the Jesuits's assertions.

In his *Foolish Path of the Papal Spirit* (*Hodomoria Spiritus Papaei*), he illustrated twelve phantasms of the Papacy caused by its positions. They included teachings that come close to but do not follow God's Word; false assertions from Trent; problems arising from the scholastic method; teaching about evil in a manner inconsistent with God's Word; upholding a false Christian anthropology; mixing and obscuring Law and Gospel; false teachings about the will of God the Father; violating the communication of attributes (*communicatio idiomatum*) and mitigating Christ's role as mediator; abolishing justifying grace through teaching free will; destroying the nature of the Sacraments to prop up the priesthood; mixing internal and external matters in Sacraments, priesthood, and sin; and teaching a false theology of the papal role in the end times.[12] In two other documents, Dannhauer sets forth his issues with the Calvinists (again in twelve points)[13] and the syncretists (in several points). Here he gives special attention to Georg Calixt's (1586–1656) teaching and the Helmstedt errors, while giving credit to Calov for defending orthodoxy.[14] In each case, Dannhauer clearly establishes his position that both the Gospel and the Word of God are compromised by the teachings of these individuals and faiths. Here Dannhauer has taken up the role of polemicist, a role he embraced for much of his career.

Preaching was another concern of Dannhauer. He was so talented that he was called to the position of cathedral preacher in Strassburg in February of 1658.[15] Undertaking various themes, Dannhauer worked tirelessly from Old and New Testament texts, incorporating the Augsburg Confession and following the example of St. Paul by encouraging the people to maintain peace and good order. Gospel themes were a hallmark of his thought and he worked to cultivate in his hearers a sincere Christian devotion toward both God and the neighbor. His preaching themes included the Gospel, the battle of Christ against the coalition

---

[12] Horning, *Der Strassburger*, 36–39.

[13] Horning, *Der Strassburger*, 40–42.

[14] Horning, *Der Strassburger*, 46ff. See also Johannes Wallmann, "Die Eigenart der Straβburger lutherischen Orthodoxie im 17. Jahrhundert. Apokalyptisches Endzeitbewuβtsein und konfessionelle Polemik bei Johann Conrad Dannhauer," in *Theologie und Frömmigkeit im Zeitalter des Barock: Gesammelte Aufsätze* (Tübingen: J. C. B. Mohr [Paul Siebeck], 1995), 87–105.

[15] Horning, *Der Strassburger*, 66.

represented by the Turk, the honor of Jesus Christ, feast day preaching, various Advent themes (including matters arising from the teaching of Balaam), Christmas and New Year sermons, sermons on the catechism, and a host of other topics. When composing his sermons, in addition to a thorough exegetical analysis of the Greek and Hebrew biblical texts, Dannhauer often drew on Luther's sermons; Chemnitz's *Harmony of the Evangelists* (*Harmoniae Evangelistarum*); and works from Leyser, Gerhard, and other distinguished commentators.

Preaching duties were not the sole change for Dannhauer in 1658. He also became the head of the Church Consistory (ruling council) of Strassburg. Here he worked to avoid the "siren song of syncretism," working with the faculties of both Leipzig and Wittenberg to address his concerns.[16] His agenda in this role was to build the church with a knowledgeable, capable, and pious spirituality. Pastors needed a preachable spirit and a true piety in order to build up a strong and stable Christian community for both the rural and urban churches of the day. He established a new parochial order by 1664 and worked to heal the wounds of the Thirty Years' War. Moreover, he was in charge of church visitation in the city and the countryside. Another major concern was the cultivation of a mature Christianity in the youth; toward this end he wrote his *Milk of the Catechism* (*Catechismus Milch*).[17] The end in mind was the formation of students to be good, upright, and ethical citizens with an eye to Christian apologetics. He had already begun this work in 1634, when he was simply a city council member.

Dannhauer died on November 7, 1666, deeply loved by many and seen as a "great one in Israel." At his funeral service on November 11, city magistrates, professors and students, the teachers of the *Gymnasium*, and many of the citizens turned out, praising him for both his theology and his deep pastoral skills and concerns. Philipp Jakob Spener (1635–1705), Dannhauer's former student, wrote:

> Here rests a man who was a magnificent pillar of the holy faith, a terror to the enemies of the truth, a brave warrior for God's cause. In the midst of struggle and complaints, of which lords always have around themselves during wars, he neither tired of them, nor did flee shamefully before any enemy. Finally, the Lord of Hosts has called him out of the tumult and he has peacefully resigned his limbs in this tomb for a brief rest. The

---

[16] Horning, *Der Strassburger*, 83.

[17] Horning, *Der Strassburger*, 89.

triumph in heaven is near; he will immediately follow at the first sound of the imminent trumpets (what a lovely sound!), and will move festively into the heavenly city with many palms of victory. Meanwhile, there hangs brightly in God's holy house, glorious trophies of his victories over Rome and Geneva. These are his works, as a mighty defender of truth.[18]

Bibliography

Works by Dannhauer in English Translation

None of Dannhauer's writings have been translated.

Select Works by Dannhauer in Latin and German

Catechismus Milch Oder Der Erklärung deß Christlichen Catechismi. 10 vols. Strassburg: Spoor, 1642–78.

Epitome Rhetorica. 2nd. Ed. Strassburg: Mülbius, Staedelius, 1651.

Idea Boni Interpretis Et Malitiosi Calumniatoris. 4th ed. Strassburg: Staedelius, 1652.

Idea Boni Interpretis Et Malitiosi Sophistae. 4th ed. Strassburg: Staedelius, 1656.

Hermeneutica Sacra Sive Methodus exponendarum S. Litterarum proposita & vindicata. Strassburg: Staedelius, 1654.

Hodomoria Spiritus Calviniani, Duodecim Phantasmatis, Academica parrhesia ac philalethea Detecti. 2 vols. Strassburg: Spoor, 1654.

Hodomoria Spiritus Papaei, Duodecim Phantasmatis, Academica Parrhesia ac Philalethea Detecti. 2 vols. Strassburg: Spoor, 1653.

Hodosophia Christiana seu Theologia Positiva. Strassburg: Spoor, 1649.

Liber Conscientiae Apertus, Sive Theologiae Conscientiae. 2 vols. Strassburg: Spoor, 1662–67.

Mysterium Syncretismi Detecti, Proscripti, Et Symphonismo Compensati. Strassburg: Spoor, 1664.

---

[18] Horning, *Der Strassburger*, 96–97.

WRITING[19]

The Summary of the Second Table [of the Law]

"You shall love your neighbor as yourself; for I am the Lord" (Leviticus 19:18).

First Chapter: On the Love of the Neighbor in General.

"Whoever dwells in love, dwells in God and God in him."

John is perfectly aware of this, therefore he has not only set this forth in his written epistles, but he also has set forth orally in his old age nothing more than love, and he always takes care to say: "Children, love one another." And when he was asked by his disciples why he repeated the same thing so often, he answered, "Because it is the command of the Lord. Whoever has fulfilled it, has fulfilled everything." This is truly love, which is the fullness of love and the summary of all virtue, the root from which they all, as twigs and branches, spring, blossom, and grow, the master and ruler of all works and acts of a Christian, which compels the Christian to do good. These things arise from the chief commandment, on which the entire Law and prophets depend, as Christ teaches in Matthew 22:38–40.

And this is also the reason why in the holy Ten Commandments, the commandment to love was not expressly spoken. For all commandments aim at it as (according) to their center, and flow from this commandment of love and are contained in it as in one summary. We should, before we move to the rest of the commandments of the other table, treat the love of the neighbor in general. God, give us grace, that we might not only be hearers of the Word, but that we also might be doers of the Word.

Three circumstances must be taken into consideration: the things or persons who are to be loved; the love or the commandment of love itself; and the way and manner such love is to be employed so that it pleases God. Your neighbor is now the treasure, the person, who God sets before us to love, not merely the one who is related to us in a blood bond; not only the one who is our fellow citizen, countrymen, or person of common faith; not only those who are well-disposed to us with favor, who treat us with friendship, good deeds, or all good manners. For Christ says

[19] The section below is a select translation of Johann Conrad Dannhauer's "Die Summa der zweiten Tafel." This exposition can be found in his *Katechismusmilch im Auszug*, vol. 1, *Die heiligen Zehn Gebote*, ed. A. L. Gräbner (Milwaukee: Geo. Brumder, 1888), 191–200.

in Matthew 5:46–47, "If you love those who love you, what will you have for a reward? Don't even tax collectors act like this? And if you greet only your brothers, how does that make you any different? Don't the tax collectors also do this?" "This means do not love others only so long,"—the words of Luther—"that I picture a man or two who do what I like and do what I want them to, and I am friendly and favorable to them and no one else." Moreover, he says, "It is a rogue love when I am this sort of good friend to him who can serve and help me and hold me in honor, but hate him who despises and opposes me." The Hebrew term is not only about blood bonds, but also neighbors and friends, fellow workers, accomplices, also about parties who wrangle with one another and conduct lawsuits, yes of all those we need and those who need us, those God added according to his foreknowledge and predestination, that we must manage with them. And even according to this understanding, Christ has also interpreted the law of love. "You have heard," He says in Matthew 5:43–45, "that it has been said by the elders, you should love your neighbors and hate your enemies—thus far the false Pharisaical gloss. But I say to you, love your enemies, bless those who curse you, treat well those who hate you, pray for those who lie about you and persecute you, because in this way you are children of your Father in heaven. For he lets his sun shine over the evil and the good, and allows it to rain over the righteous and the unrighteous."

The best interpretation of this command has been shown by our Lord himself in the parable of the Samaritan from Luke 10:30–37. In this scene, he sets forth a man wounded, half-dead, and accordingly in need of help. [The Lord] allows a priest and Levite to pass before him, who let him lay in his blood, but a Samaritan also arrives, who has mercy on the poor man and cares for him. "Which of these three men," the Lord asked the scribes, "was a neighbor to this one who had fallen into the hands of murderers?" He answered, "The one who had mercy on him." So Jesus said to him, "Go forth therefore, and do likewise." That is to say, just as the Samaritan did good to the Jew, although the Jews and Samaritans were enemies, so, too, you also should have compassion on the Samaritans in your life, although they are not your friends, because the Samaritan has been set forth by God as a mercy to the Jew. Therefore, the term "your neighbor" comprehends all men in it, your blood bonds, your countrymen, but also your enemies who cause you heartbreak, so far as the same have been sent to you by God to receive from you compassion and Christian love, not only as Christ did, who died for us when we were still his enemies (Romans 5:8, 10), and prayed for his enemies, but also as Christians in the Early Church faithfully followed this command.

Eusebius testifies of them. During the time of the great plague, the one that struck Alexandria in Egypt, in the midst of danger to both body and life, they [early Christians] served their own persecutors.

Do you reply, "That is a hard teaching; how shall I accomplish this, that I should do good to those who have sworn themselves as my enemies? This is perhaps an evangelical counsel given only to those who want to be something special in Christianity. It does not apply as a command for all Christians. Perhaps this is an evangelical addition." Answer: This is no evangelical addition, but it is found in various parts of the law, which even want that which Christ here commands. "When you discover your enemy's ox or donkey, which has gone astray, you shall lead it back to him" (Exodus 23:4). "If your enemy hungers, provide him with bread; if he thirsts, give him water, then you will heap coals on his head, and the Lord will reward you" (Proverbs 25:21–22). In the same way, the apostle Paul makes this clear in Romans 12:18–20, concerning all men. In addition, holy men of God have understood it in no other way than that they show works of love to their neighbor, although the latter were heathens and enemies of religion. It is true that the Jews were not to mix with the heathen peoples, to whom they have been like executioners of God, the judge of the whole world, in exiling the seven nations, and they were not to kill them as their own enemies but as God's enemies. Furthermore, this is also true, that the enemies of God and religion are not to be loved for their wickedness or are to be strengthened in the same, but one must rather pray for them that they would be converted by God. Therefore, the legal sword of war and judgment has not been taken away from the authorities. But it does not follow from this that they therefore forego all humanity, should not help enemies in need, or otherwise should render general services.

Is there some kind of enjoyment, use, advantage, favor, promotion, beautiful physical form for which I should love my neighbor? If not, then I don't love my neighbor in this manner, but rather love myself; neighbor is a word to me, I am the object. "A servant when he works"—these are Luther's words—"neither sees nor thinks further than this, 'My master gives me my wages, and for this reason I serve him; otherwise I would not even look at him.' This servant has neither a clean heart nor attitude." Moreover, "When I or another preach for a good, fat parish, moreover because I permit it to be pleasing [to me], I may preach the Gospel well there, but my heart is not pure, but pure filth." Such advantage-seeking love also does no good, for if fortune changes, then also love disappears. This is a mousey love: mice are happy about cabinets and granaries, not on account of the granaries, but on account of fodder and grain. But the fundamental reason for such love is the love of God, and it stands out in our text with clear words, "For I am the Lord." I am the Lord who makes a beginning for such love and precede you with an example. If you want to be my child, then you, too, must imitate me in this matter [of love], which I redeemed and bought both for your neighbor and you, to possess the self-same salvation, which I daily set before your eyes on the cross in my poor suffering limbs, which I daily renew through the Word and Sacrament, which I present to your neighbor both through nature and the bond of blood as well as a proof to you through all sorts of providential acts, so that he should come near to you.

But what does it mean to love your neighbor? Answer: It means to recognize the neighbor as a creature of God, as a precious possession purchased by Jesus Christ; so far as he is a Christian, look at him as a temple of the Holy Spirit, the gifts which God imparts to him, and honor him on account of this; understand both his needs and burdens, or desire to know them; make his neighbor's profit and salvation his business; wish the same from the heart; [do] not begrudge him any goods; have mercy upon the neighbor in any needs that occur; have sympathy for him like a member of our own body (1 Corinthians 12:26). Comfort him if he has stumbled or done evil, help him back onto the right path (James 5:19–20). If he has become bound by debt, forgive him (Matthew 18:27, 32). Even if he has insurmountable failures and infirmities from a lack of temperament, bear and tolerate them (1 Corinthians 13:7; 1 Peter 4:8). On the contrary, if it goes well for your neighbor and according to his wishes, if he is pious, even called to love, rejoice with him, wish him well. If further called to love, behave to him in a friendly manner, speak well with and about the neighbor, present his concerns before God in prayer, advise him on good things, deter him from what is evil and harmful, talk to him in truth, and assist him in his work and in the truth, even assail and disclose oneself in needs, so that the neighbor does well (James 2:15[–16]). That means perform all business deals not out of a desire for honor or gold, but rather from the heart for the best for one's neighbor, and serve the same one with the [spiritual] gifts, which each one receives (1 Peter 4:10). Finally, it means to give a good example in life and conduct, not [to] offend, but build up (1 Corinthians 8:13; 10:23–24).

But how should I love him? God's Word answers: as yourself. Furthermore, there are also other examples of love portrayed in Scripture: the bottomless compassion of God the Father (John 15:9; Matthew 5:44–45), the inexpressible love of the Son (1 John 3:16; Romans 15:3; Ephesians 5:2), the example of the saints. The Spirit of God emanates here from those well-known [saints] and presents to us his own love to assist as a guide for that which we recognize as the best and even feel in ourselves.

The spirit of man, which is in man, knows best what is in man (1 Corinthians 2:11), which is appointed for us as a taskmaster, who should teach us in all cases how we should love our neighbor. This same prescribes for us two rules: The first is a command and reads, "All things that you would have people do to you, also do unto them" (Matthew 7:12). The second is a prohibition, "That which you would not have someone do to you, this also you should not do to another" (Tobit 4:16). The heathen King Alexander Severus let this saying be written down in his palace and everywhere.

However, this "as you yourself" includes in itself the following examples: (1) That heartfelt love: as you think of yourself from the heart, so, too, think of your neighbor. (2) The voluntary, uncompelled love: many do something good, the moneylender opens his cabinets and his cellar, but out of fear of the streets or dishonor, or else he would allow [his goods] to become public goods. (3) The love without price: many take a wife on account of money, who do it not as the mother of Moses, who suckled her child and would have also suckled it even if Pharaoh's daughter had not promised wages. (4) The warm and active love: be gone, cold love of the tongue, because word and the heart are quite far apart from one another. Empty glasses ring well, but they pour and give nothing. (5) The persistent love that perseveres in good times and in bad: be gone, weather vane love, which twists according to the wind.

Still, the Lord does not exclude Christian wisdom. The apostle Paul says in Galatians 6:10, "Let us do good to all men, particularly to those who are known as believers." All men are in fact to be loved because actually helping all men is impossible. Thus one should still advise and help those first and foremost who God has allowed to come, added, and sent according to the circumstances of this present time.

Thus the love of neighbor is one such virtue because man ought to provide for his fellow man, whether he be friend or foe, as he would want God to accommodate and serve the same in him, who requires his help so heartily, so freely, so warmly, so constantly as he thinks of, tolerates, comforts, betters, advances, honors, and testifies even about himself with gestures, words, and works all according to the will of God.

But where does one find such love? One reads with wonder how the first Church Christians held their goods in common; but now are the latter times, because instead of love, there arises shame and vice.

(1) The neglect of neighbor, in which one in fact does no ill but also does nothing good, lives for himself, serves nobody, and still wants to

have among such people the name of a silent conscripted love. Such people create a good peace for themselves, but how will they fulfill the commandment of the love? (2) The hatred of the neighbor, where one bears ill will toward the other because he somehow stepped on his foot. Therefore, it is not from zeal against the sin, but rather he became an enemy and adverse to him out of his own self-love. Such an evil affect he secretly carries in his heart, and it emerges on occasion through gestures, words, and outward actions, probably even propagates it among friends and relatives of the neighbor. (3) The false suspicion, which judges and cuts off enemies from itself, also thinks evil of the best words, works, and gestures, [and] must call all that his neighbor does evil or adverse acts. It looks at all in accord with its false imagination, so that often the other does not know how he is held in such contempt—a true poison of brotherly unity. (4) The wickedness of other affections that so fight against love, namely avarice, envy, remorselessness, contempt of the other, rude gestures, and words. (5) The unclean love, love in words, love compelled by fear, forbidden love, self-seeking, fickleness, and disorderly love.

This is also the description of the cardinal virtue of the other table, the love of the neighbor, a wonderful virtue, for in it we find the beautiful apparel of the new man (Colossians 3:12–14), the fruit of faith (Galatians 5:6), the bond of perfection, the royal colors of Christ our King: "By this shall everybody know that you are my disciples, that you have love for each other" (John 13:35). I maintain that a true Christian can shine forth in no better jewelry and decoration.

So it is incumbent upon all to have this virtue toward one another. "Don't owe anybody anything," says the apostle in Romans 13:8, "except that you should love one another." Here is a virtue that God will not leave unrewarded, when the joyful "come here," and the felicitous praise "I was hungry, etc." is heard (Matthew 25:35–36).

Oh Sweet Love, grant us your favor.
Let us find the appeal of love,
That we should love one another from the heart.
And remain of one mind in peace.
Amen.

Johann Rist (1607–67)

"The Sweet Cross Has Squeezed Many Hymns out of Me"

by Jon D. Vieker

Life

Johann Rist[1] (1607–67) was a prominent poet and literary figure of the early Baroque era. A profound scholar and polymath, he excelled

[1] The sources consulted for this essay are as follows: Wolfgang Herbst, ed., *Wer ist wer im Gesangbuch* (Göttingen: Vandenhoeck & Ruprecht, 2001); Christian Möller, ed., *Kirchenlied und Gesangbuch: Quellen zu ihre Geschichte,* Mainzer Hymnologische Studien, no. 1 (Tübingen: A. Francke Verlag, 2000); Martin Rößler, *Liedermacher im Gesangbuch: Liedgeschichte in Lebensbildern* (Stuttgart: Calwer Verlag, 2001); *The Canterbury Dictionary of Hymnology*, s.v. "German Hymnody," accessed October 14, 2015, www.hymnology.co.uk/g/german-hymnody; *The Canterbury Dictionary of Hymnology*, s.v. "Johann Rist," accessed October 14, 2015, www.hymnology.co.uk/j/johann-rist.

equally in the study of science and mathematics as well as language and the arts. Rist was a cultured cleric who served his whole life in a single parish but rubbed shoulders with many of the leading aristocrats and artists of his day. Typical of the early Baroque period, his writings are replete with dramatic elements and an abundance of stylistic devices. Although he was an extremely popular and renowned author during his lifetime, he is remembered today mostly for his hymns.

Born in Ottensen (near Hamburg) on March 8, 1607 (just four days before Paul Gerhardt [1607–76]), Rist was the fourth of eight children born to his pastor father, Carl, and mother, Margarete née Ringemult. His earliest schooling was in Hamburg, where he subsequently graduated from *Gymnasium* in 1626 to attend university in Rinteln (an der Weser) as an aspiring law student. At Rinteln, however, he soon gravitated to the study of theology and poetry and came under the influence of the famous theologian and hymnwriter Josua Stegmann (1588–1632). He also excelled in the study of medicine, chemistry, botany, mathematics, and music (even mastering the violin). He eventually transferred to the prestigious University of Rostock. In the winter of 1628, he was bedridden there for weeks and nearly died of the plague.

Prior to assuming a pastorate, Rist began service in 1633 as tutor to a prominent family in Heide (Holstein). There he became acquainted with Gisela Stapel. Two years later, they were married, and Rist assumed the pastorate at Wedel (an der Elbe), a congregation of some two thousand souls. From the age of twenty-eight to the end of his life, Rist served the congregation in Wedel. He and his wife produced five children, two of whom died early. In 1662, Gisela preceded him in death, and two years later, Rist married his friend's widow, Anna née Badehoop. Rist died on August 31, 1667, of a severe fever.

Rist lived during the difficult period of the Thirty Years' War (1618–48), when the loss of life in Europe was unparalleled until modern times. Total casualties are estimated to have numbered more than 8,000,000. The town of Wedel was plundered by the Swedish Army in 1643. Rist's own home was also ravaged; much of his library, scientific equipment, and collections were either taken or destroyed. Fifteen years later, during the Danish-Swedish War, his home was again plundered of its belongings. Though not as profoundly afflicted as Johann Heermann, "The Silesian Job," Rist once remarked: "Viele Lieder hat mir das süße Kreuz abgepreßt" (The sweet cross has squeezed many hymns out of me).

Rist's poetic works were vast and prolific; they ranged from the secular to the sacred. Rist completely embraced the literary reforms of Martin Opitz (1597–1639) and, upon Opitz's death, became Germany's leading advocate for the standardizations of German language and poetry that Opitz had advanced. Rist composed more than thirty dramatic works (mostly operas and plays), but only a few have survived, among them: *Friede wünschende Teutschland* (Peace-longing Germany) (1647) and *Friedejauchzende Teutschland* (Peace-exulting Germany) (1648)—both dealing with the final years of the Thirty Years' War. He also authored numerous collections of poetry, including his earliest collection, *Johann Ristii Poetische Lust-Garte* (Poetic Pleasure Gardens by Johann Rist) (1638); and an ode to Christian IV (1577–1648), the King of Denmark, *Triumph-Lied alß . . . Christian der vierdte, zu Dennemarck . . . König . . . deroselben Königreich Norwegen in . . . Glückstatt . . . wiederum anlangete* (Victory Song as King Christian IV of Denmark Again Attained His Kingdom of Norway) (1631). In 1644, Rist was crowned poet laureate by Emperor Ferdinand III (1608–57) and in 1533 was ennobled by the same. In 1647, Rist was made a member of the "Fruchtbringende Gesellschaft" (Fruit-bearing Society), a prestigious literary society. Several years later, he established his own literary guild, the "Elbschwanorden" (Elbe Swan Order).

Rist is remembered today mostly for his religious poems and hymn texts. All totaled, they number more than 650 and are found in some eighteen extant collections published during his lifetime, the most important being: *Johann Risten himlischer Lieder* (Johann Rist's Heavenly Songs) (1641 and a number of subsequent editions), *Neuer himlischer Lieder sonderbahres Buch* (A Special Book of New Heavenly Songs) (1652), *Sabbahtische Seelenlust, das ist, Lehr- Trost- Vermahung- und Warnungsreiche Lieder* (Sabbath Joy of the Soul, that is, Teaching, Comfort, Admonition, and Warning Hymns) (1651), *Frommer und gottseliger Christen alltägliche Hauszmusic* (Pious and Godly Christians' Everyday House Music) (1654), *Neue musikalische Fest-Andachten, bestehende in Lehr- Trost- Vermahnungs- und Warnungsreichen Liederen, über Alle Evangelien* (New Musical Feast-day Devotions, Consisting in Teaching, Comforting, Admonishing, and Warning-rich Hymns on All the Gospels) (1655), *Neue musikalische Katechismus Andachten* (New Musical Catechetical Devotions) (1656), and a collection in two volumes, *Neues musikalisches Seelenparadis, in sich begreiffend die allerfürtreflichste Sprüche der heilgen Schrifft . . . in Liederen und Hertzens-Andachten* (A New Musical Soul-paradise, in Which Are Found the Most Complete Collection of Sayings from Holy Scripture . . . in Hymns and Heart Devotions) (1660–62).

As was the custom of the day, Rist's lengthy hymn texts were published as devotional literature for use in court and home and were seldom, if ever, sung in his own parish. Through his hymnody, Rist displayed his dual passion for poetry and pastoral care, crafting his texts *docere et delectare* (to teach and to delight). Although Rist himself was an accomplished amateur musician and ventured into musical composition on occasion, a number of famous musicians in his day composed tunes and compositions utilizing his texts, including Johann Schop (1615–64/65), Andreas Hammerschmidt (1611/12–75), and Jakob Praetorius (1586–1651); and in the generations following, Georg Philipp Telemann (1681–1767), Dietrich Buxtehude (1637–1707), Johann Sebastian Bach (1685–1750), and Carl Philipp Emmanuel Bach (1714–88).

Although his solidly doctrinal hymn texts place him squarely among the orthodox Lutherans of his day, Rist was at times inclined to favor the aesthetically pleasing over the confessional challenges of his times. For instance, he had no qualms in accepting the Article of Tolerance (prescribing that Lutheran and Reformed preachers not preach against each other's doctrine) mandated by the Great Elector, Friedrich Wilhelm, (1620–88) in Berlin. This is the same document that Paul Gerhardt had rejected and for which he was eventually forced from his pulpit at the St. Nicholas Church and finally exiled in his old age to out-of-the-way Lübben.

By the eighteenth century, forty of Rist's most important hymns could be found in the most significant regional and devotional hymn collections in Germany. Today, five are found in the German Protestant hymnal, *Evangelisches Gesangbuch* (1993), four in *Christian Worship* (1993); five in *Evangelical Lutheran Hymnary* (1996); two in *Evangelical Lutheran Worship* (2006); and four in *Lutheran Service Book* (2006).

BIBLIOGRAPHY

Works by Rist in English Translation

"Johann von Rist (1607–67)." In *Seventeenth-Century Lutheran Meditations and Hymns*, edited and translated by Eric Lund, 294–301. New York: Paulist Press, 2011.

"Rist: O Living Bread from Heaven." In *Documents from the History of Lutheranism, 1517–1750*, edited and translated by Eric Lund, 274. Minneapolis: Fortress Press, 2002.

Select Works by Rist in German and Latin

Himmlische Lieder. Hildesheim and New York: Georg Olms, 1976.

Neue Himmlische Lieder (1651). Edited by Johann Anselm Steiger. Berlin: Akademie Verlag, 2013.

Rist, Johann, and Johann Schop. *Himmlische Lieder (1641/42)*. Edited by Johann Anselm Steiger. Berlin: Akademie Verlag, 2012.

Rist, Johann, and Martin Coler. *Neue Hochheilige Passions-Andachten (1664)*. Edited by Johann Anselm Steiger. Berlin: Walter de Gruyter, 2014.

WRITING[2]

To the most revered in God and noble lord,
Lord Hans Heinrich of Haselhorst,[3] lord of the house,
chosen and confirmed abbot of
St. Michael's in Lüneburg of the Principality of Braunschweig-Lüneburg,
most distinguished ruler,
heir of the houses of Hermansburg and Oldendorf,
My gracious lord.

Most worthy in God, gracious Lord,

It is from the heavenly books, the Old as well as New Testaments, known so well by God-loving Christians, that the saints of God, when they experience the great and many blessings from the Almighty and in due thankfulness for them, have caused to be rendered, seen, and felt the glorious, beautiful hymns and psalms of praise, written and sung in honor of the Giver of all good things.

There, Moses, a prince in Israel, led the people of God through the Red Sea and, as it were, snatched them from the jaws of death, while the terrifying punishment upon the tyrant, Pharaoh, and his Egyptians was seen. There he immediately spoke: "I will sing to the Lord, for he has done a glorious thing—the horses and wagons he has plunged into the sea" [Exodus 15:1]. . . .

Yes, what an unspeakable (yes, indescribable!) joy and splendor it will be, when we, in the next and eternal life, with the company of so

---

[2] This is a select translation of Johann Rist and Johann Schop, dedication to the first part of *Himmlische Lieder (1641/42)*, ed. Johann Anselm Steiger (Berlin: Akademie Verlag, 2012), 9–13.

[3] Johann Heinrich von Haselhorst (1582–1642) attended school at St. Michael's in Lüneburg, and later studied in Wittenberg, Helmstedt, and Leipzig. In 1629, he became abbot of the cloister of St. Michael's in Lüneburg.

many thousands of heavenly singers, will raise our totally perfected voices with the dear holy angels and the elect of God, and laud and praise the most-holy Trinity without ceasing.

In contemplation of all of this, gracious lord, I have also pressed forward and wrought several heavenly hymns—partly through cross and suffering and partly from inner joy (both of which, for any faithful Christian, constantly alternate in this troubled life). I drafted them, just for me and in private, according to proper poetic style, and intended them to be used for the awakening of Christian devotion. Later, however, several of these versified hymns accidentally fell into the hands of others, and in particular, into the hands of high [and noble] persons, among whom also was Lord Misslick,[4] his grace, baron of Hirschhof. Once several of these my gracious lords and friends, in particular the most highly thought of and gracious Lord Misslick (whose splendid virtues are known so far and wide that the poisonous envy itself has touched him [Wisdom 6:23], or, lest it master him, he must avoid it completely) graciously, generously, and kindly requested that this same Christian, poetic work might be shared in print also with other pious hearts, that God's praise might thereby be spread and increased ever further and greater.

To follow this proper, yes Christian, desire, gracious lord, I have at this time provided the first ten versified hymns with their lovely melodies (which a most excellent and famous man of our time in the area of the singing arts set, each with its proper melody). I have published them and want to pass them on—first to the glory of the Most High, then also to all who are God-loving, art-loving, and music-loving for their good and kind pleasure.

That I may, however, be further emboldened, as such, to dedicate to your grace, for the sake of its external reputation, this brief writing, a completely underestimated little work, and to present such a simple gift in allegiance to one so high, so that you without doubt will graciously think well of me. In this day and age, when so many lack all manner of discernment concerning us and our writings, in which we boldly depict the current, fiercely evil, and perverse world, we see rightly there that we [must] present our book only to such persons whom God has enlightened with a high understanding, whom he has elevated with particular gifts of discernment way above the rabble, and whom with great

---

[4] Johann Brzetislaw Mislik von Hirschhoff, to whom Part Two of Rist's *Himmlische Lieder* was later dedicated, was a Bohemian nobleman, about whom little is known and for whom no biographical dates are available. See Rist and Schop, *Himmlische Lieder,* 92n1.

knowledge, diligent pondering, and lengthy experience he has splendidly gifted with the ability to prudently judge every kind of writing.

Yet, how would I ever have been able to find or meet a high-born person [anywhere] under the sun who would do for these pieces all that your grace could do, either beforehand or even now? I [would have] sought a widely-renowned lord of a spiritual estate, one from the true Christian religion, a devoted noble churchman in Germany. I have truly found much more than I was looking for. I struggled as to how I might meet someone with a God-loving and Word-loving character (a character that has turned far away from all vanity, which exercises itself day and night, ever growing and increasing more and more in the fear of God). Moreover, I sought here a superb mind, I desired an exquisite knowledge of the many arts and of many languages—yes, I sought one such noble soul, who above all, would have a love for righteousness, sincerity, faithfulness, and truth. Truly, I have not sought in vain, but rather, these and many more [traits] are all found to be overflowing in your grace—both in common, and indeed each in particular—and I count it my good fortune that my efforts have been so splendidly successful.

Thus, I would desire to ask your grace herewith, in all obedience, whether it would please you to gather and accept with gracious eyes and hands these first ten of my heavenly hymns from the one who has daily beseeched the Almighty from the bottom of his soul that your grace, as a true Christian lord and honorable prelate for many years, might be preserved with favored prosperity, powerfully protected from all misfortunes of body and soul, and richly showered with thousands of blessings and benefits. Then also graciously allow and grant me the least of all those who are allowed to be fit to truly inwardly promote the honor of God that I may be found worthy to live and to die, gracious lord.

Your gracious, subservient, obedient servant,
Johannes Rist

Given in Wedel on the Elbe, on the day of St. Annen,
in the year after Christ's birth, 1641.

PAUL GERHARDT (1607–76)

A THEOLOGIAN SIFTED IN SATAN'S SIEVE[1]

by Gerald S. Krispin

LIFE

While not well known as a confessor of his Lutheran faith, Paul Gerhardt[2] (1607–76) is surpassed only by Martin Luther in the number

[1] "A Theologian Sifted in Satan's Sieve" is the subscript on his portrait in Lübben.

[2] This short biography is based upon the author's *Paul Gerhardt: In statu confessionis* (master's thesis, Concordia Seminary, 1987). The sources for this thesis and the text above are drawn from three main categories of publications: (1) Editions of hymns, such as: Johann Friedrich Bachmann, ed., *Paulus Gerhardts geistliche Lieder* (Berlin: L. Oehmigke's Verlag, 1866); Albert Fischer and Wilhelm Tümpel, eds., *Das deutsche evangelische Kirchenlied des siebzehnten Jahrhunderts*, 6 vols. (Gütersloh: C. Bertelsmann, 1904–16); and most notably, Eberhard von Cranach-Sichart, ed., *Paul Gerhardt: Dichtungen und Schriften* (Munich: Verlag Paul Müller, 1957). (2) Hymnological contributions: Eduard Emil Koch, *Geschichte des Kirchenlieds und Kirchengesangs der christlichen, insbesondere der deutschen evangelischen Kirche*, 3rd ed. (Stuttgart: Chr. Belser'schen Verlagshandlung, 1867), 3:239–327; Paul Gabriel, *Das deutsche evangelische Kirchenlied von Martin Luther bis zur Gegenwart* (Leipzig: Verlag Quelle und Meyer, 1935); Wilhelm Lueken, *Lebensbilder der Liederdichter und Melodisten*, vol. 2/1, *Handbuch zum Evangelischen Kirchengesangbuch*, ed. Christhard Mahrenholz, Oskar Söhngen und Otto Schlißke

of hymns that are found in German Lutheran hymnals. And while he did not write nearly as many hymns as did many of his contemporaries, the quality of his hymns in terms of both poetry and doctrine has impressed them upon the hearts and minds of all who share in his Lutheran confessional heritage.

The home into which Paul Gerhardt was born on March 12, 1607 was well rooted in the Lutheran faith of Electoral Saxony. His mother's grandfather, Master Gallus Döbler, occupied the second court-preacher position created by the Elector August (1526–86) in Dresden. From 1555 to 1570, Döbler served as the ecclesiastical superintendent of Eilenburg. Upon Döbler's death in 1570, Gerhardt's grandfather, Kasper Starke, succeeded him as superintendent. Starke's tenure at Eilenburg saw the Lutherans of the Electorate of Saxony celebrate the fiftieth anniversary of the presentation of the Augsburg Confession, as well as the signing of the Formula of Concord by the Elector August on June 25, 1580 in Dresden. Yet Starke was also to witness and suffer the consequences of a major policy change subsequent to the elector's death in 1586.

August's only son, Christian I (1560–91), came under the influence of the Reformed chancellor Nikolaus Krell (1550–1601). Krell sought to steer Electoral Saxony toward a political alliance with another territory of the Holy Roman Empire of the German Nation, the predominantly Reformed Palatinate. Amid these political maneuvers, the confessional stand of the Lutherans in Electoral Saxony came under severe attack. The Formula of Concord was all but annulled because it divided Confessional Lutherans from the Reformed on the theological front, as well as proved

---

(Göttingen: Vandenhoeck und Ruprecht, 1957); and Walter Blankenburg, "Paul Gerhardt," in *Die Musik in Geschichte und Gegenwart*, ed. Friedrich Blume (Kassel und Basel: Im Bärenreiter Verlag, 1955), 4:1790–97. (3) Biographies (including primary sources): the foundational work of Hermann Petrich, *Paul Gerhardt: Ein Beitrag zur Geschichte des deutschen Geistes* (Gütersloh: C. Bertelsmann, 1914); E. C. G. Langbecker, *Leben und Lieder von Paulus Gerhardt* (Berlin: Verlag der Sander'schen Buchhandlung, 1841), whose biography is replete with primary documents; Kurt Ihlenfeld, *Huldigung für Paul Gerhardt* (Munich: Siebenstern Taschenbuch Verlag, 1956); Karl Hessenbacher, *Paul Gerhardt: Sein Leben-Seine Lieder*, ed. Siegfried Heinzelmann (Neuffen: Sonnenweg Verlag, 1963); the most recent work by Christian Bunners, *Paul Gerhardt: Weg-Werk-Wirkung*, 4th ed. (Göttingen: Vandenhoeck & Ruprecht, 2006); and a popular introduction to Gerhardt by Hans-Joachim Beeskow, *Paul Gerhardt: 1607–1676* (Lübben: Heimat-Verlag, 2006). It is notable that Beeskow discovered the original documents relating to Gerhardt's engagement in the Berlin Colloquy as part of the estate of Martin Lubath (1621–90). These documents (in three volumes) are found in the *Zentral-und Landesbibliothek Berlin, Sammlung des Berlinischen Gymnasiums zum Grauen Kloster,* GKI Archive XII/90/123.

highly obstructive to the political aims of Christian I and Krell. On the congregational level, the language of exorcism in baptism was deemed especially offensive to the Reformed because it was thought to be a manifestly papist rite. It was consequently forbidden through an edict of the elector, much to the chagrin of Confessional Lutherans. Those of the Lutheran clergy who refused to comply with the edict were summarily removed from office. Among those who suffered this fate was Gerhardt's grandfather, Kasper Starke of Eilenburg. In July 1591, the superintendent of the village of Gräfenhainichen, Tobias Mirus, met a similar fate. It was in Gräfenhainichen that Paul Gerhardt would be born into this tradition of Confessional Lutheran faithfulness in the face of persecution.

Yet by the time of Gerhardt's birth, the tables had turned once more in favor of the Lutherans of the Saxon Electorate. Christian I had died suddenly in 1591 at the age of thirty-one; Chancellor Krell was summarily beheaded. With the return of a Confessional Lutheran presence in government, those who had been driven from their pulpits returned. Under Christian II (1583–1611), and later Johann Georg I (1585–1656), Electoral Saxony was continually on guard against any renewed Calvinist insurgency and subterfuge. Schools and congregations were required to uphold and adhere to the Book of Concord, especially the Formula of Concord; those holding the pastoral office were periodically examined as to the faithfulness to their confessional subscription. This would become Gerhardt's theological heritage.

Paul Gerhardt was the second son of Christian and Dorothea (née Starke) Gerhardt. His older brother, who bore his father's name, had been born in 1606, with his younger sister, Agnes, being born between 1612 and 1619. The destruction of church records after the sacking of the town by the Swedes in 1637 leaves some of these dates tentative.

Paul Gerhardt's father was presumed to be active as an innkeeper at the time of Paul's birth, a role that his brother later assumed in his father's stead. Paul's father also came to serve as one of the three concurrent mayors of Gräfenhainichen. Evidently Paul was a son born to a very respectable family. Attending the local grammar school, he became well versed in Latin. Upon graduation in 1622, a fifteen-year-old Gerhardt was deemed worthy by the town council to attend the Princely Academy (*Fürstenschule*) in Grimma on a village scholarship. This support was necessary, as both his parents had already died by this time: his father in 1619 and his mother in 1621.

At Grimma, Gerhardt was met by a faculty committed to the struggle against Crypto-Calvinists, that is, apparent Lutherans who held to some of John Calvin's (1509–1564) teachings, especially those regarding the

Lord's Supper. Since 1547, the instructors at the Princely Academy had been required to subscribe to the Torgau Articles, which consisted of a collection of theological opinions by the four Wittenberg theologians—Martin Luther (1483–1546), Philipp Melanchthon (1497–1560), Justus Jonas (1493–1555), and Johannes Bugenhagen (1485–1558)—that informed the Augsburg Confession of 1530. Later, in 1579, the Formula of Concord was placed before them. By 1601, a commitment by way of an oath to expose errors in doctrine was required of the entire faculty, which was superintended by rigorous visitations. These visitors had at their disposal the theological *Enchiridion* of Leonhard Hutter (1563–1616)[3], written under the mandate of Christian II. Hutter composed his influential *Compendium of Theological Topics* (*Compendium locorum theologicorum*) as something of a memory guide consisting of thirty-four articles that standardized formulations and responses for all who sought to be faithful to the Lutheran Confessions. Doubtless, Hutter's *Compendium* was foundational for Gerhardt in his early theological formation and for his further studies for the holy ministry at Wittenberg.

By the time Paul Gerhardt came to Wittenberg in 1627, the university had become an exemplary institution of confessional unity and doctrinal purity. All faculty, not just those teaching in theology, had to subscribe to the Unaltered Augsburg Confession along with the entire Book of Concord. This subscription also extended to students at the university. In Wittenberg, Gerhardt therefore received a thoroughly orthodox Lutheran education that culminated in the systematic study and analysis of the doctrines of the Formula of Concord, including its polemical thrust.

Unsurprisingly, the polemics of the Thirty Years' War (1618–48) overshadow practically all of Gerhardt's life, from his time at Grimma; to Wittenberg; his initial sojourn in Berlin as a tutor; as pastor in Mittenwalde, then Berlin, and finally in Lübben. The war had precluded his receiving an office after graduating at Wittenberg. Consequently, he had remained in Wittenberg until 1642 as a tutor in the house of the Wittenberg vicar, August Fleischhauer. He continued as a tutor in Berlin, where he lived in the house of a solicitor, Andreas Berthold, whose youngest daughter Gerhardt would marry in 1655.

In 1642, Gerhardt arrived in a Berlin devastated by a Thirty Years' War that would continue for another six years. Before the outbreak of this war in 1618, Berlin had had some 12,000 inhabitants; when Gerhardt

[3] Hutter, who had studied at the universities of Leipzig, Heidelberg, and Jena, had become a Professor of Theology at the University of Wittenberg in 1596, where he also held the office of rector three terms.

arrived, its population had been reduced to under 7,000. Yet despite the travails of war, Berlin had tremendously creative people operating within its walls. Most significant among them were those of the choirmaster of St. Nicolai's Church, Johann Crüger (1598–1662). Crüger had published a hymnal for personal devotion called the *Musical Practice of Piety* (*Praxis Pietatis Melica*) in 1640. In Crüger, Gerhardt found a friend and collaborator, as Gerhardt had proven himself an adept poet (in Latin and German) and a talented writer of hymn texts. Crüger came to add specialized melodies to Gerhardt's first set of eighteen published hymns that appeared in the 1647 edition of the *Musical Practice of Piety*. Among these first hymns were "Now Rest beneath Night's Shadow" (*LSB* 880), "Awake, My Heart, with Gladness" (*LSB* 467), and "Now Let Us Come Before Him" (*LW* 184).

Gerhardt, through his words, and Crüger, through his melodies, sought to provide consolation in the midst of want and devastation for the survivors of the war. Notably, the hymnbook of Crüger, and thus the hymns themselves, were not meant for public worship but were written for personal devotion, as evidenced by the extensive use of the first person personal pronoun. While the "I" of Gerhardt's texts is in harmony with the "musical practice of piety music" (which is what *Praxis Pietatis Melica* means), there is always a clear connection between the individual believer and the church gathered in the Divine Service. The use of hymnbooks during the Divine Service was an innovation that was not accepted until well after Gerhardt's death. Consequently, Gerhardt's hymns continued to be used in a personal and devotional manner until hymnbooks themselves became used within a congregational setting.

It was not until Gerhardt was forty-four, in 1651, that he was first called to be a pastor. This was only because of a vacancy at the death of the incumbent, Casper Göde, in Mittenwalde, a town that lies just south of Berlin. The town council had turned to the Berlin ministerium for advice, which in turn recommended Gerhardt to them. After submitting to several theological examinations, Paul Gerhardt was ordained on November 18, 1651. On the occasion of his ordination, he provided an unequivocal confessional subscription to each document within the Book of Concord, and especially the Formula of Concord, as having been established on the unshakable foundation of the prophetic and apostolic Scriptures. On November 30, 1651, he was installed in Mittenwalde by his colleague Andreas Fromm, who himself was the vicar and canon of St. Peter's Church in Berlin.

Gerhardt's time in Mittenwalde proved to be his most fruitful as a hymnwriter. In 1653, Crüger issued the fifth edition of the *Musical*

Practice of Piety, this time with the addition of sixty-four new hymns written by Paul Gerhardt. Among them were some of his best-known hymns, including "A Lamb Goes Uncomplaining Forth" (*LSB* 438) and "O Sacred Head, Now Wounded" (*LSB* 449), a hymn plausibly inspired by the predella of the altar in the church of Mittenwalde. The predella still features a depiction of the Cloth of Veronica, with a striking image of the bloodied face of Christ with the crown of thorns embedded in his brow. Aside from his hymns, several funeral sermons of Gerhardt's survive from this time—sermons that focus on the consolation of the Gospel in a manner understandable to the ordinary parishioner who may not have been theologically astute. But it is for his hymns that Gerhardt is known today, though this was not so during his century.

Three years after his arrival, in February of 1655, Gerhardt married Anna Maria Berthold (1622–68), the youngest daughter of the Berlin household in which he had been tutor. The following May, they rejoiced in the birth of their first child, a daughter, who sadly died while not yet a year old. The memorial plaque honoring their daughter remains in Mittenwalde, on the south wall of St. Moritz's church, with the inscription, "My years have been few and difficult."

For all its creativity, the time in Mittenwalde was relatively brief. In May of 1657, Gerhardt received news that he had been chosen to be the vicar of St. Nicolai's Church in Berlin. His brother-in-law, Joachim Fromm, had passed away and created the vacancy that he was called to fill. He accepted the call on June 4 and was performing his official duties in Berlin by July of 1657.

Yet these duties were performed in the shadow of the Elector Frederick William (1620–88), who sought to create a unified Reformed/Lutheran Church within Electoral Brandenburg, of which Berlin was the capital. Frederick William himself had been brought up within the Reformed tradition in the Netherlands, where he had witnessed a relatively harmonious coexistence of Lutherans among a predominantly Calvinist population. He firmly believed that the discord he came to witness between the Reformed and Lutherans in Brandenburg was attributable to two sources: the Book of Concord (particularly the Formula of Concord) and the overt influence of Wittenberg theologians and the pastors whom they taught. By the time Gerhardt had returned to Berlin, the Elector's decree of December 3, 1656, had prohibited subscription to the Formula of Concord at ordination and ordinations outside of his territory on March 3, 1657. Lutheran pastors such as Gerhardt felt compelled to take a stand. This they did through preaching and teaching the confessional faith to which they had subscribed, and consistent with their subscription, publicly rejecting the errors of the Reformed in doctrine and practice.[4]

In response, Frederick William, through the agency of his Court Chaplain, Bartholomäus Stosch (1604–86), drafted an Edict of Toleration that came into force on June 2, 1662. The edict itself was predicated on an agreement that had been reached between the Reformed and Lutherans at the 1661 Kassel Colloquy, which essentially held that whatever differences may exist between the two confessions, none are fundamental to the faith. In agreement with 1662 Wittenberg *Epicrisis De Colloqvio Cassellano Rintelio-Marpurgensium,* which denied that fundamental doctrinal agreement existed between the two confessions, the Berlin ministerium could not comply with the elector's optimistic edict.[5] Undaunted, though irritated, the Elector prescribed a "friendly colloquy" that was to promote irenic dialogue and open-minded discussion between the Reformed clergy and the Lutheran ministerium, of which Paul Gerhardt was a member. As secretary of the ministerium, Gerhardt was also the spokesman. As such, he was singled out as being the "most stubborn Lutheran", the very "soul of the resistance", and in fact, the "leader of the resistance."[6] Between 1662 and 1663, seventeen dialogues took place, producing an exchange of draft statements, many of which were punctuated with definitive rejections of the opposing position, especially on the part of the Lutherans. Gerhardt himself was convinced that any concession to the Calvinist position constituted what he termed religious syncretism and intolerable for the following reason: "That there are Christians among the Reformed members, I freely admit, but that the Reformed members are Christians as such (*quatenus tales*) and so my fellow Christians, my fellow brothers . . . this I reject. . . . I therefore cannot regard the Calvinists to be Christians."[7] At the heart of the matter was the Lord's Supper, and the attendant Christology of the real presence of Christ with his body and blood in the bread and wine to be eaten and drunk for one's salvation. Because the Reformed rejected the real pres-

---

[4] The 1662 Wittenberg *Epicrisis De Colloqvio Cassellano Rintelio-Marpurgensium's* denial of fundamental doctrinal agreement between Lutherans and Reformed helped prompt the Great Elector to finally issue his June 2, 1662 Edict of Tolerance and, on August 21, 1662, ban his populace from attending the University of Wittenberg. On August, 21, 1662, he also called the Berlin Colloquy. Regarding the Great Elector's attempts to Calvinize the Lutheran Church of his territory, see Johannes M. Ruschke, *Paul Gerhardt und der Berliner Kirchenstreit* (Tübingen: Mohr Siebeck, 2012).

[5] "Paul Gerhardt der Bekenner," *Lehre und Wehre* 53 (1907): 55–56n8.

[6] Hermann Sasse, *Was heißt lutherisch?* (Munich: Chr. Kaiser Verlag, 1936), 108.

[7] Langbecker, *Leben,* 81.

ence of Christ's body and blood in consonance with their Christology, and in turn censured the importance of the oral eating (*oralis manducationis*), Gerhardt made it clear that this alone ensures that "neither will we be able to accept them as brothers and comrades in faith, nor do they desire our brotherhood."[8]

This firm confessional stand (or recalcitrance and obstinacy in the view of the Reformed) led to the failure of this lengthy colloquy. The Elector therefore sought to enforce the silence and compliance of the Lutheran pastors by requiring sworn statements of obedience to his wishes or be deposed from office. Most pastors of the Lutheran ministerium, with Gerhardt among them, could not comply and were consequently deposed from the offices they held in Berlin. While Gerhardt's reputation as a devout pastor and hymnwriter served to protract the process of his dismissal, he was finally removed from office on February 4, 1667.[9] Gerhardt had written that any conditions imposed upon his ministry as a Lutheran pastor that militated against his confession were an assault on his conscience, which is "an atrocity before God and draws not blessing but a curse."[10]

Though deposed from office because of his confessional stand, he remained in Berlin until 1668. During the fall of that year, the town council of Lübben had lost its pastor and turned to Gerhardt to fill the post. Gerhardt consented to preach a sermon in order for the parish to get a sense of his pastoral commitment. In October of 1668, the town council sent Gerhardt a call to serve as their pastor. However, the illness of his son and negotiations about proper accommodation delayed his arrival in Lübben until June 16, 1669. This was his final parish. He died in Lübben on May 27, 1676, at the age of sixty-nine, leaving to his thirteen-year-old son, Paul Friedrich, his final testament in which he commends him to the grace of God and urges upon him the same confessional faithfulness that had carried him through life, and finally into the arms of his beloved Savior of whom he sang in his hymn "O Sacred Head, Now Wounded":

---

[8] Langbecker, *Leben,* 82–83.

[9] By this time, Johann Georg Ebeling (1637–76) of Lüneburg had replaced Crüger (who had died in 1663) as cantor at St. Nicolai. In 1666/7, Ebeling published a compendium of 120 songs by Gerhardt for which he had composed some twenty-six new melodies. This book was fittingly entitled *Paul Gerhardt's Spiritual Devotions* (*Pauli Gerhardi Geistliche Andachten*).

[10] Cranach-Sichart, *Paul,* 479; Langbecker, *Leben,* 26.

Be Thou my consolation,
My shield, when I must die;
Remind me of Thy passion
When my last hour draws nigh.
Mine eyes shall then behold Thee,
Upon Thy cross shall dwell,
My heart by faith enfold Thee.
Who dieth thus dies well. (*LSB* 450:7)

BIBLIOGRAPHY

Works by Gerhardt in English Translation[11]

"Paul Gerhardt (1607–1676)." In *Seventeenth-Century Lutheran Meditations and Hymns*, edited and translated by Eric Lund, 302–36. New York: Paulist Press, 2011.

Paul Gerhardt's Spiritual Songs. Translated by John Kelly. London: Alexander Strahan, 1867.

Select Works by Gerhardt in Latin and German

Gerhardt, Paul. *Pauli Gerhardi Geistliche Andachten Bestehend in hundert und zwantzig Liedern / Auff Hoher und vornehmer Herren Anfoderung in ein Buch gebracht / Der göttlichen Majestät zu foderst Zu Ehren / denn auch der werthen und bedrängten Christenheit zu Trost / und einer jedweden gläubigen Seelen Zu Vermehrung ihres Christenthums Also Dutzendweise mit neuen sechsstimmigen Melodeyen gezieret.* Edited by Johann Georg Elbing. Berlin: Christoff Rungen, 1667.

[11] A number of Paul Gerhardt's hymns by various translators are included in English-language Lutheran hymnals. One comprehensive compilation of all his hymns in English was published in the nineteenth century, which is now in the public domain and available online.

WRITING

Regarding the Theses of the Reformed Set before us on November 7, 1662[12]

These theses [that the matter of the oral eating is not important enough that God would fail to save *either* a lay Reformed Christian or a Reformed preacher because of their ignorance or failure to acknowledge it] lead us to confess unequivocally what we have consistently asserted: that the authority of the oral eating be given priority. However, the quest for truth will quickly reveal to us that this phrase is more than a mere opinion, by which either we will be persuaded to say that our confession is heterodox or the Reformed will be proved wrong on the basis of Christ's own institution of the oral eating.

Even if I should grant that this phrase, "the oral eating is not of such importance," is not of absolute but only of relative significance, it is nevertheless impossible for my soul to hear it expressed in this manner without pain. It may indeed be easy for the Reformed to speak and to think in this manner, since they deny this and declare the oral eating to be an illusion, indeed, to be madness. We, however, know this eating to be ordained by our most glorious Savior and as having been established upon his most clear and certain word, which has as its aim the salvation of our souls, whereby its gravity and importance is weightier than heaven and earth. But that some who are ignorant of this article are not damned, is not, I believe, the result of their defective understanding, but stems from the immense mercy of God, who overlooks this weakness in men. The seriousness behind the emphasis of the oral eating stems from Jesus Christ himself, who, being God-Incarnate, instituted and mandated it, and the fact that the elements are not common food, but the body of the Son of God, Jesus Christ himself, the eating of which ultimately leads to the blessed salvation of our souls.

This goal of the oral eating, because it is evidently done by the mouth (although it is accomplished in a supernatural and imperceptible man-

---

[12] This is a translation of Paul Gerhardt, "Ad Theses Reformatorum 7. November 1662 nobis propositas" in *Leben und Lieder von Paulus Gerhardt*, ed. E. C. G. Landbecker (Berlin: Verlag der Sander'schen Buchhandlung, 1841), 58–62. The translated is a combined effort of Gerald S. Krispin, Michael Hertwig-Jaksch, and Daniel J. Krispin. Herein Paul Gerhardt, the Lutheran ministerium's secretary at the Berlin Colloquy, articulates the primary importance of maintaining the oral eating of Christ's body and blood as fundamental to confessing the real presence in the Lord's Supper. It is a matter that had soteriological consequences for him.

ner), makes it incumbent upon us to test the sincerity of our opponents, because they evidently do not greatly desire to cast the aspersion of Capernaitic eating upon us, even though a great number of their sect have indeed unfailingly done so. But let them agree that we remove from our confession of the oral eating words such as "dismemberment," "cutting," "chewing," "swallowing," "digesting," and other such descriptors of common and natural eating.

Meanwhile, there are many [other] theses implicitly wrapped up in those stated above. For example, (1) that the oral eating is denied by the three [Reformed] confessions [the Belgic Confession, the Heidelberg Catechism, and the Canons of Dort]; (2) that the oral eating is done in a supernatural and imperceptible manner; (3) that the oral eating is not known among Reformed Christians in general; (4) and that the "oral eating is not of such great importance" that, on account of ignorance or on account of its rejection, any of the Reformed, be he one who merely hears or be he a teacher, should be condemned.

Should this be the case, however, there must be an ultimate requirement to differentiate between the voice of ignorance and the voice of those who refuse to admit [the truth of the oral eating]. There is indeed a certain type of ignorance that is pure, plain, and simple; but there is another type of ignorance that is accompanied by denial and contradiction, by an altogether stubborn, malicious, hostile, virulent, and blasphemous attitude. The former ignorance might indeed permit these theses to be pardoned. That is not the case with the latter form of ignorance. For one who is ignorant of the oral eating in a manner whereby he would simultaneously deny it and also stubbornly, maliciously—that is, in a hostile, virulent, and blasphemous manner—contradict it; such a one we clearly cannot absolve of his damnable condition. Instead we need to reiterate that which we have stated right at the outset of this amicable colloquy, namely, that he who contradicts the Word of God by constant design and deed, in the presence of sufficient and truthful information, will eventually and most assuredly receive a grave sentence in the divine judgment.

That said, since we do not deny that there are many in the Reformed churches who toil under simple, plain, and pure ignorance of the oral eating, we affirm that such as these will incur a milder judgment as stated in the prologue of our Formula of Concord, which also applies to its condemnations, reproaches, and rejections, etc. On the other hand, there are not a few, especially among the doctors and agitators of the Reformed churches, about whom it must be said unequivocally that they do not merely refuse to admit or fail to believe in the oral eating, but indeed, that their rejection is accompanied by stubborn, malicious, hostile, virulent, and blasphemous denials and objections.

Because the Reformed doctors and many of their hearers deny the oral eating and oppose it themselves, we have highlighted that the theses, in which the oral eating is denied, constitute the public confessions of the Reformed. That they would therefore stubbornly, maliciously, and in a hostile, virulent, and blasphemous manner deny and oppose [the oral eating] is clear based on their daily practice and experience which is, alas, evident and all too obvious.

I ask you: (1) Is it not stubbornness that they do not suffer themselves to be moved even a little by so many writings, teachings, responses, arguments, information, and reminders, which have [been] put forth from our side throughout approximately 150 years? Rather, they push this article away from themselves with all their strength and set themselves in opposition to it in many great literary volumes. Lest they become receptive to this dogma, they advance their own with great zeal and effort.

(2) Is it not malice that they assign to us the monstrous aspersion of Capernaitic eating by specious assertions about the spatial inclusion and concealment of a little "corpus" in the bread, a teaching that has never occurred to us? For this reason, they have not shied away from calling us Thyestian flesh-eaters.[13] That is to say the following: they call this point of our confession Oralism and they cite statements of Luther and Lutherans in favor [of the Reformed] by doing violence to the context and turn them against the former. For example, "Christ wants to be the nourishment, and feed the soul alone;" again: "He is truly worthy and well-prepared who believes in these words;" again: "He gave us His body as food, hidden in the bread, so that we might not forget Him," etc.

(3) Is it not hostility in that they claim us to be heretics because of our confession? And are the actions of the Tigurine [Swiss] Synod not senseless, which, because of their dogma, initiated independent discussions, created separate churches, and instituted separate Sacraments and altars? Yet they denounce Luther as the author of the schism primarily on the basis of this point in *their* doctrine.

---

[13] Atreus, king of Mycenae, had learned of the adultery of his brother Thyestes with Aerope (the wife of Atreus) and plotted revenge. He killed Thyestes's sons and cooked all but their hands and heads. He served Thyestes his own sons and later taunted him with their hands and heads. This is the source of phrase "Thyestean Feast," one at which human flesh is served.

(4) Is it not virulence and blasphemy that they extract from the oral eating such horrible and abominable absurdities about concoction, digestion, and expulsion; in truth, that they call the whole object of the oral eating, in summary, "bread-meat" or a pâté, as Bergius does? Is it not dishonorable that they count this most beautiful and sacred article of our religion to be wood, hay, and stubble, thinking that by such assertions our foundation in faith is cracked? Oh, the impiety, which overflows onto the very majesty of the most glorious surface of this foundation. With what kind of countenance will you eventually appear before his tribunal?

Therefore, we forthrightly oppose our adversaries. The oral eating, which indeed does occur through the physical mouth, yet in a supernatural and imperceptible manner, is of such power that, on account of ignorance and the failure to acknowledge it, when paired with an apparent malicious obstinacy, combined with a hostile and virulent denial that in turn is coupled with open opposition, not only condemns the doctors but also the Reformed listeners.

Paul Gerhardt

A Testament for His Son[14]

Having reached the seventieth year of my life, I have arrived at the joyous hope that my faithful and loving God will liberate me from this world and lead me to a life that is better than the one I have had on this earth. Firstly, I am grateful to him for all of his goodness and faithfulness, which he has given me in body and spirit beginning from the time I was within my mother's womb up to this present hour. Furthermore, I pray from the bottom of my heart that, if it be his will, he give me a peaceful release when my hour comes, receiving my soul into his loving hands while blessing my body with peaceful rest in the earth until the Day of God, when I will awaken with my friends and family; with those who have gone before me and those who will remain after me; and with my dear Lord Jesus Christ in whom I have believed unseen, yet then to see him face to face.

To you, my own son, I leave behind little in the way of earthy goods, except an honest name of which you need never be ashamed.

You know, my son, that from the time of your tender youth I have entrusted you to the Lord and given you the charge of becoming a minis-

[14] This is a translation of Paul Gerhardt, "Ein Testament für seinen Sohn" in *Leben und Lieder von Paulus Gerhardt*, ed. E. C. G. Landbecker (Berlin: Verlag der Sander'schen Buchhandlung, 1841), 226–28.

ter and preacher of his Holy Word. Remain true to this; do not worry that your days will not always be good, for the love of God knows what is needful, supplying you sufficient inner pleasure and a joyful spirit to displace the external misery.

Study sacred theology at faithful universities and take heed against those who seek to corrupt our confession. They only seek the here and now and are faithful neither to God nor people. In your daily life, do not walk in the way of evil, but seek the will and commandments of God. In particular:

> Do not engage in anything evil with the hope that it will remain hidden; for everything will come to light.
>
> Do not be vengeful in your work and vocation. Take heed, if you become filled with anger, remain utterly unmoved and refrain from speaking a word until you have earnestly reflected upon the Ten Commandments and the Christian faith.
>
> Be ashamed of the lustful flesh; when you reach a marriageable age, marry with good and sound advice from devout, faithful, and discerning people.
>
> Do good to people, regardless of whether they have done good to you. What people cannot repay, the Creator of heaven and earth has long paid; he not only created you but sent you his own beloved Son, adopted you through Holy Baptism, and made you his child and heir.
>
> Flee greed as though pursued by hell itself. Be satisfied with that which you have acquired honorably and with a good conscience, be it little or much. You are blessed that God provides for you beyond your expectations. But ask him to preserve you from the misuse of earthly goods.

In conclusion, pray diligently, study what is true, live in peace, minister earnestly, and remain steadfast in your faith and doctrine. In this way you will also one day willingly part from this world joyfully and truly blessed. Amen.

ABRAHAM CALOV (1612–86)

THE PRUSSIAN ON THE *CATHEDRA LUTHERI*

by Timothy R. Schmeling

LIFE

Leonhard Hutter (1563–1616) has been called a second Luther (*Lutherus redivivus*). But no other Lutheran ever sat upon the Chair of Luther (*Cathedra Lutheri*) and exercised its authority like Abraham Calov (1612–86). While his friends celebrated him as the "Second Athanasius," the subsequent historiography of Calov has been critical, to say the least.[1] The crescendo of this criticism was reached in August Tholuck, the mediating theologian, who wrote Calov off as the oft-married, uncompromising, myopic, and hotheaded "Grand Inquisitor" of the Syncretistic Controversy (ca. 1645–86).[2]

[1] Johann Friedrich Mayer, "D. O. M. S. Vitæ Parallelæ Athanasiorvm . . . consecratæ," in *Sacer Decadvm Septenarivs Memoriam Theologorvm Nostra Ætate . . . Theologica*, ed. Heinrich Pipping (Leipzig: Thomas Fritsch, 1705), 108–37.

[2] August Tholuck, *Der Geist der lutherischen Theologen Wittenbergs im Verlaufe des 17. Jahrhunderts* (Hamburg: Friedrich und Andreas Perthes, 1852), 185–211, 229.

A new wave of scholarship suggests that Calov should not be so quickly dismissed.[3] The leading Calov scholar today, Kenneth Appold, goes so far as to say that Calov was perhaps the most prolific Protestant theologian of all time, one of the most influential figures of his era, and that his writings are both original and ahead of their time, even when viewed from a modern perspective.[4] Building on the scholarship of Heinrich Schmid, Otto Ritschl, and Hans Leube,[5] Jörg Baur renewed Calov research on the 350th anniversary of his birth, calling attention not only to the Prussian's significance for seventeenth-century theology and philosophy, but also his importance in German history as a theologically-driven opponent of absolutism, especially the Calvinist Hohenzollern type.[6] Thereafter, Calov studies have pursued six themes. The first is Calov's value as a model for Lutheran identity.[7] The recognition of his exegetical contributions is the second theme.[8] The third is an exploration

---

[3] For an overview of Calov studies, see the following: *Religion Past and Present: Encyclopedia of Religion and Theology*, 4th ed., s.v. "Calovius, Abraham"; *Theologische Realenzyklopädie*, s.v. "Calov, Abraham (1612–1686)"; *Biographisch-Bibliographisches Kirchenlexikon*, s.v. "Calov (eigentlich: Kalau), Abraham, luth. Theologe"; *Lexikon für Theologie und Kirche*, 3rd. ed., s.v. "Calov, Abraham"; *The Encyclopedia of the Lutheran Church*, s.v. "Calov(ius), Abraham"; *Neue deutsche Biographie*, s.v. "Calov(ius), Abraham, luth. Theologe"; *The New Schaff-Herzog Encyclopedia of Religious Knowledge*, s.v. "Calovius (Kalau), Abraham"; *Realencyklopädie für protestantische Theologie und Kirche*, 3rd ed., s.v. "Calovius (Kalau), Abraham"; *Allgemeine Deutsche Biographie*, s.v. "Calovius, Abraham."

[4] Kenneth Appold, preface to *Abraham Calov's Doctrine of Vocatio in Its Systematic Context* (Tübingen: Mohr Siebeck, 1998).

[5] Heinrich Schmid, *Geschichte der synkretistischen Streitigkeiten in der Zeit des Georg Calixt* (Erlangen: Verlag von Carl Heyder, 1846); Otto Ritschl, *Dogmensgeschichte des Protestantismus* (Leipzig: J. C. Hinrichs'sche Buchhandlung, 1912–27); Hans Leube, *Kalvinismus und Luthertum im Zeitalter der Orthodoxie*, vol. 1, *Der Kampf um die Herrschaft im protestantischen Deutschland* (Aalen: Scientia Verlag, 1966).

[6] Jörg Baur, "Die Pflicht geschichtlichen Gedenkens. Anläßlich Geburtstages von Abraham Calov," *Lutherische Monatshefte* 1 (1962): 230–32.

[7] C. George Fry, "Three Lutheran Fathers of the 17th Century: The Search for Identity," *Concordia Journal* 5, no. 4 (1979): 134–40; Timothy Schmeling, "Strenuus Christi Athleta Abraham Calov (1612–1686): Sainted Doctor and Defender of the Church," *Lutheran Synod Quarterly* 44, no. 4 (2004): 357–99; Benjamin T. G. Mayes, "Syncretism in the Theology of Georg Calixt, Abraham Calov and Johannes Musäus," *Concordia Theological Quarterly* 68, no. 3/4 (2004): 291–317.

[8] Walter Menn, "Ein Kupfertitel als Personalbibliographie," *Gutenberg-Jahrbuch* (1958): 194–96; Georg Hoffmann, "Lutherische Schriftauslegung im 17. Jahrhunderts, dargestellt am Beispiel Abraham Calovs," in *Das Wort und die Wörter: Festschriften Gerhard Friedrich zum 65. Geburtstag*, ed. Horst Balz and Siegfried Schulz (Stuttgart: W. Kohlhammer, 1973), 127–42; Volker Jung, *Das Ganze der Heiligen Schrift: Hermeneutik und*

of Calov's doctrinal insights as well as his reception of Philipp Melanchthon (1497–1560) and the Church Fathers.[9] The recovery of his pastoral care and spiritual formation is the fourth theme.[10] The fifth is a reassessment of Calov's polemics in the Syncretistic Controversy, as well as against Roman Catholicism and Socinianism.[11] The final theme is Calov's place in the history of philosophy.[12]

Schriftauslegung bei Abraham Calov (Stuttgart: Calwer Verlag, 1999); Joar Haga, "Die Biblische Hermeneutik Calovs: Die Klarheit der Schrift innerhalb seiner Metaphysik," in *Hermeneutik, Methodenlehre, Exegese*, ed. Günter Frank und Stephan Meier-Oeser (Stuttgart: Frommann-Holzboog Verlag, 2011), 173–87; Mark W. Elliot, "Looking Backwards: The Protestant Latin Bible in the Eyes of Johannes Piscator and Abraham Calov," in *Shaping the Bible in the Reformation: Books, Scholars, and their Readers in the Sixteenth Century*, ed. Bruce Gordon and Matthew McLean (Leiden: Brill, 2012), 291–302; Adina M. Yoffie, "Biblical Literalism and Scholarship in Protestant Northern Europe, 1630–1700" (PhD diss., Harvard University, 2009).

[9] Robert Preus, *The Theology of Post-Reformation Lutheranism* (St. Louis: Concordia, 1970), 1:59–61, 1:157–228; Kenneth Appold, "Abraham Calov als Vater der lutherischen Spätorthodoxie?," in *Ernst Salomon Cyprian (1673–1745) zwischen Orthodoxie, Pietismus und Frühaufklärung*, ed. Ernst Koch and Johannes Wallmann (Gotha: Forschungs- und Landesbibliothek, 1996), 49–58; Appold, *Abraham*; Kenneth Appold, "Das Melanchthonbild bei Abraham Calov," in *Melanchthonbild und Melanchthonrezeption in der lutherischen Orthodoxie und in Pietismus*, ed. Udo Sträter (Lutherstadt Wittenberg: Edition Hans Lufft, 1999), 71–79; Quentin Stewart, "Catholicity or Consensus?: The Role of the Consensus Patrum and the Vincentian Canon in Lutheran Orthodoxy from Chemnitz to Quenstedt" (PhD diss., Concordia Seminary, 2006).

[10] Kenneth Appold, "Abraham Calov on the 'Usefulness' of Doctrine: Blueprints for a Theological Mind," in *Hermeneutica Sacra: Studien zur Auslegung der Heiligen Schrift im 16. und 17. Jahrhundert*, ed. Tornjörn Johansson, Robert Kolb, and Johann Steiger (Berlin: Walter de Gruyter, 2010), 295–312; Christoph Trautmann, " 'Calovii Schrifften. 3 Bände' aus Johann Sebastian Bachs Nachlaß und ihre Bedeutung für das Bild des lutherischen Kantors Bach," *Musik und Kirche* 39 (1969):145–60; Robin Leaver, "The Calov Bible from Bach's Library," *Bach Journal of the Riemenschneider Bach Institute* 7, no. 4 (1976): 16–22; Robin Leaver, *J. S. Bach and Scripture: Glosses from the Calov Bible Commentary* (St. Louis: Concordia, 1985); Howard H. Cox, ed., *The Calov Bible of J. S. Bach* (Ann Arbor: UMI Research Press, 1985).

[11] Heinz Staemmler, *Die Auseinandersetzung der kursächsischen Theologen mit dem Helmstedter Synkretismus. Eine Studie zum "Consensus Repetitus fidei vere Lutheranae" (1655) und den Diskussionen um ihn* (Waltrop: Hartmut Spenner, 2005); Johannes Wallmann, "Abraham Calov—theologischer Widerpart der Religionspolitik des Großen Kurfürsten," in *700 Jahre Wittenberg Stadt Universität Reformation*, ed. Stefan Oehmig (Weimar: Verlag Hermann Böhlaus Nachfolger, 1995), 303–11; Timothy Schmeling, "Slaying the Syncretistic Chimera: A Study of the *Consensus Repetitus* in Light of Confessionalization Theory" (PhD diss., Concordia Seminary, 2014); Timothy Schmeling, "Lutheran Orthodoxy Under Fire: An Exploratory Study of the Syncretistic Controversy and the *Consensus Repetitus Fidei Vere Lutheranae," Lutheran Synod Quarterly* 47, no. 4 (2007): 316–55; Kenneth Appold, "Abraham Calovs Auseinandersetzung mit der

On April 16, 1612, Abraham Calov(ius) (Kalau) was born in Mohrungen, Ducal Prussia (modern Morąg, Poland) into a devout and politically distinguished family.[13] Abraham and his older brother, Fabian (1610–78), a later appointee to the Ducal Prussian Chief secretariat (*Ober-Secretariat*), were fortunate to have the Hohenzollern Electors Joachim Friedrich (1546–1608), Johann Sigismund (1572–1620), and Georg Wilhelm (1595–1640) of Brandenburg-Prussia finance their education. The two received their early classical formation at the local school under Rector Daniel Ulrich. Abraham proved so talented and industrious that his parents prayed for an ecclesiastical career for him. A speech impediment almost dashed these hopes.[14]

Abraham enrolled with Fabian at the celebrated Royal Prussian *Gymnasium* of Thorn (modern Toruń, Poland) in 1624. Under its rector, Conrad Graser II (d. 1630), he received an excellent Late Renaissance humanist, Aristotelian, and even Semitic foundation. But after only half a year, plague forced him home. There the young Abraham honed all he had learned. The following year, Abraham entered the Ducal Prussian

tridentischen Rechtfertigungslehre," in *Zur Rechtfertigungslehre in der Lutherischen Orthodoxie*, ed. Udo Sträter (Leipzig: Evangelische Verlagsanstalt, 2003), 71–80; Olaf Reese,"Lutherische Metaphysik im Streit: Berichte von Calovs antisozinianischen Feldzügen" (Diss., Georg-August-Universität Göttingen, 2008).

[12] Max Wundt, *Die deutsche Schulmetaphysik des 17. Jahrhunderts* (Hildesheim: Georg Olms Verlag, 1992), 117, 133–36, 257–60; Riccardo Pozzo, "Aristotelismus und Eklektik in Königsberg," in *Die Universität Königsberg in der Frühen Neuzeit*, ed. Hanspeter Marti and Manfred Komorowski (Köln: Böhlau Verlag, 2008), 172–85; Marco Sgarbi, "Abraham Calov and Immanuel Kant: Aristotelian and Scholastic Traces in the Kantian Philosophy," *Historia Philosophia: An International Journal* 8 (2010): 55–62; Marco Sgarbi, "Metaphysics in Königsberg Prior to Kant (1703–1770)," *Trans/Form/Ação* 33, no. 1 (2010): 31–64; Marco Sgarbi, *Kant and Aristotle Epistemology, Logic, and Method* (Albany: State University of New York Press, 2016).

[13] Apart from Calov's writings and letters, the main primary sources for his life are as follows: Johann Friedrich Mayer, *Der Biß in seinen Todt Gottfürchtende . . . Abraham Calovius . . . bracht* (Wittenberg: Martin Schultzen, 1687). The *Curriculum Vitæ B. D. D. Abrahami Calovii*, (A)r–(E)1r, and Conrad Samuel Schurzfleisch's *Oratio Quam In Funere Caloviano*, (F)2r–(H)2v, are also appended to this funeral sermon. A more complete bibliography of his more than five hundred works can be found at VD17 Das Verzeichnis der im deutschen Sprachraum erschienenen Drucke des 17. Jahrhunderts: www.vd17.de/index.php. For an introduction to the recovered third volume of Calov's extensive lost correspondence and an index to his letters published in the many articles of Theodor Wotschke, see Katharina Bethge's "Epistolae theologicae: Eine Quelle zur Erforschung von Leben und Werk Abraham Calovs und der lutherischen Orthodoxie. Briefliste aus der Bibliothek des Evangelischen Predigerseminars Wittenberg," *Pietismus und Neuzeit* 22 (1996): 22–68.

[14] Mayer, *Der Biß*, (A)r–(A)2r.

Gymnasium of Königsberg (modern Kaliningrad, Russia). Once again, plague drove him home before half a year had passed.[15] Still, all his self-discipline and diligence paid off. Abraham and Fabian matriculated at the University of Königsberg (Albertina) on February 10, 1626. Boarding in the home of Sigismund Weier (1579–1661), the philosophy (or undergraduate) faculty senior (chief member), Abraham became increasingly proficient in the humanities, philosophy, mathematics, and natural science. On Trinity Fourteen 1629, he preached his first sermon. Abraham earned his master's degree in April 1632.[16]

After being accepted into the Königsberg philosophical faculty, Calov started conducting public philosophical and theological disputations. At the same time, he began to study theology under Johann Behm (1578–1648) and Coelestin Myslenta (1588–1653). For both legal and theological reasons, Reformed irenicists had long sought mutual toleration, if not the absorption of Lutheranism, on the grounds that fundamental doctrinal agreement existed between Protestants and that a combined front was needed against Roman Catholicism. After Elector Johann Sigismund converted to Calvinism in 1613, Behm and Myslenta led the resistance to attempt to remove the Book of Concord and Calvinize Hohenzollern lands. In contrast to Behm, who eventually succumbed to Hohenzollern religious policy, Myslenta remained steadfast. In fact, this Polish nobleman, Lutheran Orientalist, and ardent anti-Calvinist not only honed Calov's Semitic skills, but he also infused Calov with his uncompromising polemic disposition as he taught him the *Body of Prussian Doctrine* (*Corpus Doctrinae Prutenicum*).[17] The twenty-one-year-old Calov now authored his first theological book, the *Steadfastness to the Most Holy Testament of Christ's Will*, published in 1635. It defended the

[15] Mayer, *Der Biß*, (A)2r; Stanisław Salmonowicz, "Das protestantische Gymnasium Academicum in Thorn im 17. und 18. Jahrhunderts," in *Kulturgeschichte Preussens königlich polnischen Anteils in der Frühen Neuzeit*, ed. Sabine Beckmann and Klaus Garber (Tübingen: Niemeyer, 2001), 395–410; Lech Mokrzeki, "Protestant Grammar Schools of Royal Prussia in the Polish School System in the 16th and 17th Centuries," in *Kulturgeschichte Preußens königlich polnischen Anteils in der Frühen Neuzeit*, ed. Sabine Beckmann and Klaus Garber (Tübingen: Niemeyer, 2001), 359–70; Henryk Porożyński and Stefan Rudnik, "Lutheran Secondary School in the 16th and 17th Century Pomerania (Thorn, Elbing)," in *Luther and Melanchthon in the Educational Thought in Central and Eastern Europe*, ed. Reinhard Golz and Wolfgang Mayrhofers (Münster: LIT Verlag, 1998), 139–45.

[16] Mayer, *Der Biß*, (A)2r–(A)2v, (A)v; Georg Erler and Erich Joachim, eds. *Die Matrikel der Albertus-Universität zu Königsberg* (Leipzig: Duncker & Humblot, 1910–17), 1:292.

[17] Götz von Selle, *Geschichte der Albertus-Universität zu Königsberg in Preußen*, 2nd ed. (Würzburg: Holzner, 1956), 77–98.

real presence of Christ's body and blood in the Lord's Supper against Johann Bergius (1587–1658), the Hohenzollern court-preacher and Calvinist irenicist, and maintained that a fundamental discord existed with the Reformed.[18] Seeing in Calov a new leader against Calvinization, the nobles funded his doctoral studies at a university outside of Hohenzollern domains.[19]

In October 1634, Calov joined Rostock University's philosophical faculty and enrolled as a doctoral student. He received room and board from Johann Quistorp I (1584–1648), the Rostock theology first professor (*professor primarius*), with whom he forged a tight bond. Calov also studied under Johann Cothmann (1595–1650), Stephan Klotz (1606–68), and Thomas Lindemann II (1609–54).[20] His roommate and future Königsberg theology professor, Christian Dreier (1610–88), like others among Calov's friends, later embraced syncretism. In 1635, Calov conducted a series of disputations on the Augsburg Confession, which illustrates his lifelong interest in explicating the Book of Concord. He later revised, expanded, and published the series—like many of his disputations—as a book.[21] His Königsberg and Rostock philosophical writings reveal that he harnessed philosophy into the service of Lutheranism and was one of the most important Lutheran philosophers.[22] The Thirty Years' War (1618–48) made his dream of studying under Johann Gerhard (1582–1637) too dangerous. Instead, he made an academic excursus to Stralsund, Greifswald, Copenhagen, Frederiksberg, Roskilde, and Sorø in 1636. He returned to Rostock and received his doctorate on June 22,

---

[18] Abraham Calov, *In Nomine Jesu! Stereoma Sacratißimæ Testatoris Christi Voluntatis . . . eversionem* (Rostock: Johann Reusner, 1635).

[19] Mayer, *Der Biß*, (A)2v–(B)v.

[20] Thomas Kaufmann, *Universität und lutherische Konfessionalisierung: Die Rostocker Theologieprofessoren und ihr Beitrag zur theologischen Bildung und kirchlichen Gestaltung im Herzogtum Mecklenburg zwischen 1550 und 1675* (Gütersloh: Gütersloher Verlagshaus, 1997), 96, 715–16.

[21] Abraham Calov, *I. N. J. Exegema Augustanæ Confessionis . . . Vindicans,* 2nd ed. (Wittenberg: Johann Borckard, 1665); Abraham Calov, *Criticus Sacer . . . Procer* (Leipzig: Martin Hallervord, 1646).

[22] Calov's philosophical writings were later republished. Abraham Calov, *Scripta Philosophica . . . refellant* (Rostock: Joachim Wilde, 1651); Walter Sparn, "Schulphilosophie in den lutherischen Territorien," in *Grundriß der Geschichte der Philosophie: Die Philosophie des 17. Jahrhunderts,* vol. 4, *Das Heilige Römische Reich Deutscher Nation, Nord- und Ostmitteleuropa*, ed. Helmut Holzhey and Wilhelm Schmidt-Biggemann (Basel: Schwabe, 1983–), 475–587.

1637.[23] That same year, he married his first wife, Barbara Martini. He would outlive five of his total of six wives. They blessed him with thirteen children.[24]

That September, Calov was enthusiastically received as the new Königsberg adjunct theological professor and was a very popular lecturer. Since Königsberg was currently the most frequented German university because of the Thirty Years' War, Calov's audience was greatly expanded beyond an already diverse audience of German, Scandinavian, and Slavic Lutherans.[25] Even the mild Calvinist Elector Georg Wilhelm held Calov in such esteem (especially for his effective preaching) that when Rostock tried to call this rising star, the elector made him an extraordinary theology professor (*Extraordinarius*) in 1639/40. Calov served the faculty twice as dean, helped revise the university statutes, and served as a superintendent of Samland (part of Ducal Prussia).[26]

Calov's growing reputation prompted the poly-confessional Royal Prussian city of Danzig (modern Gdánsk, Poland) to call him in 1643 to serve as pastor of its Trinity Church and rector of its humanist *Gymnasium* (*Athenaei Gedanensis*). His acceptance meant that he would have to share the church building with the Reformed irenicist Johann Caesar (1614–53) and overcome the influence of Calvinism in the school. Here Calov helped Johann Botsack (1600–1674), the Lutheran ministerium's senior, cultivate an orthodox Lutheran character in the city.[27] As the foremost orthodox Lutheran defender of the Trinity, he also continued his philosophical and theological polemics against Polish Socinianism, climaxing in his *Wretched Socinianism* (*Socinismus Profligatus*), an Anti-

---

[23] Mayer, *Der Biß*, (B)v–(B)2r; Adolph Hofmeister and Ernst Schäfer, eds. *Die Matrikel der Universität Rostock* (Rostock and Schwerin: In Commission der Stillerschen Hof- und Universitäts-Buchhandlung and Bärensprungsche Hofbuchdruckerei, 1889–1922), 3:98, 3:111–12.

[24] Mayer, *Der Biß*, (D)r–(D)2v.

[25] Erler, *Die Matrikel*, 1:CXXIV-CXXXIII; 1:384–85; Franz Eulenburg, *Die Frequenz der deutschen Universitäten von ihrer Gründung bis zur Gegenwart* (Leipzig: B. G. Teubner, 1904), 84ff, 100–103, 153.

[26] Mayer, *Der Biß*, (B)2r–(B)2v.

[27] Mayer, *Der Biß*, (B)2v–(C)r; Theodor Hirsch, *Geschichte des academischen Gymnasiums in Danzig, in ihren Hauptzügen dargestellt* (Danzig: Wedelschen Hofbuchdruckerei, 1837), 24–28; Hans-Joachim Müller, "Streiten und Herrschen: Konfessionelle Konflikte in Danzig zwischen 1630–1650," in *Debatten über die Legitimationen von Herrschaft: Politische Sprachen in der Frühen Neuzeit*, ed. Luise Schorn-Schütte and Sven Tode (Berlin: Akademie Verlag, 2006), 125–42.

Socinian systematics.[28] He even wrote a polemic against Roman Catholicism.[29]

Hoping to reconcile and unite Polish Lutherans and Reformed with Roman Catholicism, Polish King Władysław IV (1595–1648) invited the three confessions to the Colloquy of Thorn (1645). As a Polish prince, the militant Calvinist Great Elector Friedrich Wilhelm (1620–88) of Brandenburg-Prussia recognized the opportunity here to advance Calvinism in his decidedly Lutheran lands. To achieve this end, he sent Georg Calixt (1586–1656) to the colloquy instead of his own professor, Myslenta, along with a Reformed and Lutheran delegation that favored Calixtine theology.[30] The Lutheran irenicist and Helmstedt theology professor, Calixt, had advocated mutual toleration between confessions (pejoratively dubbed "syncretism") and hoped for a God-given reunion of Christendom on the basis of adherence to the fundamental doctrine encapsulated in the Apostles' Creed and its proper explication via the theology of the first five centuries. Since Calixt believed that the Augsburg Confession was the most faithful expression of this apostolic and catholic theology,

---

[28] These works were later reprinted in his *Scripta Anti-Sociniana ... Confirmationem* (Ulm: Georg Wilhelm Kühn, 1684); Abraham Calov, *I. N. J. Socinismus Profligatus ... refellatur* (Wittenberg: Michael Wendt, 1652); Siegfried Wollgast, "Zur Widerspiegelung des Sozinianismus in der lutherischen Theologie und Schulmetaphysik im Reich, Danzig und Preussen in der ersten Hälfte des 17. Jahrhunderts," in *Socinianism and its Role in the Culture of XVI-th to XVIII-th Centuries,* ed. Lech Szczucki, Zbigniew Ogonowski, and Janusz Tazbir (Warsaw–Łodz: Polish Academy of Sciences Institute of Philosophy and Sociology, 1983), 157–68; Lech Mokrzeki, "Socinianismus in den Diskursen der Danziger Professoren im 17. und 18. Jahrhunderts," in *Socinianism and its Role in the Culture of XVI-th to XVIII-th Centuries,* ed. Lech Szczucki, Zbigniew Ogonowski, and Janusz Tazbir (Warsaw–Łodz: Polish Academy of Sciences Institute of Philosophy and Sociology, 1983), 183–92.

[29] Abraham Calov, *Matæologia Papistica . . . confutata* (Danzig: Georg Rhete, 1647).

[30] Abraham Calov, *I. N. J. Historia Syncretistica ... Büchern* (n.p.: n.p., 1685), 199–562; Hans-Joachim Müller, *Irenik als Kommunikationsreform. Das Colloquium Charitativum von Thorn 1645* (Göttingen: Vandenhoeck & Ruprecht, 2004); Janusz Małłek, "Die Sehnsuch nach Einheit. Das Colloquium Charitativm in Thorn im Jahre 1645," in *Kulturgeschichte Preußens königlich polnischen Anteils in der Frühen Neuzeit,* ed. Sabine Beckmann and Klaus Garber (Tübingen: Niemeyer, 2001), 213–26; Hans-Joachim Müller, "Irenik als Kommunikationsreform in Umfeld des Thorner Colloquium Charitativum von 1645," in *Union—Konversion—Toleranz. Dimensionen der Annäherung zwischen den christlichen Konfessionen im 17. und 18. Jahrhunderts,* eds. Heinz Duchhardt and Gerhard May (Mainz: Verlag Philipp von Zabern, 2000), 61–82; Edmund Piszcz, *Colloquium Charitativum w Toruniu A. D. 1645: Geneza i przebieg* (Toruń, 1995); 61–82; Martin Lackner, *Die Kirchenpolitik des Grossen Kurfüsten* (Witten: Luther-Verlag, 1973), 9–107, 148–82, 304–9.

he maintained that his project (which opposed the Formula of Concord on authority, Christology, ecclesiology, and soteriology) was not only catholic, but irrefutably Lutheran. Calixt was prevented from serving the Lutherans by their moderator and vice-moderator, Johann Hülsemann (1602–61), a Wittenberg theology professor, and Abraham Calov, respectively. As a result, Calixt helped the Reformed develop a confession of faith. Instead of bringing the confessions closer, the colloquy expanded the growing fissure in Lutheranism between Lutheran syncretism led by Calixt and orthodox Lutheranism eventually led largely by Calov. This breach would be compounded by the new "Jena" theology of Johannes Musaeus (1613–81), who tried to navigate a theological path between Calixt and Calov on the topics of authority, Christology, ecclesiology, and soteriology.[31] The zeal of Calov's polemics against syncretism is not only explained by the existential crisis it caused in Lutheranism, but also by the Great Elector's capitalizing on Calixtine theology to disenfranchise the Lutheranism of Calov's native land and promote Calvinization. The Great Elector wasted no time appointing and cultivating Calixtine theologians at Königsberg University, resulting in its embrace of Lutheran syncretism.[32]

As Myslenta mobilized orthodox Lutheranism against syncretism in Königsberg, Calov fought it in Danzig. The highlights of this period were his two confessions (1646–48), which bear striking similarities with the 1655/64 *Repeated Consensus of the True Lutheran Faith* (*Consensus*

---

[31] Schmeling, "Slaying," 17–168.

[32] Calov, *Historia*, 884–998; Reimund Sdzuj, "Zwischen Irenik, Synkretismus und Apostasie: Konversionen Königsberger Gelehrter im konfessionellen Zeitalter," in *Die Universität Königsberg in der Frühen Neuzeit*, ed. Hanspeter Marti and Manfred Komorowski (Köln: Böhlau Verlag, 2008), 186–225; Bernhart Jähnig, "Die Königsberger Universitätsprofessoren im 17. Jahrhundert - Eine sozial- und bildungsgeschichte Betrachtung," in *Kulturgeschichte Ostpreußens in der Frühen Neuzeit*, ed. Klaus Garber, Manfred Komorowski, and Axel Walter (Tübingen: Niemeyer, 2001), 337–74; Thomas Kaufmann, "Theologische Auseinandersetzungen an der Universität Königsberg im 16. und 17. Jahrhundert," in *Kulturgeschichte Ostpreußens in der Frühen Neuzeit*, ed. Klaus Garber, Manfred Komorowski, and Axel Walter (Tübingen: Niemeyer, 2001), 243–318; Thomas Kaufmann, "Königsberger Theologieprofessoren im 17. Jahrhundert," in *Die Albertus-Universität zu Königsberg und ihre Professoren*, ed. D. Rauschning and D. Von Nerée (Berlin: Duncker und Humblot, 1995), 49–86; Walther Hubatsch, "Das Thorner Religionsgespräch von 1645 aus der Sicht des Geistlichen Ministeriums der Dreistadt Königsberg," in *Thorn. Königing der Weichsel 1231–1981*, eds. Bernhart Jähnig und Peter Letkemann (Göttingen: Vandenhoeck & Ruprecht, 1981), 239–58.

Repetitus Fidei Vere Lutheranæ),[33] and his first great polemic against Lutheran syncretism, the 1649–50 *Digression* (*Digressio*), later reprinted in his twelve-volume *System of Theological Commonplaces* (1655–77).[34] This analytically arranged dogmatics is the most insightful, brilliant, and influential systematics after Gerhard's *Theological Commonplaces* (*Loci Theologici*), but the later volumes seem rushed and lack the comprehensiveness of Quenstedt's 1685 *Didactic-Polemic Theology or Theological System* (*Theologia Didactico-Polemica Sive Systema Theologicum*). The *Digression* more specifically revealed the presuppositional, theological, and historical problems with syncretism unlike any polemic before it.

After dedicating his 1646 *Sacred Critic* (*Criticus Sacer*) to the Swedish court, Calov was accused of conspiring with its chancellor, Axel Oxenstierna (1583–1654), to block the legal recognition of Calvinism at the 1648 Peace of Westphalia. The rumor caused such consternation that Oxenstierna denied it in a letter to the Danzig council, but it only enhanced Calov's allure in the eyes of Saxon Elector Johann Georg I (1611–56). In July of 1650, Jakob Weller (1602–64), the chief court-preacher in Electoral Saxony, persuaded his elector to call Calov to the University of Wittenberg (*Leucorea*) as its third theology professor (after Paul Röber [1587–1651] and Johann Scharf [1595–1660]).[35] Calov arrived on October 19, 1650. Since one of his chief tasks was to bring an end to syncretism, he sought to facilitate this through an inaugural oration on syncretism and the publication of the most comprehensive refutations of syncretism produced.[36]

Immediately after Calov's arrival, there was a surge in student matriculations. His lectures were so well received that up to five hundred attended them. He was greatly respected by the Saxon Elector and en-

---

[33] Eduard Schnaase, *Geschichte der evangelischen Kirche Danzigs* (Danzig: Theodor Bertling, 1863), 214–20, 286–30. The confessions are reprinted in this same work, 687–763. Hans-Joachim Müller, "Konfession, Kommunikation und Öffentlichkeiten: Der Streit um die Irenik in Danzig 1645–1647," in *Interkonfessionalität—Transkonfessionalität—binnenkonfessionelle Pluralität: Neue Forschung zur Konfessionalisierungsthese*, ed. Kaspar von Greyerz et al. (Gütersloh: Gütersloher Verlaghaus, 2003), 151–78.

[34] Calov, *Systema Locorum Theologicorum . . . exhibens* (Wittenberg: Andreas Hartmann, Johann Röhner, Michael Wendt, Christian Schroedter, and Johann Wilcke, 1655–77), 1:881–1216.

[35] Mayer, *Der Biß*, (C)r–(C)v.

[36] Calov, *Historia*, 808–35, 836–55; Abraham Calov, *In Nomine Jesu! Synopsis Controversiarium potiorum . . . expendens* (Wittenberg: Michael Wendt, 1652); Abraham Calov, *I. N. J. Syncretismus Calixtinus . . . Lutherum* (Wittenberg: Michael Wendt, 1653); Abraham Calov, *I. N. J. Harmonia Calixtino-Hæretica . . . proposita* (Wittenberg: Michael Wendt, 1655).

joyed a close friendship with Weller. It is no surprise then that Calov was soon appointed to the Wittenberg consistory. He became pastor of St. Mary's Church by Advent 1650. That March, he assumed the second ordinary theology professorship [*Ordinarius*]. The Prussian was solemnly invested as Electoral Saxon general-superintendent on February 14, 1654. He became first theology professor [*professor primaries*] in 1660 and served nineteen times as dean.[37]

Calov the polemicist and theologian has too often overshadowed Calov the pastor and cultivator of piety. In 1652, he published a study guide that spells out an ambitious, pious, and well-rounded plan for pastoral formation. Building on his longer and shorter Danzig Catechisms based on Luther's own, he authored another catechetical textbook for Wittenberg in 1658. He contributed to the 1671 *Wittenberg Hymnal.* His 1671 *Biblical Calendar* [*Biblischer Calender*], a Bible reading guide, proved especially popular.[38] He even promoted the reading of Johann Arndt (1555–1621), and supported the early work of Philipp Jakob Spener (1635–1705).[39]

The Saxon Elector and his theologians had sought a synodical solution to syncretism (i.e., by meetings of pastors and theologians), but they were repeatedly thwarted by Musaeus, Jena University, and the Saxon dukes, who forged a third way between the Lutheran syncretists and the orthodox Lutherans. Following the spread of Calixtine theology, conversions to Roman Catholicism, and the favor Calixt had garnered at the Regensburg Diet (1653–54), the Electoral Saxons began to draft the 1655/64 *Repeated Consensus of the True Lutheran Faith*, a reaffirmation of the Augsburg Confession and the Formula of Concord and refutation of syncretism. It was decisively shaped by the theology of Hülsemann and

---

[37] Eulenburg, *Die Frequenz*, 100–103; Mayer, *Der Biß*, (C)v–(C)2v, (D)2v; Bernhard Weissenborn and Fritz Juntke, eds. *Album Academiae Vitebergensis. Jüngere Reihe* (Magdeburg: Ernst Holtermann, 1934–66), 1:492, 1:532; Karl Förstemann, *Liber decanorum facultatis theologicae Academiae Vitebergensis* (Leipzig: C. Tauchnitz, 1838); Walther Friedensburg, *Geschichte der Universität Wittenberg* (Halle: M. Niemeyer, 1917), 418–30.

[38] Abraham Calov, *I. N. J. Isagoges . . . Calixtinæ*, 2nd ed. (Wittenberg: Andreas Hartmann, 1666); Abraham Calov, *Der H. Catechismus, Lutheri . . . bestettiget* (Wittenberg: Hiob Wilhelm Fincelius, 1658); *I. N. J. Wittenbergisches Gesang-Buch . . . Registern* (Wittenberg: Matthäus Henckel, 1673).

[39] Philipp Jacob Spener, *Pia Desideria*, trans. Theodore G. Tappert (Philadelphia: Fortress Press, 1964), 18, 105.

Calov.[40] Calov's efforts to unite Lutheranism behind Wittenberg's 1662 *Judgment* [*Epicrisis*], which rejected the Kassel Colloquy's (1661) affirmation of fundamental agreement between Protestants, proved so decisive that the Great Elector barred his subjects from attending Wittenberg before he attempted to force the Berlin-Cölln Lutheran ministerium to make the same affirmation at his Berlin Colloquy (1662–63). As a result, the *Repeated Consensus of the True Lutheran Faith* was finally published in a collection of Wittenberg faculty theological opinions [*Gutachten*] that asserted the university's theological oversight in Lutheranism.[41]

While Calov would posthumously win the war on syncretism, the remainder of the controversy was marked by bitter polemics (against both Musaeus and the syncretists) and the failure of the *Repeated Consensus of the True Lutheran Faith* to achieve symbolic status. Division developed in the Wittenberg faculty. An anti-syncretistic play caused great offence in the electorate. The new "Jena" theology had time to solidify. What is more, Calov lost the favor of new Saxon Electors Johann Georg II (1613–80) and Johann Georg III (1647–91), who did not share the orthodox convictions of Johann Georg I. Despite repeated prohibitions on polemics, Calov defied the elector and printed his 1682 *Syncretistic History* [*Historia Syncretistica*], omitting the publisher and place of publication. Calov even rebuked his elector's confiscation of the text in a virtually unprecedented manner for that day.[42]

Calov closed his final years with some extraordinary exegetical, systematic, and devotional writings. He had already written significant commentaries on Romans (1648), Hebrews (1649), and Genesis (1671), but none could compare with his *magnus opus*, the 1672–76 *Elucidated Bible*, a highly respected four-volume Latin Bible commentary and a correction to the annotations of the Arminian Dutch Jurist Hugo Grotius (1583–1645).[43] After completing his *System of Theological Commonplaces*, he penned two dogmatic compendiums, one of which presents the

---

[40] Calov, *Historia*, 562–94; 1090–98; "Consensus Repetitus Fidei Vere Lutheranæ . . . complices," in *Consilia Theologica Witebergensia . . . daselbsten* (Frankfurt am Main: Balthasar Christoph Wust, 1664), 1:928–95; Schmeling, "Slaying," 169–228.

[41] Calov, *Historia*, 594–97, 609–808; Schmeling, "Slaying," 229–95; Lackner, *Die Kirchenpolitik*, 111–48.

[42] Calov, *Historia*, 1099–1114; Schmeling, "Slaying," 296–325.

[43] Abraham Calov, *I. N. J. Biblia Testam. Veteris Illustrata . . . locupletissimo* (Frankfurt am Main: Balthasar Christoph Wust, 1672); Abraham Calov, *I. N. J. Biblia Novi Testamenti Illustrata . . . locupletissimo* (Frankfurt am Main: Balthasar Christoph Wust, 1676).

faith largely using Scripture alone.[44] To promote the reading of Martin Luther and the cultivation of godliness, he published his 1681–82 *The Holy Bible*, a German study Bible compiled from Luther's writings. It profoundly shaped the piety of J. S. Bach (1685–1750), whose personally annotated copy now resides at Concordia Seminary in St. Louis, Missouri.[45] Calov breathed his last on February 25, 1686, not long after republishing the *Syncretistic History*. He was buried in St. Mary's Church in Wittenberg on March 4, 1686. His picture was hung over the archdeacon's confessional chair.[46]

No one could ever really fill Luther's shoes, but in Calov, one finds a profound biblical theologian like Luther himself. Calov had a greater interest in philosophy and systematics than Luther, but he practiced an "Anti-Scholastic 'Scholasticism,'" which made scrutinizing use of the Church Fathers, Renaissance humanism, and the best tools of the day in service of the Church.[47] His writings were prolific, even pastoral and devotional, touching on nearly every subject. In addition, they were no less driven by polemic than Luther's own, and could be just as penetrating, biting, and scatological as the 1541 *Against Hanswurst*. Calov was a natural leader, possessing a powerful intellect, work ethic, and presence that exuded confidence and authority. He even facilitated the reading of Luther and was just as willing as Luther to defy the state in defense of sound doctrine. He certainly had his flaws and excesses. But who else ever sat upon the Chair of Luther like Abraham Calov?

BIBLIOGRAPHY

Works by Calov in English Translation

"Thoughts on Objective Justification: Selections from *Biblia Illustrata* 2 Corinthians 5:18–19; Romans 3:23–24; 4:25; 5:18–19." Translated by

[44] Abraham Calov, *I. N. J. Theologia Positiva ... Theologici* (Wittenberg: Christian Schroedter, 1682); Abraham Calov, *I. N. J. Apodixis Articulorum Fidei ... Confirmandi* (Lüneburg: Johann Kelp and Kaspar Gruner, 1684).

[45] Abraham Calov, *I. N. J. Die Heilige Bibel ... ist* (Wittenberg: Christian Schroedter, 1681–82).

[46] Mayer, *Der Biß*, (D)2v–(E)r; Johann Christoph Erdmann, *Lebensbeschreibungen und litterarische Nachrichten von den Wittenbergschen Theologen seit der Stiftung der Universität 1502, bis zur dritten hunderjährlichen Säkularfeyer 1802 ...* (Wittenberg: Samuel Gottfried Zimmermann, 1804), 88–91.

[47] See also Ulrich Leinsle, *Introduction to Scholastic Theology*, trans. Michael Miller (Washington, DC: The Catholic University of America Press, 2010), 306–7.

Souksamay K. Phetsanghane. *Wisconsin Lutheran Quarterly* 111, no. 3 (Summer 2014): 195–213.

"Thoughts on Objective Justification Part II: Selections from *Biblia Illustrata* Romans 3:23–24; 4:25; 5:18–19." Translated by Souksamay K. Phetsanghane. *Wisconsin Lutheran Quarterly* 111, no. 4 (Fall 2014): 243–74.

Select Works by Calov in German and Latin

I. N. J. Apodixis Articulorum Fidei . . . Confirmandi. Lüneburg: Johann Kelp and Kaspar Gruner, 1684.

I. N. J. Biblia Novi Testamenti Illustrata . . . locupletissimo. 2 vols. Frankfurt am Main: Balthasar Christoph Wust, 1676.

I. N. J. Biblia Testam. Veteris Illustrata . . . locupletissimo. 2 vols. Frankfurt am Main: Balthasar Christoph Wust, 1672.

Criticus Sacer . . . Procer. Leipzig: Martin Hallervord, 1646.

Der Catechismus, Lutheri . . . bestettiget. Wittenberg: Hiob Wilhelm Fincelius, 1658.

I. N. J. Exegema Augustanæ Confessionis . . . Vindicans. 2nd ed. Wittenberg: Johann Borckard, 1665.

I. N. J. Harmonia Calixtino-Hæretica . . . proposita. Wittenberg: Michael Wendt, 1655.

I. N. J. Die Heilige Bibel . . . ist. 3 vols. Wittenberg: Christian Schroedter, 1681–82.

I. N. J. Historia Syncretistica . . . Büchern. N.p.: n.p., 1685.

I. N. J. Isagoges . . . Calixtinæ. 2nd ed. Wittenberg: Andreas Hartmann, 1666.

Matæologia Papistica . . . confutata. Danzig: Georg Rhete, 1647.

Scripta Anti-Sociniana . . . Confirmationem. Ulm: Georg Wilhelm Kühn, 1684.

Scripta Philosophica . . . refellant. Rostock: Joachim Wilde, 1651.

I. N. J. Socinismus Profligatus . . . refellatur. Wittenberg: Michael Wendt, 1652.

In Nomine Jesu! Stereoma Sacratißimæ Testatoris Christi Voluntatis . . . eversionem. Rostock: Johann Reusner, 1635.

I. N. J. Syncretismus Calixtinus . . . Lutherum. Wittenberg: Michael Wendt, 1653.

In Nomine Jesu! Synopsis Controversiarium potiorum . . . expendens. Wittenberg: Michael Wendt, 1652.

Systema Locorum Theologicorum . . . exhibens. 12 vols. Wittenberg: Andreas Hartmann, Johann Röhner, Michael Wendt, Christian Schroedter, and Johann Wilcke, 1655–77.

I. N. J. Theologia Positiva . . . Theologici. Wittenberg: Christian Schroedter, 1682.

WRITING[48]

I. N. I.

A Well-Founded Christian Consideration of Good Church Peace and Christian Unity in the Blessed Doctrine of the Heavenly Truth

Introduction

There are almost as many writings about the union of the churches and about peace and unity in these days as there are those who are found under [the name of] Christian. [There are] especially [writings] concerning the reconciliation and agreement of the true evangelicals (those who adhere to the Unaltered Augsburg Confession), and those who call themselves Reformed, as well as the Roman Catholics or papists. Very many *Irenica* or irenic writings, proposals, considerations, and counsels have been issued from the Reformed side for the union of our [Lutheran church] with their churches. Encouragements [have also been issued] through writings to ecclesiastical and secular persons, as well as to leading governmental figures, and in part in the name of higher leaders, that such church-peace petitions may happen. But many among the Roman Catholics, and in fact even among the Jesuits, have also put forward via various writings to higher places and elsewhere how a reconciliation and union could take place and be demonstrated with those adhering to the Augsburg Confession for the sake of peace and unity. Such books and writings are public and are so well known that it is not necessary to introduce them all here. In addition to this, a new and different party has come about, which confesses neither those [doctrinal positions of] the Reformed, nor those [doctrinal positions of] the papists, but wants to

[48] This is a translation of Abraham Calov's "*Eingang*" and "*das Erste Praeliminar-Capitel*" from his *Historia*, A4r–B4v.

adhere to the Augsburg Confession. However, [this party] ignores not a few doctrinal positions, sometimes those of the Calvinists and sometimes those of the papists. For this reason, we would like to call [this party] the Calixtiner for the sake of distinction, so that we can speak and treat particularly of them, although such opinions were not first established by [Georg] Calixt, but were picked up by him and clothed in new dress in these recent years. The [Calixtiner] also do not exactly agree in all aspects, rather each almost has his own mind, although they come close to expressing agreement just for the sake of being able to establish a common position as is well established by the Rintelner, several Königsberg professors, and others. A good part of the Calvinists are at peace with the [Calixtiner] proposals for peace, as the [1661 Kassel] colloquy especially testifies, which, together with the resulting writings about it, began almost twenty years ago at Kassel. However, [the Calixtiner] got no thanks from the papist side for their writings, except that the papists make use of what is conducive out of their doctrinal positions for the Roman Church. Therefore, because the [Calixtiner] do not abide by the Unaltered Augsburg Confession and by the Christian Book of Concord, they are a new and distinct party.

If then pious Christians of high and low estate seem to desire a more thorough report [about the potential for reconciliation] because of these manifold peace proposals, what should they [then] hold according to the inerrant rule of God's Word? [What should they then hold about] whether it is not then possible and could happen with a good conscience that one unites himself [with] or at least steps closer together [to the other confessions], particularly now because the ill-disposed party even petitions peace and peace proposals? One should take care in treatises seeking peace and proposals for unity in worldly matters, not to refuse the means of peace, much less that it should happen by the cutting up or tearing apart of the church through highly tragic disunity and division. Therefore, we are thus compelled to open our Christian theological consideration from God's Word in a timely fashion without bitterness and in all meekness, not to widen the unholy division, but for the purpose of Christian, God-pleasing agreement in the spirit through the bond of peace.

Christ Jesus, you who are truth and peace itself, give us and all who read such the spirit of truth and peace to the honor of His holy name and for the assured rest and for the binding together of His believers in the Word of divine truth, that we praise God together and with one mouth, here in time and there forevermore.

The First Preliminary Chapter

Pious Christians should search from the heart for true church peace and help promote it according to their abilities just as dearly as God's grace is to them.

§ I. There is no doubt among all that all pious Christians are duty bound to promote true Christian peace, not so much with public writings and explanations, as with inner fervent desire and from the bottom of their heart in integrity and truth. First of all, in fact, [we are] to promote with heartfelt prayer to God, who alone has in his divine hand beloved church peace, these true gifts which Christ has acquired, gifted, and preserved for us through his Spirit and power, [just as] our high priest Christ himself has fervently groaned to God his Father for the sake of peace. John 17:[11, 20–21]:

> Holy Father, keep them in your name, which you have given me, that they may be one, even as we are one. [. . .] I do not ask for these only, but also for those who will believe in me through their word, that they may all be one, just as you, Father, are in me, and I in you, that they also may be in us.

§ II. But next, so that each one can lend the hand of and not neglect his estate and his vocation, take care with the highest diligence to drive and direct into work what may be useful and of service for the preservation of good unity in the Christian Church, so that one does not give cause for division and disunity. God's earnest will and command should always be before the eyes of us all. Romans 12:18: "If possible, so far as it depends on you, live peaceably with all." Hebrews 12:14: "Strive for peace" (as wild game, which one must pursue with special diligence when one wants to obtain it) "and for the holiness without which no one will see the Lord." Ephesians 4:3: "Eager to maintain the unity of the Spirit in the bond of peace." Philippians [2]:1–3: "So if there is any encouragement in Christ, any comfort from love, any participation in the Spirit, any affection and sympathy, complete my joy by being of the same mind, having the same love, being in full accord and of one mind. Do nothing from selfish ambition or conceit." How could St. Paul admonish us in a more loving manner? How could he commend to us more emphatically that we devote ourselves diligently to seeking love and unity than with the Holy highly-praiseworthy Trinity? Who else [than] He, who is our peace, should allow us some exhortation in Christ? Who [else than] he, who is the God of peace, should allow us some comfort of the love of God the Father? Who [else than] he, who is the Spirit of love, should allow us some communion of the Holy Spirit, and so execute in truth heartfelt love and mercy over us?

§ III. We should set before ourselves what peace cost Jesus Christ, our Prince of Peace, who spent his own precious blood on it that "thereby killing the hostility and making peace, . . . he might create in himself one new man" out of Jew and Gentile (Ephesians 2:[16,] 15), so that "[t]here is neither Jew nor Greek, there is neither slave nor free, there is no male and female, for you are all one in Christ Jesus" (Galatians 3:28). Therefore, the first word to his disciples after his resurrection was "Peace be with you," which, after he showed them his hands and his side, he repeated again, "Peace be with you" (John 20:21), to show that peace was acquired for them through the wounds in his hands and his side. Therefore, he has testified and notified us of this peace also in his testament. John 14:27: "Peace I leave with you; my peace I give to you." Who would then not regard this peace highly and worthily?

§ IV. We should hold up before ourselves God the Holy Spirit's beautiful encomium of peace so that he may be decorated with blessing and salvation. Psalm 133:1–3: "Behold, how good and pleasant it is when brothers dwell in unity! It is like the precious oil on the head, running down on the beard, on the beard of Aaron, running down on the collar of his robes!" Just as this holy oil, the precious balsam, poured out on the high priest's head, gave a felicitous, comely aroma and made fragrant his high priestly clothing, so, too, for God, peace and unity is a precious balsam and gives a beloved, pleasant aroma. "It is like the dew of Hermon, which falls on the mountains of Zion," which otherwise has no water, and gives it moisture, making it fruitful. Thus beautiful, beloved fruit comes out of the lovely dew of peace. "For there the Lord has commanded the blessing, life forevermore." He has made and ordered a command that the blessing must follow those [who] love because it is also a proper life and foretaste of eternal life. Matthew 5:9: "Blessed are the peacemakers, for they shall be called sons of God." Second Corinthians 13:11: "Live in peace; and the God of love and peace will be with you."

§ V. Our vocation should awaken us to peacefulness because "God has called you to peace" (1 Corinthians 7:15). "Walk in a manner worthy of the calling to which you have been called, . . . [B]e eager to maintain the unity of the Spirit" (Ephesians 4:[1–]3). "Put on love, which binds everything together in perfect harmony. And let the peace of Christ rule in your hearts, to which indeed you were called in one body" (Colossians 3:14[–15]). The putting on of Christ should also bind us into his spiritual body and the Holy Sacraments through which the Holy Spirit binds and arranges us as members of his Body among one another. "There is one body and one Spirit—just as you were called to the one hope that belongs to your call—one Lord, one faith, one Baptism, one God and Father of all, who is over all and through all and in all" (Ephesians 4:4–6). "For in one Spirit we were all baptized into one body" in the Sacrament of Holy Baptism and "all were made to drink of one Spirit" in the Holy Lord's Supper so that we are one in the Spirit as we all enjoy one blessed cup and one blessed bread, which belongs to this spiritual Body (1 Corinthians 12:13). "Because there is one bread, we who are many are one body, for we all partake of the one bread" (1 Corinthians 10:17). "Speaking the truth in love, we are to grow up in every way into him who is the head, into Christ, from whom the whole body, joined and held together by every joint with which it is equipped, when each part is working properly, makes the body grow so that it builds itself up in love" (Ephesians 4:15–16). If we do not want to hold on to peace, how can the spiritual Body of Christ exist? "If one member suffers, all suffer together; if one member is honored, all rejoice together. Now you are the body of Christ and individually members of it" (1 Corinthians 12:26–27).

§ VI. Whoever does not want to be aroused to seek peace, he should consider how those who have a desire for contentiousness and controversy are regarded in the Church of God. First Corinthians 11:[16]: "If anyone is inclined to be contentious, we have no such practice, nor do the churches of God." Such do not belong in the communion of saints and cannot be true members of the Church. They are not spiritually, but fleshly minded: "For while there is jealousy and strife among you, are you not of the flesh and behaving only in a human way?" (1 Corinthians 3:3) They are not true upright Christians, but falsely pass themselves off as such. They are not driven by a good, but by an evil spirit. "But if you have bitter jealousy," says James in 3:14[–15], "and selfish ambition in your hearts, do not boast and be false to the truth. This is not the wisdom that comes down from above, but is earthly, unspiritual, demonic." They have not enjoyed the fruits of peace, but as "one who sows to his own flesh will from the flesh reap corruption" (Galatians 6:8). "But for those who are self-seeking and do not obey the truth, . . . there will be wrath and fury," affliction and anxiety (Romans 2:8). They exclude themselves from the inheritance of the kingdom of God because these are the public works of the flesh: "strife, jealousy, fits of anger, rivalries, dissensions, divisions, envy . . . things like these. I warn you, as I warned you before, that those who do such things will not inherit the kingdom of God" (Galatians 5:20–21). They despise the sour sweat and the precious blood of Christ Jesus together with his salvific prayer through which he acquired and asked for peace for his Church. They want nothing of God, who is a God of peace and is love itself. "God is love, and whoever abides in love abides in God, and God abides in him" (1 John 4:16). Therefore, it is easy to conclude who they must be. "By this it is evident who are the children of God, and who are the children of the devil: whoever does not practice righteousness is not of God, nor is the one who does not love his brother" (1 John 3:10).

§ VII. Therefore, Gregory of Nazianzus writes correctly and effectively in his Twelfth Oration. All those who pursue peace and hate discord draw themselves near to God through this and to the holy angels. In contrast, those who delight in controversy and only want to make a reputation for themselves through innovation, and therefore boast of their scandal, are antagonists devoted to Satan: [Satan] pits both against each other; and as a murderer from the beginning and as an enemy of the good, he works such things in others. [He does this] so that he enters under the darkness of derision the common Body of the Church and hides himself in division and once more secretly opens for himself a place that he might completely and thoroughly break through with all power in no way different than a courageous army [breaks] through a fallen wall or through an enemy army.

Who would not gladly want to restrain Satan, that hellish peace destroyer? Who would want to be his companion and help perpetuate and preserve disorder? Yes, who would not wish to plead and groan and in its place help advance, according to all one's abilities, that the love of peace (without which the kingdom of Christ cannot exist) may be established everywhere, particularly in [God's] treasured Christendom that "the wolf shall dwell with the lamb, and the leopard shall lie down with the young goat. . . . The cow and the bear shall graze; their young shall lie down together; and the lion shall eat straw like the ox" (Isaiah 11:6–7). What a glorious gift of God's grace it would be to behold, if only a true God-pleasing unity could also blossom from those three groups in the West [*occident*]: the papists, Lutherans, and Reformed! And who indeed would want to be so un-Christian that he would not be prepared to purchase, if it were possible, such goods also with his own blood? "We ought to lay down our lives for the brothers" (1 John 3:16). Who would not allow for so many million Christians that life be joyous!

JOHANN ANDREAS QUENSTEDT (1617–88)

THE CONSENSUS BUILDER

by Timothy R. Schmeling

LIFE

In his critical account of Wittenberg Lutheran Orthodoxy, August Tholuck, a mediating theologian, once called Johann Andreas Quenstedt (1617–88) the "bookkeeper" of the Lutheran tradition.[1] But Quenstedt was more than a mere archivist; he made it his project to help rebuild the Lutheran consensus that had collapsed in the Syncretistic Controversy (ca. 1645–86).[2] His great systematics not only refers to the Lutheran

[1] August Tholuck, *Der Geist der lutherischen Theologen Wittenbergs im Verlaufe des 17. Jahrhunderts* (Hamburg: Friedrich und Andreas Perthes, 1852), 247.

[2] See also Kenneth Appold, *Orthodoxie als Konsensbildung: das theologische Disputationswesen an der Universität Wittenberg zwischen 1570 und 1710* (Tübingen: Mohr Siebeck, 2004).

syncretists with the more amiable term "innovators,"[3] but it also presented the received Lutheran tradition with such systematic precision, comprehensiveness, and exegesis that Robert Preus wrote the following:

> There is no question that after the *Loci Theologici* of Martin Chemnitz and Gerhard (who was his uncle) the *Systema* [*Theologia*] of Quenstedt ranks as the greatest dogmatics book ever written by a Lutheran. Although this enormous volume would have cost a pastor many weeks' salary, it went through five editions between 1685 and 1715. One might say that Quenstedt's *Systema* killed systematic theology in the period of Lutheran orthodoxy as Michelangelo killed Renaissance art by the unexcelled quality of his work. Quenstedt's lifework is so big, so concise and systematic, and so excellent that no later Lutheran ever came close to equaling it.[4]

To be sure, Quenstedt was not the greatest Lutheran theologian of his day.[5] Still, it is not only Lutherans who have felt the need to wrestle with Quenstedt.[6] Protestant theologians and church historians of all stripes have continued to engage him as well. Friedrich Schleiermacher,

---

[3] Johann Andreas Quenstedt, *Theologia Didactico-Polemica, Sive Systema Theologicum . . . Divisum* (Wittenberg: Johann Ludolph Quenstedt, Elert Schumacher, and Matthäus Henckel, 1685).

[4] Robert Preus, *The Theology of Post-Reformation Lutheranism* (St. Louis: Concordia, 1970), 1:62–63.

[5] For an overview of Quenstedt studies, see the following: *Religion Past and Present: Encyclopedia of Religion and Theology*, 4th ed., s.v. "Quenstedt, Johann Andreas"; *Biographisch-Bibliographisches Kirchenlexikon*, s.v. "Quenstedt, Johannes Andreas; lutherischer Dogmatiker"; *Lexikon für Theologie und Kirche*, 3rd ed. s.v. "Quenstedt, Johann Andreas"; *The Encyclopedia of the Lutheran Church*, s.v. "Quenstedt, Johannes-Andreas"; *The New Schaff-Herzog Encyclopedia of Religious Knowledge*, s.v. "Quenstedt, Johannes Andreas"; *Realencyklopädie für protestantische Theologie und Kirche*, 3rd ed., s.v. "Quenstedt, Johannes Andreas"; *Allgemeine Deutsche Biographie*, s.v. "Quenstedt, Johann Andreas."

[6] Robert Preus, "The Vicarious Atonement in John Quenstedt," in *Doctrine is Life: The Essays of Robert D. Preus on Justification and the Lutheran Confessions*, ed. Klement I. Preus (St. Louis: Concordia, 2006), 55–78; Quentin Stewart, "Catholicity or Consensus?: The Role of the Consensus Patrum and the Vincentian Canon in Lutheran Orthodoxy from Chemnitz to Quenstedt" (PhD diss., Concordia Seminary, 2006). See also "Lebensregeln für Prediger, genommen und übersetzt aus Quenstedt's Ethica pastoralis," *Lehre und Wehre* (1872): 18, no. 8:225–40; 18, no. 9:270–76; 18, no. 10:304–7; 18, no. 11:340–47; 19, no. 6:181–3; 19, no. 7:206–10; 19, no. 8:248–51; 19, no. 10:300–304; 20, no. 6:182–85; 20, no. 8:241–48; 20, no. 9:278–80; 21, no. 2:51–54; as well as Luther Poellet's English translation of selections of Quenstedt's *Theologia* in the bibliography.

the father of classical liberalism, read Quenstedt closely as he formulated his dogmatic lectures for the University of Berlin.[7] Mediating theologians like Isaak Dorner attempted to subvert Quenstedt's theology of the immutability of God in order to develop a kenotic Christology.[8] Karl Barth, the father of neo-orthodoxy, highly prized Quenstedt, quoting him in his *Church Dogmatics* more than he quoted any other Protestant orthodox theologian with the exception of Amandus Polanus von Polansdorf (1561–1610).[9] Helping correct the negative caricature of Lutheran Orthodoxy, church historian Jörg Baur used Quenstedt to illuminate the role of reason within one of its most important theological systems.[10] One recent church historian has even attempted to read Quenstedt anew through the eyes of Ludwig Wittgenstein.[11]

Johann Andreas Quenstedt was born in Quedlinburg on August 13, 1617.[12] He grew up in an environment that was not unprecedented in Lutheranism, but generally speaking uncommon. The city and the sur-

---

[7] B. A. Gerrish, *Continuing the Reformation: Essays on Modern Religious Thought* (Chicago: The University of Chicago Press, 1993), 194n70.

[8] Zachary Purvis, "The New Ethicist and the Old Bookkeeper: Isaak Dorner, Johann Quenstedt, and Modern Appropriations of Classical Protestantism," *Zeitschrift für Neuere Theologiegeschichte* 19, no. 1 (March 2012): 14–33.

[9] Rinse H. Reeling Brouwer, *Karl Barth and Post-Reformation Orthodoxy* (Burlington, VT: Ashgate Publishing Company, 2015), 8, 16.

[10] Jörg Baur, *Die Vernunft zwischen Ontologie und Evangelium: Eine Untersuchung zur Theologie Johann Andreas Quenstedts* (Gütersloh: Gütersloher Verlagshaus, 1962).

[11] Michael Coors, *Scriptura efficax Die biblisch-dogmatische Grundlegung des theologischen Systems bey Johann Andreas Quenstedt: Ein dogmatische Beitrag zu Theorie und Auslegung des biblischen Kanons als Heiliger Schrift* (Göttingen: Vandenhoeck & Ruprecht, 2009); Michael Coors, "Theologische Texttheorie: Theologische Erkundungen zur Textualität der Heiligen Schrift zwischen Ludwig Wittgenstein und Johann Andreas Quenstedt," *Neue Zeitschrift für Systematische Theologie und Religionsphilosophie* 51, no. 4 (January 2009): 400–426.

[12] Apart from Quenstedt's own writings, the main primary sources for his life are as follows: Caspar Löscher, *Reine / Theologische und Johannitische Bekäntnis ... Johanne Andrea Qvenstedten ... wiederholet* (Wittenberg: Johann Ludolph Quenstedt, 1688). The *Curriculum Vitæ Dn. D. Joh. Andreæ Qvensted* and Christian Röhrensee's *Ad Exeqviatores Logos Eucharis Tikos* are also appended to this funeral sermon. Andreas Sennert, "Rector Academiæ VVittenbergensis ... Johannis Andreae Qvenstedii ... indicit," in *Sacer Decadvm Septenarivs Memoriam Theologorvm Nostra Ætate ... Theologica*, ed. Heinrich Pipping (Leipzig: Thomas Fritsch, 1705). A bibliography of seventy-one of his works can be founded in Jean-Pierre Nicéron, *Nachrichen von den Begebenheiten und Schriften berümter Gelehrten mit einigen Zusätzen*, ed. Siegmund Jacob Baumgarten (Halle: Christoph Peter Franckens, 1749–77), 20:130–38. A more complete bibliography can be found at VD17 Das Verzeichnis der im deutschen Sprachraum erschienenen Drucke des 17. Jahrhunderts: www.vd17.de/index.php.

rounding territory were dominated by a famous medieval autonomous imperial abbey from which princess-abbesses ruled this land. Under the protection and influence of Albertine Saxony, these princess-abbesses came to embrace the Reformation in 1540, establishing a Lutheran territorial church wherein Lutheran canonesses lived an evangelical religious life in accordance with the Augsburg Confession.[13]

The day after his birth, Quenstedt was baptized and named Johann Andreas in honor of his two uncles. He descended from an old, patrician family that was very much part of the Quedlinburg social fabric. Ludolph Quenstedt (d. 1654), his father, was a Lutheran canon of Halberstadt's Blessed Virgin Mary Collegiate Church. Dorothea née Gerhard, his mother, was a sister of Dr. Andreas Gerhard (1580–1623), princely Saxon Chancellor at Arnstadt (*fürstl. Sächß. Cantzler zu Arndstad*), and Dr. Johann Gerhard (1582–1637), a professor of theology at the University of Jena.[14]

The "prudence and moderation" attributed to Quenstedt by Andreas Sennert (1606–89), his funeral orator, had its roots in Quedlinburg.[15] His early theological acumen, piety, and peaceful nature were not only influenced by Gerhard, the most renowned Lutheran theologian of the day, but also by Johann Arndt (1555–1621), his uncle's early spiritual mentor and Quedlinburg's most famous pastor. But it was during the reign of Princess-abbess Dorothea Sophia of Saxony-Weimar (1587–1645) that he learned the real meaning of the cross. In Quenstedt's formative years, Quedlinburg was inundated by the armies of the Thirty Years' War (1618–48).[16]

For the first thirteen years of his life, the young Quenstedt was educated at home. The new city deacon, Jacob Hartmann; St. Wiperti Pastor Johann Vielitz; and St. Aegidius Pastor Daniel Heimbürger oversaw the next three years of his formation in the home of Dr. Friedrich Lentz (1591–1659), the chancellor of the Quedlinburg Abbey. In 1633, the sixteen-year-old Quenstedt entered Quedlinburg's *Gymnasium illustre* where he studied for the next four years. Under the lead of Rector Johann Prätorius from 1620 to 1656, this already superregional *Gymnasium* (upper school) flourished, so much so that there was talk of making it a

---

[13] Peter Kasper, *Das Reichsstift Quedlinburg (936–1810): Konzept—Zeitbezug—Systemwechsel* (Göttingen: V & R unipress, 2014), 27–156.

[14] Löscher, *Reine*, Fr–F2r.

[15] Sennert, "Rector," 229.

[16] Johann Heinrich Fritsch, *Geschichte des vormaligen Reichstifts und der Stadt Quedlinburg* (Quedlinburg: Gottfried Basse, 1828), 2:28–33, 204, 212–13, 242.

university in 1677. Here, Quenstedt made good progress in the liberal arts, particularly in Hebrew, Greek, and Latin. The school, moreover, was a feeder for the universities of Wittenberg, Leipzig, and Helmstedt.[17]

Quenstedt had already made plans to study with Gerhard at the University of Jena. When his uncle died on August 17, 1637, Quenstedt chose instead to study at Braunschweig's unorthodox University of Helmstedt because it was closer to his parents and because of the war.[18] The Lutheran irenicist and Helmstedt theology professor Georg Calixt (1586–1656) developed a new kind of theology at this time that promoted mutual toleration between the three confessions on the basis of adherence to the fundamental doctrine encapsulated in the Apostles' Creed and its proper explication via the theology of the first five centuries. The orthodox Lutheran opposition to Helmstedt theology as syncretism, which was largely led by Abraham Calov (1612–86), also revealed another rift in Lutheranism, that is, the new "Jena" theology of Johannes Musaeus (1613–81). Quenstedt's career was dominated by the vying of these three schools of thought for the Lutheran hearts of his day.[19]

Johann Gerhard raised some of the first flags against Helmstedt theology at a 1621 Saxon Conference.[20] Naturally, it would prove a great boon for Helmstedt's orthodoxy if Gerhard's own nephew could be won over to Calixtine theology. Quenstedt matriculated at Helmstedt on September 30, 1637. He received room and board at the home of Conrad Horneius (1590–1649), Calixt's chief collaborator. For the next six years, Quenstedt studied the liberal arts under Helmstedt's renowned Late Renaissance humanist philosophical faculty. But it was Calixt and Horneius who made the greatest impression on him. Caspar Löscher (1636–1718), his funeral preacher, reported that Quenstedt never wanted to miss one of their theological lectures and meticulously wrote down all that they

---

[17] Löscher, *Reine*, F2r–F3v; Fritsch, *Geschichte*, 2:226, 251, 255, 267–72; Thomas Wozniak, *Quedlinburg im 14. und 16. Jahrhundert. Ein sozialtopographischer Vergleich* (Berlin: Akademie Verlag, 2013), 323–24, 353.

[18] Löscher, *Reine*, F2v.

[19] Timothy R. Schmeling, "Slaying the Syncretistic Chimera: A Study of the *Consensus Repetitus* in Light of Confessionalization Theory" (PhD diss., Concordia Seminary, 2014); Heinz Staemmler, *Die Auseinandersetzung der kursächsischen Theologen mit dem Helmstedter Synkretismus. Eine Studie zum "Consensus Repetitus fidei vere Lutheranae" (1655) und den Diskussionen um ihn* (Waltrop: Hartmut Spenner, 2005).

[20] Schmeling, "Slaying," 92.

said.[21] On April 11, 1637, he defended a philosophical disputation on habits of the mind presided over by Heinrich Julius Scheurl (1600–1651). More importantly, on August 26, 1643, he defended a theological disputation on transubstantiation that was presided over by Georg Calixt.[22] He earned his master of arts degree on January 3, 1643, and was encouraged to teach geography at Helmstedt the next semester.[23]

His parents' ailing health drew him home. There Quenstedt cared for his parents, studied, and preached. The Quedlinburgers enjoyed his sermons enough that they called him to serve the abbey, but he turned down this call to continue his theological studies. Instead of returning to Helmstedt, he made a danger-filled trek to the University of Wittenberg, where he enrolled on August 22, 1644, to study theology. In October of 1644, he earned the right to join the philosophical (or undergraduate) faculty with a disputation on a Dutch polar expedition's (1596–97) observation of what would become known as the Novaya Zemlya effect (polar mirage), and began lecturing on geography, logic, ethics, and metaphysics.[24] Whether it was new misgivings about Calixtinism or naïveté that caused him to enroll at Wittenberg, the hostility he encountered enrolling as a Helmstedt alumnus so bothered him that he wrote Horneius a letter about his deflating experience.[25]

He lived in the home of Wilhelm Leyser I (1592–1649), who was a former student of Johann Gerhard. Repaying the favor Gerhard once showed him, Leyser treated Quenstedt like a son, privately conversed with him for many hours a day, let him use his personal library, and was primarily responsible for winning him over to orthodox Lutheranism. Besides Leyser, Quenstedt studied theology under Jakob Martini (1570–1649), Paul Röber (1587–1651), and Johann Hülsemann (1602–61), who further shored up his orthodoxy.[26] In a 1655 travel report, Valentin

---

[21] Walther Spieβ, Werner Hillebrand, and Herbert Munhenke, eds., *Die Matrikel der Universität Helmstedt* (Hildesheim: Verlag August Lax, 1955–79), 2:3; Löscher, *Reine*, F2v–F3v.

[22] Johann Andreas Quenstedt, *De Transsvbstantiatione Contra Pontificios ... Praesidio Georgi Calixti ... Islebiensis* (Helmstedt: Henning Müller, 1643). Some printings date the disputation October 25, 1643.

[23] Löscher dates his M.A. July 3, 1643 in his *Reine*, F3r–F3v.

[24] Löscher, *Reine*, F3v–Gr; Bernhard Weissenborn and Fritz Juntke, eds. *Album Academiae Vitebergensis. Jüngere Reihe* (Magdeburg: Ernst Holtermann, 1934–66), 1:432.

[25] Quenstedt's letter to Horneius is cited in Georg Calixt's *Wiederlegung Der vnchristlichen vnd vnbilligen Verleumbdungen ... ecclesiasticæ* (Helmstedt: Henning Müller, 1651), Cr.

[26] Löscher, *Reine*, F4v–Gr; Tholuck, *Der Geist*, 215; Walther Friedensburg, *Geschichte der Universität Wittenberg* (Halle: M. Niemeyer, 1917), 427.

Crüger, a Quedlinburg-born Helmstedt student, suggested to a fellow Helmstedter that Quenstedt's theological shift was symptomatic of a weak character.[27] In contradistinction, Luther Poellet argues, "So he held the views set forth as his in his *Theologia* out of conviction based on experience and personal study—and not, as some might think, because he was, so to say, born and bred that way."[28]

By October 28, 1646, he had become a Wittenberg adjunct philosophy professor. Now that the Syncretistic Controversy had begun to rage, Quenstedt was asked by the theological faculty to draw up an explanation of the points of controversy between Helmstedt and Wittenberg. No doubt just happy to have Gerhard's nephew on their side, the supreme consistory received it so favorably that Quenstedt was allowed to give a private collegium (a course in the form of disputations) on Helmstedt errors. Yet, his disputations from these times did not just touch on syncretistic themes. Instead he maintained a wide liberal arts focus, as evident by his oft-reprinted study of ancient burial customs.[29]

In 1649, he turned down a call to serve as deacon for the County of Mansfeld because of his weak constitution. He declined another call that same year to be a pastor at the Halberstadt St. Martin's Church because Wilhelm Leyser had died on February 8, 1649. As a result, Johann Scharf, Abraham Calov, Johann Meisner (1615–81), and Andreas Kunad (1602–62) became first, second, third, and fourth ordinary professors (*Ordinarii*), respectively. Quenstedt, conversely, became an ordinary professor of philosophy (*Ordinarius*) (logic and metaphysics) and extraordinary theology professor (*Extraordinarius*) by September of 1649. On February 20 and 21, 1650, he defended his licentiate disputation on 1 Samuel 23, which was presided over by Johann Scharf. He was made a doctor of theology on November 12, 1650.[30] The following year he married for the

---

[27] August Tholuck, *Das akademische Leben des siebzehnten Jahrhunderts, mit besonderer Beziehung auf protestantische-theologischen Facultäten Deutschlands* (Halle: Eduard Anton, 1853–54), 2:144.

[28] Luther Poellet, preface to *The Nature and Character of Theology: An Introduction to the Thought of J.A. Quenstedt from Theologia Didactico-Polemica Sive Systema Theologicum*, by Johann Andreas Quenstedt, abr., ed., and trans. Luther Poellet (St. Louis: Concordia, 1986), 10.

[29] Weissenborn and Juntke, *Album*, 1:432; Löscher, *Reine*, Gr–G2v. The final version of this 1647–48 disputation is appended to his *Antiqvitates Biblicæ Et Ecclesiasticæ ... emendates* (Wittenberg: Johann Ludolph Quenstedt, 1699).

[30] Löscher, *Reine*, G2r–G3r; Weissenborn and Juntke, *Album*, 1:492–93; Karl Förstemann, *Liber decanorum facultatis theologicae Academiae Vitebergensis* (Leipzig: C. Tauchnitz, 1838), 95–96.

first time. (He later remarried after the death of his first wife, and again after the death of his second wife.)[31]

On June 22, 1660, Quenstedt became fourth ordinary theology professor after the death of Scharf. In Easter of 1662, he became the third professor after the death of Kunad. Following the death of Meisner in 1684, he became second professor, Provost of All Saints (Castle) Church, and consistorial assessor (a member of the consistory). Due to his old age, Johann Friedrich Mayer (1650–1712), the fourth Wittenberg theology professor, became his adjunct to help him preach some of the sermons. He became first professor (*professor primarius*) a year before his death. He was rector of the university five times.[32]

Throughout his life, Quenstedt was a sickly individual who often suffered from stomach ailments and hypochondria. These afflictions all took their toll on his health. On May 22, 1688, he died, surrounded by the singing and praying of his family. He was buried in the All Saints Church in Wittenberg. His epitaph was recorded on the burial stone that hangs on the great church door. His picture also once hung with an inscription over the sacristy door.[33]

During the second half of the seventeenth century, Abraham Calov and his war on syncretism came to dominate the University of Wittenberg. While Calov's influence can clearly be seen in the writings of Quenstedt, he was more diplomatic than Calov and shows more originality than is often claimed. Later, Quenstedt and Johann Meisner even distanced themselves from the 1655/64 *Repeated Consensus of the True Lutheran Faith* (*Consensus Repetitus Fidei Vere Lutheranæ*), an Electoral Saxon confession against syncretism, but generally remained faithful to Calov's theology. Quenstedt was particularly disturbed by the later feud

[31] Löscher, *Reine*, G3v–Hr; Weissenborn and Juntke, *Album*, 3:268; Johann Christoph Erdmann, *Lebensbeschreibungen und litterarische Nachrichten von den Wittenbergschen Theologen seit der Stiftung der Universität 1502, bis zur dritten hunderjährlichen Säkularfeyer 1802; aus den Matrikeln und andern glaubwürdigen Urkunden. Ein Beitrag zur Kursächs. Reformations- und Kirchengeschichte* (Wittenberg: Samuel Gottfried Zimmermann, 1804), 87–88; Tholuck, *Der Geist*, 216–17.

[32] Löscher, *Reine*, G3r; Johann Christoph Erdmann, *Biographie sämtlicher Pröpste an der Schloß- und Universitätskirche zu Wittenberg vom Anfange des XVI. Jahrhunderts bis auf gegenwärtige Zeit aus glaubwürdigen Urkunden. Ein Beitrag zur Chursächs. Reformations- und Kirchengeschichte* (Wittenberg: Samuel Gottfried Zimmermann, 1802), 25–26; Weissenborn and Juntke, *Album*, 3:593–94.

[33] Löscher, *Reine*, Hr–H2v; Erdmann, *Biographie*, 25–26.

between Calov and Meisner over the articles of the faith in the Wittenberg faculty.[34]

The number of theological works he published was smaller than other theologians of his day, but the contributions he did make were significant. The first work for which he is known is his *Pastoral Ethics* (1678), a pastoral theology and preaching manual. Herein one sees the Lutheran conviction that theology can never be severed from pastoral care. Quenstedt's moderation, prudence, and piety likewise bleed through the pages.[35] He produced two noteworthy works of history, his 1654 *Dialogue concerning the Fatherlands, Learning, and Writings of Illustrious Men* (*Dialogus De Patriis Illustrium Doctrina Et Scriptis Virorum*) and his 1688 *Biblical and Churchly Antiquities* (*Antiqvitates Biblicæ Et Ecclesiasticæ*), the latter of which included his oft-reprinted work on burial customs.[36] His most important work of all was his massive 1685 *Didactic-Polemic Theology or Theological System* (*Theologia Didactico-Polemica Sive Systema Theologicum*), published a year before Calov's death. It was based on the outline of Johann Friedrich König's (1619–64) *Advanced Positive Theology* (*Theologia positiva acroamatica*) and employed the analytical method. Each locus was divided into a didactic and polemic section. It is intended in large part to help formulate consensus in Lutheran Orthodoxy in the wake of the Syncretistic Controversy.[37]

BIBLIOGRAPHY

Works by Quenstedt in English Translation

The Church. Abridged, edited, and translated by Luther Poellet. Malone, TX: Repristination Press, 1999.

The Holy Ministry. Abridged, edited, and translated by Luther Poellet. Fort Wayne: Concordia Theological Seminary Press, 1991.

The Nature and Character of Theology: An Introduction to the Thought of J. A. Quenstedt from Theologia Didactico-Polemica Sive Systema

[34] Tholuck, *Der Geist,* 400–406.

[35] Johann Andreas Quenstedt, *Ethica Pastoralis . . . conficiendi* (Wittenberg: Tobias Mevius, Elert Schumacher, and Michael Wendt, 1678).

[36] Johann Andreas Quenstedt, *Dialogus De Patriis Illustrium Doctrina Et Scriptis Virorum . . . descriptions* (Wittenberg: Tobias Mevius, Elert Schumacher, and Michael Wendt, 1654); Quenstedt, *Antiqvitates.*

[37] Quenstedt, *Theologia*; Johann Friedrich König, *Theologia positiva acroamatica (Rostock 1664),* ed. and trans. Andreas Stegmann (Tübingen: Mohr Siebeck, 2006).

Theologicum. Abridged, edited, and translated by Luther Poellet. St. Louis: Concordia, 1986.

Select Works by Quenstedt in German and Latin

Antiqvitates Biblicæ Et Ecclesiasticæ . . . emendates. Wittenberg: Johann Ludolph Quenstedt, 1699.

De Transsvbstantiatione Contra Pontificios . . . Praesidio Georgi Calixti . . . Islebiensis. Helmstedt: Henning Müller, 1643.

Dialogus De Patriis Illustrium Doctrina Et Scriptis Virorum . . . descriptions. Wittenberg: Tobias Mevius, Elert Schumacher, and Michael Wendt, 1654.

Ethica Pastoralis . . . conficiendi. Wittenberg: Tobias Mevius, Elert Schumacher, and Michael Wendt, 1678.

Theologia Didactico-Polemica, Sive Systema Theologicum . . . Divisum. Wittenberg: Johann Ludolph Quenstedt, Elert Schumacher, and Matthäus Henckel, 1685.

WRITING[38]

Chapter X. Concerning the Cross

Section I. Didactic

Thesis I. The affliction of the pious is called the cross (Matthew 10:38; 16:24; Mark 8:34; Luke 9:23; 14:27), from the cross of Jesus Christ, through which it is sanctified and which it imitates.

Note: The calamites and afflictions of the pious are expressed with various words in the Sacred Scripture. The word *cross* holds first place, (Matthew 10:38; 16:24; Mark 8:34; Luke 9:23; 14:27), by an allusion to the cross of Christ, through which it is sanctified and which it imitates. All afflictions of the pious, I say, fall under the name of the cross because they are conformed through the same to the crucified Christ. Christ sanctified and consecrated by his cross all our suffering so that we may be saved. The cross of the pious is also called the yoke of Christ (Matthew 11:29), *thlipsis*, [which means] affliction [or] pressing, because it grinds, presses, and burdens the body just like the soul (1 Thessalonians 3:3), and

[38] This is a translation of Johann Andreas Quenstedt's *Theologia*, part IV, chapter 10, 348–51. It is his chapter on the cross.

distress, because the anguish of the soul is the companion of the cross and calamity (1 Peter 1:6; Romans 8:35).

Thesis II. In other places, it is called temptation (1 Corinthians 10:13), not for evil, but for good (James 1:13).

Note: The affliction of the pious is also called temptation (1 Corinthians 10:13); God is faithful, and he will not let you be tempted beyond your ability, but with the temptation he will also provide the way of escape, that you may be able to endure it. Here can be considered: (1) the certainty of temptation, (2) the nature of temptation, (3) the significance of its causes (God clearly sends temptations for certain reasons), and (4) that the temptation is: (a) bearable and (b) able to be stopped. This temptation is also never for evil, but always for good. "Let no one say when he is tempted, 'I am being tempted by God,' for God cannot be tempted with evil, and he himself tempts no one" (James 1:13). Observe: The apostle does not treat here those temptations, by which faith, steadfastness, and the patience of the pious are tested, but concerning those by which James affirms man is stirred up and prompted to evil or sin, and those not the product of God's action. *To Peipazomai* [I am being tempted] is the same in this place as to be prompted and stirred up to sin. In the contrary manner, the father will test his son, the master his servant, the husband his wife, the master his disciple in order to search out, sharpen, and arouse talents, affects, and zeal. Augustine says in *De Consens[u] Evangel[istarum]*, book 2, chapter 30, "Temptation is to be understood in one way, when it is said, God tempts no one, and in another way when it is said, the Lord your God tempted you to know if you loved Him (Deuteronomy 13). The former is [the temptation of] seduction, the latter is [the temptation of] trial." Compare [Salomon] Gesner *[Commentationes In] Psalm.*, Psalm 17, page 157 concerning the accompaniment of the yoke of the cross and faith.

Thesis III. It is in fact called *paideia* [discipline] (Hebrews 12:5–9, 11), also *dokimasia* [testing] in 1 Peter 1:7.

Note I: In Hebrews 12:6, it is called *paideia kyrios,* the discipline of the Lord (see also verses 7–9, 11). Moreover, *paideia* signifies an instruction that is undertaken, bound together with a correcting of vices, even called *dokimasia* and *dokimion*, testing of faith (1 Peter 1:7), [and] *pathêmata,* [sufferings] of this present time (Romans 8:18), because the cross of the pious is momentary. It is limited in this present life (2 Corinthians 4:17), the cup of the Lord, because God measures out a certain measure of affliction to each one (Psalm 75:[8]; 116:13; Mark 10:38ff.; Matthew 26:39).

Note II: But *paideia* and *dokimasia* differ from *timôria* [punishment] and punishment properly speaking. For *timôria* is inflicted by God as an angry judgment upon men, especially the disgraced, but *paideia* and *dokimasia* are a test and trial with which the pious are afflicted, not on account of previous sins, which are remitted, but on account of the consent of the divine will to test their faith, patience, and steadfastness. Punishment, properly speaking, is called a decree not to remit fault. It departs from the judiciary forum of God by an act of justice with the intention of imposing the penalty merited by sin. The cross of the pious moreover truly follows the remission of fault as a paternal correction and reproof or is imposed *kata epeikeian* [according to forbearance] by an act of paternal providence of God and is only directed to the good, suitable, and salutary correction of man.

Thesis IV. God is the principle efficient cause of the cross, even while he strikes and injures as a good father ought to test (Isaiah 45:7; Amos 3:6; Lamentations 3:37–38; Hebrews 12:6–8).

Note: God is the principle efficient cause of the cross. Clamities and hardships are sent from God by his will and providence. But even when he strikes and injures, he is a good Father. Augustine [says] of Psalm 98, "And when you fawn, you are father, and when you strike, you are father." Isaiah 45:6–7: "I am the LORD, and there is no other. I form light and create darkness, I make well-being and create calamity." Tertullian says more eloquently: "They are called evils of trespasses and sufferings: By separating evils of trespasses from evils of sufferings, evils of fault from evils of punishment,[39] we confine to each part its own author, the devil as the author of the evils of sin and fault, and God as the author of the evils of sufferings and punishment." Amos 3:6: "Does disaster come to a city, unless the Lord has done it?" It is clear from the context that the sense is really about evils, not [of] fault, but rather punishment. Confer Lamentations 3:37–38 [and] Hebrews 12:6ff, "For the Lord disciplines the one he loves." In these words, consider: (1) the hand of correction, namely of God, the most Good and Greatest, (2) the intention of correction is a paternal correction; "God is angry against the one whose sin he does not whip," Augustine says of Psalm 98, and (3) Clement of Alexandria says in *Strom*[ata], book 2, that the objects of correction are the pious: "Near to God is he who is fully whipped."

Thesis V. The ministerial cause is sometimes Satan (Luke 22:3; 1 Peter 5:8; Revelation 12:13; Ephesians 6:11–12; 2 Corinthians 12:7), the

---

[39] In contrast to Thesis III, Quenstedt is using the Latin *poena* or punishment here in its improper sense, that is, as a paternal chastisement of the cross.

world (John 15:19; Galatians 4:29), or our flesh (Romans 7:23; James 1:14; 1 Peter 2:11).

Note: The ministerial cause of the cross is sometimes the devil when God occasionally uses him as an official attendant and instrument of his correction of the pious. God does not always send the cross and calamities immediately, but he often unlooses the bridle of the devil, the world, and the flesh in order to afflict man. It can clearly be proved both from examples (Job 1–2) and especially from clear passages of Scripture that the devil is certainly the cause of many evils by divine permission, as Luke 22:31 states: "Behold, Satan demanded to have you, that he might sift you like wheat." Observe: This sieve of affliction, persecution, and temptation is turned by Satan. This power is not obtained first by his will, but by God. First Peter 5:8: "The devil prowls around like a roaring lion, seeking someone to devour." See the preceding chapter IX, section I, thesis XV, number 3. Second Corinthians 12:7: "A thorn was given me in the flesh, a messenger of Satan to harass me, to keep me from becoming conceited." Observe: Dr. [Johann Conrad] Dannhauer says in his *[Christeis Sive] Dram[a Sacrum]*, act 1, page 128 that God knows what the *skolops* [thorn in the flesh] will be, which Paul bemoans with such great emotion [in] verse 3, but that there is nothing else here for us except the remaining conjecture [about what that thorn actually was]. Dr. Gesner agrees in his *Exegesis Epist. Domin. Sexages.*, page 504, saying, "What, properly speaking, has given this thorn to the flesh of Paul, what has inflicted him with the fist blow of Satan, we judge that no one knows. Some indeed understand by this thorn the concupiscence of the flesh, or too much of a propensity for women, which Satan arouses often in the apostle. Many of the papal party hold to this opinion, [Robert] Bellarmine, *De Monach[is]* [in *Disputationes de controversiis*], tome 2, book 2, chapter 30; Cornelius À Lapide; [Giovanni Stefano] Menochio; and Jacob Tirinus, *Com[mentarivs]* on this locus. Nevertheless, Paul does not complain about some vexation common to all, but of an extraordinary one, not the innate, but a [vexation] that has been given. It is by no means like the concupiscence of the flesh as it remains in Paul. It is so infested and unrestrained in him that it is a test not to succumb. It was necessary to pray to God three times so that he might be freed from it. Others understand by the thorn, a sickness of the head, from the devil with divine permission infecting Paul, in fact a *kephalalgiav* in appearance. That is a headache as Jerome says; a suffering from a colic as Lyra and Thomas say; or a kidney ailment, also a debilitation of the joints, or gout as Nicetas says; sickness of the stomach as Vincent and others say. But neither this opinion about the sickness of the whole body, nor some part of it is able to stand: (1) because no complaint occurs elsewhere about this from Paul, (2) because to be assailed with sickness does not agree very well with traveling perpetually (which Oecumenius contends for from the word *kolaphizē* [you harass] in his *Comment[arii]*) via land and sea, and in addition, preaching to people publically as well as privately. Others explain these words as the persecutions and abuse of bad men who were having daily dealings with Paul, but they did not agree in everything. See [Wolfgang] Franz *[Tractatus Theologicus Novus & Perspicuus] De Interpret[atione Sacrarum] Scriptur[arum], oracul.* 78, page 572. Still, the messengers of Satan are different. Men are clearly wicked and impious, but the angel Satan himself is different, since he once attacked Job *atoprôsôpos* [in his own person without a mask] (Job 2:7). Later, he taunted Christ, his Lord and God, time and time again (Matthew 4:3). However, the apostle recognized that the angel Satan had given this to him ("It has been given to me as a thorn in the flesh," he said, therefore Satan himself is not able to assume this himself, but it has been given to him), namely by God or Christ. [God or Christ] concedes or permits it to him, but restricts the power to a certain measure so that he [Satan] attacks and strikes Paul in the form of the thorn in the flesh, and so in this way (to this end), the spirit suppresses the things filling up in him on account of the *apokalupseôn huperbolên* [surpassing greatness of the revelations]. The way in which it has been used by Satan in this conflict is as a *kolaphismês* [harassment], for Paul says so, *hina me kolaphizê* [in order to harass me]. For he in whom this satanic *kolaphismos* lingers, it is the greatest difficulty. Dr. Georg König explains in an extended explanation of the locus in his *Vindici[ae] S[acræ]*, locus 113, page 692, wherein he is disposed to this opinion that Paul was beaten in a bodily and perceptible fashion by a messenger of Satan. The late [Friedrich] Balduin explains in his *Comm[entarius In Omnes Epistolas]* on this passage in a certain place about his most severe affliction of body and soul in which Satan without doubt recalled into [Paul's] memory the blood of Christians innocently shed at his inquisitions when he was still Saul. Dr. Dannhauer says in the locus already cited, "In Paul, God permits what once happened to Job, whom Satan afflicted with ulcers from the outside and with inestimable afflictions from the inside. He takes Paul prisoner with blows from the outside, and he harasses his character from inside by the perpetual scratching open of the memory of his most severe persecutions." Compare Dr. Joh[ann] Schmidt *[Viertzig Christliche Conscients oder] GewissensPredig[ten]*, sermon 16, page 315 and sermon 22, page 442. The world is the second ministerial cause, that *Organon* [instrument] of Satan, which he uses for persecuting the good.

Christ says here in John 15:19, "The world hates you." Compare Galatians 4:29, our flesh, which is as troublesome for us as possible. Paul bemoans this in Romans 7:23; James 1:14; 1 Peter 2:11.

Thesis VI. The pious and the faithful are the suffering subject (Sirach 2:2; Tobit 12:13; Hebrews 12:6ff; Revelation 3:19), with regards to the soul (Psalm 18:5–6; 2 Corinthians 12:7ff), the body (Job 2:7), the abilities (Job 1:14–17), the family (Job 1:18–19).

Note: God so loves pious and faithful men that he wishes that they be *symmorphous* [conformed] to the image of his Son through the cross (Romans 8:29), "near to God, full of lashes," says Clement of Alexandria, *Stromat[a]*, book 2. Sirach 2:1: "Prepare yourself for suffering." Tobit 12:13: "Because you were dear to God," etc. Hebrews 12:6ff: "The one he loves [he] chastises." Compare Revelation 3:19. But the pious are afflicted in the body as much as the soul. Some afflictions are internal. Others are external. The internal ones crucify the soul. Psalm 18:5–6: "The cords of death entangle me completely," namely like water. With these words, the Messiah bemoans his internal and infernal torture. See 2 Corinthians 12:7 above. External calamities afflict the body, family, and abilities, as in the example of Job. It is told in [Job] 1 of cows and donkeys stolen by the Sabeans in verses 14–15, the consumption of the sheep through fire from heaven (verse 16), of the camels stolen by the Chaldeans in verse 17, the striking down of his children through the collapse of his house in verses 18–19, and finally his body is struck with ulcers by Satan in [Job] 2:7.

Thesis VII. The form is a painful, temporary, and salutary suffering.

Note: The form of the cross is suffering: (1) painful, for affliction is always joined with suffering, pain, and annoyance; (2) having closely connected [to it] a paternal *dokimasian*; (3) temporary, for it is never forever, but lasts for a reserved time; (4) and salutary—it is not sent for our destruction, but salvation.

Thesis VIII. The purpose of the cross is either final or intermediate, either final without qualification or qualified in some respect. Final without qualification is the glory of God (John 9:1–3). Qualified in some respect refers to the salutary nature of being corrected (Acts 14:22; Romans 8:17–18; 2 Timothy 2:21). Intermediate is (1) the rebuke owed sin (Jeremiah 30:11; 46:28; 1 Peter 4:17), (2) the testing of our faith, (Genesis 22:1; Deuteronomy 8:2; Psalm 66:20; 1 Peter 1:6–7; James 1:12), and (3) the mortification of the flesh (Jeremiah 31:18–19; 1 Peter 4:1–2; Romans 6:6; Psalm 119:71; 2 Corinthians 4:16–17).

Note: In John 9:1–3, [it says:] "He saw a man blind from birth." Observe: This blindness was considered in itself to be a *timôria* until the event truly becomes an *aphormê* [starting point] of a manifest work of

God. In Romans 8:17ff, the apostle sets forth three comforts in adversity, of which: (1) is the consideration of future glory, (2) the aid of the Spirit (verse 14ff), [and that] (3) "we know that God directs all evil and adversity for our salvation." Second Corinthians 4:17: "For this light momentary affliction is preparing for us an eternal weight of glory beyond all comparison." That which is crucified for a moment will find delight for eternity. Truly the apostle does not speak about his own essential glory, but about the sublime weight, that is, about the elevated grades of glory. But affliction is not a cause of divine reward or of heavenly glory *per se* and *per consequens*. It does not have the regard of an efficient or meritorious cause, to merit or effect, but only the regard of an antecedent to a consequence. The apostle greatly exults the worth and excellence of heavenly glory when he says *kath huperbolên eis huperbolên* [beyond all comparison], that is, incomprehensible exulting, greatily exulted, surprisingly above every way in the highest sublime level of glorious weight. (Such excessive talk is not to be found in the entire Bible, says the late [Johann] Hülsemann in *Myrt[us] Lipsiensi[a]*, page 593 on this locus). But the Hebrews are accustomed to use a doubling of one expression to signify vehemence, abundance, or excellence. Therefore, this antithesis of affliction and consequence of heavenly glory (which plainly excludes all merit) is exceedingly emphatic, as Chrysostom and Theodoret note on this locus. For afflictions do not belong to rest, but are opposed to glory, as eternity to the course of time, weight to levity, and sublimity and excellence to vileness, as this verse and the subsequent ones oppose sight to not seeing, eternity to time. But having been divinely ordered by this, glory is opposed to affliction, not as rewards are to merit, but as an event is to its middle. Compare Hebrews 6:12; James 1:12; and 2 Timothy 2:21. The intermediate purpose of affliction is: (1) The rebuke and correction owed by sin so that we namely acknowledge our sins and avoid and shun them in the future. Jeremiah 30:11 [states], "I will discipline you in just measure, and I will by no means leave you unpunished." Compare [Jeremiah] 46:28 [and] 1 Peter 4:17. (2) The proving and testing of our faith; the cross tests and strengthens faith (1 Peter 1:6–7). Where there is faith, its testing through the cross is compared with corruptible gold that it may be proved by fire (James 1:12). Some so set forth this purpose of the cross that it is a confirmation of faith, a rooting having been more firmly confirmed, and a direction having been rooted for the purpose of illuminating divine grace and glory (1 Peter 1:7; Ephesians 3:18; Luke 8:15; 1 Corinthians 1:8; 9:10; 1 Peter 4:14). (3) The mortification of our corrupt flesh. Our old man is crucified (Romans 6:6), killed, and corrupted (2 Corinthians 4:16–17).

Thesis IX. This is the definition. The cross of the pious is painful suffering sent by God, as from a benevolent father, to believers at a certain time for the glory of the stricken and the salvation of the afflicted.

Note: Dr. J[ohann] F[riedrich] König defines the cross in this way in his *Theolog[ia] Posit[iva Acromatica]*. The cross is a suffering sent by God. But other theologians distinguish between the cross divinely sent and the cross divinely permitted. The latter is that which God himself imposes on his own for a blessed end, indeed he effects it so that the desired outcome follows. This is as God determines so that their faith is tempted by the flesh, the world, and the devil, not so that they are defeated, but so that they are tested, corrected, and glorified. But when it is asked whether a cross, which is permitted by God, is even sent by God, they respond not *energêtikôs*, but only *sugchôrêtikôs* [not active, but only permitted], not *thetikô*s, but *aphairetikôs* [not arbitrarily prescribed, but fit for removal]. This is the fuller definition of Dr. [Jesper] Brochmand from a locus cited later. "The cross is the calamity by which man is weighed down: (1) immediately by God, (2) or with divine permission by the devil, the world, or the wicked flesh, (3) various external pressures indeed press down, but [also] interior melancholy or anxieties of the heart, (4) or so that one suffers the just punishments of sin, or so that his heart is tested, or so that what is changed from life is for the better, one thinks maturely, or finally that God be glorified." Nevertheless, Brochmand appears to mix *timôrian* or punishment, properly speaking, with *dokimasia* or the cross of the pious as it appears in number 4; for the form of the cross of the pious is not penal, but a paternal correction, not a leaving behind of fault after remission, [but] an accusation of temporal punishment having been expiated for all the faithful.

Thesis X. Quantity, duration, utility, diversity, and necessity are the characteristics of the cross.

Note: Concerning quantity: a measure and quantity of affliction is divinely shown to every one of the faithful. To each one is measured out congruently his own cross. Concerning duration: it appears long to the pious, [see] Psalm 13:1, where David repeats his "Lord, how long,"etc. It is nevertheless brief, difficult to understand, and quickly passing; it is limited by time and changes because it happens for the better.

Section II. Polemic

Questions, which are accustomed to be offered here, are partially examined elsewhere and are partially not therefore of great importance. Nevertheless, Dr. Brochmand in his *System[a Universae] Theolog[ia]*, article XLI, chapter 2, and Dr. [Abraham] Calov in his *System[a Locorum] Theol[ogicorum]*, tome. X., article, XI., chapters 1–2 explain them, to which I also add the blessed Martin Luther.

SEBASTIAN SCHMIDT (1617–96)

SEVENTEENTH-CENTURY "JEROME"

by Joshua J. Hayes

LIFE

Sebastian Schmidt (1617–96)[1] was born and baptized on the Feast of the Epiphany in Lampertheim, a community near Strassburg, to humble parents. His father was a wheelwright; his mother died when he was only

[1] Most of these biographical facts may found in the biography written after his death by his friend and colleague at the University of Strassburg, Johann Joachim Zentgraf, "Seb[astiani] Schmidii D. Vita," in *Commentarii in Epistolas D. Pauli Ad Romanos, Galatas et Colossenses Una cum Paraphrasi Epistolae Prioris ad Corinthios, . . . Luc. I. v. 46. seqq.*, ed. Sebastian Schmidt (Hamburg: Schillerus, 1704). See also Wilhelm Horning, *Dr. Sebastian Schmidt von Lampertheim* (Strassburg: Bomhof, 1885).

five. From boyhood, he was mentored by his pastor, Bartholomäus Oehr, who started him in his Latin studies. He attended the *Gymnasium* in Strassburg with his father's support and excelled in his studies. Though his father died, Schmidt continued his studies and took up Hebrew. Orphaned, he left for Marburg to continue his studies there but did not remain long since that city would be devastated by the Thirty Years' War (1618–48). Threat of violence forced Schmidt to leave for Wittenberg in the summer of 1636, where he studied theology for two years under Jakob Weller von Molsdorf (1602–64). He also studied in Königsberg before returning to Strassburg in 1638. There, he was received by Johann Georg Dorsche (1597–1659) and the leading theologians of the University of Strassburg. At their encouragement, Schmidt devoted himself to the study of Eastern languages and in 1640 determined to go to Basel to study under the great Reformed scholar of Hebrew, Johann Buxtorf the Younger (1599–1664), until 1643. After completing his studies in Basel—his "Reformed exile" as his friends called it—he was made pastor at Ensheim briefly before being called to be the rector of the *Gymnasium* at Lindau in 1644. He served there for nearly a decade and wrote a grammar of Greek and Latin for the school as well as a textbook on philosophy. In 1653, Schmidt was called to fill an opening at the University of Strassburg as a theology professor and served among the canons of St. Thomas Church. He was made a doctor of theology, and though he would receive many prestigious calls, he chose to stay in his hometown of Strassburg as pastor and professor for the rest of his life, saying, "I always loved the same city and the same church."[2] He was made church president there in 1666.

Schmidt was known for being sedulous in giving public and private lectures on the Scriptures and the Lutheran Confessions. He frequently held disputations and regularly preached, in addition to voluminous publishing. The surge of commentaries published in the last fifteen years of his life indicates that his commentaries were the direct results of his life's work in lectures and disputations.[3] He attributed much to Martin Luther (1483–1546), Johannes Brenz (1498/99–1570), Martin Chemnitz (1522–86), Johann Gerhard (1582–1637), and Johann Georg Dorsche. An orphan who was married twice and widowed twice, he died just after his seventy-ninth birthday, on January 10, 1696, having long suffered from

---

[2] Sebastian Schmidt, preface to *In prophetam Hoseam commentarius* (Frankfurt am Main: Zunner, 1687).

[3] Schmidt, preface to *In prophetam Hoseam commentarius*, where he says that his work on Hosea began when "learned young men" asked him to lecture on Hosea privately.

the effects of a stroke, and having just put the finishing touches on his Latin translation of the Bible with Apocrypha.

His biographer remembers him as a seventeenth-century "Jerome," a translator and exegete of the Hebrew Scriptures. Indeed, Schmidt was remembered for these exegetical works and for his efforts in Hebrew biblical theology. Schmidt's emphasis on solid exegesis of the biblical text deeply affected many of his students, including Philipp Jakob Spener (1635–1705), the father of Pietism who greatly admired him.[4] One could hardly do better as pastor of the time than to have a set of Schmidt's massive commentaries or his smaller "paraphrases." Andreas Adam Hochstetter (1668–1717), for example, recommends all of Schmidt's commentaries, but surprisingly highlights not a commentary on the Old Testament, but Schmidt's paraphrase on John. "This," says Hochstetter, "above all his other works should be commended to our theologians."[5] Therefore, limiting Schmidt's fame and influence to his Hebrew works alone would be a mistake. Moreover, after his death, he was also remembered as a great Lutheran dogmatician, for exegetical and dogmatic theology were largely inseparable at the time. He was well known for his support of and participation in the disputations, as well as his *Compendium Theologiae* (1697), which was "an abridged Gerhard" (*Gerhardum contractum*).[6] It was especially helpful for theological students who were expected to gain a good grasp of the commonplaces through lectures and private reading.

Today, Schmidt is mostly remembered for his exegetical works and depth of learning in Hebrew. He has been called "the most thorough biblical exegete of Lutheran orthodoxy."[7] In fact, Schmidt's exegesis does stand as a convenient epitome for exegesis in the period of Lutheran Orthodoxy. Scholars see him as a figure to mark the near end of that period because his student, Spener, conveniently marks the beginning of

---

[4] Edmond Jacob, "L'oeuvre exégétique d'un théologien strasbourgeois du 17e siècle: Sébastien Schmidt," *Revue D'histoire Et De Philosophie Religieuses* 66, no. 1 (January 1986): 71. See also Johannes Wallmann, *Philipp Jakob Spener und die Anfänge des Pietismus* (Tübingen: Mohr Siebeck, 1986), 88–100.

[5] Andreas Hochstetter, "A Short Treatise on How to Preach Aright and How to Expound and Apply the Sacred Text," trans. Joshua J. Hayes, in Wilhelm Loehe, *The Pastor*, trans. Wolf Knappe (St. Louis: Concordia, 2015), § 15.

[6] Isaac Faust, preface to *Compendium Theologiae,* by Sebastian Schmidt (Strassburg: Dulsseckeri, 1697).

[7] Johannes Wallmann, "Schmidt, Sebastian," in *Religion Past & Present: Encyclopedia of Theology and Religion*, ed. Hans Dieter Betz (Boston: Brill, 2012), 11:498.

Pietism.[8] Still, one should not forget his efforts as a pastor and dogmatician. As naturally happens with prolific authors, some will favor one aspect of his work over others.

Schmidt commented on Genesis, Joshua, Judges, Ruth, 1–2 Samuel, 1–2 Kings, Job, selected prophetic Psalms, Ecclesiastes, selections of Isaiah, Jeremiah, Lamentations, Hosea, John, Romans, 1 Corinthians, Galatians, Ephesians, Colossians, 1–2 Thessalonians, 1 Timothy, Titus, Philemon, Hebrews, James, 1 John, Jude, the *Magnificat*, the Sermon on the Mount, and the Canticle of Zechariah. Of all the Lutherans to comment on the Scriptures, Johann Georg Walch (1693–1775) considers Schmidt to have the best commentary on Judges, 1–2 Samuel, Job, Ecclesiastes, Jeremiah, Hosea, and Hebrews.[9] His commentaries are noted for the abundance of references on every page,[10] including references from the Church Fathers, pre- and post-Reformation commentators, rabbinic scholars, and Talmudic writings. This displays his masterful grasp of the history of the exegesis of the text. Even as he is able to show where there has been a difference of interpretation of a text, he does not shy away from offering a decisive opinion. For example, there is a question on the beginning of Hosea 13:14 as to whether it should be read as indicative or interrogative or even conditional. Schmidt strongly sides with those who take this indicatively as, "I shall redeem them from the hand of hell," as a promise pointing to the New Testament fulfillment in Christ's death and resurrection. He further notes that this is the common position of Lutheran theologians, and at the same time vindicates the Luther Bible.[11] While he is not enslaved to Luther's translation, he frequently displays fondness for it and defends it. Schmidt aims always to read Christocentrically, seeing the fulfillment of the Old Testament in Christ and his Church. His commentaries follow the same general structure with slight variation: Latin translation (sometimes with a brief paraphrase), verse-by-verse annotations on issues of philology and interpretation, and then a list of various "commonplaces" or points of teaching that can be brought out of the text with explanation. Often these commonplaces are applications of the text that one might make in a

[8] Jacob, "L'oeuvre exégétique," 78; John H. Hayes and Frederick C. Prussner, *Old Testament Theology: Its History and Development* (Atlanta: John Knox Press, 1985), 5.

[9] Johann Georg Walch, *Bibliotheca Theologica Selecta* (Jena: Viduae Croeckerianae, 1765), 4:470, 475, 483, 519, 544–45, 569, 728.

[10] Jacob, "L'oeuvre exégétique," 74.

[11] Schmidt, *In prophetam Hoseam*, 590–92.

sermon. Schmidt's skill in listing these applications reveals his concern that faithful exegesis lead to faithful preaching and teaching.

The crown of Schmidt's efforts in exegesis, and his life's work, was his complete translation of the Scriptures into Latin. Though other Lutherans had corrected the Latin Vulgate or translated parts of Scripture, Walch notes that Schmidt is the only Lutheran "to attempt a truly new translation [into Latin] of the Holy Book."[12] He labored on this translation for forty years, aiming to be as clear, faithful, and literal as possible to the divinely inspired text.[13] It was received with great enthusiasm, especially by the theologians in Strassburg who prefaced it with his eulogy, but it also gained a reputation for sometimes being "more transcription than translation."[14] Walch notes that it is most useful when used as a literal interlinear for those learning Hebrew since it brings out the exact force of each word and particle.[15]

A convenient work by which to transition to a discussion of Schmidt as dogmatician is his particularly famous *Collegium Biblicum* (1670). This collection of exegesis, disputation, and commentary on various statements of Scripture, organized by the theological commonplaces—one volume for each Testament—is unique for its character as a dogmatic book but also a biblical commentary. For each commonplace, Schmidt discusses passages of Scripture that support Lutheran doctrine (*dicta probantia*). He does not necessarily choose to discuss the seat of each doctrine in Scripture, especially if he feels it has been thoroughly treated elsewhere, but selects passages that require explanation or which may be particularly useful for teaching or in the disputations.

The corollary to this work and his best known dogmatic text is his *Compendium Theologiae* (1697), published shortly after his death. In 567 octavo pages, Schmidt summarized all of Lutheran dogmatics, and, as said above, it served as an "abridged Gerhard," as the author of the preface claims:

> In this book you will find an abridged Gerhard. This abridgment of blessed Gerhard's *Theological Commonplaces* does not omit a single commonplace. Among these, the volume *On Marriage* is massive, and the commonplaces *On the Holy Supper, On the Church's Ministry, On Civic Office, and On*

[12] Walch, *Bibliotheca*, 4:76.

[13] Jacob, "L'oeuvre exégétique," 75.

[14] Jacob, "L'oeuvre exégétique," 75.

[15] Walch, *Bibliotheca*, 4:76.

> *Eschatology* are quite prolix. Yet even these have been abridged with such skill that nothing is lacking that is necessary for the student who needs to be formed in the basic pattern of theology. . . . Therefore, we shall call this compendium an introduction to Gerhard's volumes and a guide to reading and understanding Gerhard for those who need to learn the first foundations of theology.[16]

In addition to these dogmatic works, Schmidt's disputations and lectures on the symbolic writings and key Lutheran texts, such as Luther's *Bondage of the Will*,[17] were also collected and published. All of his works are of value to Christians today, especially with respect to philology and Schmidt's ability to make the transition from academic exegesis to right preaching and teaching based upon the Word of God alone.

The selection that follows is taken from the Old Testament volume of *Collegium Biblicum*, "On the Church's Ministry" (*De ministerio ecclesiastico*), and is representative for a variety of reasons. First, this exegesis and discussion on Psalm 68:11 displays Schmidt's exegetical prowess with Hebrew and his grasp of the various ways a passage has been interpreted and translated. After laying out the philological problems and history of interpretation, he offers a solution to this exegetical knot and expounds on the significance of this verse for the life of the Church. Second, we see here Schmidt's intention to interpret the Scriptures Christologically, finding the Old Testament fulfilled in the New. Yet he seeks to do so on the basis of Scripture itself and the interpretations of the apostles themselves. Finally, the ministry is a commonplace to which Schmidt often applies Scripture in his commentaries, for his commentaries were usually born from his lectures to theological students who were preparing to enter the preaching office.

BIBLIOGRAPHY

Works by Schmidt in English Translation

None of Schmidt's writings have been translated.

---

[16] Faust, preface to *Compendium Theologiae*.

[17] See Theodor Mahlmann, "Die Interpretation von Luthers *De servo arbitrio* bei orthodoxen lutherischen Theologen, vor allem Sebastian Schmidt (1617–1696)," in *Luthers Erbe* (Tübingen: Mohr Siebeck, 2005), 73–136.

Select Works by Schmidt in Latin and German

Articulorum Formulae Concordiae Repetitio. Strassburg: Staedel, 1696.

Beati Patris Martini Lutheri Liber De Servo Arbitrio, contra Desid[erium] Erasmum Roterodamum: Cum brevibus Annotationibus, quibus B. Vir ab accusatione, quasi absolutum Calvinianorum, vel durius aliquod Dei decretum in libro ipso statuerit, praecipue vindicatur. [Strassburg]: Pastorius, 1664.

Biblia Sacra sive Testamentum Vetus et Novum. Strassburg: Spoor, 1696.

Collegium Biblicum. Strassburg: Tidemann, 1670.

Collegium Disputatorium In Articulos XXI. Aug[ustanae] Conf[essionis] et Martini Becani Manuale Olim in gratiam Studiorum Theologiae habitum in Acad. Argent. nunc vero editum. Schleswig: Eckstorfius, 1694.

Commentarii Super Librum Prophetiarum Jeremiae Tomus. Frankfurt am Main: Zunner, Haasius, 1685.

Commentarius in librum Salomonis regi, ebraice koheleth, graece et latine ecclesiastes dictum. Strassburg: Spoor, 1691.

Compendium Theologiae, in quo Capita Christianæ Fidei, iuxta Causarum Seriem, per Thesin et Antithesin, Plenè, et Perspicuè Traduntur, Scripturæque Fundamentis Confirmantur. Strassburg: Dulssecker, 1697.

Disputatio Inauguralis De Antiquissima Fide Mosaica, circa Mysterium Sacrosanctae Trinitatis. Strassburg: Thilo, 1654.

In Epistolam D. Pauli Ad Hebraeos Commentarius: In Quo Textus Non Modo, quoad Cohaerentiam et sensum, cum praecipuis Interpretibus expenditure, sed singulis etiam Capitibus Loci, quos vocant, Communes ex textu petiti subiunguntur. Strassburg: Spoor, 1680.

In Librum Jobi Commentarivs, In Quo, Cum Optimis Quibusque Commentatoribus, tum Hebraeis tum Christianis, cohærentia et vocabula diligenter expenduntur, et sensus studiose eruitur. Strassburg: Spoor, 1670.

In librum Judicum commentarius. Strassburg: Spoor, 1684.

In Librum Posteriorem Samuelis, Commentarius exhibens ad Singula libri Capita Versionem Textus Hebraei Latinam, Analysin, Annotationes, Quaestiones Et Locos Communes. Strassburg: Spoor, 1687.

In Librum Priorem Samuelis, Commentarius exhibens ad Singula libri Capita Versionem Textus Hebraei Latinam, Analysin, Annotationes, Quaestiones Et Locos Communes. Strassburg: Spoor, 1687.

In prophetam Hoseam commentarius. Frankfurt am Main: Zunner, 1687.

Resolutio brevis cum paraphrasi verborum Evangelii D. Johannis Apostoli. Strassburg: Spoor, 1684.

WRITING[18]

Commonplace XVII: On the Church's Ministry

Saying I: Psalm 68:[11]

§ 1. We, along with our theologians and others, take Psalm 68:11 as being about the Church's ministry. However, this verse has its unique difficulties. (I) People construe it in different ways, as one can readily see from the translations. The Chaldaic paraphrase would sound like this in Latin: "The Lord gave the words of the Law to his people, but Moses and Aaron announced God's Word to the great host of Israel." In the latter half of the verse, the Chaldaic translator supplies the nominatives "Moses and Aaron," and makes the participle a verb, in addition to supplying a dative *lamed* with *tsava*, "host," besides other additions. This is farfetched. The Septuagint translators render it: "The Lord will give the word to those who announce the good news with great power." Thus they combine two hemistiches into one and add a dative *lamed* with the participle *hamevasseroth*. This is also harsh, but nonetheless the Vulgate follows them verbatim. Blessed Luther did some transposition and fitting together: *Der Herr gibt das Wort mit grossem scharen der Evangelisten.* Pagninus does the same, but supplies a substantive verb so as to form two hemistiches: "The Lord gave the word; the host of those who announced it was great." Others leave the order of the words in the second hemistich but supply a verb. Thus Diodatus: "The Lord gave the matter of the word; those who brought the good news were a great host." Thus the Belgians: *De Heere gaf te spreken: Der Boodschappers von Goede tijdingen was een groote Heirschar.* Moreover, Tremmelius and Piscator supply a verb and a preposition, rendering it: "The Lord gave the word; those who announced spoke in great number." Abben-Ezra combines everything

[18] Sebastian Schmidt, *Collegium Biblicum* (Strassburg: Tidemann, 1670), 352–58.

together! He says: "The Lord will give (fulfill) the word of those preaching good news to a great host."

§ 2. The variety is obviously astounding. And I am surprised that it never occurred to anyone how Scripture, especially in the Psalms, has a very frequent habit of repeating the verb of the preceding construction. Thus the simplest rendering would be: "The Lord will give the word; preachers of good news [*Evangelizantes*]"—read: He will give—"as a great army." That is to say, He will give or cause evangelists to multiply until they become a great army. The version by blessed Luther agrees with the meaning of this rendition quite nicely.

§ 3. (II) But now a new difficulty arises: to what is our verse referring? The Chaldaic paraphrase cited above seems to have taken it with reference to Old Testament times, specifically to the giving of the Law when Moses and Aaron presented the words of God to the people of Israel. Abben-Ezra notes that most Hebrew interpreters explain it in reference to the giving of the Law at Mount Sinai, but he admits that this explanation does not fit the context of the words. So he would rather take it with reference to David's war with the uncircumcised. . . .

§ 4. However, our theologians simply interpret it about the New Testament, and we subscribe to their position wholeheartedly. For our psalm is not speaking in the past tense in this verse and the following, but in the future tense. David Kimchi also recognized that this psalm is prophetic and speaks about a future event. Paul's citing [of this psalm] in Ephesians 4:10–11 interprets this future event to be about Christ and the New Testament. Moreover, even the events fit the words in the simplest way. For in the New Testament, the Lord gave the Word, that is, the Gospel. He gave in great number his apostles and teachers, preachers of good news. Nowhere in the Old Testament do we read of any such occurrence. Considering this as being about the choruses of girls who announced the victories (about which see below), that is slipshod. Those girls did not "evangelize" or bring good news; rather they rejoiced over God and the victors upon hearing the news from others. Therefore, we hold that this verse is a prophecy about the Gospel in the New Testament being promulgated through Christ and about his evangelists.

§ 5. (III) Who is "the Lord"? Here, the simplest and best understanding of *Adonai*, "the Lord," is the Messiah, or, Christ. For he is this *Elohim, Jah, Adonai* who "ascended on high" (v. 18). Thus the divinity of Christ can also be shown from this verse, since the noun *Adonai* with a *qames* can only mean the true God, especially since verse 18 adds to him the names *Jah* and *Elohim*. . . .

§ 8. (VI) But this word *hamevasseroth*, "of those preaching good news, evangelists" has a unique difficulty in the Hebrew idiom, where it is feminine. There are some who take this as about the feminine sex just as grammatically it is of the feminine gender. They generally interpret this as being about choirs of girls singing about victories (Exodus 15:20; Judges 5:1ff; 11:[34]; 1 Samuel 18:[6]). So [say] Calvin, Piscator, Junius, Diodatus, and others. However, a little earlier we noted that the term "evangelists" is not an accurate term for those girls because they did not actually announce new news, but had received new news from others and celebrated it with songs of praise. This is why I have not found any Hebrew scholar who dared to interpret this as about those girls. The Chaldaic paraphrase preferred to explain it as about Moses and Aaron delivering and explaining the Law of Israel. Rabbi Salomon and Abben-Ezra interpret it about women foretelling and announcing things to come. David Kimchi interprets it with regard to women being led into captivity by Sennacherib who, once freed, announced his destruction. Therefore, I am astonished that Christian interpreters have been so bold. We understand that the truest preachers and evangelists are the teachers of the New Testament. For the subject matter in the context is nothing other than the New Testament of Christ. We cannot discuss this further.

§ 9. Therefore, may women preach the Gospel in the New Testament? Certainly the apostle forbids women to speak in the church. The Belgians approach this difficulty, which drives others away, by saying that it is a Hebraism where the word is conceptually about souls, that is persons—that is to say, the souls [*animae*] or persons [*personae*] preaching good news were a great host. But I would like to see them cite similar instances; then we would easily agree. But I do not see any instances that are like this passage. One of our own, Brenz, seems to read in "crowds" [*turbas*]—that is, "He will give crowds preaching the Gospel in great number." Clearly this would be good, even better, if only we could have a word somewhere in the context meaning "crowds."

As for us, it seems that the Church of Christ has been established in the likeness of a mother, who has daughters in great number under her, who are nothing other than believers. From these daughters of hers stands a great host of daughters, that is believers, who preach the Gospel. Thus the feminine gender is not used literally of the feminine sex but figuratively of those people who are members of the Church and who are portrayed and represented in the likeness of virgin daughters ministering to their mother and bringing the news. What follows next convinces us of this explanation of this word [v. 12]: "The woman at home, or house-mother, will divide the spoils." So also Jerusalem and Zion are portrayed in the likeness of a woman preaching good news (Isaiah 40:9). Also in Psalm 45, the Church is portrayed as the Bride of Christ in the likeness of a king's daughter, and believers [are portrayed] in the likeness of virgins (Psalm 45:9–14). Furthermore, I think that here in the likeness of virgins are portrayed the teachers of the New Testament for teaching the grace of the Gospel. You see, the appearance of virgins is most pleasing, and their words are sweet and welcome. So also the Gospel of New Testament evangelists is very sweet and pleasing, and is experienced as such by all those who receive it by faith. One can also consider the most faithful care involved in caring for men's salvation. On this account, the apostle Paul compares himself to "a nursing mother caring for and nourishing her children" (1 Thessalonians 2:7). At the same time, that these preachers of the Gospel should be male is clear from the following verse, in which the image of virgins is resolved and they are called "kings of the armies"—that is, the first teachers of all the army of those evangelists. For such is the habit of Scripture, to mix figures of speech together, or figurative words and literal words together, so as to provide a mutual explanation of itself. Clearly these kings of the armies are none other than the apostles and apostolic men who went out into the world. See Brenz on this passage. . . .

§ 11. Now let us discuss a few things about the Church's ministry. (I) There is and must be an ecclesiastical ministry in the New Testament. This is proved because the Scripture must be fulfilled. But now, in this passage [Scripture] foretells that there will be a ministerium in the New Testament since Christ will give the Word and evangelists of the Word. Note also that in Romans 10:14–15, Scripture concludes from this kind of prophecy that the Church's ministry is necessary, that ministers of the Church must be sent by Christ, and that the Word of God cannot be heard ordinarily except through the minsters of the Church. "How," he says, "will they hear without a preacher? But how will they preach unless they are sent? Just as it is written: 'How serviceable are the feet of evangelists,' " etc. But now, our passage here seems even more powerful since it expressly says that the Lord will give the evangelists. . . .

§ 12. (II) The Church's ministry is and must be a distinct order in Christ's Church so that not all Christians are or should be evangelists indiscriminately. This is proved (1) because the army of their evangelists and kings is clearly distinguished from the housemother, that is, the Church herself or the community of the rest of the believers. "The Lord," it says, "gives the Word, evangelists as a great army. Kings of the armies are spread abroad, going about, and the housemother divides the spoils." It also shows (2) that the name "evangelists" is distinct, because it clearly denotes a distinct order. For if all were supposed to preach indiscriminately, there would be no need to call certain men "evangelists." The same is meant (3) by the term "army," since it denotes certain men chosen for military service.

§ 13. (III) The chief cause of the Church's ministry is Christ. . . .

§ 14. (IV) The most proper teaching of the New Testament ministry is the Gospel. This is proved because from this the Church's ministers are all called "evangelists." Yet let this be only a metonymy because of their chief role. And so they certainly also preach the Law, but to lead people to Christ, and as a rule for living. (V) There are distinct classes of ministers. Proof: They are an army, which has been well ordered. (VI) The rule of teaching is the Word that Christ gives or reveals, as is seen clearly enough in our words above.

CHRISTIAN SCRIVER (1629–93)

ON THE INSTITUTION, NATURE, AND SINGING OF HYMNS

by Jon D. Vieker

LIFE

Christian Scriver[1] (1629–93) was a Lutheran pastor and forerunner of German Pietism. An esteemed preacher and widely published author,

[1] The sources consulted for this essay are as follows: *Allgemeine Deutsche Biographie*, s.v. "Scriver: Christian"; "Vorwort des Herausgebers," *Der Lutheraner* 2, no. 1 (September 6, 1845): 1; "Die heilige Absolution," *Der Lutheraner* 2, no. 15 (March 21, 1846): 59; "Gibt es Alt- und Neu-Lutheraner?", *Der Lutheraner* 2, no. 19 (May 16, 1846): 74; Joel R. Baseley, trans., *C. F. W. Walther's Original Der Lutheraner, Volumes One through Three (1844–47): The LCMS in Formation* (Dearborn, MI: Mark V Publications, 2012); Martin Brecht, Ulrich Gäbler, Hartmut Lehmann, eds. *Geschichte des Pietismus,* 4 vols. (Göttingen: Vandenhoeck & Ruprecht, 1993–2003); Eric Chafe, *Tears into Wine: J. S. Bach's Cantata 21 in Its Musical and Theological Contexts* (New York: Oxford University Press, 2015);

Scriver pioneered the genre of daily devotional collections. He also authored a number of hymns within those devotional writings. As with many Lutheran theologians during his time, Scriver was influenced greatly by the proto-Pietist thought of Johann Arndt (1555–1621) and was also a frequent counsel and correspondent with Philipp Jakob Spener (1635–1705), the father of Pietism. Scriver strove to combine orthodox Lutheran doctrine and practice with an intentional renewal of church life and a focus on the individual spiritual life of the believing soul.

Scriver was born on January 2, 1629, in Rendsburg (Schleswig-Holstein) during the middle of the Thirty Years' War (1618–48). His father, also named Christian, and two of his sisters perished six months after Scriver was born, leaving a widow, Abigail née Guden, with five remaining children. Soon remarried to the local pastor, Gerhard Kuhlmann, Abigail was widowed again in 1635. In later years, Scriver noted the impact his mother's faith made on him during these difficult times.

Through the generous support of a wealthy relative, young Christian was enabled to attend *Gymnasium* in Lübeck in 1645 and then the university in Rostock in 1647. His chief influences during his university years were Joachim Lütkemann (1608–55) in theology and Andreas Tscherning (1611–59), a student of Martin Opitz, in philology. Scriver earned his master's degree there in 1649 and became a tutor in nearby Segeberg. In 1653, he was called and ordained as archdeacon to Stendahl, where he served until 1667, when he was called as pastor at St. Jakobi in Magdeburg. He subsequently held a number of offices in the regional consistory.

Scriver was in poor health the last two decades of his life, and his pastoral and ecclesial duties were at times overwhelming. At one point, he considered a call to Sweden, where his devotional writings were widely read, but elected to stay in Germany. Finally, in 1690, he accepted a call to serve as court preacher to the Princess-Abbess of Quedlinburg, Anna

---

Wolfgang Herbst, ed., *Wer ist wer im Gesangbuch* (Göttingen: Vandenhoeck & Ruprecht, 2001); Eric Lund, ed., *Documents from the History of Lutheranism, 1517–1750* (Minneapolis: Fortress Press, 2002); Eric Lund, ed., *Seventeenth-century Lutheran Meditations and Hymns* (New York: Paulist Press, 2011); Christian Möller, ed., *Kirchenlied und Gesangbuch: Quellen zu ihre Geschichte,* Mainzer Hymnologische Studien, no. 1 (Tübingen: A. Francke Verlag, 2000); Holger Müller, " 'Seelsorge und Tröstung': Christian Scriver (1629–1693) Erbauungsschriftsteller und Seelsorger," (Diss., Heidelberg University, 2003); *Religion in Geschichte und Gegenwart*, 4th ed., s.v. "Scriver, Christian"; F. Ernest Stoeffler, *The Rise of Evangelical Pietism,* Studies in the History of Religions, no. 9 (Leiden: E. J. Brill, 1965).

Dorothea (1657–1704). Spener had recommended his name, and Scriver served there until his death on April 5, 1693, from a stroke. Scriver was married four times during his sixty-four years, with all of his wives preceding him in death and only two of his fourteen children surviving him.

The suffering, sorrow, and illnesses in Scriver's life shaped the prodigious amount of devotional literature he produced. One of his earliest collections, titled *Chrysologia catechetica, oder Gold-Predigten* (Golden Catechetics, or Golden Sermons) (1658), flowed out of the chaotic aftermath of the Thirty Years' War. At this time, Scriver was trying to get the young catechumens of Magdeburg back on track with a traditional week-long sermon series on the Small Catechism, delivered during the octave of Holy Trinity. At the encouragement of his parishioners, he later had his sermons published as a collection. In his *Gottholds zufälligen Andachten* (Gotthold's Occasional Devotions) (1663–71), Scriver published some four hundred daily devotions based on a similar work, *Occasional Meditations* (1630) by the English bishop and literary figure Joseph Hall (1574–1656). With this collection, Scriver focused each devotion around a brief description of a natural object or event from daily life, which he then used as a symbol for the problems believers face in living the Christian life. In this work, Scriver was clearly influenced by the genre of emblem literature, which presents a series of printed images that are then ascribed an allegorical interpretation with the accompanying text. In the case of Scriver's work, a "word-emblem"—a prose description of a scene or object—takes the place of a printed image. Scriver's *opus magnum* was his monumental *Seelen-Schatzes* (Soul Treasures) (1675–92), published in five volumes of several hundred pages each. Based on an extensive reworking of seventy of his sermons, Scriver describes the progress of the believing soul. Finally, toward the end of his life, Scriver published his *Gottholds Siech- und Siegsbett* (Gottholds Sick- and Victory-bed) (1687/94), an introspective focus on physical and spiritual sickness (Part I) and victory (Part II). In both this work and his earlier work with a similar title, Scriver uses the reference to "Gotthold" as a kind of everyman, yet one who is shaped through the experiences of Scriver's own personal battles with sickness and sorrow.

Scriver's devotional writings became classics during the centuries following and were reprinted well into the twentieth century. Although none of his hymns are in common usage among American Lutherans today, one (*Der lieben Sonne Licht und Pracht* ["The Lovely Sun's Light and Splendor"]) is still included in the German Protestant hymnal, *Evangelisches Gesangbuch.* Scriver was held in high esteem by the early fathers of the Missouri Synod and is quoted positively a number of times in early issues of *Der Lutheraner.* Although Scriver held traditional, orthodox Lutheran teaching in high esteem, he was also concerned with the concrete social and moral conditions of his day. Above all, his chief concern was the believing soul—that through repentance and conversion, it would come to a marriage with Christ and lead a blessed and holy life. Some of those blessings come in the shape of crosses—of sorrow, poverty, weaknesses, marital problems, oppression, and hostility. Scriver's influence upon Lutheran piety in the centuries that followed was of major importance.

BIBLIOGRAPHY

Works by Scriver in English Translation

"Christian Scriver (1629–1693)." In *Seventeenth-Century Lutheran Meditations and Hymns*, edited and translated by Eric Lund, 245–47. New York: Paulist Press, 2011.

"Christian Scriver (1629–1693): Gotthold's Occasional Devotions (1667)." In *Seventeenth-Century Lutheran Meditations and Hymns*, edited and translated by Eric Lund, 228–57. New York: Paulist Press, 2011.

"Christian Scriver (1629–1693): The Treasure of the Soul (1675)." In *Seventeenth-Century Lutheran Meditations and Hymns*, edited and translated by Eric Lund, 258–73. New York: Paulist Press, 2011.

Gotthold's Emblems, or, Invisible Things Understood by Things That Are Made, translated by Robert Menzies. Edinburgh: T. & T. Clark, 1857.

"Gotthold's Occasional Devotions (1663–69)." In *Documents from the History of Lutheranism, 1517–1750*, edited and translated by Eric Lund, 267–71. Minneapolis: Fortress Press, 2002.

Select Works by Scriver in German and Latin

Chrysologia catechetica, oder Gold-Predigten, Darinnen die Seligmachende Catechismus-Lehre aufs kürtzeste gefasset mit der Betrachtung des Goldes erkläret und allem vergänglichen Golde und Schätzen derWelt vorgezogen wird. . . . Magdeburg, 1658.

Gottholds Siech- und Siegs-Bette, beschrieben und zum Trost und Erbauung der christlichen Kirchen in 2 Th. Ausgefertiget. Nuremberg, 1694.

Gottholds zufällige Andachten: bey Betrachtung mancherley Dinge der Kunst und Natur, in unterschiedenen Veranlassungen . . . geschöpffet. Leipzig, 1671.

Seelen-Schatzes Kern und Stern, oder, Dessen nochmahls übersehene, vermehrete und vollkommene Registe : ingleichen Richtige Anweisung, wie aus diesem herrlichen Buche die aus denen Sonn- und Festtäglichen Epistolischen und Evangelischen, auch Passions-Texten nach allen vier Evangelisten, und dem Catechismo Lutheri allerhand herausgezogene auch rare Usus erbaulich auszuführen, darneben auch die emphatischen Wörter und Redens-Arten aus dem Grund-Text wohl erörtert warden. Leipzig, 1711.

Writing[2]

Part Two. The Second Meditation—"Teach and admonish one another with psalms and hymns and lovely spiritual songs, and sing to the Lord in your hearts" (Colossians 3:16).

§ I. These words of the apostle are to be understood in a threefold way: regarding the institution of hymns and songs of praise in the Christian Church, then also regarding the nature of such hymns and songs, and finally regarding their application, which they can produce through the grace of the Holy Spirit. Regarding the first, it is evident that already in the Old Testament the singing of the psalms and hymns is quite common. . . . [Examples and Bible citations follow.]

§ III. So also many [individuals] can be named from the writings of church history who have served the community of God with the preparation of beautiful spiritual songs. These gifts have come to our forefathers and also to us today. Luther left behind many hymns in which we clearly perceive his high and rich spirit, and which also have such power and vigor that they are thus far without compare. They are his own, and nothing has been put forward like Luther's [hymns] among all the others, as experienced and reasonable hearts know well. Yet, there have also been other gifted and spiritually endowed people who have produced songs,

[2] This is a select translation of Christian Scriver, *Gottholds Siech- und Siegs-Bette / Anderer Theil* (Nuremberg: Hoffmann, 1694), 61–102, quoted in Christian Möller, ed., *Kirchenlied und Gesangbuch: Quellen zu ihre Geschichte,* Mainzer Hymnologische Studien, no. 1 (Tübingen: A. Francke Verlag, 2000), 166–69.

which one finds collected together in common and oft-printed hymnals, and which are in daily use.

§ IV. Thus, I cannot help but recall that it is good what one finds in the Saxon Visitation Articles, formerly given for instruction, where it says that there should not be made a rule about how each German hymn should be used in the church. Rather, care should be taken that in every respect such hymns are a gift and bestow grace; and that not just anyone should be able to gather his hymns together in print, much less introduce them into the church, until they have first been examined by learned, God-fearing, and spiritual men, and be found to be well-written, edifying, and comforting. Wherever this has not happened, the church has in lesser times become so overwhelmed with songs and hymns that the simple do not know which ones to choose. . . . I have also recently noticed that certain prominent theologians in the church are accustomed to altering established hymns, trying to improve the rhymes, which are not always suitable to the rules of today's delicate and artful poetry. In the fear of God and with sincere love of neighbor, I have wondered whether these alterations and improvements actually serve the betterment and edification of the church, and peace in general. The division and disruption is unfortunately widespread and not good when individual communities, also in songs and hymns, are thereby made to be divided and disunited. When some of our young people maintain the old hymns unchanged, but others are accustomed to improving them, and then they travel—from here to another region, from one church to another, to this house or to that workplace—and confusion occurs from one place to the other, as one person wants to defend his version, and another wants to defend a different version; annoyance, bickering, and animosity surely follow as a result of it. This is something for those in the church who handle these sorts of things to give some mature and thoughtful reflection about.

§ V. As for the second part, the nature of hymns and songs in the community of God, in the assembly of saints, and also concerning the Christian, how such hymns should otherwise be used, the apostle said that they should be spiritual and lovely—that is, they should flow from the Spirit, be full of the Spirit, of power, grace, comfort, and edification, and that they should create a spiritual, godly, and heavenly stirring and activity in man. . . .

§ VIII. I hasten, however, to the third part that I proposed to discuss—namely, the blessed and great use which the spiritual and lovely hymns in the church are accustomed to create, a use which has at all times been certain, right, and great, and still is! The holy apostle gives us a threefold use: first, for our own edification; second, for the betterment of our neighbor; and third, for the glory and praise of God. Concerning the first, he says: "Teach and admonish one another with psalms and hymns of praise" (Colossians 3:16). It is reported by a godly teacher that the ancients considered such spiritual hymns to be the "milk of the soul," which is truly well said. I would suggest, in addition, that they are also the wine, the medicine, the gentle breeze or wind, the noblest pastime, the flowering bush, and the refreshment of the God-fearing soul. . . .

§ IX. The apostle teaches that the betterment and edification of the neighbor can and must be promoted through such spiritual and lovely hymns. . . . He makes it quite clear that our hymns can be a fitting means of fellowship in the Spirit and a brotherly encouragement and edification. . . . There is many a child born to poor, simple, and often also godless parents, and with a great lack of means. But as soon as something decent is provided in the household, it is halted on account of the great ignorance and recklessness of the child's fleshly inclined parents. Then at school, good teaching is also not maintained, so that the child knows all too little about divine and spiritual matters, and with the catechism's teachings, he has certainly not grasped everything. Such a child, however, learns in the home or the church, from husband and wife, or from other Christian people, the customary spiritual hymns—hymns concerning repentance, concerning the justification of a poor sinner before God, concerning the Lord Jesus and his holy suffering and death, concerning the triune God, and other such matters—and thereby such hymns create much edification and comfort. . . . [Additional examples follow.]

§ XI. A famous and learned man of our time once said: "The sound of strings bound to a clear voice is like the wind that governs the waves of the sea, be it stormy or calm."[3] However, string playing is not even necessary, but rather only the singing of a spiritual and lovely hymn in a clear, pure, and pleasant voice. Such hymns can often, through the power and strength of the heavenly Pentecost wind, so bestir and direct the hearts of men that one cannot help but be astonished. . . . [Additional stories of the power of hymns follow.]

§ XVII. I have remaining, then, the third part, wherein the holy apostle desires to know the spiritual and lovely hymns, in which he says: "And sing to the Lord in your hearts" [Colossians 3:16]. The Lord who has created, redeemed, and sanctified us likes it that one serves him with a joyful heart. . . .

---

[3] This is attributed to Georg Philipp Harsdörffer (1607–58), a German poet and translator, whose knowledge of languages earned him the appellation "the learned." His writings in German and Latin fill fifty volumes.

§ XIX. It follows, according to what we have thus far provided and maintained concerning spiritual hymns and songs, that a God-loving, Christian heart, as often as it possibly can, should let be heard such hymns to glorify his most gracious God—for the encouragement and edification of his neighbor, and for his own comfort and betterment. On the occasion of the holy Sabbath days and festival days of the Lord, all hearts, all homes, all churches, every avenue, every gathering should be full of joy, full of singing and praise. Such gatherings should not be held haphazardly, but rather all at the same time, according to the ringing of the bells, where the entire community should sing heartily, prayerfully, and unanimously, so that their voices might be as a gently blowing breeze and as the rustling of water. I cannot begin to describe how the blowing and rustling of the God-sanctified and united voice in the Spirit prepares and at times bestirs a preacher's heart to proclaim the Word of the Lord, so that he proceeds with an all-the-more zealous and holy desire and expounds the Word with a joyful opening of his mouth. On account of the little children, the sick, and all the other occupations that must unavoidably remain at home, they should also thus unite their hearts in spirit with the congregation, and even as little as they are able, praise God and enliven and edify themselves with those spiritual and lovely hymns. Likewise, the soldiers on the watchtowers and sentry posts, the shepherds with their flocks, those traveling by wagon and on the highways, the nurse by the cradle, the one who cares for the sick at the bedside—all of these should lift up their voices and sing these blessed hymns.

At the conclusion of the Divine Service, the churches as well as homes in the city, in towns and in villages, should flutter and resound from the praise of God, and every lane should ring forth with those spiritual and lovely hymns. One should have a holy and affectionate foresight—particularly toward the simple, the children, and the servants—that they be devoted to the knowledge of God and the salutary doctrine contained in those graceful, lovely hymns, and be infused with their sweet melody. Well, that is how it should be, but what unfortunately happens these days calls for grieving with hot tears: O righteous and holy God, how we have fallen! Amend our faults and curb every vexful and unchristian nature!

§ XX. The occasion for this contemplation of the spiritual and lovely hymns of the church is this: our Gotthold,[4] in his difficult illness and great weakness, treasured these very same hymns, amid other reliefs, to

---

[4] In Scriver's writings, "Gotthold" is a kind of everyman, narrated through Scriver's own experiences with sickness and suffering.

serve as his comfort and strength. He would leave his bedcovers now and again to stroll about and to linger with his fellow lodgers (more than once, only a single boy), to sing with a measured and pleasant voice. . . . Oh, how much sweet consolation flowed to him by the Holy Spirit into his heart! How powerfully was he enlivened and strengthened through them from God's Word and Spirit-animated sound! So it is without a doubt an extraordinary blessing from God that he has given so many glorious, Spirit-laden, doctrine-laden, and comfort-laden hymns to the evangelical church, for which also a special and hearty thanks is due him. I must, however, finally say this: I do not know what those who, in such a famous church, remain so ignorant and wretched, will find for an excuse on that great Judgment Day of the Lord, when the hymns alone could be sufficient to persuade them from their willful ignorance. O Lord Jesus, help us not to receive your grace in vain!

HEINRICH MÜLLER (1631–75)

THE DEVOTIONAL WRITER FOR LUTHERAN RENEWAL

by Gaylin R. Schmeling

LIFE

Heinrich Müller (1631–75) is not the most familiar name in Lutheran history. If one searches for his name online, the first result is a Nazi who became the chief of the Gestapo, the secret state police of Nazi Germany. However, this is not the Heinrich Müller who is being considered here.

Heinrich Müller was a Lutheran pastor and theologian in the Arndtian tradition during the seventeenth century. He was part of a cohort of men serving in the Mecklenburg city of Rostock on the Baltic Sea in northern Germany who desired renewal in Lutheran Orthodoxy. This group included Johann Quistorp the Elder (1584–1648), Johann Quistorp the Younger (1624–69), Joachim Schröder (1613–77), and Theophil Großgebauer (1627–61).[1]

Heinrich Müller was born in Lübeck, Germany, on October 18, 1631.[2] Here his family, originally from Rostock, fled for temporary refuge during the Thirty Years' War (1618–48).[3] The first years of his education occurred in Lübeck. In 1644, his parents were able to return to Rostock, where he continued his education. Later he attended the University of Greifswald, but he received his master's degree in Rostock in 1650. Müller was influenced in his education by Joachim Lütkemann (1608–55),[4] who was an influential conveyer of Arndtian piety through his own devotional writings.[5] After receiving his master's degree, Müller made the customary educational tour of the major universities in northern Europe, spending time with Cölestin Myslenta (1588–1653) in Königsberg and visiting Johann Benedict Carpzov I (1607–57), Johann Hülsemann

---

[1] Ernst Koch, *Das konfessionelle Zeitalter-Katholizismus, Luthertum, Calvinismus (1563–1675)* (Leipzig: Evangelische Verlagsanstalt, 2000), 221.

[2] Apart from Müller's own writings, the chief primary source for his life is the following: Ludwig Barclay, *Klagstimm Uber den unheilbahren Schaden Babels . . . gegeben* (Freiberg: Zacharias Becker, 1675). Barclay's *Personalia* of Müller is also appended to this funeral sermon. See also Albert Hauck, "Heinrich Müller," in *Realencyklopädie für protestantische Theologie und Kirche*, 3rd ed. (Leipzig: J. C. Hinrichs'sche Buchhandlung, 1896–1913), 13:521–23; Hermann Beck, "Heinrich Mueller," in *The New Schaff-Herzog Encyclopedia of Religious Knowledge* (Grand Rapids: Baker Book House, 1977), 8:40; Ingetraut Ludolphy, "Heinrich Mueller," in *The Encyclopedia of the Lutheran Church* (Minneapolis: Augsburg, 1965), 2:1, 670; Ingeborg Dorchenas, "Müller, Heinrich," in *Biographisch-Bibliographisches Kirchenlexikon* (Nordhausen: Verlag Traugott Bautz, 1975–), 6:250–54.

[3] This was during Wallenstein's occupation of Mecklenburg.

[4] Joachim Lütkemann was born in Demmin, Pomerania. He attended university in Greifswald and later in Strassburg, where he was influenced by the teachings of Johann Conrad Dannhauer. In 1639, he became archdeacon of St. Jakob's Church in Rostock and taught at the university. Later, he was court-preacher and general superintendent in Braunschweig-Wolfenbüttel and Abbot of Riddagshausen Abbey. In 1649, he defended the thesis that during Christ's three days in the tomb, he was not truly human since his soul and body were separated. Lütkemann's intention was to emphasize that the Son of God truly died, but his terminology was confusing. He is best known as a devotional writer who followed in the tradition of Johann Arndt and influenced Heinrich Müller and Christian Scriver. His most important work is *Foretaste of Divine Goodness* (*Der Vorschmack göttlicher Güte*).

[5] Constantin Große, *Die Alten Tröster: ein Wegweiser in die Erbauungsliteratur der evang.-luth. Kirche des 16. bis 18. Jahrhunderts* (Hermannsburg: Missionshandlung, 1900), 236.

(1602–61), and Martin Geier (1614–80) in Leipzig.[6] He concluded this trip in Wittenberg, where he lodged with Abraham Calov (1612–86).[7]

Upon his return to Rostock, the twenty-two-year-old Müller became the youngest member of the Rostock clergy when he was appointed archdeacon of St. Mary's Church in 1653. This was his family's parish. Shortly after his appointment as pastor, he married Elizabeth Margarete Siebrand,[8] the daughter of a Rostock merchant. They were blessed with five sons and a daughter.

Throughout his career, Müller was ambitious and, at times, outspoken. Because of his youth and possibly his assertiveness, he was not immediately awarded a doctorate of theology in Rostock, even though he had fulfilled all the requirements. Exasperated by the theologians in Rostock, he turned to the University of Helmstedt, which conferred a doctorate to him in December 1660.[9] Although Helmstedt was suspect in the eyes of Lutheran Orthodoxy because of the syncretistic theology of Georg Calixt (1586–1656) and its nonacceptance of the Book of Concord,[10] still Müller, who rejected these viewpoints, was well received in Rostock. In 1659, he was approved as professor of Greek in Rostock and became a professor of theology in 1662. He was a professor at the University of Rostock and at the same time was the head pastor of St. Mary's Church, the most prestigious church in Rostock.

Among the leading German preachers of the second half of the seventeenth century, Heinrich Müller has always been held in particular honor.[11] His sermons were eloquent and popular. They are written in a simple and interesting style, complete with picturesque language and illustrations. He was definitely in touch with his congregation and touched his people with Law and Gospel.

With unanimous consent of both the civil and ecclesiastical leaders of Mecklenburg, he was elected superintendent and confirmed in this high office by the Duke of Mecklenburg. He was solemnly installed by

---

[6] Otto Krabbe, *Heinrich Müller und seine Zeit* (Rostock: Adler, 1866), 81–86.

[7] Jonathan Strom, *Orthodoxy and Reform: The Clergy in Seventeenth Century Rostock* (Tübingen: Mohr, 1999), 223; Johann Anselm Steiger, *Das Gebet im Zeitalter der Reformation und des Barock* (Neuendettelsau: Freimund-Verlag, 2013), 36.

[8] The alternate spelling is Sibrand.

[9] Barclay, *Klagstimm*, 73; Strom, *Orthodoxy and Reform*, 225; Steiger, *Das Gebet*, 36.

[10] Timothy R. Schmeling, "Slaying the Syncretistic Chimera: A Study of the *Consensus Repetitus* in Light of Confessionalization Theory" (PhD diss., Concordia Seminary, 2014).

[11] F. Ernest Stoeffler, *The Rise of Evangelical Pietism* (Leiden: E. J. Brill, 1965), 223–24; Hughes Oliphant Old, *The Reading and Preaching of the Scriptures in the Worship of the Christian Church* (Grand Rapids: Eerdmans, 1998–2007), 4:393.

Jacob Sommerfeld in Parchim in 1671. Always frail of constitution, he died at the age of forty-four on September 23, 1675. Shortly before his end, he received the Holy Supper of Christ's body and blood. Thus he was united with his Redeemer and Savior and assured of the blessed hope of everlasting life.[12]

The ultimate purpose of the ministry of Müller and his associates in Rostock was to remedy the social and moral devastation in the church caused by the Thirty Years' War and to revive spiritual life. The war had disastrous effects on the organization of the church and the spirituality of its members. These men were particularly concerned with spiritual renewal of both the laity and the clergy through a heartfelt devotional life.

This movement has occasionally been referred to as Lutheran reform-orthodoxy (*Reformorthodoxie*).[13] Müller, however, would have considered himself no different from the other Lutheran theologians in seventeenth-century Lutheran Orthodoxy. He did not deviate from any of the doctrines of the Lutheran Confessions. The concept of reform-orthodoxy has been properly criticized for its lack of precision and its tendency to divide orthodox Lutheran theologians of the seventeenth century. As scholarship reveals more and more Lutheran Orthodox theologians to have been interested in piety, it becomes harder to identify those who could not belong to a so-called reform-orthodoxy.[14] All the Lutheran theologians of the time would have encouraged reform and spiritual renewal to a greater or lesser degree. Abraham Calov, known for his strict orthodoxy, was just as interested in renewal as Müller.

The concept of reform-orthodoxy seems to have developed from a view that desires to find the origin of Lutheran Pietism in Johann Arndt (1555–1621) and the Rostock pastors around Müller, rather than in Philipp Jakob Spener (1635–1705), who is usually considered to be the father of Pietism.[15] Unlike the later Pietists who overemphasized sanctification and devalued the Means of Grace, the devotional writers held that the Means of Grace, the liturgy, personal devotions, and piety went hand-in-hand.

---

[12] Barclay, *Klagstimm*, 78; Heinrich Müller, *Hours of Spiritual Refreshment*, trans. Maximilian Geneste (London: The Religious Tract Society, 1840), XXII.

[13] An example of this is to be found in Stoeffler, *Rise of Evangelical Pietism*, 217–25.

[14] Johannes Wallmann, *Pietismus-Studien: Gesammelte Aufsätze* (Tübingen: Mohr Siebeck, 2008), 2:9–10; Lowell C. Green, "Duke Ernest the Pious of Saxe-Gotha and his Relationship to Pietism," in *Der Pietismus in Gestalten und Wirkungen*, ed. Heinrich Bornkamm et al. (Bielefeld: Luther Verlag, 1975), 189–91.

[15] Strom, *Orthodoxy and Reform*, 13–14.

A number of Müller's associates in Rostock criticized the outward practices of the church, especially in the area of church discipline. In his sermons and devotional writings, Müller generally did not criticize the outward practices of the church of Rostock or his parishioners. Rather he emphasized the inner spiritual life of his members. He feared that Christians were substituting outward spiritual ritual for inner belief. Through the Law and the Gospel, he desired to awaken the inner spiritual life of his parishioners based on a confident faith or trust in Jesus as the Savior, which was evident in love. His concern was the renewal of the spiritual life of the individual, not necessarily the outward ecclesiastical forms of the church.

The statement for which Müller is most criticized and most infamous from an orthodox Lutheran perspective is found in his epistle sermon for the Tenth Sunday after Trinity. Here he states, "Also, present-day Christianity has four dumb church idols which they follow: the baptismal font, the pulpit, the confessional, and the altar. They comfort themselves in their outward Christianity that they are baptized, hear God's Word, go to confession, and receive the Lord's Supper, but the inner power of Christianity they deny."[16] These words seem to be denigrating the Means of Grace of the Lutheran Church. Yet this was not Müller's intent. Elsewhere he speaks of the effectual nature of the Means of Grace. He clearly teaches that the Word is powerful and that Baptism is regenerational (i.e., it works faith).[17] Concerning the Supper, he writes, "Out of love, he gives me in the Holy Supper his flesh to eat, his blood to drink so that my feeble heart is refreshed, my weak faith strengthened, my cold love ignited, my wavering hope confirmed."[18] In his controversial statement, Müller is rather criticizing the substitution of institutional ritual for true inner faith in the Savior. One is not saved by going through the outward motions of worship if there is no faith in the Redeemer in the heart.

---

[16] "*Auch hat die heutige Christenheit vier stumme Kirchen-Götzen, denen sie nachgehet, den Tauffstein, Predigstul, Beichtstul, Altar, sie tröstet sich ihres äusserlichen Christenthums, daß sie getaufft ist, Gottes Wort höret, zur Beichte gehet, das Abendmahl empfängt, aber die innere Krafft des Christenthums verleugnet sie.*" See Heinrich Müller, *Apostolische Schluß-Kette Und Krafft-Kern Oder Gründliche Auslegung der gewöhnlichen Sonn- und Fest-Tags-Episteln: worinnen ... befördert* (Frankfurt am Main: Balthasar Christoph Wust, 1671), 271. See also Johann Bernhard Krey, *Beiträge zur Mecklenburgischen Kirchen und Gelehrtengeschichte* (Rostock: Adlers Erben, 1818), 1:351; Heinrich Müller, *Geistliche Erkwick-stunden, Oder Dreyhundert Hauß- und Tisch-Andachten: Vor diesem ... Bestraffung* (Frankfurt am Main: Balthasar Christoph Wust, 1673), no. 152, 512–20.

[17] Müller, *Apostolische Schluß-Kette*, 224.

[18] Müller, *Apostolische Schluß-Kette*, 168.

Müller's sermons and devotional literature usually do not criticize the outward practices of the church in Mecklenburg as his associates did. There was, however, one exception. He was extremely averse to the confessional penny (*Beichtpfennig*) and wanted to see it abolished. Private absolution was not strictly demanded in Rostock, but it remained the norm. After receiving absolution, the individual would customarily present the confessor with a monetary gift, the confessional penny, to help provide for the support of the clergy. Müller saw the confessional penny as virtual bribery and would not accept it.[19] It made it look as though the parishioner was paying for the absolution. In addition, it caused the pastors to appear avaricious.

Müller produced many doctrinal treatises on subjects like justification, Baptism, and the Lord's Supper, as well as refutations of the errors of the Reformed and Roman Catholics.[20] But he is best known as a prolific writer of devotional literature. His devotional books were written in the tradition of Arndt, Lütkemann, and Scriver after him. For these writers, as for all Lutherans, the blood of Christ is counted as the all-sufficient sacrifice for sin: "How precious and how powerful is the blood of Christ, which is shed for your sins. A little drop is worth more than all human sin."[21] Müller maintained the central doctrine of the Lutheran Church—that a person is justified or declared righteous by nothing that he does, but alone on the basis of Christ's redemption, received through faith in the Savior, worked by the Means of Grace. At the same time, he held that faith should always show forth itself in love. The Christian mirrors God's great love in creation and redemption to those around him.[22]

These devotional writers viewed Luther's prayer, meditation, and the cross (*oratio,*[23] *meditatio,*[24] *et tentatio*[25]) as the Christian school of spirituality and formation. Müller even made the intriguing statement that

---

[19] Heinrich Müller, *Vermehrter und durchgehends verbesserter Himmlischer Liebes-Kuß, Oder: Göttliche Liebes-Flamme . . .* (Nuremberg: Joh. Ernst Adelbulner, 1732), 184–85; Strom, *Orthodoxy and Reform*, 114.

[20] Krabbe, *Heinrich Müller*, 210–17, 245–53, 289–97.

[21] Müller, *Geistliche Erkwick-stunden*, no. 117, 374.

[22] Müller, *Himmlischer Liebes-Kuß*, 2–9; Müller, *Apostolische Schluß-Kette*, 167–68.

[23] Müller, *Geistliche Erkwick-stunden,* no. 8, 21–22; no. 294, 1183–88.

[24] Müller, *Geistliche Erkwick-stunden,* no. 121, 392–96; no. 293, 1178–83.

[25] Müller, *Apostolische Schluß-Kette,* 168, 224; Steiger, *Das Gebet,* 44. Müller composed a homiletics manual entitled *Orator Ecclesiasticus* (1659), which made use of Luther's *oratio, meditatio,* and *tentatio.*

God has bound his presence to prayer.[26] One is to pray fervently to the triune God, meditate continually on the Word, and be trained through affliction or the cross that the loving Father sends. In this way, the interior life of the Christian is fortified and revived. Their devotional literature (*Erbauungsliteratur*) was to encourage proper meditation on the Word and contemplation of the loving Savior through reading, marking, learning, and inwardly digesting the Word. Seeing his parishioners suffering great losses through terror, disease, and hunger in the wake of the Thirty Years' War, Müller viewed his decisive task as renewal and comfort for his people.

Müller was an eloquent preacher of the mystical union, that is, the believer's union and communion with Christ and the entire Trinity through the Means of Grace, the Word and the Sacraments.[27] When an individual is brought to faith in Christ, there is a mystical communion between the Christian and Christ in which Christ takes up residence in the believer's heart and influences the person's life. In this connection, he makes use of a number of pictures like the nuptial motif (*Brautmystik*) to illustrate the union between the deity and the individual in typical Bernardian mysticism.[28] Union with Christ brought great comfort. Christ is dwelling in the believer; what can be against him? In addition, the indwelling of Christ was a force of renewal. It gave strength and motivation for the Christlike life.

Themes such as union with God,[29] marriage between Christ and the soul,[30] partaking in the divine,[31] and the benefits of the cross run through his writings. They are filled with pithy statements that are easy to remember and memorize. For example, he makes statements such as, "A bit of bread easily satisfies the body if the soul is already nourished with God's Word,"[32] and, "Better sad in God than happy in the world."[33]

---

[26] "*Daß Gott seine Gegenwart ans Gebet gebunden habe.*" See Müller, *Himmlischer Liebes-Kuß*, 385.

[27] John 14:17, 23–24; FC SD III 54.

[28] Johannes Wallmann, *Theologie und Frömmigkeit im Zeitalter des Barock: Gesammelte Aufsätze* (Tübingen: J. C. B. Mohr, 1995), 15–19.

[29] Müller, *Apostolische Schluß-Kette*, 169, 225; Müller, *Geistliche Erkwick-stunden*, no. 138, 467–70.

[30] Müller, *Apostolische Schluß-Kette*, 172; Müller, *Geistliche Erkwick-stunden*, no. 138, 467–70.

[31] Müller, *Apostolische Schluß-Kette*, 168, 173.

[32] Müller, *Geistliche Erkwick-stunden*, no. 248, 953.

[33] Müller, *Geistliche Erkwick-stunden*, no. 20, 63.

His sermons were more devotional than many sermons of the era. They explicated the doctrinal content of the historic pericopes, but they were more meditative and contemplative in nature. The hearer was pointed to true repentance and new life in Christ. They caused one to ponder on the life-giving Word. His sermon books were avidly read in the generations following him in Germany and Scandinavia[34] and were brought to America in the "Old Lutheran" immigrations to help shape the piety of the New World Lutheran.[35]

A number of hymns were written by Müller and used in the German-speaking world,[36] but none of them have been translated into English. Themes from Müller's writings, however, were used by Bach in portions of *St. Matthew Passion*.[37] These themes were mainly from Müller's passion sermons.

The major sermonic writings of Müller include *Apostolic Chain of Reasoning* (*Apostolische Schluß-kette*), *Gospel Chain of Reasoning* (*Evangelische Schluß-kette*), *Festival Gospel Chain of Reasoning* (*Fest-evangelische Schluß-kette*), and *Gospel Mirror of the Heart* (*Evangelischer Hertzens-Spiegel*). These are sermons on the historic Gospels and Epistles of the Church Year. His most important devotional book was *Spiritual Hours of Refreshment* (*Geistliche Erkwick-stunden*). It contains three hundred devotions on a variety of topics, including true repentance and faith in the Savior, growth in faithlife, meditation on the Word, and union with Christ.[38] Another well-known devotional of Müller is *The Heavenly Kiss of Love or The Divine Flame of Love* (*Himmlischer Liebes-Kuß, Oder: Göttliche Liebes-Flamme*). The first chapter of this book encourages meditation on God's love, which ignites the flames of our love toward him. In twenty-five chapters, Müller illustrates God's love in creation,

---

[34] Steiger, *Das Gebet*, 37.

[35] L. F. E. Krause, *The Chronicle of Pastor L. F. E. Krause: First Lutheran Pastor to Work in Wisconsin*, ed. and trans. Roy A. Suelflow (Freistadt: Trinity Lutheran Church, n.d.), 3, 6; Carl S. Meyer, ed. *Moving Frontiers* (St. Louis: Concordia, 1964), 126–27.

[36] Eduard Emil Koch, *Geschichte des Kirchenlieds und Kirchengesangs der christlichen, insbesondere der deutschen evangelischen Kirche*, 3rd ed. (Stuttgart: Chr. Belser'schen Verlagshandlung, 1866–77), 4:67–75.

[37] Elke Axmacher, "Ein Quellenfund zum Text der Matthäus-Passion," *Bach-Jahrbuch* 64 (1978): 181–91.

[38] A translation of a number of these devotions can be found in Heinrich Müller, "Spiritual Hours of Refreshment (1664)," in *Document from the History of Lutheranism, 1517–1750*, ed. and trans. Eric Lund (Minneapolis: Fortress Press, 2002), 263–67; Heinrich Müller, "Spiritual Hours of Refreshment (1664)," in *Seventeenth-Century Lutheran Meditations and Hymns*, ed. and trans. Eric Lund (New York: Paulist Press, 2011), 207–27.

redemption, rebirth in Baptism, the preaching of the Word, the Lord's Supper, and the indwelling of God in us. The second part of the book centers in the flame of our love, which shows forth itself in the praise of God, denial of self, and in love and mercy toward our neighbor.[39] Among his other devotional writings are *Cross, Repentance, and Prayer School* (*Creutz- Buß- Und Bet-Schule*), *Tears and Comfort Source* (*Thränen- und Trost-Quelle*) and *The Heavenly Kiss of Love or The Practice of True Christianity* (*Himmlischer Liebes-Kuß, oder Übung des wahren Christentums*), which shows the close connection to Arndt's *True Christianity* (*Wahres Christentums*).[40]

Heinrich Müller was a Lutheran pastor and theologian in the Arndtian tradition. While he was an orthodox Lutheran who bound himself to the Lutheran Confessions, he desired spiritual renewal in seventeenth-century church life following the ravages of the Thirty Years' War. Prayer, meditation on the Word, and training in the cross were the center of his theology and pastoral endeavor. The Father's love in Christ's redemptive work ignites the flame of the Christian's love through the Means of Grace. That flame, ablaze through the Means of Grace, will show forth itself in love for Christ and other Christians. This was Müller's practice of true Christianity.

BIBLIOGRAPHY

Works by Müller in English Translation

"Spiritual Hours of Refreshment (1664)." In *Documents from the History of Lutheranism, 1517–1750*, edited and translated by Eric Lund, 263–67. Minneapolis: Fortress Press, 2002.

"Spiritual Hours of Refreshment (1664)." In *Seventeenth-Century Lutheran Meditations and Hymns*, edited and translated by Eric Lund, 207–27. New York: Paulist Press, 2011.

Hours of Spiritual Refreshment. Translated by Maximilian Geneste. London: The Religious Tract Society, 1840.

[39] Udo Sträter, *Meditation und Kirchenreform in der lutherischen Kirche des 17. Jahrhunderts* (Tübingen: J. C. B. Mohr, 1995), 115.

[40] Johannes Wallmann, *Pietismus-Studien: Gesammelte Aufsätze* (Tübingen: Mohr Siebeck, 2008–10), 3:114.

Select Works by Müller in German and Latin

Apostolische Schluß-Kette Und Krafft-Kern Oder Gründliche Auslegung der gewöhnlichen Sonn- und Fest-Tags-Episteln: worinnen nicht allein der Buchstab nach dem Sinn des Geistes erkläret, sondern auch die Glaubens-Stärckung und Lebens-Besserung aus den Kraft-Wörtern der Grundsprachen heraußgezogen vorgetragen wird, In Öffentlichen Predigten vorgestellet nunmehr aber auf sehr vieler Gottsliebenden Hertzen flehentliches Anhalten zum Druck befördert. Frankfurt am Main: Balthasar Christoph Wust, 1671.

Creutz- Buß- Und Bet-Schule: Vorgestellet Von David / Im Cxliii. Psalm: Und der Gemeine Christi zu S. Marien in Rostock In zweyjährigen Bet-Stunden geöffnet. Rostock: Joachim Wilde the Elder, 1674.

Evangelische Schluß-Kette, Und Krafft-Kern, Oder Gründliche Auslegung der gewöhnlichen Sonn- und Fest- Tags- Evangelien: worinnen nicht allein der Buchstab, nach dem Sinn des Geistes, erkläret, sondern auch die Glaubens-Stärckung und Lebens-Besserung, aus den Krafft-Wörtern der Grundsprachen heraußgezogen, vorgetragen wird. Hiebevor in Öffentlichen Predigten vorgestellet und auf sehr vieler Gott-liebenden Hertzen flehentliches Anhalten zum Druck befördert. Frankfurt am Main: Andreà, Hort, Fleischer, Möller, and Varrentrapp, 1734.

Evangelischer Hertzens-Spiegel, In Öffentlicher Kirchen-Versammlung, bey Erklärung der Sonntäglichen und Fest-Evangelien, Nebst beygefügten Passion-Predigten, Der Gemeine Gottes, zu S. Marien vorgestellet. Edited by Johann Caspar Heinisius. Frankfurt am Main: Balthasar Christoph Wust, 1679.

Geistliche Erkwick-stunden, Oder Dreyhundert Hauß- und Tisch-Andachten: Vor diesem eintzel in dreyen Theilen nacheinander herauß gegeben, jetzo aber durch und durch wieder vermehret, und in ein Wercklein, auff vielfältiges Begehren, zusammen getragen, und zu lieb den alten und blöden Augen in diesem groben Druck herauß gegeben. Sampt angehengtem Register auch Theologischen Bedencken von der Abgötterey der heutigen MaulChristen und von der brüderlichen Bestraffung. Frankfurt am Main: Balthasar Christoph Wust, 1673.

Himmlischer Liebes-Kuß, Oder Übung des wahren Christentums, fliessend aus der Erfahrung Göttlicher Liebe. Frankfurt am Main and Leipzig: Joachim Wilden, 1669.

Thränen- und Trost-Quelle: Bey Erklärung der Geschichte von der Grossen Sünderin Luc. VII. v. 36. 37. etc. Allen armen Sündern geöffnet. Frankfurt am Main: Balthasar Christoph Wust, 1675.

Vermehrter und durchgehends verbesserter Himmlischer Liebes-Kuß, Oder: Göttliche Liebes-Flamme: Das ist: Aufmunterung zur Liebe Gottes: Durch Vorstellung dessen unendlichen Liebe gegen uns. Mit vielen schönen Sinn-Bildern gezieret, und mit nöthigen Registern versehen. Nuremberg: Joh. Ernst Adelbulner, 1732.

WRITING[41]

Sermon for the Sixth Sunday after Trinity, concerning the Blessed Death to Sin . . .

Beloved in the Lord! After the apostle Paul plants the tree of faith in the five first chapters of the Epistle to the Romans, he also begins to seek fruits. Among the fruits of justifying faith is the new obedience. By discussing the same, the apostle gives occasion for the secure, worldly crowd—who, like toads, suck poison out of a flower and misuse the doctrine of justification by faith—to cover the old man nice and warm with it and to persist in sin. . . . When Paul very comfortingly teaches that where sin is, there the grace of God also is powerful [Romans 6:1],[42] this is to be understood not as nurturing sin, but rather as driving it out. Still the coarse crowd goes on and infers, "Ah, we are permitted to comfortably heap sin upon sin that the grace of God is able to prove its power in us," as someone would conclude that where sickness is present, there medicine is proven powerful. Therefore, I always want to be sick that the medicine be confirmed in me. Still, the medicine is not given to allow sickness in the body, but to drive it out. . . . The grace of God does not nourish and increase sin, but is contrary to it and kills it. Paul teaches this in today's epistle when he convinces the Romans that through their Baptism they have died to sin and still must die daily. This is a lovely death! . . .

We are baptized into his death because in Baptism we partake in the power of his death as if we ourselves were already dead to sin. Through such power of Christ's death, not only are our sins forgiven, but also we

[41] This is a select translation of Heinrich Müller's "Epistel am VI. Sonntag nach Trinitatis, Von dem seligen Sünden-Tod," based on Romans 6:3–12. The sermon comes from the *Apostolische Schluß-Kette*, 219–25.

[42] Bible references alluded to but not in the text or the marginal notes are in [brackets].

receive the Holy Spirit and the works of the flesh are put to death and suppressed [extinguished] in us. . . .

Since Baptism is so necessary that ordinarily no one can be a member of the Christian Church unless he is baptized, Christian parents rightly should not hinder their children's Baptism, but rather lead them to the Lord Christ.

This is especially true because Baptism is so very profitable. For we are baptized into Christ, that is, we are united with him in Baptism as also Paul teaches in Galatians 3[:27], "As many of you as are baptized—have put on Christ," that is, they are as close and intimate with Christ through faith as clothes with the body. They become the children of God in Christ, for the one who is clothed with the adoption of God is a child of God. Christ is their protection and adornment as the clothes of the body. We are also baptized into the death of Christ because through Baptism, we participate in all good things and the gracious treasures which Christ obtained with his death. This is what your young children answer when they are asked, "What does Baptism give or profit?" "It works," they answer, "forgiveness of sin, delivers from death and the devil, and gives eternal salvation."

First, it takes away sin. When you were born, you were flesh born of flesh, sinful fruit out of sinful seed, a sinful child from sinful parents. No one is so noble and holy that he does not need to lament with David, "Behold, I was begotten out of sinful seed and my mother conceived me in sin" (Psalm 51[:5]).[43] The baptismal water does not wash away the filth of sin totally and completely so that sin no longer dwells in us or should stir in our members; rather, it is that sin can no longer condemn us or rule in us, for we are baptized into Christ. Now there is nothing that condemns those who are in Christ Jesus (Romans 8[:1]). We are baptized into the death of Christ. Here the death of Christ is so powerfully imputed to us by God, as the forgiveness of our sin, that it is as if we ourselves died for sin. Here we receive the Holy Spirit, who, according to the pattern and through the power of the death of Christ in us, puts to death the works of the flesh so that sin cannot rule in our mortal body.

Next, Baptism takes away death, not in this way that we do not die, but rather that we do not feel the pain of death and remain in death eternally. For we are baptized into Christ. On Christ and those who are in Christ, death has lost its claim. Through the death of Christ, we have the forgiveness of sins. Where sin is forgiven, there death has no more power, for the sting of death is sin [1 Corinthians 15:56]. What harm can a

[43] Bible references in the marginal notes are in parentheses.

bee do that has lost its sting? We die daily to sin through the Spirit of Christ; where sin does not rule, there death does not rule. In Christ, death is not our lord, but our servant. It must serve us in this, that we lay aside the earthly tent and be clothed with a heavenly tent [2 Corinthians 5:1–2].

Finally, Baptism redeems us from the devil, for the devil's kingdom is sin and death. Where sin and death cease, there the devil loses all his authority. Therefore, we can boast with Paul: "Thanks be to the Father, who has qualified us for the inheritance of the saints in light and has delivered us from the dominion of darkness and transferred us into the kingdom of his beloved Son, in whom we have redemption through his blood, namely, the forgiveness of sin" (Colossians 1[:12–14]).

Not only does Baptism take evil from us, but does it not also, above all else, give us benefits and salvation? We are baptized into Christ and into the death of Christ so that in him we obtain the forgiveness of all sins. For through his death, we were reconciled with God and in his blood we find cleansing from all our sins. We are baptized into Christ so that we are born anew in him and become the children of God. Accordingly, Paul may rightly conclude in Galatians 3[:26–27], "We are all children of God through faith, for as many of you as are baptized have put on Christ." We are baptized into Christ so that we are partakers of his Spirit. The same one is richly poured out over us through the bath of rebirth and renewal, as Paul writes in Titus 3[:5]. We are baptized into the death of Christ so that through him we are received into the gracious covenant of God, for he is the mediator of the New Testament and has ratified the gracious covenant with his death (Hebrews 9:15). We are baptized into Christ's death that through him we are saved eternally, for through his death, those who are called receive the promised eternal inheritance. Out of these benefits of Holy Baptism, we draw rich comfort in every need and anxiety. Because we are baptized into Christ and his death, Christ is completely ours with everything that he is, has, and is able to do.

No sin can condemn us because he is our righteousness. Who will accuse the elect of God? God is here who justifies [*gerecht machen*]. Who will condemn? Christ is here who has died (Romans 8:33–34). No cross can trouble us, for we are clothed with Christ in Baptism. Who can harm the one who indeed is preserved in Christ? Death cannot frighten us because Christ is our life and death is our gain [Philippians 1:21]. The devil may not venture anything against us. If Christ is for us, who may be against us [Romans 8:31]? We are redeemed from sin, death, and the devil through Baptism. God has already saved us in Baptism and we need to do nothing for our salvation, only see to it that we do not again lose this inheritance through our ungodly life.

Therefore, by virtue of our Baptism, we are pledged to die to sin. We are baptized into the death of Christ so that his death should work in us the putting to death of our flesh. The one who lives in sin denies the power of his Baptism, loses Christ, and is living in death until he, through repentance, is again renewed and Christ's death, through dying to his sins, is allowed to be powerful in him. This is typified through circumcision in the Old Testament as Paul teaches in Colossians 2[:11–12] when he states, "You are circumcised in Christ with the circumcision without hands through the putting off of the sinful body of the flesh, namely with the circumcision of Christ, in that you are buried with him through Baptism." As the foreskin of the flesh is taken away through circumcision, thus the sinful flesh must be put off through Baptism so that sin ceases to reign in the flesh (Genesis 17:11).

Baptism is a bath of rebirth and renewal (Titus 3:5). Therefore, it is not proper that a baptized Christian walk in the old birth of the lusts of his flesh. Through Baptism, faith is worked in us. Through faith, our hearts are cleansed (Acts 15:9). Just as it is impossible that a fig tree bears thorns, so, too, it is impossible for faith's tree to bear the fruits of sin. In Baptism, the forgiveness of sins is imparted to us; therefore, it is not appropriate that we stain ourselves with new sins. No wild animal runs willfully into the restraints out of which it once escaped, and no little lamb after washing in the watering place wallows in the mire, as Peter states, "If they have escaped the filth of the world through the knowledge of the Lord and Savior Jesus Christ but again are entangled and overcome, the last state with them is worse than the first" (2 Peter 2:20). Through Baptism, we are received in the gracious covenant of God, not only that we receive the benefits of God, but also that we serve God in a holy life. Therefore, Baptism is called a covenant of good conscience with God (1 Peter 3:21), both because through it we are assured in the conscience of God's grace in Christ Jesus and also because through it we are bound to practice a good defense [*Ritterschaft*] to preserve faith and a good conscience.

God has saved us through the bath of rebirth and renewal (Titus 3:5). Therefore, it would not be proper that we live in [carnal] security and sin, so that we do not again forfeit the inheritance. How sad! How little is their Baptism considered! And how much they vainly boast of their Baptism, living not as baptized Christians but as unbaptized heathens. I dare not hesitate to say that in the midst of Christianity there are many more heathens than Christians. Were we not all baptized and became Christians on the basis of this covenant, so that we should renounce the devil and his works and ways? And still all the estates are so full of the satanic conduct against all the commandments of God that it cannot be mourned enough with fervent tears. Are we not all baptized into Christ? But where do you find the footsteps of the holy life of Christ? Yet it is almost as if gentleness and humility have completely vanished. Are we not baptized into the death of Christ? Still sin is allowed to rule in us, living only according to our lusts. O you covenant-breaking and perjuring Christians, what will be said when you knock on the gate of heaven? "Depart from me, you evildoers, for I have not known you" [Matthew 7:23]. This will happen to you justly. Because you have denied Jesus before men, so also will Jesus deny you before his heavenly Father [Matthew 10:33]. Those of you who would be true Christians and uphold your baptismal vow should put to death the activity of the flesh and not allow the root of sin to bear fruit in you. You will feel sin so long as you have flesh and blood, but do not permit it to live and reign. But since it was put to death in Christ, put it to death again. Be as the dead who do not stir and do not give your members to obey the lusts of sin.

Upon such blessed death must follow burial. The deceased Jesus was buried partly to confirm the truth of his death and partly to sanctify our graves. Baptism is our grave. We were buried with Christ through Baptism into death [Romans 6:4].

Through Baptism, the Holy Spirit works faith in us. He buries the sin carcass in the wounds of Jesus as in a deep grave. In addition, he restrains the sinful enticements of the flesh so that they may not come to light through words or deeds but remain hidden in the heart as their estate and grave. The old man must decay and be destroyed more and more in the spiritual grave and prison in which he is laid. The sin that stirs within us must more and more be suppressed and lose its power, that it does not raise its head and break forth in outward fruit. . . .

Upon this burial follows the resurrection. Christ did not remain in the grave but was raised from the dead through the glory of the Father. Christ indeed arose through his own indwelling divine power. Still, Paul applies this work to God the Father partly because in the works wherein God reveals himself outwardly to the creation, all three persons work together and partly so that we are assured that God has accepted Christ's death as a complete ransom for our sins. Otherwise he would not have released him from the bonds of death. What St. Paul here calls the glory of God, he refers to elsewhere as the power of God when he writes in 1 Corinthians 6(:14), "God has raised the Lord and will also raise us through his power." It is referred to as glory because it has proven itself glorious in the resurrection of Christ.

We also must arise spiritually with Christ, for life and death hang together. The more the old man dies and sinks, the more glorious the new [man] rises. The more the outward is decaying, the more the inward is renewed. The more the flesh is put to death, the more powerfully the spirit is raised and made alive. The more the works of darkness are laid aside, the brighter the works of light appear. The more the world, with its love and lusts, its cares and fears are given up, the more lovingly Christ penetrates within with his Spirit, light, and power. Through Baptism we were raised spiritually that we walk in a new life. As God gave Christ into death according to his holy counsel, so also he puts to death our old man. The dying to sin and the overcoming of the bad behavior of the flesh is God's power and work in us. We are able to do nothing through our own abilities. Accordingly, as God raised Christ, so he awakens us also through his Spirit to a new life in Christ. As little as a dead corpse may awaken itself, so we ourselves are not able to do anything good. It is God who works in us both the will and the accomplishment [Philippians 2:13]. God works faith in us through Baptism by which we are united with Christ. In such a union, there exists spiritual life, for we receive from Christ a new life, new spirit and mind. Such life shows itself through works as the natural life through conduct and the life of the tree through the fruits. In works, we do not reach perfection; still, we strive thereafter until we come to the point [*Pünctlein*] of eternity; there all is full [*rund*] and complete. . . .

AUTHORS

Rev. Gerhard H. Bode, Ph.D., is assistant professor of historical theology and archivist at Concordia Seminary, St. Louis, MO.

Matthew Carver, M.F.A., is an independent scholar and translator in Nashville, TN.

Otfried Czaika, Dr. theol., is professor of church history with concentration on the history of the Reformation at the private Teologiske Menighetsfakultet (Norwegian School of Theology) in Oslo, Norway.

Rev. Timothy Dost, Ph.D., is associate professor of historical theology at Concordia Seminary, St. Louis, MO.

Rev. Joshua J. Hayes, M.Div., M.A., is pastor of University Lutheran Chapel in Boulder, CO.

Rev. Robert A. Kolb, Ph.D., is missions professor of systematic theology (emeritus) at Concordia Seminary, St. Louis, MO.

Rev. Gerald S. Krispin, Th.D., is professor of religious studies and president and vice-chancellor at Concordia University of Alberta in Edmonton, Alberta, Canada.

Rev. Jason D. Lane, Dr. theol. (*designatus*), is assistant professor of theology at Concordia University Wisconsin.

Rev. Benjamin T. G. Mayes, Ph.D., is assistant professor of historical theology at Concordia Theological Seminary, Fort Wayne, IN.

Rev. Jonathan Mumme, Dr. theol., is assistant professor of theology at Concordia University Wisconsin.

Rev. Steven R. J. Parks, M.Div., is a doctoral candidate at the University of Bristol in Bristol, England, and assistant professor of theology at Concordia University, Irvine, CA.

Rev. David R. Preus, M.Div., is a missionary to the Dominican Republic and Ph.D. candidate at Concordia Seminary, St. Louis, MO.

Rev. Gaylin R. Schmeling, M.Div., S.T.M., is president and professor of historical and systematic theology at Bethany Lutheran Theological Seminary, Mankato, MN.

Rev. Timothy R. Schmeling, Ph.D., is assistant professor of theology and history at Bethany Lutheran College, Mankato, MN.

Rev. Jon D. Vieker, Ph.D., is senior assistant to the president of The Lutheran Church—Missouri Synod.

Rev. William R. Wangelin, M.Div., is senior pastor of Our Savior Lutheran Church and School, Lansing, MI.

Rev. Armin Wenz, Dr. theol., is pastor of St. Maria-Magdalena Lutheran Church in Halle/Saale, Germany, and a guest professor of systematic theology at Lutherische Theologische Hochschule in Oberursel, Germany.

Rev. Roland F. Ziegler, Dr. theol., is the Rev. Dr. Robert D. Preus associate professor of systematic theology and confessional Lutheran studies at Concordia Theological Seminary, Fort Wayne, IN.